CW00741386

The Making of British Socialism

The Making of British Socialism

Mark Bevir

PRINCETON UNIVERSITY PRESS

PRINCETON AND OXFORD

Copyright © 2011 by Princeton University Press

Requests for permission to reproduce material from this work should be sent to Permissions, Princeton University Press

Published by Princeton University Press, 41 William Street, Princeton, New Jersey 08540

In the United Kingdom: Princeton University Press, 6 Oxford Street, Woodstock, Oxfordshire OX20 1TW

press.princeton.edu

All Rights Reserved

Library of Congress Cataloging-in-Publication Data

Bevir, Mark.
The making of British socialism / Mark Bevir.
p.   cm.
Includes bibliographical references and index.
ISBN 978-0-691-15083-3 (hardcover : alk. paper)
1. Socialism--Great Britain--History. 2. Labor unions--Great Britain--History.
I. Title.
HX241.5.B4 8 2011
335'.1–dc22   2010052050

British Library Cataloging-in-Publication Data is available

This book has been composed in Sabon

Printed on acid-free paper. ∞

Printed in the United States of America

10 9 8 7 6 5 4 3 2 1

To Bill and Phebe

Contents

Part Three: *The Ethical Socialists*

Preface

THIS BOOK HAS BEEN a long time in the making. I first began working on the history of British socialism in the late 1980s. Back then, Margaret Thatcher's governments loomed large over my political world. Critics portrayed socialism as a discredited statist ideology. Even socialists sometimes implied that it was an outdated class-based ideology. Yet, I wanted to recapture the diversity of socialism and thereby find inspiration for a radical democratic and transformative politics that rejected market individualism for egalitarian fellowship. I thought British socialists needed a new narrative with which to respond to neoliberalism.

One reason this book has been so long in the making is that in the 1990s the Labour Party provided just such a narrative. New Labour presented itself as adhering to historic socialist "ends" while adopting new "means." The old socialist "means" had allegedly been made irrelevant by the rise of new times. The advancement of socialism now supposedly required supply-side economics, capacity building, and networks and partnerships delivering services. Although I was impressed by the energy and vigor of the New Labour project, its narrative and politics were not what I had had in mind. I got distracted from the history of British socialism by the desire to come to terms with its present.

The reader will find that this book still echoes my early aim of providing a more diverse portrait of socialism. Socialism has never been just about class-based politics and state intervention. It has never been the caricature depicted by Mrs. Thatcher; nor has it been the preserve of the Labour Party and its leaders. On the contrary, British socialism has always included radical democratic, pluralist, and utopian strands. Many socialists have promoted nongovernmental visions of personal and social transformation. They have envisaged more simple and cooperative ways of life.

I hope this book will help to correct widespread misconceptions about the history and nature of socialism. I also hope that it will contribute, even if only ever-so slightly, to attempts to forge more fulfilling ways of living with one another and the natural world of which we are part.

Acknowledgments

BECAUSE THIS BOOK has been a long time in the making, my list of debts is correspondingly long. I began working on the history of British socialism while studying for a D.Phil. at the University of Oxford. José Harris and Alan Ryan supervised my thesis, and I am grateful to them for their light touch, advice, and support.

The Economic and Social Research Council funded my original doctoral research. Later financial support came from the University of Newcastle, the Leverhulme Trust, the Harry Ransom Humanities Research Center, and the University of California, Berkeley. Without their support, I could not have visited and revisited archives, studied rare newspapers and pamphlets, or found sufficient time to think and write.

As I continued with my research, I published pieces as specialist academic articles. These articles are the bases for several chapters in this book. For permission to draw on them, I thank the editors and publishers of *English Historical Review, Historical Journal, Historical Research, History of European Ideas, History of Political Thought, International Review of Social History, Journal of British Studies, Journal of the History of Ideas, Journal of Modern History*, and *Review of Politics*.

I have had so many fruitful conversations about British socialism with so many people that I would be bound to neglect some of them were I to attempt to list them all; but I want specifically to mention James Meadowcroft and Frank Trentmann for reading and commenting on several of my earlier writings on British socialism. More recently, Ian Malcolm was both an effective and a perceptive editor. I thank him and all the people at Princeton University Press who have helped to produce the final book.

As always, I am immensely grateful to Laura; she drove me up to Oxford when I first went there, and now, all these years later, she has prepared the index of this book.

Mum and Dad—my books, especially this one, took too long; thanks, thanks for everything.

Abbreviations

BLPES	British Library of Political and Economic Science
BSP	British Socialist Party
DF	Democratic Federation
HRC	Harry Ransom Center
ILP	Independent Labour Party
LCC	London County Council
LRC	Labour Representation Committee
MP	Member of Parliament
MSL	Manhood Suffrage League
NRL	National Reform League
SDF	Social Democratic Federation
TUC	Trades Union Congress

The Making of British Socialism

CHAPTER ONE

Introduction: Socialism and History

"WE ARE ALL SOCIALISTS NOW: The Perils and Promise of the New Era of Big Government" ran the provocative cover of *Newsweek* on 11 February 2009. A financial crisis had swept through the economy. Several small banks had failed. The state had intervened, pumping money into the economy, bailing out large banks and other failing financial institutions, and taking shares and part ownership in what had been private companies. The cover of *Newsweek* showed a red hand clasping a blue one, implying that both sides of the political spectrum now agreed on the importance of such state action.

Although socialism is making headlines again, there seems to be very little understanding of its nature and history. The identification of socialism with "big government" is, to say the least, misleading. It just is not the case that when big business staggers and the state steps in, you have socialism. Historically, socialists have often looked not to an enlarged state but to the withering away of the state and the rise of nongovernmental societies. Even when socialists have supported state intervention, they have generally focused more on promoting social justice than on simply bailing out failing financial institutions.

A false identification of socialism with big government is a staple of dated ideological battles. The phrase "We are all socialists now" is a quotation from a British Liberal politician of the late nineteenth century. Sir William Harcourt used it when a land reform was passed with general acceptance despite having been equally generally denounced a few years earlier as "socialist." Moreover, *Newsweek*'s cover was not the first echo of Harcourt's memorable phrase. On 31 December 1965, *Time* magazine had quoted Milton Friedman, a monetarist economist who later helped to inspire the neoliberalism of the 1980s and '90s, as saying, "We are all Keynesians now." During the twentieth century, conservative and neoliberal ideologues encouraged "red scares" by associating not just Soviet communism but also socialism, progressivism, and Keynesianism with totalitarianism. All kinds of benevolent and ennobling projects were thus decried. The Appalachian Trail was the first completed national scenic trail in the United States. It is managed by a volunteer-based organization and maintained by trail clubs and multiple partnerships. It houses and protects some two thousand rare and endangered species of plant and animal life. This trail was first proposed in 1921 by Benton MacKaye, a progressive and an early advocate of land preservation for ecological and recreational uses.[1] MacKaye's inspiring vision was of a hiking trail linking self-owning communities based on cooperative crafts, farming, and forestry and providing inns and hostels for city dwellers. Critics complained that the scheme was Bolshevist.

The Bolshevik Revolution and the cold war helped entrench particular ways of thinking about socialism. Socialism became falsely associated with state ownership, bureaucratic planning, and the industrial working class. As a result, before the financial crisis, socialism appeared to some to be disappearing into the history books. There were numerous empty celebrations of the triumph of capitalism. The fall of the Berlin Wall in 1989 became a popular marker for the end of "real socialism." Few communist states remained, and they were communist in little more than the official title of the ruling political party. Socialism, progressivism, and Keynesianism seemed to be faring little better. In Britain the Labour Party rebranded itself as "New Labour." The party's leaders accepted much of the neoliberal critique of the Keynesian welfare state. They explicitly rejected old socialist "means," including state ownership, bureaucratic planning, and class-based politics. Moreover, although they suggested that they remained true to socialist "ends," this change in means entailed a shift in ends, with, for example, the greater role given to markets pushing the concept of equality away from equality of outcome and toward equality of opportunity.[2]

Perhaps an adequate response to current and future problems depends on a rejection of the caricatures of old ideological battles. Perhaps we would be better placed to consider possible responses to problems—such as those posed by the financial crisis and ecological preservation—if we had a more accurate understanding of the nature and history of socialism. Perhaps we should treat the pulling down of the Berlin Wall not as a sign of the triumph of capitalism but as the end of the conceptual dichotomy that had pitted socialism against capitalism.[3] Perhaps we should see the collapse of real socialism not as justifying an empty neoliberal triumphalism in which global capitalism has swept all before it but as an opportunity to reconsider the history of socialism.

---

[1] L. Anderson, *Benton MacKaye: Conservationist, Planner, and Creator of the Appalachian Trail* (Baltimore: Johns Hopkins University Press, 2002).

[2] M. Bevir, *New Labour: A Critique* (London: Routledge, 2005), esp. pp. 54–82.

[3] M. Bevir and F. Trentmann, eds., *Critiques of Capital in Modern Britain and America: Transatlantic Exchanges, 1800 to the Present Day* (Basingstoke, UK: Palgrave Macmillan, 2002); and M. Bevir and F. Trentmann, eds., *Markets in Historical Contexts: Ideas and Politics in the Modern World* (Cambridge: Cambridge University Press, 2004).

Today, as the cold war recedes into the past, we might do well to retrieve lost socialist voices, their histories, and their continuing legacy and relevance. In this book, I rethink socialism by looking back to the late nineteenth century, before ideological lines became hardened by political parties and cold-war warriors. I explore creative exchanges between socialism and other traditions, including popular radicalism, liberal radicalism, and romanticism. I show that socialism was closely associated with progressive justice, radical democracy, and a new life. In doing so, I hope to offer a fruitful history that will inspire further research. And I hope also to retrieve neglected socialist ideas that might inspire political action today. The era of state ownership, bureaucratic planning, and the industrial working class may perhaps be behind us. But even if it is, many socialist ideas remain viable and exciting—perhaps necessary, definitely worth fighting for.

HISTORIOGRAPHY

My account of the making of British socialism participates in a historiographical revolution. Just as the end of a simplistic dichotomy between socialism and capitalism makes it possible to retrieve alternative socialist pasts, so rejecting that dichotomy contributes to the rise of new ways of narrating those pasts. The old historiography suggested that socialism arose as the working class became conscious of itself as a class. Historians told the story of workers and their socialist allies reacting to the rise of capitalism by founding political parties, taking power, and building socialist and welfare states. Ideas generally appeared as mere reflections of socioeconomic developments. Today, however, political events, social movements, and theoretical arguments have all combined to dismantle the old historiography. Historians have adopted more fluid concepts of socialism and demonstrated a greater concern with the role of ideas in the construction of social and political practices. They point the way to a new historiography that shows how people actively made socialism by drawing on diverse traditions to respond to dilemmas and to inspire new practices. This chapter discusses this historiographical revolution as it relates to the making of British socialism.

The old historiography emerged in the late nineteenth century alongside the socialist movement, and it remained largely unchallenged until the 1980s. The old historiography attracted Marxists, laborists, and progressives, ranging from G.D.H. Cole to the Hammonds and on, most famously, to Eric Hobsbawm and E. P. Thompson.[4] These historians told

---

[4] On non-Marxist traditions of social history, see M. Taylor, "The Beginnings of Modern British Social History," *History Workshop* 43 (1997): 155–76.

a unified and linear story about capitalism and its socialist critics. They argued that capitalism possessed an innate, largely natural trajectory defined by its inner laws. Initial opposition to capitalism took the form of a Luddite resistance, which was soon exposed as naive.[5] Socialists and workers had to learn the nature of a capitalist society that had arisen independently of their beliefs and actions. As the workers caught up with the reality of capitalism, so they developed class consciousness.[6] Working-class consciousness appeared and developed through Chartism, the trade unions, the socialist movement, the Labour Party, and the welfare state. This old historiography thus defined a clear research agenda around the topics of class, production, trade unions, the Labour Party, and the central state as an agent of socioeconomic transformation.

While the old historiography sometimes drew on a materialism and determinism associated with Marxism, it also fitted easily into general accounts of the Victorian age as a time of unprecedented growth. Most social historians believed that the Industrial Revolution brought a rapid entry into modernity during the early nineteenth century. The Industrial Revolution marked a clear break with traditional society. It introduced a world of factories, the bourgeoisie, political reform, an organized working class, and thus class conflict and class accommodation.[7] Even after Thompson encouraged social historians to emphasize human agency in contrast to a crude Marxist determinism, they continued to study the ways in which people had made this modern world. Thompson himself studied "the poor stockinger, the Luddite cropper, the obsolete hand-loom weaver, the utopian artisan," not only to rescue them "from the enormous condescension of posterity," but also to show how they made a modern, organized, and politically conscious working class.[8] Although Thompson emphasized the role of Protestantism, he presented working-class agency as a response to more or less pure experiences of socioeconomic reality. The turn to agency thus left the old historiography intact even as it broadened the research agenda to encompass more subjective aspects of the past.

---

[5] E. Hobsbawm, *Primitive Rebels: Studies in Archaic Forms of Social Movement in the 19th and 20th Centuries* (Manchester, UK: Manchester University Press, 1959).

[6] E. Thompson, *The Making of the English Working Class* (Harmondsworth, UK: Penguin, 1981).

[7] A. Briggs, *The Age of Improvement, 1783–1867* (London: Longman, 1959); G. Kitson Clark, *The Making of Victorian England* (Cambridge, MA: Harvard University Press, 1962); H. Perkin, *Origins of Modern English Society, 1780–1880* (London: Routledge, 1969); and G. Young, *Victorian England: Portrait of an Age* (London: Oxford University Press, 1936).

[8] E. Thompson, *Making of the English Working Class*, p. 12.

Challenges to the old historiography reflected both the limitations and the successes of Thompson's intervention. Historiography still privileged a teleological narrative of the rise of the working class, and it still centered on topics such as class, production, unions, socialist parties, and the central state. It thus seemed unable to extend itself to cover widespread changes in the social and political landscape, including deindustrialization, neoliberalism, identity politics, and the new social movements. The forward march of labor had come to an abrupt halt.[9] Of course, Marxist historians had long grappled with the failure of the working class to fulfill its revolutionary role; they tried to explain this failure by appealing to theories about the peculiar nature of British society, social control, and hegemony.[10] By the 1980s, however, the changing social and political landscape posed a more general dilemma for social historians. The dilemma was that the theoretical bases of the old historiography—with its focus on class, production, trade unions, political organization, and the state—appeared more and more implausible as the dominant story of modernity. The theory lurking behind much social history had failed. Some social historians responded to this dilemma by rejecting theory. Thompson conflated his turn to agency with a rhetorical dismissal of theory in favor of an empirical focus on people's experiences of the past.[11] Other historians turned to new theories, including many that treated language and ideas as relatively autonomous from the development of capitalism.

Parallel challenges to the old historiography arose out of the very successes of Thompson's intervention. Thompson's success in conferring voice and agency on hidden figures of the past inspired numerous historians. Thompson himself echoed an idealized view of a robust, masculine working class engaged in public bodies and didactic self-improvement. Yet, many of the historians he inspired began to retrieve other voices. For a start, even when historians stuck with the male working class, they often shifted their attention from production to consumption. Historians explored the voices of workers interested in the music hall, football,

[9] For an attempt to adapt the old historiography to deal with this difficulty, see E. Hobsbawm et al., *The Forward March of Labour Halted* (London: New Left Books, 1981).

[10] E. Hobsbawm, "The Labour Aristocracy in Nineteenth-Century Britain," in *Labouring Men: Studies in the History of Labour* (London: Weidenfeld and Nicolson, 1964), pp. 272–315; T. Nairn, "The Fateful Meridian," *New Left Review* 60 (1970): 3–35; G. Stedman Jones, *Outcast London: A Study in the Relationship between Classes in Victorian Society* (Oxford: Oxford University Press, 1971); and S. Hall, "The Great Moving Right Show," in *The Politics of Thatcherism*, ed. S. Hall and M. Jacques (London: Lawrence and Wishart, 1980), pp. 19–39.

[11] E. Thompson, "The Poverty of Theory; or, An Orrery of Errors," in *The Poverty of Theory and Other Essays* (London: Merlin Press, 1978), pp. 1–210.

and private leisure activities.[12] In addition, this interest in sites of consumption recast the study of cultural and political identities.[13] Historians explored consumption in part because they had become interested in voices other than those of the male working class. New social movements helped shift attention from the factory floor to the family household, the department store, and the imperial museum. Historians explored the voices of women, gays, and colonial subalterns. In doing so, moreover, they pointed to frequent contrasts and tensions between these people and male workers. Joan Scott explicitly argued that the Victorian working class was a masculine construction defined in contrast to a middle class that was accordingly given a feminine identity.[14] A new generation of imperial historians highlighted the racist elements in movements for social and political reform.[15] A greater awareness of consumption, gender, sexuality, and ethnicity undermined the old historical narrative of the working class spearheading demands for the people's rights and interests along the path to industrial modernity and socialist government. It increased the appeal of new theories that gave a greater autonomy and role to discourses and beliefs.

The transformation of social history continued throughout the 1990s, and it had important consequences for the study of socialism. The greater attention paid to language and ideas spread to the history of socialist thought. The rise of new topics such as gender encouraged a more fluid concept of socialism. Today, therefore, socialism often appears less as the natural outcome of workers' reacting to the prior formation of capitalism and more as a contingent and variegated cluster of political theories.

Historians of socialism now pay more attention to language and ideas. They are less ready to accept that socioeconomic changes necessarily lead to class consciousness, recognition of the social causes of social evils, and so laborism and socialism. Instead, they look more closely at language and the written evidence of radical movements in order to recover people's beliefs. One of the earliest and most prominent examples was

---

[12] P. Bailey, *Popular Culture and Performance in the Victorian City* (Cambridge: Cambridge University Press, 1998); and C. Waters, *British Socialists and the Politics of Popular Culture, 1884–1914* (Manchester, UK: Manchester University Press, 1990).

[13] J. Walkowitz, *City of Dreadful Delight* (Chicago: University of Chicago Press, 1992); and E. Rappaport, *Shopping for Pleasure: Women in the Making of London's West End* (Princeton, NJ: Princeton University Press, 2000).

[14] J. Scott, *Gender and the Politics of History* (New York: Columbia University Press, 1988). Also see A. Clark, *The Struggle for the Breeches: Gender and the Making of the British Working Class* (Berkeley: University of California Press, 1995).

[15] A. Burton, *Burdens of History: British Feminists, Indian Women, and Imperial Culture, 1865–1915* (Chapel Hill: University of North Carolina Press, 1994); and C. Hall, *White, Male, and Middle Class: Explorations in Feminism and History* (Cambridge: Polity Press, 1992).

Gareth Stedman Jones's study of Chartism.[16] The old historiography portrayed Chartism as the first expression of the class consciousness of the workers; the Chartists broke with popular Luddite forms of resistance and initiated a modern social outlook. In contrast, Stedman Jones treated the language of protest as relatively autonomous from the development of capitalism. He suggested that the language of the Chartists pointed to a political movement as much as a social one. Chartism was less the inauguration of a modern working class looking forward to the twentieth century than the end of a popular radicalism reaching back to the eighteenth century.

When other social historians have examined language and ideas, they too have stressed continuity and populism. Intellectual historians of the eighteenth century have explored the diverse, complex languages within which social theorists and economists responded to the rise of capitalism, commercialism, and market society.[17] Historians of radicalism and socialism have then traced the continuing legacy of these languages in the nineteenth century. Soon after Stedman Jones traced continuities through the Chartists, Greg Claeys did something similar for the Owenites and the radical economists.[18] Other historians traced continuities between eighteenth-century ideas and liberal radicalism, thereby highlighting the overlaps and continuities between the Chartists, Owenites, and later liberal radicals.[19] It now seems clear that the early critics of capitalism drew on diverse strands of radicalism that resembled eighteenth-century republicanism at least as much as they resembled twentieth-century socialism. Even the socialism of the 1880s, 1890s, and early years of the Labour Party echoed themes drawn from popular and liberal radicalism.[20] The continuity between eighteenth-century republicanism and nineteenth-

[16] G. Stedman Jones, "Rethinking Chartism," in *Languages of Class: Studies in English Working-Class History, 1832–1982* (Cambridge: Cambridge University Press, 1983), pp. 90–178.

[17] J. Pocock, *Virtue, Commerce, and History: Essays on Political Thought and History, Chiefly in the Eighteenth Century* (Cambridge: Cambridge University Press, 1985); and D. Winch, *Adam Smith's Politics* (Cambridge: Cambridge University Press, 1978).

[18] G. Claeys, *Machinery, Money, and the Millennium: From Moral Economy to Socialism, 1815–60* (Princeton, NJ: Princeton University Press, 1987), and *Citizens and Saints: Politics and Anti-politics in Early British Socialism* (Cambridge: Cambridge University Press, 1989).

[19] E. Biagini and A. Reid, eds., *Currents of Radicalism: Popular Radicalism, Organised Labour, and Party Politics in Britain* (Cambridge: Cambridge University Press, 1991); and E. Biagini, ed., *Citizenship and Community: Liberals, Radicals and Collective Identities in the British Isles, 1865–1931* (Cambridge: Cambridge University Press, 1996).

[20] J. Lawrence, "Popular Radicalism and the Socialist Revival in Britain," *Journal of British Studies* 31 (1992): 163–86; and D. Tanner, "The Development of British Socialism, 1900–1918," *Parliamentary History* 16 (1997): 48–66.

century radicalism appears most clearly in a type of populism. Historians now suggest that the Chartists and Owenites thought less in terms of modern social classes than of the people. Some historians argue that "the people" or "demos" provided the main frame of collective identity for workers throughout the nineteenth century.[21]

Historians of socialism also now pay more attention to topics associated with consumption, leisure activities, gender, postcolonialism, and race. Studies of these topics in the early and mid-nineteenth century add nuance and detail to accounts of the persistence of eighteenth-century republicanism and related populist languages. For a start, historians have returned to the idea of civil society as a relatively autonomous space capable of fostering toleration and difference through voluntary associations. They have retrieved radical visions, akin to Thomas Paine's, of a vibrant civil society and a minimal state.[22] They have shown how cooperators and radicals embraced policies such as free trade in the hope of strengthening their own autonomy and that of a broader civil society against commercial capitalism.[23] Radicals often directed their collective action not to the state but to self-governance and the reform of society from within. Historians have thus shown how consumption and leisure acted as sites of social identity, contest, and reform. In addition, historians have explored identities that prevented class from simply subsuming populist concepts. Class appears as just one identity, created and maintained in tandem with others. Historians have not limited themselves here to identities and categories tied to gender, ethnicity, and sexuality. They have also paid more attention to the impact of religious, aesthetic, and patriotic beliefs on socialist politics.[24]

Victorian social history has been energized by the new interest in ideas and by the rise of new topics. However, the new historiography leaves significant questions largely unaddressed. It may even appear to be little more than a series of particular insights and interests, lacking an overarching theory and narrative. The interest in ideas has created a greater

[21] P. Joyce, *Visions of the People: Industrial England and the Question of Class* (Cambridge: Cambridge University Press, 1991); and J. Vernon, *Politics and the People: A Study in English Political Culture* (Cambridge: Cambridge University Press, 1993).

[22] J. Keane, "Despotism and Democracy: The Origins and Development of the Distinction between Civil Society and the State, 1750–1850," in *Civil Society and the State*, ed. J. Keane (London: Verso, 1988), pp. 35–71. Also see G. Claeys, *Thomas Paine: Social and Political Thought* (London: Unwin Hyman, 1989).

[23] F. Trentmann, *Free Trade Nation* (Oxford: Oxford University Press, 2008).

[24] See respectively S. Yeo, "A New Life: The Religion of Socialism in Britain, 1883–1896," *History Workshop* 4 (1977): 5–56; I. Britain, *Fabianism and Culture: A Study in British Socialism and the Arts, c. 1884–1918* (Cambridge: Cambridge University Press, 1982); and P. Ward, *Red Flag and Union Jack: Englishness, Patriotism, and the British Left, 1881–1924* (Woodbridge, UK: Royal Historical Society, 1998).

awareness of continuities running from eighteenth-century republican-ism through the radical movements of the mid-nineteenth century and beyond. But the presence of these continuities raises questions about how and when nineteenth-century radicalism fed into twentieth-century socialism. Of course, socialism continued to overlap considerably with both popular and liberal radicalism. Nonetheless, by the early twentieth century, Britain was home to a range of Marxist groups, other avowedly socialist and anarchist groups, and a Labour Party that combined some of these groups with the trade unions. How was British socialism made in the late nineteenth century? How are we to explain the discontinuities as well as the continuities with earlier radical ideas and movements? Here the new studies of topics such as consumption, gender, and patriotism are of only limited use. They impressively expand our understanding of the ways in which socialism interacted with other ideas and activities, but they arguably lose sight of British socialism as a movement. They focus on a particular theme in socialism, rather than the rise and shape of the socialist movement as a whole. Inevitably, they fragment the ideas and activities of socialist groups. What general narrative should we tell about the making of British socialism? What aggregate concepts best explain the rise of the British socialist movement out of mid-nineteenth-century radicalism? This book aims to provide a general account of the making of British socialism in continuity and discontinuity with earlier radicalisms.

THEORY

The new historiography needs aggregate concepts that can cover its frag-mented studies of particular topics and that allow for historical continuity and discontinuity. The task of building these aggregate concepts is in part a theoretical one.[25] Historians need theories that avoid the determinism and essentialism of the old historiography. Their concepts cannot reduce socialist thought to socioeconomic terms. Nor can their concepts rely on appeals to a "true socialism" or class consciousness. Instead, their concepts should allow that socialism is diverse and contingent. There may seem to be a tension here. On the one hand, aggregate concepts necessarily clump particular beliefs and events together; they suggest a pattern, privileging some features and some cases while neglecting others; and so they might seem inevitably to elide diversity and contingency. On the other hand, the more historians refuse all aggregate concepts and focus instead on the diversity and contingency of particular cases and topics, the less able they

---

[25] For the philosophical groundwork of this theory, see M. Bevir, *The Logic of the History of Ideas* (Cambridge: Cambridge University Press, 1999).

are to explain what happened in the past. Clearly the solution lies with aggregate concepts that avoid determinism and essentialism.

Unfortunately, the vigor and sophistication of the new historiography has not been replicated in new historical theories. On the contrary, historians have often retreated into a naive empiricism that dismisses the need for theory, or they have used structuralist and post-structuralist tropes that merely displace determinism and essentialism into the linguistic sphere.[26] When Thompson conflated his turn to agency with a dismissal of all theory, he was explicitly attacking the structuralist Marxism of Louis Althusser.[27] Other historians, equally misleadingly, have tried to seem theoretically sophisticated by using concepts (or at least words) derived from structuralism and post-structuralism.[28] Many of these historians rightly worry that Thompson's naive empiricism tacitly assumes that the individual agent has pure experiences uncorrupted by the effects of power. But they wrongly conclude that the proper alternative is a theory that gives pride of place to concepts of language or discourse that neglect agency.

Structuralism and post-structuralism encourage historians to reify language. They suggest that meanings arise not from the ways agents use words but from the relations of difference among semantic units. The meanings of "male" and "working class" result not from the ways in which people use these words, but from the differences between these words and other words such as "female" and "middle class." Language thus appears to be a reified semiotic code that generates meaning quite apart from the activity of human beings. This reified view of language then reintroduces determinism and essentialism. A reified language determines the meanings, beliefs, and so actions of individual agents. And any particular language consists essentially of a particular set of relationships among its semantic units.

By no means has every contributor to the new historiography been bewitched by a reified view of language. Yet, when historians do use post-structuralist concepts, their linguistic determinism and essentialism undermine their ability, respectively, to explain ideational change and to recognize the diversity of populism. Consider the problem of change. The new historiography ascribes to language a relative autonomy in relation to capitalism, thereby rendering problematic any direct appeal to experience as a source of change. When post-structuralists go on to reject the

[26] G. Stedman Jones, "The Determinist Fix: Some Obstacles to the Further Development of the Linguistic Approach to History in the 1990s," *History Workshop* (1996): 19–35.

[27] E. Thompson, "Poverty of Theory."

[28] Very little (if any) of the literature on postmodern and post-structuralist approaches to British social history is worth reading. The heatedness of the debate was matched only by its lack of philosophical literacy. For an overview, see W. Thompson, *Postmodernism and History* (Basingstoke, UK: Palgrave Macmillan, 2004), esp. chap. 6.

"real," they undermine even indirect appeals to experience. Moreover, their emphasis on language as constitutive of all subjectivity undermines any appeal to agency as a source of change: if individuals merely construct their selves in terms given to them by a social discourse, they must lack the capacity to modify such discourses. When post-structuralists invoke reified languages as productive of both the social and agency, without in turn being produced by either of these, it is hard to grasp how and why languages might change. A related problem stems from the neglect of the diversity of populist discourse, or the confusion of diversity with difference. A reified concept of language encourages historians to look for a common set of meanings as opposed to the diverse beliefs that agents express in speech and action. Populism can act as little more than a broadening out of the concept of class. When post-structuralists do explore diversity, they generally do so in terms of the different connotations given to binary concepts by a reified language. Much less attention is paid to the diverse beliefs that agents hold for reasons of their own.

So, the new historiography is often caught between naive empiricism and reified concepts of language. What historians need is a theory that takes agency seriously while not reducing it to the pure experience of an independent social reality. The key idea here is that individuals are situated agents; they are agents who can act innovatively for reasons of their own, but their agency is situated in that they are necessarily influenced by social inheritances. The past consists of people and their activity. Languages and discourses do not exist as reifications. They are just abstract concepts that should refer back to the beliefs, utterances, and actions of particular individuals. When historians appeal to such abstract concepts, they might think about—and ideally specify—who precisely held the relevant beliefs. They might situate meanings more precisely in the relevant social ecology. And they might recognize that individuals may have held very different beliefs even if they used the same words—they might allow for diversity as well as binary differences.

To reject reified concepts of language is to highlight the importance of individuals and their activity. However, it is not necessarily to appeal to an autonomous subjectivity. Some post-structuralists set up a false dichotomy between, on the one hand, "theory" with its appeal to reified languages based on the difference among semantic units within them and, on the other, a naive empiricism that tacitly appeals to an autonomous subjectivity. Historians can escape this false dichotomy simply by insisting that agency is necessarily situated.

As agency is inevitably situated, so historians need a concept such as tradition to capture the social context as it affects the individual subject. The concept of tradition implies that people never can have pure experiences and unmediated knowledge. People necessarily encounter the world against the background of an inherited set of beliefs and meanings. Individuals construct their experiences and reach their beliefs influenced by inherited traditions. As the role of traditions is to situate agency, traditions should not be reified. Historians should not define traditions by reference to allegedly core ideas, and then locate people in traditions according to whether or not they hold these core ideas. Traditions are contingent and changing objects. They are products of individuals and their activity. Historians can specify the content of a tradition and trace its development only by following the ways in which people inherit and modify a loose collection of changing themes. So conceived, tradition is more than a tool of high intellectual history. It is an ontological concept that captures the social context of agency. Tradition is the background to all human activity. Tradition appears throughout social life, embedded in actions, practices, and social movements just as much as within texts.

A concept of tradition has the advantage over those of language and discourse that it allows for agency. Historians can conceive of change arising from the local reasoning of agents in the context of tradition. Yet, just as "tradition" captures the situated nature of agency, so historians need a concept such as "dilemma" to explain why agents modify traditions. A dilemma arises for individuals or groups whenever they adopt a new idea or action and so have to accommodate it in their existing beliefs and practices. Dilemmas here explain change without postulating a teleological process or a universal rationality. Dilemmas do not have historically necessary solutions. On the contrary, people respond to dilemmas in a creative and contingent process. The concept of a dilemma does not involve postulating pure experience of a prior social reality, and it also avoids dismissing the importance of lived experience. People modify traditions in response to their new beliefs irrespective of whether or not these beliefs reflect material changes in the world. Yet, people do have experiences of the world, and their interpreted experiences often constitute the dilemmas to which they respond. Just as tradition is more than a tool of high intellectual history, so dilemma provides a means of integrating language with the world. Beliefs and traditions are not reified discourses lurking in a detached linguistic realm uninfluenced by changes in the world. Beliefs and traditions are the properties and products of agents who revise them in response to historical dilemmas that often consist of interpreted experiences of social relationships.

SOCIALISM

A new historiography could narrate the history of socialism in terms of a diverse cluster of ideas and the traditions and dilemmas from which they emerged. In doing so, it would raise questions about how to define socialism as an object of inquiry. The old historiography typically gave socialism stable content and then projected that content back through history. Sometimes socialism was defined by one or more core ideas, such as common ownership of the means of production. At other times it was defined as the ideological expression of a certain group, such as the working class. And at still other times it was defined by reference to an allegedly scientific theory of history and society. The general point is that the old historiography included an explicit or implicit account of the key features of socialism. Historians were able to define socialism in terms of the key features that their historiography ascribed to it.

How should historians define socialism after they reject the teleological and reductionist impulses of the old historiography? If socialism has no essence, how can historians decide whether something is part of a history of socialism? What working definition of socialism can guide the selection of organizations, authors, and texts for inclusion in any history of socialism? To focus on these questions, we might distinguish between two roles that are played by aggregate concepts such as tradition and dilemma. Aggregate concepts can be descriptive or explanatory. Historians can evoke socialism descriptively as an object of inquiry, but they also can evoke a socialist tradition as a background context to explain the beliefs and actions of particular socialists. When historians appeal to an explanatory concept, they can offer a pragmatic justification of its content. They can say that they define a tradition one way rather than another, to include these things but not those, because doing so best explains the particular objects that they want to explain. Clearly, however, when historians appeal to a descriptive concept that does not do explanatory work, they cannot define it pragmatically by reference to what they want to explain. The problem is, therefore, not how to define this or that tradition of socialism so as to explain something; it is how to define socialism in order to describe an object of inquiry.

This problem arises insofar as the new historiography rejects essentialism and so reified definitions of socialism. Socialism has no necessary core. There are no ideas and actions such that when they are present, we have an instance of socialism, and when they are absent, we do not have an instance of socialism. On the contrary, socialism is a fluid set of beliefs and practices that people are constantly making and remaking and in which no one idea or action has a fixed or necessary place. Historians can define socialism only by tracing how it develops over time as its exponents inherit, debate, and modify beliefs and practices before passing them on to others. Of course, people often try to stipulate what is and is not socialism, to dismiss a person or group for being socialist or for not being properly socialist, but these stipulations are just part of political struggles involving words and their meanings. There is no "true socialism" against which to judge instances as proper or improper. Yet, if there is no "true socialism" by which to judge instances, then neither is there a true or natural definition of socialism by which to decide what organizations, authors, and texts to include in a history of socialism.

Perhaps the lesson is that historians should be more relaxed about defining their objects of inquiry. Maybe it is enough to say that we are inquiring into the organizations, authors, and texts that happen to have caught our attention or that happen to interest us. Be that as it may, I have tried in this book to be receptive to the ways in which British socialists understood themselves. My aim is to understand the British socialists of the late nineteenth century in their own terms—to recover the meanings of socialism for people who thought of themselves as socialists at a time before the political parties and global conflicts of the twentieth century arguably narrowed the range of meanings that were regularly associated with the word "socialist."

As the new historiography undermines stipulative definitions of socialism, it allows historians to pay greater attention to the varied ways in which past socialists have defined themselves. Instead of imposing a particular concept of socialism back on the past, historians might concentrate on recovering the various meanings, feelings, and ways of life that people have attached to socialism. The best way to grasp both the nature and the appeal of socialism is perhaps to portray it as a lived experience, or rather as an open-ended series of lived experiences. Socialism is not a given thing—a natural kind—with a prescribed and bounded content. Rather, socialists made plural socialisms by drawing on inherited traditions to respond imaginatively to cultural, social, and political dilemmas. Socialism emerged as diverse and fluid phenomena that included a vast range of beliefs, feelings, and activities. One task for historians is to recover the diversity of this movement—the different meanings it had for the people who were part of it.

When we take a more relaxed approach to defining objects of historical inquiry, we can allow that different histories of socialism can begin at different places. The word "socialism" derives from the Latin *sociare*, meaning "to combine" or "to share," and political thinking about community and fellowship has a very long history. Nonetheless, the word "socialism" emerged only after the French Revolution through the 1820s and 1830s. At that time the Owenites became the first people in Britain to use the word self-consciously to describe themselves. Yet, after the Owenite movement collapsed, people in Britain rarely described themselves as "socialists," preferring a word such as "radical" or "republican." It was only later, beginning in the 1880s, that terms such as "socialist" and "social democrat" began to gain wider currency in Britain. By the 1890s, numerous organized groups in Britain self-consciously avowed "socialism." Different histories of British socialism might go back to early modern communal utopias, focus on the Owenites, or look at what has been called "the socialist revival" of the 1880s.

This book focuses on the 1880s and 1890s. My narrative often stretches beyond those two decades, especially when I trace the later fortunes of various thinkers and groups. Even then, however, the relevant thinkers and groups are those that dominated British socialism in the 1880s and 1890s. I focus on the late nineteenth century because those years were the immediate context for the birth of the Labour Party. Although I do not try to narrate the formation of the Labour Party, I am interested in how different British socialists came to relate to it. My questions are about the diverse strands of British socialism that existed before the Labour Party and their relationship to the party. My story addresses questions such as: Which strands of socialism fed into the Labour Party? Which did not? What webs of meaning and actions did the Labour Party embrace? Which were forgotten or marginalized?

In selecting and arranging strands of British socialism during the 1880s and the 1890s, I have again taken a relaxed and receptive approach. So, my division of British socialists into Marxists, Fabians, and ethical socialists is not an attempt to provide a formal classification in which each category is defined by an allegedly distinctive and defining set of properties. Of course, there are family resemblances among the members of each category, and those resemblances are typically greater than those across categories. Equally, however, there were heated disagreements within each category, and some members of each category had more in common with some members of other categories than they did with members of their own category. Each of these three categories is, like the more general category of socialism, a diverse and fluid movement, the character of which historians should not stipulate but rather recover by exploring the beliefs, feelings, and activities of the relevant people.

Far from stipulating a definition of Marxism, Fabianism, or ethical socialism, I try to recover the meanings of these categories for the people who belonged in them. The categories themselves arise from the self-understandings of late nineteenth-century British socialists. These categories constantly recurred in discussions of socialism and debates among socialists. British socialists typically saw themselves as Marxists, Fabians, or ethical socialists promoting a new religion, although several identified themselves with more than one of these categories, consciously locating themselves, for example, on the ethical wing of the Fabian Society.

The categories of Marxism, Fabianism, and ethical socialism have an additional advantage. They capture, more or less in chronological order, the self-understanding of the leading socialist groups that arose in Britain during the 1880s and 1890s. The first socialist groups to appear in Britain in the 1880s were Marxist—the Social Democratic Federation and the Socialist League. Next followed the Fabian Society, which arose out of the Fellowship of the New Life. Finally there emerged various groups—often located in the provinces—that explicitly set out to promote "the religion of socialism." In using the categories of Marxism, Fabianism, and ethical socialism, I am thereby able to embed the history of socialist thought in the history of socialist groups. Socialism was a set of ideas, but these ideas were embedded in organizations, practices, and ways of being. When I discuss individual thinkers, I generally do so because they were seen by fellow British socialists as the leading theorists of groups—the intellectual inspirations for personal transformations and collective actions.

Making Socialism

The Making of British Socialism traces the ways in which people collectively made various socialist projects in a complex world of mass literacy and popular politics. It explores the traditions against the background of which people turned to socialism and the dilemmas that prompted them to do so. It asks how people crafted and conceived of the diverse socialisms to which they adhered. Throughout, I concentrate on the period from 1880 to 1900. The bulk of the book consists of three parts, each covering one of the main strands of British socialism recognized at that time, namely, Marxism, Fabianism, and ethical socialism. Each part contains four chapters dealing with the leading theorists and organizations of the relevant strand of British socialism. The aim is in part to narrate the rise of British socialism as a belief system that later gained some kind of expression in an organized party and a state formation. However, the aim is also to show how the diversity of British socialism was poorly captured by that party and state formation.

The next chapter explores the Victorian context in which people made British socialism. The Enlightenment and romanticism following rapidly on one another transformed early modern political thought with its republican humanism and natural jurisprudence. By the mid-nineteenth century, Enlightenment and romantic themes had intermingled in Britain to inspire a culture dominated by liberalism and evangelicalism. Liberalism, with its ties to classical political economy, and evangelicalism, with its basis in atonement theology, inspired ideals of individualism, laissez-faire, and free trade in public policy, as well as prudence, truth, and duty in personal and social relations. By the 1870s, however, this Victorian culture faced two major dilemmas: the collapse of classical economics and the crisis of faith. British socialism emerged largely in response to these dilemmas. The crisis of faith led people to break with evangelicalism and to adopt ethical positivism and immanentist theologies that inspired moral emphases on humanitarianism and fellowship. The collapse of classical economics led people to explore new policy instruments and utopian visions.

Much of British socialism fused an ethic of fellowship with calls for society or the state to use new policies to improve the well-being of the poor. Equally, however, people with backgrounds in different traditions responded to the crisis of faith and the collapse of classical economics in various ways, thereby forging different socialisms, notably Marxism, Fabianism, and ethical socialism.

The first part of *The Making of British Socialism* discusses the Marxists. It highlights the continuing debt of Marxists to republican traditions with their vision of a popular and participatory democracy. Chapter 3 focuses on E. B. Bax, probably the leading socialist philosopher in Britain during the late nineteenth century. Bax argued that Marxism was an economic and historical science that lacked a philosophical and ethical basis. He wanted to base the Marxian dialectic on German idealism, arguing that the dialectic was a fact about reality. And he wanted to base an ethical defense of Marxism on the republican positivism of the French Revolution.

Whereas Bax fused Marxism with German idealism and republican positivism, H. M. Hyndman drew on a radical Toryism that overlapped with several republican themes. Hyndman founded and then dominated the Social Democratic Federation (SDF), the first socialist organization of the 1880s. Chapter 4 shows how Hyndman's discovery of Marx provided a scientific basis for his Tory historiography and politics, suggesting that they reflected both the economic laws governing capitalism and the dialectic of history. His Tory inheritance still lingered in his Marxism, inspiring a medievalist historiography, a fear of anarchy, a commitment to statesmanship, and a belief in peaceful social change.

Not every Marxist echoed republican themes. Yet, when other Marxists, notably William Morris, drew on other traditions that were skeptical of politics, they typically were pushed to the margins of the main Marxist organizations of the late nineteenth century. Chapter 5 highlights the place of romanticism and Protestantism in Morris's socialism. His romanticism led him to seek self-realization through an art based on naturalness and harmony. His Protestantism led him to do so in the everyday worlds of work and home. Morris inherited from John Ruskin a sociology that linked self-realization in daily life to the quality of art in a society. Even when Morris turned to Marxism, he still defined his socialist vision in terms of good art produced and enjoyed within daily life. His overriding concern to promote a new spirit of art then led him to a purist rejection of political action.

Morris's purism attracted little support among the early Marxists largely because they drew on republican traditions that overlapped at key points with Hyndman's radical Toryism. Chapter 6 provides a detailed investigation of the background, thought, and politics of the members of the SDF. Several of the early members of the SDF were followers of James Bronterre O'Brien, based in the radical workingmen's clubs of London. Even after they came to accept the need for collective ownership of the means of production, their political strategy remained that of O'Brien. They believed in political action to create a properly democratic state through which the people might then promote social reforms. This account of the O'Brienites helps to explain various unsolved problems in the history of British Marxism, notably why most members remained with Hyndman rather than follow Morris into the Socialist League, and why the SDF adopted an ambiguous attitude to trade unions and palliatives.

The republican inheritance of many Marxists inspired a commitment to radical democracy. This commitment helps to explain why they came to have only a marginal and oppositional role in British socialism. British socialism soon became dominated by more liberal concepts of democracy. The second part of *The Making of British Socialism* explores the principal source of this liberalism: Fabianism. As the Fabian Society broke away from the Fellowship of the New Life and rejected Marxism and anarchism, its leading members reworked liberal radicalism to respond to the collapse of classical economics.

Yet, Fabianism contained diverse viewpoints that drew on different economic theories as well as, to varying degrees, Marxism and positivism. The early history of the Fabian Society saw lively disputes and compromises between those with different viewpoints and the political strategies that these inspired. Chapter 7 thus challenges the idea that there was a single Fabian socialism based on a shared theory of rent. The late nineteenth century saw numerous attempts to reformulate political economy. Different Fabians were attracted to marginalism, neoclassical theory, and more historical and ethical approaches. Their different analyses of economic surpluses inspired varying beliefs as to the extent to which the state could and should intervene either to redistribute these surpluses or to use them for the collective good.

Chapters 8 and 9 explore in more detail the thought of the two leading Fabian socialists. Chapter 8 concerns the famous playwright George Bernard Shaw. Shaw's biographers consistently discuss his debt to Marx, but intellectual historians have found little sign of this debt. I show how Shaw's Marxism becomes visible if we look for the kind of Marxism found among his contemporaries, as opposed to the kinds of Marxism that became prominent later in the twentieth century. In the mid-1880s,

Shaw shared many of the Marxist ideas of the SDF. Even later, after he rejected Marxist economics for marginalism, he continued to defend several Marxist themes in ways that distanced him from the other leading Fabians, most importantly Sidney Webb.

Webb was the single most important thinker and actor in the development of Fabian socialism. Chapter 9 looks in detail at his political thought, rejecting the often repeated claim that he was a descendant of the utilitarians and a representative of a new managerial class. Webb's intellectual background lay in the liberal radicalism of the 1870s, which combined ethical positivism with evolutionary sociology. Webb first became a socialist because of his positivist ethic. He soon defined his socialism in terms of an evolutionary philosophy. He later adopted collectivism when he turned away from neoclassical economics to positivist sociology. And his collectivism always remained an ethical ideal embedded in an evolutionary sociology.

Chapter 10 discusses Shaw's and Webb's respective political strategies and their roles in inspiring Fabian policy. The Fabians did not share a commitment to permeating other parties in order to promote incremental measures of socialism. For a start, Shaw would have liked an independent socialist party, but for much of the 1880s and 1890s he did not think that such a party was possible. Moreover, insofar as the leading Fabians came to agree on "permeation," they defined it differently. Shaw thought of permeation in terms of luring Radicals away from the Liberal Party in order to form an independent party to represent workers against capitalists. In contrast, Webb defined permeation in terms of giving expert advice to the political elite. The response of the Fabian Society to the formation of the Independent Labour Party (ILP) reflected the interplay of these different strategies.

The conference that formed the ILP was spearheaded by socialist groups from the north of England. Many of these groups were inspired by an ethical socialism. The third part of *The Making of British Socialism* describes the rise of ethical socialism and its relationship to the crisis of faith. Chapter 11 shows how various welfare liberals and ethical socialists adopted immanentism in an attempt to reconcile religion and science. They located God in evolutionary processes here on earth. They suggested that each person contains a divine spark and so is related to all others in fellowship. Many of them experimented with new ways of living in an attempt to realize the divine in themselves and in their relations with others and nature.

Chapter 12 highlights some of the themes that distinguish ethical socialism from welfare liberalism as well as other strands of socialism. Several ethical socialists owed a distinctive debt to American romantics such as Ralph Waldo Emerson, Henry David Thoreau, and Walt Whitman. American romanticism initially entered British socialism through the wandering scholar Thomas Davidson, who inspired the Fellowship of the New Life. When Davidson continued on his travels, several of the socialists associated with the Fellowship took their ideals out of London and into the provinces. The most notable example was the libertarian poet Edward Carpenter, who set up the Sheffield Socialist Society and inspired numerous other local groups all across Britain, from Bristol to Nottingham and on to Bolton.

One of the most distinctive features of ethical socialism was the place it gave to personal transformation and communal utopianism. Chapter 13 explores the intersections between this type of socialism and a new anarchism. For most of the nineteenth century, anarchists were individualists, favoring clandestine organization and violent revolution. Yet, at the turn of the century, there arose a new communal anarchism associated with sexual liberation and moral experiments. The prophets of the new anarchism were Peter Kropotkin and Leo Tolstoy, not Mikhail Bakunin. Its organizational homes included the Freedom Group and the Brotherhood Church. It inspired agricultural and urban utopias in places such as the Cotswolds, Essex, Leeds, and London. And it appeared in discussion groups aimed at transforming personal and private relationships, including the Men and Women's Club.

Chapter 14 looks more closely at the main organizational expression of the religion of socialism, namely, the Labour Church movement. Previous historians have usually explained the rise of the Labour Church as part of a transfer of religious energy to the political sphere and then explained its demise by reference to the continuing process of secularization. In contrast, I focus on the religious self-understanding of the Labour Church. To begin, I explain the rise of the movement by reference to the immanentist theology with which so many Victorians and Edwardians responded to the crisis of faith. Thereafter, I appeal to the ideas of the movement in order to explain its appeal, structure, and activities and to suggest that the decline of the movement reflected the weaknesses of its theology as a political theory.

The final chapter explores the later roles of Marxism, Fabianism, and ethical socialism in the ILP, the Labour Party, and the social democratic state. The dominant strand of socialism fused Fabianism with ethical socialism. It promoted a labor alliance to win state power within a liberal, representative democracy, and then to use the state to promote social justice. Later in the twentieth century, the rise of modernist social science·altered the type of knowledge on which the Labour Party relied, with Fabian approaches to the state and policy giving way to planning, Keynesianism, and other formal expertise. Whatever type of knowledge the Labour Party relied upon to guide state intervention, it was constantly challenged by socialists opposed to its liberal concept of democracy and the role it gave to the state. These latter socialists often advocated the democratization of associations within civil society itself.

Socialism arose as part of a broad cultural shift away from the evangelicalism and classical liberalism of the mid-nineteenth century, initially toward immanentism and social welfarism, and then on to the modernist approaches to public policy that became a prominent feature of the twentieth century. The rise and trajectory of socialism is thus part of a wider progressivism apparent in other movements such as the New Deal in the United States and the new liberalism in Britain. There is no clear boundary between socialists and other progressives, nor is there one "true" socialist view of justice and how to realize it. Some socialists have brought to progressivism a particular concern with class-based politics and state intervention. Others have brought different emphases on radical democracy and personal transformation.

CHAPTER TWO

The Victorian Context

IN *DOMBEY AND SON*, THE FAMOUS VICTORIAN NOVELIST Charles Dickens described a London suburb:

> The first shock of a great earthquake had, just at that period, rent the whole neighbourhood to its centre. Traces of its course were visible on every side. Houses were knocked down; streets broken through and stopped; deep pits and trenches dug in the ground; enormous heaps of earth and clay thrown up; buildings that were undermined and shaking, propped by great beams of wood. Here, a chaos of carts, overthrown and jumbled together, lay topsy-turvy at the bottom of a steep unnatural hill; there, confused treasures of iron soaked and rusted in something that had accidentally become a pond. ... Hot springs and fiery eruptions, the usual attendants upon earthquakes, lent their contributions of confusion to the scene. Boiling water hissed and heaved within dilapidated walls; whence, also, the glare and roar of flames came issuing forth; and mounds of ashes blocked rights of way, and wholly changed the law and custom of the neighbourhood. In short, the yet unfinished and unopened Railroad was in progress; and, from the very core of all this dire disorder, trailed smoothly away, upon its mighty course of civilization and improvement.[1]

For many Victorians, the railroad symbolized industrialization, with its civilization and improvement and yet its destruction and chaos—its unnatural end to historic custom.

Recent studies show that industrialization was a gradual and uneven process.[2] Workshops rather than modern factories continued to dominate across much of Britain well into the nineteenth century. Older trades, such as the wool industry, still flourished and, along with finance and trade, contributed as much to growth as did newer industries. A recogni-

---

[1] C. Dickens, *Dombey and Son* (London: Bradbury and Evans, 1848), p. 46.

[2] N. Crafts, *British Economic Growth during the Industrial Revolution* (Oxford: Clarendon Press, 1985); M. Daunton, *Progress and Poverty: An Economic and Social History of Britain, 1700–1850* (Oxford: Oxford University Press, 1995); J. Jaffe, *Striking a Bargain: Work and Industrial Relations in England, 1815–1865* (Manchester, UK: Manchester University Press, 2000); and R. Samuel, "The Workshop of the World: Steam-Power and Hand-Technology in Mid-Victorian Britain," *History Workshop* 3 (1977): 6–72.

tion of the continuing importance of workshops, domestic trades, and imperial finance shifts attention away from a historiography dominated by the workers' becoming conscious of the nature of capitalism and of themselves as a class. It draws attention to a new historiography focused on how Tory aristocrats, romantic poets, popular radicals, and others forged traditions of social and economic thought that, by the late nineteenth century, constituted the historical background to the making of socialism.

Industrialization and urbanization are still important in this new historiography, but their importance arises largely from the ways in which contemporaries conceived of them and reacted to them. Like some of their eighteenth-century predecessors, Victorians experienced the gradual and uneven rise of the railroad, industry, and cities as a profound transformation of their world. As a society, and sometimes as individuals, they had an ambiguous response to this transformation. On the one hand, Victorians linked this transformation to the deepening of a prosperous and dutiful civilization and to the further spread of this civilization through trade and empire. On the other hand, they expressed caution and pessimism about the destruction rent by this transformation. Sometimes they looked back nostalgically to a more tranquil world based on established customs and relations. At other times they looked with horror on the ugliness, dirt, poverty, and squalor of the new industries and growing cities. Victorian culture and British socialism were products of the ways in which people made sense of industrialization, urbanization, and the social relations and processes associated with them.

This chapter explores Victorian culture using the concepts of tradition and dilemma to highlight both continuities and discontinuities. Continuities arose from the persistence of traditions from the late eighteenth century right through the late nineteenth century. Discontinuities arose as people responded to dilemmas in ways that transformed these traditions. More specifically, the dominant traditions in Victorian Britain were liberalism and evangelicalism, both of which had constitutive places in a wide range of domestic, social, political, and imperial practices. However, by the 1880s and 1890s, these two traditions confronted dilemmas such as the collapse of classical economics and the crisis of faith. People responded to these dilemmas in ways that decisively changed social practices, altering the manner of religious worship, inspiring a new trade unionism, and fragmenting the Liberal Party. The British socialist movement developed in the context of these changes, sometimes benefiting from them, sometimes contributing to them, and at other times struggling to respond to them.

Traditions

Historians have described two main traditions of political thought in early modern Britain. These traditions—natural jurisprudence and republican humanism—persisted into the Enlightenment. For example, Adam Smith inherited these traditions even as he initiated what has become known as classical political economy; he developed his science of the legislator by examining the operation of sympathy and prudence in the context of psychological and moral theories.[3] Equally, Enlightenment thinkers altered the traditions of natural jurisprudence and republican humanism as they grappled with dilemmas such as those posed by metropolitan and commercial life. For example, Smith and others rethought the nature of liberty so as to make it less dependent on self-sufficiency and more compatible with sociability and exchange, where an Enlightenment science of society explained sociability in terms of a conjectural "stadial" historiography, and exchange in terms analogous to the movement of the planets.

This revised view of the Enlightenment blurs the widespread distinction between its rationalism and a later romanticism. However, historians can still treat romanticism as a second wave of dramatic intellectual innovation that came hard on the heels of the Enlightenment. Romanticism heightened interest in imagination, creativity, and the inner life of the mind.[4] To some extent, romanticism was a response by people with religious faith to the secular histories of the Enlightenment. However, romanticism was less about a narrow counter-enlightenment than about a broad organicism. It took inspiration from new discoveries in anatomy

---

[3] D. Forbes, "Sceptical Whiggism, Commerce, and Liberty," in *Essays on Adam Smith*, ed. A. Skinner and T. Wilson (Oxford: Clarendon Press, 1976), pp. 179–201; K. Haakonssen, *The Science of a Legislator: The Natural Jurisprudence of David Hume and Adam Smith* (Cambridge: Cambridge University Press, 1981); D. Winch, *Adam Smith's Politics* (Cambridge: Cambridge University Press, 1978); and, for a greater emphasis on change, J. Robertson, "Scottish Political Economy beyond the Civic Tradition: Government and Economic Development in *The Wealth of Nations*," *History of Political Thought* 2 (1983): 451–82. Also see, more generally, I. Hont and M. Ignatief, eds., *Wealth and Virtue: The Shaping of Political Economy in the Scottish Enlightenment* (Cambridge: Cambridge University Press, 1983); J. Pocock, *Virtue, Commerce and History* (Cambridge: Cambridge University Press, 1985); and D. Wooton, *Republicanism, Liberty and Commercial Society, 1649–1776* (Stanford, CA: Stanford University Press, 1994).

[4] See I. Berlin, *Political Ideas in the Romantic Age: Their Rise and Influence on Modern Thought*, ed. H. Hardy, introd. J. Cherniss (Princeton, NJ: Princeton University Press, 2006); and for the specific case of Britain, D. Forbes, *The Liberal Anglican Idea of History* (Cambridge: Cambridge University Press, 1952); J. Mendilow, *The Romantic Tradition in British Political Thought* (London: Croom Helm, 1986); and J. Morrow, *Coleridge's Political Thought: Property, Morality and the Limits of Traditional Discourse* (London: Macmillan, 1990).

and biology and rejected the Enlightenment view of the mind as passive and inert. The romantics stressed the living nature of the inorganic world, and especially the ability of living beings to create a fluid and changing order through activity infused with purpose, thought, and imagination. Romantic themes appeared throughout the sciences in the nineteenth century as questions of time, dynamics, and evolution challenged those of system, statics, and balance.[5]

Enlightenment and romantic thought intermingled. Victorian thinkers restated themes from Jeremy Bentham and Smith in the context of organic concepts associated with historical evolution, cultural variety, and human agency. Enlightenment social science continued to inform accounts of the inner workings of modern society, but a romantic organicism encouraged social theorists to locate their analyses of modern societies in developmental narratives. The liberal and evangelical traditions in particular continued to cling to Enlightenment economic ideas in a way that muted romanticism.

The liberalism of the nineteenth century differed from Whiggism in its debt to an Enlightenment utilitarianism and a romantic organicism.[6] J. S. Mill and other liberals generally adopted utilitarianism with its individualistic and associational psychology. This individualistic psychology inspired novel arguments against state intervention and for democratic reform. Liberals discussed liberty and democracy in terms of individuals recognizing and safeguarding their own interests. They paid less attention to a security and regularity based on sociability, commerce, the rule of law, and constitutionalism. Liberalism also differed from Whiggism in the organicist twist it gave to social theory. When Mill pondered the problems of a naively individualistic view of human nature, he suggested that the solution lay neither in Whiggism nor in utilitarianism but in the cultural theories of the romantics. Historians might neglect the distinction between liberalism and Whiggism if they conflate utilitarianism with classical political economy. Although liberals rejected the psychology and ethics of the Whigs, they still defended the classical political economy of the Enlightenment in a way that simply bypassed utilitarianism. Even David Ricardo doubted Bentham's soundness as a political economist. To the extent that the liberals moved away from the political economy

[5] B. Hilton, "The Politics of Anatomy and an Anatomy of Politics," in *History, Religion, and Culture: British Intellectual History, 1750–1950,* ed. S. Collini, R. Whatmore, and B. Young (Cambridge: Cambridge University Press, 2000), pp. 179–97.

[6] N. Capaldi, *John Stuart Mill: A Biography* (Cambridge: Cambridge University Press, 2004); M. Milgate and S. Stimson, *After Adam Smith: A Century of Transformation in Politics and Political Economy* (Princeton, NJ: Princeton University Press, 2009); and W. Thomas, *The Philosophic Radicals: Nine Studies in Theory and Practice, 1817–1841* (Oxford: Clarendon Press, 1979).

of the Enlightenment, they were inspired by organicism, not by utilitarianism. Whereas Smith had treated labor as representing a certain amount of value, Ricardo understood labor in terms of the toil, energy, and time of living people. Ricardo thereby opened the way to a less static and more dynamic political economy. Political economy became less about an equilibrium arising from a hidden hand and more about the surpluses, slumps, and booms caused by the changing amounts of labor at work in society.

Nineteenth-century evangelicalism was a response not only to commercialism and trade cycles but also to later concerns associated with the French Revolution and English Jacobinism. Evangelicals dealt with these dilemmas by fusing classical economics with an atonement theology.[7] Evangelical moralists understood commercial upheavals as akin to other calamities, including wars, revolutions, famines, and pestilence. All calamities were a type of divine justice. Evangelicals argued that God had created natural laws that operated to reward virtue and punish sin. They suggested, for example, that Thomas Malthus's theory of population was the discovery of laws established by a benevolent God. In their view, Malthus had shown that God had made a social order in which the idle pursuit of pleasure brings disaster and poverty, whereas acting prudently in accord with God's will brings rewards. Evangelicals thought that any attempt to protect improvident workers or businessmen who went bankrupt from the natural consequences of their sin was bad economics and also contrary to the will of God. Poverty constituted a form of atonement by which people paid for their sins. Evangelicalism thus overlapped with Enlightenment economy while constituting a distinct movement of thought wedded to Protestant notions of character, duty, sacrifice, and truth. It linked economic concepts to these Protestant ones far more strongly than to the Enlightenment ones of sociability, manners, and sympathy. Evangelicalism also established a distinct domestic ideology. Social order and individual character depended on sacrifice and duty, both of which had to be defined by the church and instilled by the family. Strict notions of appropriateness defined familial relationships; for example, women were generally restricted to the roles of obedient daughters, wives, and mothers.[8]

Liberalism and evangelicalism dominated Victorian thought. Classical political economy and atonement theology inspired the individual-

---

[7] B. Hilton, *The Age of Atonement: The Influence of Evangelicalism on Social and Economic Thought, 1785–1865* (Oxford: Clarendon Press, 1991). Also see P. Mandler, "Tories and Paupers: Christian Political Economy and the Making of the New Poor Law," *Historical Journal* 33 (1990): 81–103.

[8] C. Hall, "The Early Formation of Victorian Domestic Ideology," in *Fit Work for Women*, ed. S. Burman (London: Croom Helm, 1979), pp. 15–32.

ist, laissez-faire, and free-trade beliefs that prevailed in the first half of the nineteenth century. Victorian culture was saturated with liberal economics, evangelical notions of truth and duty, and endeavors to raise the moral tone of the individual members of society.[9] The popular liberalism of William Gladstone was perhaps the clearest political expression of this culture.[10] More generally, Whigs and Liberals were typically the most indebted to Enlightenment ideas. Tories owed more to evangelicalism. The Liberal Tories of the Clapham Sect believed that nature was regular in a way that enabled them to adopt the political economy of the Enlightenment. The more extreme evangelicals, such as Lord Shaftesbury, believed that God intervened continuously in human affairs, so they were less comfortable with the mechanistic ideas and tropes of the Enlightenment.

PRACTICES

The early Victorians responded to the expansion of commerce, industry, and cities by developing Enlightenment and romantic themes and thus forging a culture saturated with liberalism and evangelicalism. This culture was not an inevitable reflection of prior social changes. It was a contingent response to perceived dilemmas. And it, in turn, then inspired shifts in religious, social, economic, and political practices. In 1851 the Great Exhibition showcased a self-confident Britain that identified itself with individual duty, social industriousness, scientific inventiveness, and competition and trade.[11]

The evangelical revival of the early nineteenth century spread belief in the divine inspiration and literal truth of the Bible, the supernatural and transcendent nature of God, and the importance of personal holiness and duty. The main religious organizations of the time were the Church of England, nonconformist Protestantism, and the Catholic Church.[12] The census

[9] S. Collini, *Public Moralists: Political Thought and Intellectual Life in Britain, 1850–1930* (Oxford: Oxford University Press, 1991). On the continuing tensions between evangelicalism and classical economics, see G. Searle, *Morality and the Market in Victorian Britain* (Oxford: Clarendon Press, 1998).

[10] E. Biagini, *Liberty, Retrenchment, and Reform: Popular Liberalism in the Age of Gladstone, 1860–1880* (Cambridge: Cambridge University Press, 1992). Also see D. Bebbington, *The Mind of Gladstone: Religion, Homer and Politics* (Oxford: Oxford University Press, 2004).

[11] J. Auerbach, *The Great Exhibition of 1851: A Nation on Display* (New Haven, CT: Yale University Press, 1999).

[12] D. Bebbington, *The Nonconformist Conscience: Chapel and Politics, 1870–1914* (London: Allen and Unwin, 1982); O. Chadwick, *The Victorian Church*, 2 vols. (London: A. and C. Black, 1971); and A. Gilbert, *Religion and Society in Industrial England: Church, Chapel and Social Change, 1740–1914* (London: Longman, 1976).

of 1851 provided denominational data based on attendance at places of worship. The statistics for England and Wales suggested that a quarter of the population belonged to the Church of England, a quarter attended other churches, and the remaining half did not attend any place of worship. Contemporaries were shocked by how few people went to church, as well as by how few of those who did attended the Church of England. Today we know that church attendance was actually at something of a historical high; throughout the first half of the nineteenth century, the growth in church attendance seems to have outstripped the more general rise in population. Today it also seems that the Church of England was increasingly holding its own: from 1800 to about 1830 or 1840, there arose a new type of dissent associated primarily with Methodism, and nonconformists probably were the main beneficiaries of the evangelical revival; but in the latter half of the nineteenth century, the Church of England experienced an even greater rise in the numbers of clergy and laypeople.

Although both nonconformity and the Church of England thrived in the context of a shared evangelical revival, they often seemed to share little socially. Victorian society was divided between chapel and church. The congregations at nonconformist chapels consisted mainly of people from the lower middle and working classes, such as clerks, shopkeepers, and skilled workers. The congregations at Anglican churches consisted more of people from the middle and upper classes and older industries such as brewing. During the nineteenth century, many nonconformists grew wealthier and more socially confident. Their confidence led them to describe themselves less often as dissenters and more often as Free Churchmen. The growing pride of nonconformity ran up against both the social exclusiveness of some Anglicans and the continued legal privileges that were granted to the Church of England. Until the passing of the University Tests Act in 1871, for example, teaching fellows at the Universities of Cambridge and Oxford still had to swear allegiance to Anglican articles of faith. As nonconformists became more socially confident, they looked to the Liberal Party to advance their cause, even calling for the disestablishment of the Church of England.

The Liberal Party had emerged in the 1830s as an alliance made up of Whigs in the House of Lords and Radicals in the House of Commons, both of whom wanted to promote free trade in opposition to the Conservatives. Ironically, when the Conservatives returned to government, their leader, Sir Robert Peel, repealed the Corn Laws, thereby effectively splitting his party and committing Britain to free trade. Thereafter, free trade dominated Victorian economic and foreign policy.[13] Economically, Brit-

[13] F. Trentmann, *Free Trade Nation* (Oxford: Oxford University Press, 2008). Also see Biagini, *Liberty, Retrenchment, and Reform*; Daunton, *Progress and Poverty*; M. Edelstein, *Overseas Investment in the Age of High Imperialism: The United Kingdom, 1850–1914*

ain was well placed to benefit from free trade. For a start, British banking had been through a long boom and now dominated global trade, and so Britain benefited immensely from global trade simply by financing it. In addition, Britain's massive empire and plentiful trade ports gave it easy access to (and, at times, control over) many of the resources that were imported to Europe and then used to manufacture other commodities for export. Finally, the content of global trade strongly favored Britain. Food and raw materials came from distant parts of the empire, parts that then needed the textiles and iron in which Britain specialized. On most estimates, global trade more or less doubled in the mid-nineteenth century, and for a while Britain played a part in almost half of that trade. It seems probable that the ratio of Britain's foreign trade to its national income has never been so high and that no other state has ever taken such a large share of global trade.

Coincidentally or not, Britain experienced a prolonged period of industrial growth and economic prosperity without a corresponding rise in population. As population levels remained steady or even decreased slightly while incomes rose, more people had surplus wealth to devote to leisure activities. Increasing numbers of the middle classes visited theme parks, exhibitions, museums, and other curiosities. The aristocracy built summer homes, took up hunting, and engaged in ostentatious consumerism. At the apex of society, the monarchy became a symbol of the wealth, power, and grandeur of the nation.

Over time, free-trade policies further altered British economic and social life. Free trade combined with improvements in transportation to drive down prices, especially for agricultural goods. Domestic producers found it hard to compete. Some agricultural workers moved to the cities and towns, where they usually found work in manufacturing, banking, and clerical occupations. Britain came to depend on cheap imports to feed its population. Moreover, British investment was often tied to overseas enterprises. Studies of the slow and uneven process of industrialization have revealed the extent to which British entrepreneurs generated their own long-term capital. Yet, if the banks and stock markets raised surprisingly little money for domestic industrialists, they were extremely active in securing funds for governments and large public utilities at home and abroad. By the 1870s, the income earned from foreign investments was greater than the continuing flood of such investments. Britain benefited greatly from interests and dividends paid on loans abroad.

Britain's dependence on imports made its trade relations crucial. And its loans to foreign governments made the stability of those governments

(London: Methuen, 1982); and A. Howe, *Free Trade and Liberal England, 1846–1946* (Oxford: Clarendon Press, 1997).

almost as crucial. Many of the wars and military engagements of the Victorian era were about securing trade routes and foreign investments. The British Empire expanded in a rather hesitant and unplanned manner, with little conscious direction. Of course, there were repeated attempts to reduce the expense of the empire's defense and administration, debates about whether empire was profitable, and discussions of the viability of securing trade without taking direct control of a territory. Nonetheless, Britain's economic interests and belief in free trade continued to give rise to a hesitant imperialism and at times to a bellicose and aggressive foreign policy.[14] Lord Palmerston's gunboat diplomacy embodied the link between free trade and an aggressive foreign policy. More typically, however, Britain did not explicitly seek out conflict so much as fall into it as a result of its foreign investments and commitment to free trade. The occupation of Egypt is just one example. When the Suez Canal opened in 1869, it vastly increased the speed and efficiency of trade between Europe and Asia, but it also increased nationalist hostility to European interference and to the local rule of Khedive Tawfiq. Conflict flared in 1882. Britain and France sent warships to Alexandria to support the khedive. The nationalists gained control of the country in June, but a British expeditionary force arrived in August and won a decisive battle at Tel el Kebir in September, thus putting Tawfiq back in power. The British military occupation of Egypt arose from the dictates of overseas investments and free trade.

DILEMMAS

British socialism had continuities with Victorian traditions, including, as we will see, popular radicalism, liberal radicalism, and romanticism. Equally, British socialism emerged as contemporaries responded to dilemmas in ways that modified the traditions they inherited. Socialism marked a rupture with the evangelicalism and classical political economy (if not liberalism) that had dominated so much of the Victorian age. The rise of socialism was, from this perspective, part of a much broader and more protracted cultural shift. The nineteenth century owed much to a mixture of classical political economy and evangelical ideas about truth, duty, and individual character. The twentieth century owed more to a so-

---

[14] For different variations on the theme, see P. Cain and A. Hopkins, *British Imperialism: Innovation and Expansion, 1688–1914* (London: Longman, 1993); J. Darwin, "Imperialism and the Victorians: The Dynamics of Territorial Expansion," *English Historical Review* 112 (1997): 614–42; R. Robinson and J. Gallagher, *After the Victorians* (London: Macmillan, 1961); and B. Semmel, *The Rise of Free Trade Imperialism* (Cambridge: Cambridge University Press, 1970).

cial welfarism infused with expert knowledge applied to ever more finely divided areas of society.

Two main dilemmas led people from the late nineteenth century onward to break with the dominant traditions of the Victorian age. These dilemmas were the collapse of classical economics and a crisis of faith. Most early British socialists grappled with these problems. Just as their debt to various traditions explains the continuities between socialism and earlier radicalisms, so their response to these dilemmas explains the discontinuities between socialism and earlier traditions.

Classical political economy collapsed in large part because statistical evidence showed that the 1850s and 1860s had involved the simultaneous growth of trade unions, wages and living standards, and population levels. This statistical evidence undermined the two main pillars of the classical theory of distribution. First, the idea that trade unions might raise wages undermined the wages-fund doctrine, according to which there was in the short term a fixed amount of savings to pay wages. Second, the concurrence of rising living standards and a population boom undermined the Malthusian idea that population growth responded to wages so as to create a natural tendency toward subsistence wages. Tories and romantics had often complained about the immorality of classical political economy. Now the economists themselves seemed to doubt its validity as a science. By the end of the 1860s even Mill had rejected the wages-fund doctrine.[15] When the British economy slumped in the 1870s and 1880s, observers complained that it suffered from all kinds of ills, including technological obsolescence, insufficient investment, poor management, and a lack of support from the state. Walter Bagehot pronounced political economy "dead in the public mind."[16]

Throughout the 1870s and 1880s, economists continued to decry the state of their discipline while exploring new theories.[17] William Jevons's marginalism was the most forceful of the new theories. Jevons redefined value in terms of marginal utility, thereby encouraging economists to turn away from questions of dynamics and toward more formal analy-

[15] J. Mill, "Thornton on Labour and Its Claims," in *The Collected Works of John Stuart Mill*, ed. J. Robson (Toronto: University of Toronto Press, 1963–91), vol. 5: *Essays on Economics and Society*, pp. 631–68.

[16] W. Bagehot, "The Postulates of English Political Economy," in *The Collected Works of Walter Bagehot*, ed. N. John-Stevas (London: Economist, 1965–86), vol. 11: *The Economic Essays*, p. 223.

[17] T. Hutchison, *A Review of Economic Doctrines, 1870–1929* (Oxford: Oxford University Press, 1953); Milgate and Stimson, *After Adam Smith*, esp. chap. 13; and for a more continuous narrative of revision that challenges any simple division between classical and neoclassical economics, D. Winch, *Wealth and Life: Essays on the Intellectual History of Political Economy in Britain, 1848–1914* (Cambridge: Cambridge University Press, 2009).

ses. However, most economists were more attracted to positivist attempts to incorporate history, social institutions, and ethics within their discipline. The collapse of classical economics created the space for the rise of avowedly historical and ethical approaches that owed a clear debt to romantic organicism. Historical economics flourished through the late nineteenth century until the neoclassical alternative finally acquired its hegemonic status. Indeed, even as Alfred Marshall developed his neoclassical synthesis, he argued that it was too abstract and that economists should pay more attention to historical and social factors in order to allow for reality.[18]

Victorian thought was transformed as people responded to the crisis of faith as well as the collapse of classical economics. The Victorian crisis of faith included several distinct challenges to Christianity and especially the evangelical belief in the literal truth of the Bible.[19] Geological discoveries falsified the historical timeline of life on earth that Christians deduced from the Old Testament. Historical criticism of the Bible suggested that the gospels could not be reconciled with one another. A romantic sensibility led to a growing revulsion over doctrines such as the vicarious atonement. Many Christians had already confronted one or more of these dilemmas before the 1859 publication of Charles Darwin's *On the Origin of Species*. Darwin's work then emphasized the gap between faith and science, including earlier evolutionary theories. (Few Victorians grasped the extent to which natural variation and random selection eroded the possibility that appeals to God might do any explanatory work whatsoever.)

When historians locate Darwin's discovery in the context of earlier biological thought, they suggest that his evolutionary theory emerged out of a broader organicism. In many ways, the Victorian crisis of faith represented the fall of evangelicalism before the onslaught of romanticism. Certainly, historians now recognize that the crisis of faith did not lead inexorably to secularization but, rather, to a change in the nature of religious faith.[20] Religious faith shifted away from a concept of God as a transcendent judge to a belief in a God who worked through evolution-

---

[18] M. Marshall, *What I Remember* (Cambridge: Cambridge University Press, 1947), p. 20; and for an example, A. Marshall, *Industry and Trade: A Study of Industrial Technique and Business Organisation* (London: Macmillan, 1919).

[19] Chadwick, *Victorian Church*, esp. vol. 2, chap. 2; J. Moore, *The Post-Darwinian Controversies: A Study of the Protestant Struggle to Come to Terms with Darwin in Great Britain and America, 1870–1900* (Cambridge: Cambridge University Press, 1979); G. Rowell, *Hell and the Victorians* (Oxford: Clarendon Press, 1974); and F. Turner, *Between Science and Religion: The Reaction to Scientific Naturalism in Late Victorian Britain* (New Haven, CT: Yale University Press, 1974).

[20] J. Harris, *Private Lives, Public Spirit: A Social History of Britain, 1870–1914* (Oxford: Oxford University Press, 1993); and Moore, *Post-Darwinian Controversies*.

ary processes within the world. Christians stressed God's incarnation in Jesus, the importance of the church he established, and the basis for faith provided by our inner moral voice. Other immanentisms flourished within spiritualism, pantheism, and idealism, all of which typically taught that the divine was present in everyone, uniting humanity in a single spiritual whole and guiding this whole to spiritual fulfillment.

The collapse of classical economics and the crisis of faith prompted numerous people to turn away from classical liberalism and evangelicalism. Various forms of romantic organicism rushed in to fill the space. Romantic organicism had already influenced much of Victorian social theory; it had contributed to restatements of Whig historiography against utilitarian rationalism and to the emergence of evolutionary themes in anthropology and sociology.[21] By the 1870s and 1880s, many people believed that the rise of organicism and evolutionary theories constituted an intellectual revolution. They thought that their mental world had to be completely different from that of their parents. Everything seemed up for grabs. Edward Pease, an early socialist, later recalled:

> It is nowadays not easy to recollect how wide was the intellectual gulf which separated the young generation of that period from their parents. *The Origin of Species*, published in 1859, inaugurated an intellectual revolution such as the world had not known since Luther nailed his Theses to the door of All Saints Church at Wittenberg. ... The young men of the time grew up with the new ideas and accepted them as a matter of course. ... Our parents, who read neither Spencer nor Huxley, lived in an intellectual world which bore no relation to our own; and cut adrift as we were from the intellectual moorings of our upbringings, recognising, as we did, that the older men were useless as guides in religion, in science, in philosophy, because they knew no evolution, we also felt instinctively that we ... had to discover somewhere for ourselves what were the true principles of the then recently invented science of sociology.[22]

Pease's generation thus turned to socialism and related movements, including philosophical idealism, the new liberalism, spiritualism, and theosophy. It broke with classical liberalism and evangelicalism, but it still accepted romantic organicism with its historicist restatement of Enlightenment ideas of reason and progress. Almost all the early socialists believed in progressive evolution, historicist approaches to social inquiry, and holistic accounts of the self and its social duties. It is true that the Vic-

[21] J. Burrow, *Whigs and Liberals: Continuity and Change in English Political Thought* (Oxford: Clarendon Press, 1988); J. Burrow, *Evolution and Society: A Study in Victorian Social Theory* (Cambridge: Cambridge University Press, 1966).

[22] E. Pease, *The History of the Fabian Society* (London: A. Fifield, 1916), pp. 17–18.

torian crisis of faith began to inspire a modernist skepticism that could make evolutionary narratives of progress seem overly optimistic and ambitious. Nonetheless, it was not until the First World War that modernism seriously challenged romantic organicism. The First World War shattered the belief in progress, destroying people's faith in the power of truth and reason and undermining accounts of the historical development of spirit and purpose.

RELIGION

British socialism and related movements, including philosophical idealism, the new liberalism, spiritualism, and theosophy, arose in an interlude between the heyday of Victorian culture and the modernism of the twentieth century. The collapse of classical economics and the crisis of faith had eroded the classical liberalism and evangelicalism of the earlier nineteenth century, but the First World War had not yet undermined romantic organicism and thereby created the space for an incipient modernism to come to the fore. During the 1880s and 1890s, social theorists were often responding less to commerce and industrialization than to the dilemmas besetting the liberalism and evangelicalism with which they had previously made sense of modernity. Their beliefs and actions disturbed the religious, economic, and political settlements of the mid-nineteenth century. In religion, scientific discoveries unsettled many, simultaneously spreading doubt and fostering alternative approaches to spirituality and faith. In economic affairs, there was a general sense of living through a depression, a growth of protectionist sentiment, and a new trade unionism. In politics, the Liberal Party began to creak as its factions pulled apart from one another and imperial entanglements alienated Radicals.

Darwin did not use the word "evolution" until the fifth edition of *The Origin of Species* came out in 1869, but his work had immediately reinforced the widespread use of evolutionary explanations of the natural and social worlds. Darwin's main innovation was to propose natural selection as the mechanism governing evolutionary developments. Generally, the Victorians treated Darwinism as the highest expression of a growing set of scientific and evolutionary ideas. Victorians increasingly discussed the world in terms of "evolution," using it to postulate a progressive tendency in nature and to express lurking doubts about contemporary society. Historical and comparative studies of societies often put Victorian Britain at the apex of advancement, but they also could express fears about regression and collapse.[23] In political theory, for example,

---

[23] Burrow, *Evolution and Society*; and M. Fichman, *Evolutionary Theory and Victorian Culture* (New York: Humanity Books, 2002).

Bagehot deployed evolutionary language simultaneously to postulate a law of progress and to express quasi-scientific concerns about the future prospects of progress.[24] On the one hand, Bagehot presented the history of civilization as an evolutionary development from despotism to the adaptive growth he associated with contemporary Britain. On the other hand, he expressed his fear, especially given the apparent rise of mass democracy, that a suppressed atavism might overwhelm custom and lead to backsliding and chaos.

Evolutionary theory unsettled many Victorians not only because the language of development raised the possibility of backsliding but also because scientific discoveries provided a contrast to older religious truths. As we will see throughout this book, it is a mistake to assume that science and evolution led inexorably to secularization. However, it is still quite clear that many educated Victorians believed, with good reason, that science was spreading religious doubts. The age included extensive discussions of the apparent conflict between faith and reason and of how the two might be reconciled with one another. The attempt to bridge faith and reason energized quasi-scientific approaches to the soul, death, the afterlife, and the divine.[25] The Theosophical Society, founded by Madame Blavatsky, was just one of many organizations to use the language of science and evolution to discuss paranormal and mystical experiences. The Society for Psychical Research was formed in 1882 by Frederick Myers, an Oxford philosopher who had lost his Christian faith. Its members included prominent academics, politicians, and writers, including Henry Sidgwick, Arthur Balfour, and Sir Arthur Conan Doyle. Some spiritualists actively believed in a spirit world that mediums could enter to contact the dead or a kind of ether that mediums could manipulate to produce action at a distance. Others focused on rigorous observation and experimentation to investigate and measure possible examples of psychic phenomena.

Science was not the only source of unease among Victorian Christians. As we have seen, the census of 1851 surprised many by revealing that half the population did not attend church. The census suggested that attendance was especially low among the working classes in cities and large towns. Mid-Victorians increasingly began to worry about the moral and spiritual health of the poor and the failure of churches to connect with them.[26] By the end of the 1880s, the message of the census

[24] W. Bagehot, "Physics and Politics," in *Collected Works*, vol. 7: *The Political Essays*, pp. 15–144.

[25] J. Dixon, *Divine Feminine: Theosophy and Feminism in England* (Baltimore: Johns Hopkins University Press, 2001), and J. Oppenheim, *The Other World: Spiritualism and Psychological Research in England, 1850–1914* (Cambridge: Cambridge University Press, 1985).

[26] K. Inglis, *Churches and the Working Classes in Victorian England* (London: Routledge, 1963); and for what follows, S. Meacham, *Toynbee Hall and Social Reform, 1880–*

had been echoed by the social surveys of Charles Booth, Henry Mayhew, and others. Several churches tried to engage the urban poor by means of missionary programs that combined social work and evangelizing. In 1883 Arnold Toynbee, an Oxford historian, gave a sermon asking that the workers forgive the higher classes for neglecting them and calling on the youth of those higher classes to devote themselves to the service of the poor. A year later, Samuel Barnett, an Anglican vicar, founded Toynbee Hall in the Whitechapel district of London as a place where students from Oxford and Cambridge could live among the workers. The Settlement Movement aimed to bring relief and uplift to the poor. The members of Toynbee Hall and other similar settlements offered to the poor practical assistance such as free legal aid, educational lectures, and boys' clubs. The crucial inspiration, however, was the idea of creating a bridge between the social classes by fostering a shared spirituality.

ECONOMY

Many Victorians experienced the 1880s as a time of economic depression. It is true that historians have often questioned the correctness of this experience, emphasizing Britain's continuing prosperity throughout the late nineteenth century.[27] Historians grant that Britain's effective monopoly of many manufacturing industries came to an end as foreign competition caught up, but they argue that industrialization abroad also reduced the cost of imported raw materials and of consumer prices. Still, whatever the facts of the matter, many contemporaries believed that they were living through a "Great Depression." In 1885 the government formed the Royal Commission on the Depression of Trade and Industry. When the Royal Commission sent requests for information to fifty chambers of commerce, thirty-eight of the replies said that their local industries were in serious distress.

Members of the middle and upper classes suffered as profit margins were squeezed between price-reducing competition from abroad and the need for increasingly expensive plant machinery at home. Feelings of gloom spread, feeding on and stimulating the crumbling confidence in classical economics and its historic policy prescriptions. New economic

---

1914: The Search for Community (New Haven, CT: Yale University Press, 1987); and N. Scotland, *Squires in the Slums: Settlements and Missions in Late Victorian London* (London: I. B. Taurus, 2007).

[27] S. Saul, *The Myth of the Great Depression, 1873–1896* (London: Macmillan, 1969). Also see C. Feinstein, "What Really Happened to Real Wages? Trends in Wages, Prices, and Productivity in the United Kingdom, 1880–1913," *Economic History Review* 43 (1990): 329–55.

theories multiplied; economists adopted historical and positivist theories often in an explicit attempt to close the perceived gap between theory and reality. Social surveys and social statistics provided ample newsworthy evidence of poverty. The authority of free trade seemed to unravel as the fair trade movement expanded and protectionism became almost respectable.

The making of British socialism was, at least initially, a middle-class affair; there was little enthusiasm among the workers. Yet, middle-class socialists were often reacting to their perceptions of the poverty and distress of rural and urban workers. The Great Depression was especially severe across the agricultural sector.[28] By the early 1890s, the price for agricultural commodities was often nearly half of what it had been back in the 1870s. During the 1890s, almost five hundred farmers went bankrupt each year, and still more quit in desperation. Although livestock farmers fared better than those specializing in cereals, all forms of farming suffered the effects of foreign competition. Wide tracts of land ceased to be cultivated. Large numbers of farmworkers migrated to the cities or even emigrated abroad. Farmers and landlords typically saw their income fall sharply. Radicals, and some liberals, blamed the troubles of the rural economy on the system of land ownership. Historically, they had long complained that because the supply of land was more or less fixed, landowners had a kind of monopoly that enabled them to exploit others. Now, as the Great Depression set in, programs of land reform spread.[29]

Urban workers too were affected by the Great Depression. Even if there was no general decline in living standards, unemployment rose as the loss of market share to foreign competition led to cutbacks in production.[30] By the mid-1880s, trade-union unemployment was around 10 percent. Workers marched and protested, and some of the early socialists played a prominent role in mobilizing them. The most famous protest was organized by the London Workingmen's Committee and Social Democratic Federation (SDF) for Monday, 8 February 1886. The demonstration began peacefully in Trafalgar Square, but after the speeches, the crowd marched down Pall Mall, smashing windows and looting shops. After pausing in Hyde Park, much of the crowd then returned down Oxford Street, again breaking windows and looting, until it was dispersed by the police using a baton charge.

---

[28] R. Perren, *Agriculture in Depression, 1870–1940* (Cambridge: Cambridge University Press, 1995), pp. 7–16.

[29] P. Jones, "Henry George and British Socialism," *American Journal of Economics and Sociology* 47 (1988): 473–91; and P. Readman, *Land and Nation in England: Patriotism, National Identity and the Politics of Land, 1880–1914* (Woodbridge, UK: Boydell and Brewer, 2008).

[30] J. Harris, *Unemployment and Politics, 1886–1914* (Oxford: Clarendon Press, 1972).

As the depression eased, a new style of trade unionism arose among the workers. Previously trade unions had largely been restricted to skilled workers, since they alone could afford to sustain unions through membership fees. During the late 1880s, however, with wages rising, trade unions began emerging among unskilled workers. The New Unionism recruited a far wider range of workers than had the elder craft ones, aspired to a general trade union open to all, appeared more militant and ready to take industrial action, and relied for much of its leadership on socialists.[31] The New Unionism dates from 1888, when Annie Besant, a member of the Fabian Society, helped the match girls at Bryant and May's factory to go on strike. In 1889 Will Thorne, a member of the SDF, led a successful strike by gasworkers for an eight-hour working day. The most famous example of New Unionist action came in the summer of 1889 when some ten thousand dockers, led by another socialist, Ben Tillett, went on strike, demanding a minimum of four hours of continuous work at a rate of sixpence an hour. The employers initially held firm, but socialist and other groups raised money to support the strikers, and after five weeks, the employers gave in to more or less all of the dockers' demands. The dockers then formed the new General Labourer's Union, with Tillett as its general secretary and Tom Mann, another socialist, as its president.

POLITICS

The Liberal Party was formed as a parliamentary alliance composed of Whigs and Radicals.[32] During the 1860s, new social movements began to look to this parliamentary alliance to represent their political views. These social movements included a provincial liberalism linked to the rise of local daily newspapers, an increasingly outspoken nonconformity, and the liberal-minded elite within organized labor. The Liberal Party had consisted of an alliance dominated by a Whiggish faith in administrative reform, the transcendence of sectional interests, and civil society as the locus of progress. Now it faced a crisis. Leading Liberals had to reconcile and satisfy the competing programs of the diverse movements

---

[31] For discussions of the New Unionism and its relation to socialism, see D. Howell, *British Workers and the Independent Labour Party, 1888–1906* (Manchester, UK: Manchester University Press, 1983); A. Reid, *The Tide of Democracy: Shipyard Workers and Social Relations in Britain, 1870–1950* (Manchester, UK: Manchester University Press, 2010); and P. Thompson, *Socialists, Liberals and Labour* (London: Routledge, 1967).

[32] On contemporary liberalism, see Biagini, *Liberty, Retrenchment, and Reform*; D. Hamer, *Liberal Politics in the Age of Gladstone and Roseberry* (Oxford: Oxford University Press, 1972); and J. Parry, *The Rise and Fall of Liberal Government in Victorian Britain* (New Haven, CT: Yale University Press, 1994).

that expected its help in realizing their ambitions and ideals. The difficulties of accommodating such diverse programs triggered a series of conflicts during the 1870s and early 1880s. The nonconformists opposed the 1870 Education Act because it increased state grants to Anglican schools, whereas they expected the Liberals to support a secular educational system. Trade-union leaders quarreled with the Liberal Party over legislation that failed to confer the right of peaceful picketing. The Liberal government of 1880 angered the radicals by almost entirely ignoring every aspect of their progressive program.

During the 1880s, the Liberal alliance cracked, and arguably collapsed, over foreign policy and Ireland. Britain viewed the Ottoman Empire as an ally from the Crimean War and as a buffer against Russian expansion in the Balkans. When, in 1876, the Ottomans suppressed an uprising in Bulgaria, the Conservative government continued to support them, with the prime minister, Benjamin Disraeli, seeming to downplay the atrocities. In contrast, various Liberals and Radicals called for Britain to end economic support to the Ottomans, and as the conflict between the Ottomans and Russia deepened, they called for peace and British neutrality. Gladstone campaigned across the country delivering a series of fierce and emotional speeches on foreign policy. His Midlothian Campaign brought him back into politics, and in April 1880 he became prime minister, presiding over a new Liberal government. Yet, in the wake of victory, Gladstone's administration then appeared—at least to many radicals—to pursue just the sort of jingoistic and imperialistic policies against which he had campaigned. Gladstone initiated the occupation of Egypt, and although earlier he had denounced the annexation of Transvaal, he now refused to grant it self-government, thereby sparking the first Boer War of 1880–81.

Irish affairs proved even more contentious than foreign policy. Failing harvests had resulted in the eviction of many Irish tenant farmers because they could not afford to pay their rent. In the spring of 1880 the government introduced a bill to compensate the tenant farmers, only to see it fail in the House of Lords. The Irish National Land League, led by Charles Stewart Parnell, began encouraging tenant farmers to refuse to pay their rents and to resist evictions. Violence spread rapidly. English-owned farms were burned and English people attacked. The government decided that special coercive powers were needed, and so it suspended habeas corpus in Ireland and restricted people's right to hold arms. Although Parliament finally passed Gladstone's Second Land Act in August 1881, the Irish agitation and violence continued, and Parnell was later arrested and jailed. Parnell was soon released and further land reform was introduced, but the unrest persisted. After a seven-month interlude of Conservative rule, Gladstone returned to government in February 1886, explicitly to look into the possibility of home rule for Ireland. When his

Home Rule Bill failed, he resigned and called an election, which he lost to the Conservatives. The Conservatives remained in office for most of the next ten years, during which their Irish policy appeared to consist largely of coercion coupled with the intermittent suspension of various civil rights.

The Liberals' maneuverings on Ireland alienated both Radicals and Whigs. The Radicals deplored the intermittent reliance on special powers and coercion throughout the 1880s. Many joined a growing number of socialists to protest government policy under both Liberal and Conservative rule. Bloody Sunday is just one well-known example of these protests. On 13 November 1887, the Irish National League and the SDF organized a demonstration to demand the release from jail of William O'Brien. Ten thousand protesters approached Trafalgar Square from various directions. They were met by police and soldiers, infantry and cavalry. Four protesters died, and two hundred, including women and children, were hospitalized. Other opposition to Gladstone's Irish policy was even more damaging to the Liberal Party. Gladstone may have favored home rule, but the aristocratic Whigs did not, and many of them split with the Liberal Party and joined Joseph Chamberlain in forming the Liberal Unionist Party, which would eventually merge with the Conservatives.

By 1890 yet more problems loomed for the Liberal Party. Once workingmen began to get the vote, some wanted to enter the world of party politics, and their political aspirations sometimes offended the prejudices of local Whig and Liberal grandees.[33] The Reform Act of 1884 exacerbated the problem. Many county constituencies had previously returned multiple members of Parliament, often one Whig and one Radical. Now the Reform Act divided them into single-member constituencies that reflected population patterns. Those new constituencies with large working-class majorities began to field Lib-Lab candidates who could get the endorsement of trade unions.

CONCLUSION

During the 1880s, the churches seemed to be reorganizing themselves, the economy appeared to be in a severe depression, and the Liberal Party seemed to be falling apart. British socialism emerged in this context as people reworked Victorian traditions in response to the dilemmas posed by the collapse of classical economics and the crisis of faith. The first

[33] J. Brown, "Attercliffe 1894—How One Local Liberal Party Failed to Meet the Challenge of Labour," *Journal of British Studies* 14 (1975): 48–77; and P. Thompson, *Socialists, Liberals and Labour*, chap. 5.

socialist societies were small Marxist groups in London. The early British Marxists were generally secularists and either Tory or popular radicals. These traditions fed into their socialism. Typically, they argued that Karl Marx had created an economic and historical science, proving that capitalism entailed exploitation and that the collapse of capitalism was inevitable. Older radical ideas sometimes entered their accounts of Marx's economic theory. More importantly, their understanding of Marx suggested that he had relatively little to say about metaphysics, ethics, and politics. The early Marxists often supplemented their Marxism with philosophical and political ideas derived from radicalism and romanticism. Even the disagreements among British Marxists often reflected their earlier commitments to different traditions, with the Tory and popular radicals lining up against those with more liberal and romantic inheritances.

Most Fabians drew on a tradition of liberal radicalism. They typically responded to the crisis of faith by adopting an evolutionary and ethical positivism. They moved away from the individualism of much midcentury liberalism and evangelicalism and turned instead to reformist humanitarianism. The Fabians' humanitarian concern with social duty led them to explore a range of movements for social reform, including land reform, Marxism, Christian socialism, and anarchism. In the mid-1880s, several Fabians studied political economy extensively; they read widely, joined discussion groups, gave lecture courses, and published articles. They got caught up in the collapse of classical economics. Different Fabians espoused, to various degrees, marginalist, neoclassical, and positivist approaches to political economy. These economic ideas inspired much of their socialism.

The Marxists and the Fabians began as metropolitan groups. They made efforts at propaganda elsewhere. Some members went to live in towns in the Midlands and farther north, and they even made converts and founded provincial branches. But their overall membership remained small. Socialism became a widespread movement only when a noticeably more ethical socialism spread through the provinces. This ethical socialism was a response to the crisis of faith. Idealists and other romantic organicists forged immanentist theologies, according to which the divine was present in the world working through evolutionary processes. Some evangelicals also adopted immanentism as a new faith. This immanentism then encouraged a new ethic of fellowship. It gave divine sanction to various utopian projects of personal and social transformation. Some ethical socialists even argued that God was present in the labor movement; God was using the movement to realize his purpose.

As socialists transformed their Victorian inheritance, they crafted the traditions that appeared in the formation of the Labour Party and that still echo in debates about the future of socialism. Many Fabians and ethical socialists came to favor a labor alliance with the industrial working class. Together they forged the social democratic tradition, with its emphasis on an active state based on expert knowledge. Although some Marxists held similar ideas, they were often more reluctant to dilute socialism in order to appeal to trade unions. They began to forge an alternative communist tradition, stressing the importance of a vanguard socialist party leading the workers in revolutionary industrial and political action. Finally, nongovernmental ethical socialists, and a few Marxists, forged yet other socialisms. These nongovernmental traditions rejected state ownership, bureaucratic planning, and even the industrial working class. They gave pride of place to a new life based on personal transformation, collaborative governance, and radical democratic politics.

PART ONE

The Marxists

CHAPTER THREE

Ernest Belfort Bax

SOCIALISM FLOURISHED AS PEOPLE from diverse traditions responded to dilemmas such as the crisis of faith and the collapse of classical political economy. In the early nineteenth century, evangelicalism and classical political economy had lent considerable intellectual legitimacy to capitalism. Yet, evangelicalism and classical political economy were never ubiquitous; they were always contested. Secularists were skeptical of all forms of faith, including evangelicalism. Popular radicals combined secularism with a republican politics that challenged liberalism and especially the political power of landowners and finance capitalists. Tory radicals denounced classical political economy for its association with an urbanization and industrialization that they believed undermined customary social bonds.

Early recruits to the socialist movement had backgrounds in secularism, popular radicalism, and Tory radicalism. Part 1 explores the pathways from these traditions to the first Marxist organizations to appear in Britain. The Marxists remained few in number throughout the late Victorian and Edwardian eras. A few Tory and popular radicals read Karl Marx and understood him in terms set by these traditions. Chapters 3 and 4 explore the two people who first introduced Marx to the British public. Ernest Belfort Bax fused his Marxism with German idealism and republican positivism. Henry Mayers Hyndman fused his Marxism with Tory radicalism. Chapter 5 examines the other leading figure in the early Marxist movement: William Morris. Morris turned to Marxism against the background of a romantic medievalism that echoed themes from Tory radicalism. Chapter 6 looks at the popular radicals who provided so many of the members of the early Marxist organizations.

This chapter begins to show how British Marxism arose out of traditions that stood aside from the evangelicalism and liberal economics that had dominated much of the nineteenth century. It begins by looking at the traditions and movements that fed into British Marxism, including republican positivists and exiled anarchists as well as Tory and popular radicals. Bax came to Marxism through his contact with these groups and his interest in German idealism. Later in the chapter, we will find that

A version of this chapter appeared as "Ernest Belfort Bax: Marxist, Idealist, Positivist," *Journal of the History of Ideas* 54 (1993), 119–135. Published by The Johns Hopkins University Press.

Bax's Marxism continued to echo themes that came from these groups and the traditions of thought that inspired them.

THE BACKGROUND TO MARXISM

Throughout the middle of the nineteenth century, Tory radicals, popular radicals, and republican secularists toyed with socialist ideas. Tory radicals harked back to a hierarchical social order in which the aristocrats led the people in a spiritual and moral life. They denounced industrialism and commercialism as dangerously unstable. F. D. Maurice and the other early Christian socialists called for a social and communal order while remaining hostile to democracy.[1] Popular radicals saw "old corruption" as the source of social ills. The ruling class had a monopoly of political power, which they used to enforce legal bonds on the people. Democracy would secure the political rights of the people, enabling them at last to overturn corruption and monopoly. Some Chartists joined the avowedly socialist groups associated with Robert Owen.[2]

British Marxism arose against the background of traditions of secularism and radicalism, especially the republican strand of popular radicalism. Popular radicals asserted the democratic rights of the common people and at times demanded economic justice. They made their claims for political representation through appeals to natural rights and a historiography according to which these rights had been established in Saxon or medieval times. The clear enemy of democracy was privilege. Privilege corrupted those who possessed it, leading them to act for their own interests and against the rights of the people. The propertied interest controlled both political and legal power. The rulers used their power to protect the interests of property by, for example, enforcing land rights and manipulating public finances. Popular radicals thus called for democratic reforms to prevent these abuses of power. Yet, their proposed reforms rarely challenged property more generally. Rather, they believed in a Lockean right to the fruits of one's own labor. They wanted a republic of free citizens who were economically independent. Their ideal was a commonwealth of farmers and craftsmen owning their land and tools.

Secularism overlapped considerably with popular radicalism.[3] The two traditions shared a rationalist and antiestablishment outlook. Thomas Paine and G. H. Holyoake inspired them both. If people rejected the dog-

[1] E. Norman, *The Victorian Christian Socialists* (Cambridge: Cambridge University Press, 2002).

[2] G. Claeys, *Citizens and Saints: Politics and Anti-politics in Early British Socialism* (Cambridge: Cambridge University Press, 1989).

[3] E. Royle, *Radicals, Secularists, and Republicans* (Manchester, UK: Manchester University Press, 1980).

matic evidence for Christianity, they could become liberal Christians or even syncretists. Generally, they adopted a more militant secularism only if they had an active hostility to the established church. Secularists and popular radicals fought for freedom from the restraints of legal bonds imposed by the landed and clerical authorities of the feudal era.

The republican movement of the 1860s and 1870s illustrates the close connections between secularism and popular radicalism. Charles Cattell had to remind the secularists that although many republicans supported free thought, it was not necessary to be a secularist in order to be a republican.[4] The republican movement also illustrates the extent to which popular and liberal radicals intermingled throughout the middle of the nineteenth century. By and large, liberal radicals wanted political reforms to promote democracy, but they did not believe that a democratic state would or should lead to legislative challenges to the landlords and money lords.

In 1871 the division between liberal and popular radicals led to a schism over the Paris Commune. The leaders of the republican and secularist movement adopted a liberal position opposed to the Commune. They formed the National Republican League, led by Charles Bradlaugh. Support for the Commune came instead from the popular radicals of the London clubs. The Stratford Dialectical and Radical Club even broke with the local secularist group over the need to promote social reform rather than continue with mere antitheological propaganda. The popular radicals who supported the Commune came together with British positivists, such as E. S. Beesly, Henry Compton, and Frederic Harrison, to organize rallies in its support.

If the Paris Commune split popular radicals from their liberal counterparts, its failure led to an influx of socialist and anarchist exiles into London.[5] A further influx followed from Germany in 1878 after the passing of antisocialist laws. The exiles were typically craftsmen: Johann Most was a bookbinder, Hermann Jung a watchmaker, and Andreas Scheu a furniture designer. Many of them knew of Marx's writings; Adam Weiler even addressed the Manhood Suffrage League on Marx and Engels's *Communist Manifesto*.[6] However, their loyalty was not to Marxism but to mutualism and nongovernmental communism. When they reached Britain, they formed various organizations, including, most importantly, the General Communist Workers' Educational Union, which was attached to the Rose Street Club. In 1879 Frank Kitz, an English dyer,

---

[4] *National Reformer*, 6 October 1872.

[5] H. Oliver, *The International Anarchist Movement in Late Victorian London* (London: Croom Helm, 1983).

[6] *Labour Standard*, 1 October 1881.

formed a British section of the Rose Street Club. In 1880 Kitz's group merged with Joseph Lane's Homerton Social Democratic Club. Then, in 1882, after the police closed the Homerton Club, Kitz and Lane formed the Labour Emancipation League.

Much of the membership of Britain's early Marxist organizations came from the popular radicals of the London clubs and the British associates of the European exiles. We will return to them in chapter 6. But at least in the early 1880s, their politics were either republican or vaguely anarchist forms of radicalism. So, chapters 3 through 5 will look at the rise of overtly Marxist ideas among the early philosophical and political leaders of British Marxism. These leaders were secularists and either Tory radicals or republican positivists who had met and cooperated with the popular radicals and European exiles of the British clubs.

THE PARADOXICAL BAX

In 1881 Bax wrote the article that Karl Marx regarded as the first one to introduce his ideas to Britain.[7] That article, along with another by Hyndman, marked the start of the socialist movement in Britain.[8] Hyndman's article borrowed extensively from Marx but, much to Marx's annoyance, did not mention him by name. Pride of place thus goes to Bax. Marx told Friedrich Sorge that Bax's article was "the first publication of that kind which is pervaded by a real enthusiasm for the new ideas themselves and boldly stands up against British philistinism"; but he also complained that "the biographical notices the author gives of me are mostly wrong" and "in the exposition of my economic principles and in his translations (i.e., quotations of the *Capital*) much is wrong and confused."[9]

Bax was born in 1854 to a nonconformist and lower-middle class family.[10] His father and uncle had become moderately wealthy by running a wholesale and retail business in the mackintosh trade. The growing prosperity of the family enabled them to move from Lemington, where Bax was born, to fashionable Brighton and then to leafy Hampstead. As a child, Bax accepted, apparently without much thought, the evangelical

---

[7] E. Bax, "Leaders of Modern Thought—XXIII: Karl Marx," *Modern Thought* 3 (1881): 349–54.

[8] H. Hyndman, "The Dawn of a Revolutionary Epoch," *Nineteenth Century* 9 (1881): 1–18.

[9] K. Marx and F. Engels, *Letters to Americans, 1848–1895*, trans. L. Mins (New York: International Publishers, 1953), p. 131.

[10] Biographical details are scanty. The main source is Bax's remarkably impersonal autobiography. See E. Bax, *Reminiscences and Reflexions of a Mid and Late Victorian* (London: Allen and Unwin, 1918). For a discussion, see J. Cowley, *The Victorian Encounter with Marx* (London: British Academic Press, 1992).

Christianity and Manchester School economics of his family. As he began to read more widely, evolutionary theory undermined his religious faith. He turned to positivism, with its religion of humanity and republican politics. His earliest article, written for *Modern Thought*, described his new ideas. Bax wrote that religion should lose its theological implications. He claimed that religion was not about God but about the ideal and so the infinite extension of all that is valuable. In his view, the religious aspect of ethics "points to an infinitely extended development of social feeling," whereas the religious aspect of aesthetics points to an infinite extension of beauty.[11] Bax then argued that religion is, like social feeling and beauty, necessarily tied to consciousness, and because the highest form of consciousness is humanity, the religion of the future must be the religion of humanity.

During the 1870s, Bax's republican positivism led to his becoming friendly with some of the European exiles living in London, including old Communards such as Pascal Grousset, Charles Longuet, and Albert Reynard. Bax also met Jung and Most at the London Dialectical Society in Poland Street. These exiles were not Marxists, but they introduced him to socialism. When Bax read *Capital* in 1879, he began to consider himself a Marxist, and thinking that Marxism lacked a philosophy, he set out to provide it with one by drawing on German idealism and republican positivism.

Clearly, Bax did not correspond to the caricature of British Marxists as people who reject theory and replace the dialectic with naive empiricism. On the contrary, he attempted to bolster Marxism by recourse to the metaphysics of German idealism and the ethics of French positivism. When a correspondent criticized one of Bax's articles on socialism, Bax advised him to read not only Marx but also Immanuel Kant.[12] At the turn of the century, relatively few of Marx's works had been published. Marx was known as the revolutionary of *The Communist Manifesto* and the economist of *Capital*, but not as the philosopher who was later revealed in his earlier writings.[13] Bax himself believed that Marx's economic theory was "comparable in its revolutionary character and wide-reaching implications to the Copernican system in astronomy," but it lacked a philosophy.[14] He thought that Marx had used the dialectic in *Capital* without giving it any metaphysical grounds, and "the dialectic method without metaphysic is a tree cut away from its roots"—"it has no basis

---

[11] E. Bax, "The Word 'Religion,'" *Modern Thought* 1 (1879): 68.

[12] E. Bax, "Reply to Criticism of Modern Socialism," *Modern Thought* 1 (1879): 197. The original article was E. Bax, "Modern Socialism," *Modern Thought* 1 (1879): 150–53.

[13] On the availability of Marx's writings in Britain, see S. Macintyre, *A Proletarian Science: Marxism in Britain, 1917–33* (London: Lawrence and Wishart, 1986), pp. 91–93.

[14] Bax, "Marx," 350.

and therefore no justification as an instrument of research."[15] He argued that German idealism could provide the Marxist dialectic with a metaphysical basis. Bax also thought that Marx had neglected the ethical aspect of socialism, where socialism was a new worldview appearing "in economy as co-operative communism; in religion as anti-theistic humanism; and in politics as cosmopolitan republicanism."[16] He argued that French positivism could provide Marxism with a suitable humanist and republican ethic.

Few historians have studied Bax's ideas. Those who have describe them as irrational. Stanley Pierson concluded, "Bax exhibited attitudes, or a style of thought, which were simply irrational," and "his peculiar fixations on the Victorian family suggest anxieties, resentments or desires which, in the absence of much information of Bax's personal life, are beyond the reach of the historian."[17] E. P. Thompson suggested that "there was something odd about Bax," for he "kept plunging off after the spectacle of hypocrisy, rather than the fact of exploitation."[18] Earlier, in Bax's own lifetime, Friedrich Engels dismissed him as a "chaser after philosophical paradoxes."[19] All these critics make much the same point: Bax's social commentary neglects politics and exhibits a strange obsession with social hypocrisy, reflecting his idiosyncratic psychological makeup. In contrast, I explain Bax's obsessions by placing them in the context of his wider web of beliefs, that is, his mixture of Marxism, idealism, and positivism.

AN IDEALIST METAPHYSICIAN

As a youth, Bax wanted to become a composer. He studied music at the conservatorium in Stuttgart, where he also developed an interest in German philosophy. Later, in 1880, Bax became assistant correspondent in Berlin for the *Standard*. He met Eduard von Hartmann, with whom he had long discussions about idealist metaphysics. By the time Bax returned to Britain, he had come to believe that the solutions to "all the more comprehensive problems in philosophy" must begin with Kant's concept of the unity of apperception as expressed in the self-conscious act "I

[15] E. Bax, *Outlooks from the New Standpoint* (London: Swan Sonnenschein, 1891), p. 187.

[16] Bax, "Marx," 354.

[17] S. Pierson, "Ernest Belfort Bax, 1854–1926: The Encounter of Marxism and Late Victorian Culture," *Journal of British Studies* 12 (1972): 58–59.

[18] E. Thompson, *William Morris: Romantic to Revolutionary* (London: Lawrence and Wishart, 1955), p. 439.

[19] Marx and Engels, *Letters to Americans*, p. 154.

think."[20] Bax attempted to resolve philosophical problems that he found in the tradition of German idealism. His philosophical work represented his attempt to grapple with issues raised by this tradition. Bax's view of German idealism thus provides the context for a proper understanding of the philosophical tasks that he set himself.

Bax argued that Kant's metaphysics contained two possible paths of development. The history of German idealism consisted of the working out of these two paths.[21] G.W.F. Hegel took one path. He stressed the "think" of the unity of apperception and so fell prey to the intellectualist fallacy, reducing reality to reason. However, Hegel's dialectic caught the true dynamic nature of the world. The dialectic was a revolutionary concept that showed all fixed distinctions were merely temporal. Whereas Kant's categorical imperative postulated a transcendental, quasi-religious source of morality, the dialectic showed that morality depended on the needs of society, although unfortunately Hegel had reined in the radical implications of the dialectic by portraying the state, not society, as the arbiter of social needs. Arthur Schopenhauer took the other path. His concept of the "will" overturned Hegel's panlogism and reasserted the "I" of Kant's unity of apperception by deriving thought from a deeper, nonconscious reality. However, Schopenhauer argued that all willing implied wanting and all wanting implied suffering, so the best hope was for the will to live to recognize its own futility. His philosophy thereby ends in a pessimistic asceticism that negates the "will." Besides, Bax continued, Schopenhauer's "will" could not be the root principle of reality, since, according to Schopenhauer's own ethical theory, the "will" negated itself, and negation implied the destruction of the original substance: "The Will as thing-in-itself would seem to be not merely a basal element, but itself a concrete."[22] Bax turned here to von Hartmann, who, he argued, had managed to overcome the problems attendant on Schopenhauer's concept of the will by replacing it with the concept of the unconscious but had unfortunately rejected Hegel's dialectic in favor of Schopenhauer's pessimism.[23]

Hopefully Bax's philosophical aims are now clear. He wanted, first, to develop the idea of the unity of apperception in a way that steered clear of Hegel's panlogism by emphasizing that subject and object coexisted in a world understood in terms of a concept resembling von Hartmann's notion of the unconscious. He wanted, second, to develop a metaphysics

[20] E. Bax, introduction to *Kant's Prolegomena and Metaphysical Foundations of Natural Science* (London: George Bell, 1883), p. cix.

[21] E. Bax, *A Handbook of the History of Philosophy* (London: George Bell, 1886).

[22] E. Bax, introduction to *Selected Essays of Arthur Schopenhauer* (London: George Bell, 1891), p. xlv.

[23] Bax, *Handbook*; and E. Bax, "Hartmann's 'Religious Consciousness of Humanity,'" *Modern Thought* 4 (1882): 177–81.

that would secure the dialectic with what he considered to be its radical implications. Let us explore how Bax drew on German idealism in an attempt to meet these aims.

Bax's philosophy begins with the assertion that reality is the Kantian unity of apperception.

> The warp of which reality consists cannot be space or extension, for this is a mere blank form of external objects; it cannot be matter (in the physical sense), for this is merely a name for a synthesis of qualities in space which are perceived or thought, and which have no meaning apart from their perceivedness, as old Berkeley showed; it cannot be mind, for this is made up of "impressions and ideas" derived from external experience. . . . What then is more fundamental than all these? The answer is the *act of apprehension*.[24]

The act of apprehension contains two terms, the subject, or "I," and the object, or "think." Bax argued that because an unknown reality is a contradiction in terms, the object must be consciousness, and because reality must constitute a single whole, the object must be "consciousness-in-general," where consciousness in general is a universal, all-embracing consciousness presupposed by the particular consciousness of each individual. Bax then argued that just as any particular consciousness must have an individual or "particular-I" as its subject, so consciousness in general must have a "universal-I" as its subject. Indeed, he suggested that these two terms exist as one. He described them as interdependent, not divisible: "We may, if we like, define the 'Ego' as the potentiality of Consciousness, or Consciousness as the actuality of the 'Ego,' since the two are correlative."[25] Bax was therefore an idealist for whom reality consisted of a primary unity between a universal object, consciousness in general, and a universal subject, the universal-I. He combined the objective idealism of Hegel with a Kantian subject in a fundamental unity of apperception.

According to Bax, there is a basic unity between consciousness in general and the universal-I. But all phenomena and experience involve the negation of this basic unity. All experience presupposes the division of reality into subject and object (into "Ego" and "feltness"). This division undermines the indissoluble relation of subject to object. The subject now regards the object, consciousness in general, as external to itself. Moreover, because the individual subject regards itself as separate from the

---

[24] Bax, *Outlooks*, p. 180. His main philosophical works are *The Problem of Reality* (London: Swan Sonnenschein, 1892), *The Roots of Reality* (London: Grant Richards, 1907), and *The Real, the Rational and the Alogical, Being Suggestions for a Philosophical Reconstruction* (London: Grant Richards, 1920).

[25] Bax, *Problem of Reality*, p. 153.

object, it distinguishes itself from the universal subject. The particular-I or individual asserts its independence from the universal-I. A primary negation thus divides reality into a subject or "ego" and an object or "feltness" that includes other subjects. Bax explained, "A feltness, although ultimately referred to the 'Ego,' is referred to it by Antithesis; the 'Ego' is *Sub*ject, the Feltness is *Ob*ject."[26]

Bax then argued that the primary negation is itself negated by thought. Thought thus appears as the third term of the original synthesis. Thought shows that subject and object are interdependent, thereby reaffirming the unity of all against the primary negation implied in all phenomena and experience. Thought establishes that subject and object are united in a single whole, and so also that the particular-I is just a part of a universal-I. Bax's argument was that although our immediate intuition suggests the individual is absolute, thought or philosophy shows it is not. Thought reduces the particular-I to a "particular representative of a universal class," revealing the particular-I as a pseudo-unity, or one of many in contrast to the universal-I, which is a genuine unity, or one in many.[27] Thought reconciles the opposing terms of the primary negation. As Bax explained:

> The essence of every real-qua-real consists in these three elements or momenta, a thatness or matter (= "I"), a whatness or form (= negation of "I" or feltness), and the limitation of each by each, whence results the relation or logical category, which, so to say, suffuses with its light the alogical process behind it, which it completes. Every real contains a non-rational as well as a rational element.[28]

Bax's metaphysics thus presents both the primary unity and the primary negation as prior to thought. In his view, the primary unity and primary negation are thus alogical in that to describe them is necessarily to bring logical categories to bear and so to distort them. The alogical refers, like von Hartmann's concept of the unconscious, to a reality beyond thought, a reality that thought can never perfectly capture, a reality that cannot be caught in logical categories.

The foregoing analysis of a primary synthesis provided Bax with a basis with which to introduce the dialectic as the proper scientific method. For a start, Bax argued that the alogical lies beyond thought, so our logical categories cannot fully capture reality, and thus we must develop our categories through a dialectical process. Nondialectical thinking gives us only the consistency we find in formal logic. It describes the logical side of reality as if it were static. To grasp reality properly, we must embrace the

[26] Ibid., p. 154.
[27] Ibid., p. 24.
[28] Bax, *Outlooks*, p. 182.

alogical as well as the logical; we have constantly to redefine and extend our categories in a dialectical process. In addition, however, Bax implied that the dialectic constitutes a scientific mode of thinking because reality is dialectical. Thought begins with the unity of apperception before building up dialectically through the primary negation to the primary synthesis. Reality understood as thought or consciousness in general, without reference to feeling, conforms to the dialectic. Reality is dialectical, in other words, because thought obeys the laws of the dialectic: "We find, throughout the whole range of Reality, that activity of the Subject, which we call Thought, universalising, defining and reducing to its special forms or categories the a-logical element of feeling."[29] What is the result of philosophy? For Bax, "The result is dialectic—contradiction and its resolution—which is nothing more than the continuous positing of the alogical and its continuous reduction to reason; in other words, to the forms of the logical concept."[30]

Bax's metaphysics drew on von Hartmann's idea of a fundamental reality lying beyond thought to provide the dialectic with a metaphysical basis in idealism. He argued that reality consisted of a unity of apperception that was beyond thought in the realm of the alogical. Our immediate experience negates this unity by suggesting that we are distinct beings separate from a world around us that appears to us to consist of external objects. Then, when we apply logical categories to our experience in an attempt to understand it, we enter a realm of thought, which, through philosophy, reasserts the fundamental unity of apperception. Reality is thus dialectical; it consists of thesis (unity of apperception), negation (experience), and synthesis (thought). So we must adopt a dialectical method if we are to make sense of reality.

Although Bax provided Marx's dialectic with a metaphysical basis, he did so by appealing to a curious version of idealism. His commitment to this idealism inspired a philosophy of history very different from that of Marx himself. In some respects, Bax's philosophy of history closely resembled Hegel's and especially the Young Hegelians, who argued that contemporary conditions were far from rational. Like Hegel, Bax argued that the dialectic was a logical truth about reality itself. History logically must conform to the laws of the dialectic. Indeed, history is the logical movement of the dialectic manifested in reality; history is the dialectical progress of consciousness in general as it constantly resolves its own contradictions. Unlike Hegel, however, Bax claimed that the end of the dialectical movement of history would be socialism: socialism was the rational form of society and so the end of the dialectical process of consciousness in general. Thus, Bax concluded that socialism was inevitable

---

[29] Bax, *Problem of Reality*, p. 155.
[30] Ibid.

in the strong sense of being a logical necessity deducible a priori from the nature of reality itself. Bax reached this conclusion because, like Hegel, he believed that philosophy established the fact that reality is consciousness in general (albeit that the universal object is linked indissolubly to the universal subject), so reality must conform to the laws of the mind. The dialectic must result in socialism because socialism is rational. And reality must end in socialism because reality must conform to the dialectic.

In other respects, however, Bax's philosophy of history had little in common with Hegel's. The similarities appear when Bax considers reality only logically from the perspective of thought. Bax followed von Hartmann in arguing that behind thought there is an alogical dimension of reality. When Bax considered the alogical, he differed notably from Hegel. Bax believed that logical explanations subsume an event under a category that provides a general law covering that event. Logical explanations work by abstraction, so they are true only in a timeless sense. We can grasp Bax's meaning by imagining a given mathematical truth that needs to be worked out through history. The mathematical truth is a logical truth even in the present. But it is true only outside of time. It would not yet have become an actualized truth worked out through history. For Bax, therefore, history and reality must conform to the dialectic and logic, but they must do so only in a logical and so timeless sense. The alogical means that socialism is inevitable only apart from time. As Bax explained, "The Category must be realised; the logical course of human development must obtain; but the individual working in his own element, so to say, the form of all quantitative Particularity—Time, to wit—can indefinitely delay or accelerate its realisation."[31] Bax's concept of the alogical implied that determinism was part of the intellectualist fallacy that was Hegel's error.

So, whereas the logical dimension of history appears as "law," the alogical appears as "chance," "the ceaseless change of events in time."[32] The past creates the alogical forces that govern the constant unfolding of the present. Bax argued that these alogical forces involved an interaction between material and ideological forces.

> Of course "ideological" conception to bear fruit must be planted in suitable economic soil, but this economic soil, as such, is merely a negative condition. The active, formative element lies in the seed, i.e., the "ideological" conception. . . . Economic conditions, let them press never so hardly, require the fertilising influence of an idea and an enthusiasm before they can give birth to a great movement, let alone a new society.[33]

[31] Ibid., p. 161.
[32] Ibid., p. 157.
[33] E. Bax, *Outspoken Essays on Social Subjects* (London: W. Reeves, 1897), pp. 55–56.

Within time, the triumph of socialism depended on a suitable conjunction of material and ideological circumstances.

Once we grasp Bax's distinction between the logical pattern of history and the alogical forces of history, we can understand the apparently contradictory positions he took in the revisionist controversy. On the one hand, Bax called on the German Social Democratic Party to expel Eduard Bernstein for denying almost every principle of socialism.[34] But on the other hand, Bax attacked the economic determinism of Karl Kautsky, insisting that ideology played an independent role in history.[35] Historians such as Pierson have noted Bax's apparently contradictory views on Kautsky and Bernstein, but they have been unable to explain them precisely because they do not distinguish Bax's logical and alogical accounts of history.[36] Generally there is a contradiction between asserting the inevitability of socialism and denying economic determinism. Yet, Bax could reconcile the two because when he considered reality from a logical perspective, he was an idealist-determinist, and when he considered reality from an alogical perspective, he believed that chance and ideology played a role.

A REPUBLICAN POSITIVIST

Bax was a youth in 1871, but the Paris Commune made "a deep and ineradicable impression" on him, which "nothing else could make again."[37] The Commune led him to the positivism of Auguste Comte. Later he recalled:

> I can well recall the tears I shed during those days, in secret and in my own room, over this martyrdom of all that was noblest (as I conceived it) in the life of the time. Henceforward I became convinced that the highest and indeed only true religion for human beings was that which had for its object the devotion to the future social life of humanity.[38]

---

[34] E. Bax, *Essays in Socialism: New and Old* (London: Grant Richards, 1906), pp. 254–55.

[35] E. Bax and H. Hyndman, "Socialism, Materialism and the War," *English Review* 19 (1914): 52–69.

[36] Pierson, "Bax," 55.

[37] E. Bax, "How I Became a Socialist," in *How I Became a Socialist: A Series of Biographical Sketches,* ed. H. Hyndman et al. (London: Twentieth Century Press, n.d.), p. 11.

[38] Bax, *Reminiscences,* pp. 29–30. Also see E. Bax, *A Short History of the Paris Commune* (London: Twentieth Century, 1895).

Bax noticed that the British positivists were "the only organised body of persons" with "the courage systematically to defend the movement of which the Commune was the outcome."[39] He even began to attend positivist meetings. Later, as we have seen, he became friendly with a number of Communards living in London, and it was they who introduced him to Marxism.

Comte's positivism offered a linear theory of history.[40] Society progressed from theology through metaphysics to science, and morality progressed from egoism to altruism. The contemporary age was on the verge of a transition from metaphysics to science; it foreshadowed the end of religion and all other speculations about the infinite. In the future scientific age, the technical elite of industrial entrepreneurs would govern society for the welfare of all. Later Comte argued from his belief in the decline of all metaphysics to the need for a religion of humanity to act as a spiritual force in the society of the future.[41] Later still, he added liturgical elements to his Church of Humanity.[42] So, we can distinguish at least three sets of positivists in Britain. The first set consisted of the republicans mentioned earlier.[43] Beesly, Compton, and Harrison rejected Comte's religion while adhering to a less authoritarian version of his social theory. They strove for a democratic and social republic based on the revolutionary trinity of liberty, equality, and fraternity, a republic in which social sympathies would replace class sympathies and in which labor and capital would unite behind enlightened captains of industry. They joined enthusiastically in the battle for legal rights for trade unions. The second group consisted of evolutionary and ethical positivists, including George Eliot and Beatrice and Sidney Webb. Typically they responded to the Victorian crisis of faith by accepting evolution as the pinnacle of science and transferring the evangelical sense of sin and duty from God to man.[44] The final group was a small band of religious positivists, such as Richard Congreve, who adopted Comte's liturgies.[45]

---

[39] Bax, Reminiscences, p. 30. For the positivists' defense of the Commune, see R. Harrison, ed., The English Defence of the Commune 1871 (London: Merlin Press, 1971).

[40] A. Comte, The Positive Philosophy, trans. H. Martineau, 2 vols. (London: George Bell, 1853).

[41] A. Comte, System of Positive Polity, trans. J. Bridges, 4 vols. (London: Longmans, 1875–77).

[42] A. Comte, The Catechism of Positive Religion, trans. R. Congreve (London: Chapman, 1858).

[43] R. Harrison, Before the Socialists (London: Routledge and Kegan Paul, 1965), and, more generally, T. Wright, The Religion of Humanity (Cambridge: Cambridge University Press, 1986).

[44] B. Wiley, Nineteenth Century Studies (Harmondsworth, UK: Penguin, 1964), pp. 214–60; B. Webb, My Apprenticeship (Harmondsworth, UK: Penguin, 1938).

[45] W. Simon, "Auguste Comte's English Disciples," Victorian Studies 8 (1964): 161–72.

Unfortunately, historians sometimes fail to distinguish between these three groups of positivists and so mistakenly treat Bax as an ethical positivist. For example, Pierson describes both Bax's concept of consciousness in general and ethical theory as attempts to replace the Christian idea of God while retaining "important features of the traditional faith."[46] Yet, Bax disagreed profoundly with ethical positivists. Where they lamented the loss of faith and worried about how morality would fare in a post-Christian world, he was a confessed secularist who attacked Christianity for sustaining the false morality of the bourgeoisie. Bax was a republican and a secularist who detested not only Christianity but also Christian morality. He did not think of positivism as a way of keeping the good features of Christianity alive in an age when the dogmas of Christianity were no longer tenable. On the contrary, he denied that Christianity had any good features, and he saw positivism as opposed to Christian religion and Christian ethics. Bax was an iconoclast who defended new artistic expressions, such as the music of Wagner, on the grounds that they challenged the moral complacency of bourgeois society.[47] He belongs with other secularist converts to socialism, including Edward Aveling and George Bernard Shaw, who promoted Henrik Ibsen as a critic of contemporary morality.[48] More particularly, Bax was a republican positivist who drew inspiration from the French Revolution and especially the Paris Commune, praising Jean-Paul Marat for his work "in the service of Humanity and Progress."[49] Republican positivism could provide Marxism with a suitable ethic.

Bax based his moral theory in his metaphysics. He argued that because feeling and the alogical are metaphysically prior to reason and the logical, "the basis of the Rationality in human action is always Feeling."[50] The telos of human action is feeling. Moreover, Bax continued, although "we are not able to formulate this telos in its totality, we are nevertheless immediately conscious beyond all dispute of the fact that happiness, or pleasure, using the words in their widest sense, is at least its essential attribute."[51] Action aims at happiness conceived as satisfied impulse or completed feeling. However, moral individualism involves a contradic-

[46] Pierson, "Bax," 57–58.

[47] E. Bax, "Leaders of Modern Thought—XX: Richard Wagner," *Modern Thought* 3 (1881): 243–49.

[48] E. Aveling, "'Nora' and 'Breaking a Butterfly,'" *To-day* 1 (1884): 473–80; G. Shaw, *The Quintessence of Ibsenism* (London: Walter Scott, 1891).

[49] E. Bax, *Jean-Paul Marat: The People's Friend* (London: Charing Cross, 1882); and for a discussion, see R. Kinna, "The Jacobinism and Patriotism of Ernest Belfort Bax," *History of European Ideas* 30 (2004): 463–84.

[50] Bax, *Problem of Reality*, p. 90.

[51] Ibid., pp. 90–91.

tion that proves altruism exists: individualism teaches that we should seek our own good, and so individualists can define what we ought to do, as opposed to what we actually do, only by assuming that we do not always act out of self-interest and that altruism exists.

Bax believed both that human action necessarily aims at happiness and that altruism exists. He argued here that because happiness guides human action and yet individuals constantly act against their own interest, we must conclude that the happiness that constitutes the telos of life is social, not individual. If all actions aim at happiness, we can explain actions of deliberate sacrifice only with the hypothesis that the happiness aimed at is the happiness of something "intrinsically more comprehensive" than the particular-I. Bax concludes:

> May not the true significance of Ethics . . . the conviction that the *telos* of the individual lies outside of himself as such, consist in the fact that he is already tending towards absorption in a Consciousness which is his own indeed, but yet not his own, that this limited Self Consciousness of the animal body with the narrow range of its memory synthesis is simply subservient and contributory to a completer and more determinate Self Consciousness of the Social Body as yet inchoate in Time? If this be so, the craving of the mystic for union with the Divine Consciousness in some transcendental sphere would be but the distorted expression of a truth . . . that . . . the human animal is yet not the last word of Self Consciousness, but is in its nature subordinate to a higher Self Consciousness, his relation to which the individual human being dimly feels but cannot formulate in Thought.[52]

Bax's ideal is an idealist rendition of Comte's social morality, an "ethic of human solidarity."[53]

Again, Bax believed that the primary negation is one between subject and object during which the particular-I asserts itself as separate from the universal-I. Bax defined socialism as the resolution of this primary negation. Socialism consists of the particular-I or individual recognizing itself to be not a discrete identity but rather an intrinsic part of the universal-I or society. Bax evoked a "higher instinct which, though on face it has the impress of a class, is in its essence above and beyond class; which sees in the immediate triumph of class merely a means to the ultimate realisation of a purely human society, in which class has disappeared."[54] Bax's ideal is, like Comte's, a positive social ethic that goes beyond class.

[52] Ibid., pp. 56–58.
[53] E. Bax, *Problems of Men, Mind, and Morals* (London: Grant Richards, 1912), p. 39.
[54] E. Bax, *The Ethics of Socialism* (London: Swan Sonnenschein, 1889), p. 104.

Bax appealed to the republican positivism of the French Revolution and the Commune to give content to his social ethic. He argued that the revolutionary trinity of liberty, equality, and fraternity describes the true relationship between the particular-I and the universal-I. Liberty is "the freedom of the individual in and through the solidarity of the community."[55] However, Bax continued, liberty is not majority rule. The will of the majority is a mere collection of individual prejudices. True liberty depends on a concept of the general will derived from Bax's idealist metaphysics. It consists of the realization of one's relationship to society. It requires people to recognize that their interests are the same as those of the community. Bax's account of the universal-I here implied that "the perfect individual is realised only in and through the perfect society."[56] The ideal of liberty thus embodies those of equality and fraternity.

According to Bax, the realization of a social ethic requires a new principle of justice. Society must have a right to "all wealth not intended for direct individual use."[57] Bax argued that property is an essential prerequisite for liberty. So, whereas capitalism provides liberty for the few through private property, socialism will provide liberty for all through collective property. Bax again postulated a dialectical movement. He argued that "individual autonomy, or the liberty of private property—once the only conceivable form of liberty at all—implied the negation of the bonds arising directly or indirectly out of the crude homogenous solidarity of tribal society; the liberty of the future implies the negation of this negation."[58]

Bax's ethic thus entailed the Marxist goal of common ownership of the means of production. He provided the ethical justification that he thought Marxism needed by arguing that his idealist metaphysics supported a positivist ethic and by showing that the Marxist goal of abolishing private property was a necessary corollary of this positivist ethic. The need to subordinate the particular-I to the universal-I pointed to the social morality of Comte, and the social morality of Comte required that we establish a socialist commonwealth.

[55] E. Bax and J. Levy, *Socialism and Individualism* (London: Personal Rights Association, 1904), p. 47. Also see E. Bax, "The 'Collective Will' and Law," *Social-Democrat* 1 (1897): 368–71.

[56] E. Bax and C. Bradlaugh, *Will Socialism Benefit the English People?* (London: Freethought Publishing, 1887), p. 10.

[57] Bax, *Ethics*, p. 75.

[58] Bax, *Outlooks*, p. 88.

BOURGEOIS HYPOCRISY

Bax believed that Marxism lacked a philosophy, and he tried to fill this gap by appealing to idealist metaphysics and republican positivism. His metaphysics and positivism inform his social theory, explaining why he often focused on social hypocrisy rather than exploitation. Bax argued that because the primary opposition is between the particular-I and the universal-I, "the most salient relation in history" is the antagonism between the individual and society.[59] Similarly, because the primary opposition involves the individual's asserting itself against a supposedly external object, the antagonism between the individual and society is mirrored in the antagonism between mind and nature. Bax thus concluded that "the oppositions wherein history . . . consists, may, I think, be reduced to two chief pairs, i.e., *the opposition or antagonism between Nature and Mind, and the opposition or antagonism between the Individual and the Society*."[60] What of class? The class struggle is just "a special manifestation of the antagonism between individual and community."[61]

No wonder, then, that Bax found the explanation of history in the changing nature of humanity's ethical consciousness. He described the logical course of history primarily in terms of the changing dialectical relationships between the individual and society and between mind and nature, not changes in the means of production and class relations.[62] Initially the antagonisms between individual and society and between mind and nature were latent. An unconscious social solidarity reigned supreme; land was held in common, and individuals identified their interests with the interests of the tribe. Similarly, people worshiped nature, but only insofar as nature affected their own tribe. The antagonisms asserted themselves in the current era of liberal individualism. Individuals see their links to the community as fetters from which they want to break free, and they are obsessed with their own rights. Similarly, people distinguish themselves from nature conceived as inert matter ruled over

---

[59] Bax, *Problems of Men*, p. 56.

[60] E. Bax, *The Religion of Socialism* (London: Swan Sonnenschein, 1887), p. 7.

[61] Ibid., p. 51.

[62] On the logical course of these antagonisms, see Ibid., pp. 1–37. Pierson, in "Bax," 52, complains that "even when Bax discussed the subject with which he was most concerned, the growth of a new ethic, he tended to apply the categories and expectations supplied by his interpretation of history in an *a priori* manner." Pierson is right, but he does not recognize that Bax's idealist metaphysics implied that if one considered history from a logical point of view, one should treat it in an a priori manner. For an example of a more concrete study in which Bax considered alogical as well as logical factors, see E. Bax, *The Social Side of the Reformation in Germany*, 3 vols. (London: Swan Sonnenschein, 1894–1903).

by a transcendent God who is distinct from them. So, in the modern era, Christianity has resulted in the "severance of the individual from nature and society."[63] In the future, however, a conscious social solidarity and a conscious religion of humanity will arise, reuniting the individual with society and mind with nature. The particular-I will recognize its integral relationship to the universal-I, and people will no longer distinguish religion from politics, the sacred from the profane.

So, Bax believed that the most important antagonisms in history are between the individual and society and between mind and nature. His social commentary thus focuses on the state of these antagonisms, rather than on the class struggle. Bax argued that the most important point about contemporary society was that it represented the most acute point in the history of these antagonisms, and the main expression of these antagonisms was the ethos of individualistic Christianity. His social commentary thus consists largely of virulent polemics against Christianity. He refused to accept the Social Democratic Federation's official policy of neutrality on matters of religion.

According to Bax, we should consider behavior from an ethical perspective if it is "definitely social" and from an aesthetic perspective if it "merely concerns individual taste."[64] Christian ethics do the exact opposite, concentrating on the subjective virtues of personal piety, rather than the objective virtues of a social consciousness. Bax's social commentary describes the nature of this ethic and its malign ramifications. He argues constantly that Christianity leads to hypocrisy because people are more concerned to appear to be good than to do good deeds—the bourgeoisie are "vulgarity in a solution of hypocrisy."[65] As a result, Bax directed his critique of contemporary society at the teachings of Victorian Christianity, arguing that it alienated individuals from society by leading them to worship a transcendent God, not the humanity of the positivists, and that it alienated mind from nature by leading people to look on the material world as full of sin as compared with a pure spiritual world. He concentrated his fire on the ways in which a Christian ethic led people to act contrary to a proper social ethic. He exposed moral humbug and social hypocrisy.

Bax argued that Victorian morality, symbolized by the middle-class family and the capitalist "hearth," was the "perfect specimen of the complete sham."[66] For example, monogamous marriage is incompatible with natural affection. Personal relations are an aesthetic matter, so people

---

[63] Bax, *Handbook*, p. 402.
[64] Bax, *Problems of Men*, p. 203.
[65] Bax, *Ethics*, p. 101.
[66] Bax, *Religion of Socialism*, p. 141.

should be free to abandon the shackles of such a marriage if they wish to do so. But Christianity teaches instead that personal relations are a moral matter and that people should conform to the Christian ideal of monogamous marriage. The result is hypocrisy; people piously pretend to be living in accord with the ideal of a monogamous marriage while doing nothing of the kind. Similarly, interior decoration is clearly an aesthetic matter that should be left to individual taste, but the bourgeoisie asserts that a certain style of decoration is a sign not only of good taste and good breeding but also of upright morals. The result is "jerry-built architecture," "cheap art," "shoddy furniture," "false sentiment," and "pretentious pseudo-culture."[67] Bax's infamous attitude to the woman question follows the same pattern. Whereas relations between the sexes should be an aesthetic matter, Christianity imposes a strict moral code on them. Once again the result is a sham, with appearance dramatically diverging from reality. Men seem to dominate, but behind this facade the Christian moral code enables women to exercise almost complete control.[68]

We should note, finally, that Bax's metaphysics suggested that exposing moral shams and hypocrisies was a crucial form of political action. He believed that the logical triumph of socialism was inevitable. Action was necessary in the alogical dimension of history. Within the alogical dimension, economic factors were a necessary backdrop to socialist victory, but it was ideology that would lead to socialist revolution. The main task was thus to spread the socialist ideal. But what was the socialist ideal? Well, as we have seen, Bax described the socialist ideal as the synthesis of individual and society and of mind and nature. Thus, effective political action consisted in polemical pieces of social criticism that showed how contemporary civilization divorced the individual from society and mind from nature. Bax focused on philosophical paradoxes—on hypocrisy rather than exploitation—because that was how he thought socialism would come about.

CONCLUSION

Bax's synthesis of Marxism, idealism, and positivism resulted in an original and complex, if eccentric, philosophy. His views often appeared to run directly contrary to the Marxism of his time. He propounded an ide-

[67] Ibid., p. 145.
[68] E. Bax, *The Legal Subjection of Men* (London: New Age, 1908); and E. Bax, *The Fraud of Feminism* (London: Grant Richards, 1913). On British Marxism and feminism, see K. Hunt, *Equivocal Feminists: The Social Democratic Federation and the Woman Question, 1884–1911* (Cambridge: Cambridge University Press, 1996).

alist and a priori metaphysics while Engels was popularizing a rigidly empirical and materialist version of the dialectic, while the world's leading Marxist party—the German Social Democrats, inspired by Kautsky—was enshrining views very like Engels's as the orthodox Erfurt Program, and while, as we will see in chapters 4 and 6, Hyndman's equally materialist and empiricist philosophy was coming to dominate the Social Democratic Federation, to which Bax belonged for most of his life.[69] Small wonder that Bax complained Marxism had become identified with a "crude and dogmatic materialism."[70] His views may appear to have more in common with those later Marxists who reassessed the relationship between Marxism and German idealism. Indeed, his interest in the relationship between Kant and Marx and his concern with the ethical foundations of Marxism influenced the Austro-Marxists. Victor Adler translated a number of Bax's essays into German while imprisoned for involvement in the train strike of 1889. Yet, in some respects, Bax was very much a Marxist of his time. For a start, Bax's belief that Marxism needed a philosophical basis was characteristic of his time. Engels's scientism and Bax's idealism were alike attempts to fill a perceived gap in Marx's work. Their work differs noticeably here from the later humanist Marxists who tried to find a Marxist philosophy in the early writings of Marx himself. In addition, Bax's belief that the dialectic applied to all of reality places him firmly among his contemporaries. Like Engels, Kautsky, and Hyndman, he believed that in a sense the future was determined. He rejected their economic determinism for idealist determinism rather than a humanist emphasis on agency.

---

[69] F. Engels, *Anti-Dühring* (Moscow: Progress Publishers, 1947) and *Dialectics of Nature* (Moscow: Progress Publishers, 1972).

[70] Bax, *Reminiscences*, p. 46.

CHAPTER FOUR

Henry Mayers Hyndman

IN 1881 TWO ARTICLES introduced Karl Marx's ideas to the British public. The one by Ernest Belfort Bax provided a reasonable introduction to Marx's ideas. The other, by Henry Mayers Hyndman, did not mention Marx by name and advocated a very different politics, but it borrowed extensively from Marx's analysis of capitalism. Over time, Bax may have become the recognized philosopher of the Marxist court in Britain, but it was Hyndman who built what there was of a Marxist movement. He founded and long dominated the Social Democratic Federation (SDF), which was the first socialist society of the 1880s, for many years the largest and most famous Marxist organization in Britain, and the most prominent forerunner of the Communist Party of Great Britain.[1]

Despite Hyndman's illustrious position in the history of British socialism, he has been widely castigated. His personal failings are often blamed for the SDF's inability to attract the working class. The critics fall into two main schools. The Marxist critics argue that Hyndman's reformism, jingoism, and authoritarian personality divided British Marxists, thereby preventing the emergence of a truly socialist alternative to the Labour Party.[2] The other socialist critics argue that Hyndman was too radical to attract the British working class; the SDF was alien to British political culture and so lost out to the Independent Labour Party (ILP); the SDF failed not to provide an alternative to the Labour Party but to become the Labour Party.[3] The two schools of criticism originated among Hyndman's contemporaries. Tom Mann, a Marxist who became a syndicalist, attacked Hyndman for neither appreciating the significance of the trade

A version of this chapter appeared as "H. M. Hyndman: A Rereading and a Reassessment," *History of Political Thought* 12 (1991), 125–145. Published by Imprint Academic.

[1] M. Crick, *The History of the Social Democratic Federation* (Keele, UK: Keele University Press, 1994); and G. Johnson, *Social Democratic Politics in Britain, 1881–1911* (Lampeter, UK: Edwin Mellen, 2002).

[2] H. Collins, "The Marxism of the Social Democratic Federation," in *Essays in Labour History, 1886–1923*, ed. A. Briggs and J. Saville (London: Macmillan, 1971); and E. Thompson, *William Morris: Romantic to Revolutionary* (London: Lawrence and Wishart, 1955).

[3] S. Pierson, *Marxism and the Origins of British Socialism* (Ithaca, NY: Cornell University Press, 1973); and W. Wolfe, *From Radicalism to Socialism* (New Haven, CT: Yale University Press, 1975).

unions nor working among trade unions to create a genuine socialist movement.[4] John Bruce Glasier, an ethical socialist and a member of the ILP, criticized Hyndman for his dry presentation of the socialist ideal: "There was hardly a ray of idealism in it"; "capitalism was shown to be wasteful and wicked, but socialism was not made to appear more practicable or desirable."[5]

The various criticisms of Hyndman emphasize his idiosyncrasies. They often focus on his personality. He "lacked many of the essential political virtues, such as tact, a willingness to listen to other people, and a capacity to suffer fools gladly," and the same weaknesses affected the SDF, which "bore the imprint of Hyndman's personality."[6] He was "a natural gambler and adventurer who delighted in political crisis, he totally lacked the personal tact and strategic skill which a successful politician needs."[7] When critics occasionally mention Hyndman's beliefs, they portray them as personal attitudes not part of a wider intellectual tradition, thereby leaving them without a historical explanation. They criticize his neglect of the "impulse towards a qualitatively different way of life," or they argue that his belief in an iron law of wages led him mistakenly to reject the trade unions, but they do not explain his attachment to these beliefs.[8] Obviously personal attitudes can express a belief system. However, we cannot explain attitudes unless we put them in the context of the relevant belief system. Hyndman's beliefs were not private attitudes. They were extensions of an intellectual tradition of Tory radicalism. To understand Hyndman, we should situate him against the background of this tradition.

Tory Radicalism

Tory radicalism began with Edmund Burke and links Samuel Taylor Coleridge and Robert Southey with Thomas Carlyle and Benjamin Disraeli. Certainly there are differences between these thinkers, often profound ones—particularly in the case of Carlyle; but these thinkers none-

---

[4] T. Mann, *Memoirs* (London: Labour Publishing, 1923), esp. pp. 56–58.

[5] J. Glasier, *William Morris and the Early Days of the Socialist Movement* (London: Longmans, 1921), p. 30.

[6] C. Tsuzuki, *H. M. Hyndman and British Socialism* (Oxford: Oxford University Press, 1961), p. 273. Also see D. Howell, *British Workers and the Independent Labour Party, 1888–1906* (Manchester, UK: Manchester University Press, 1983), p. 284.

[7] P. Thompson, *Socialists, Liberals and Labour* (London: Routledge and Kegan Paul, 1967), p. 113.

[8] Pierson, *Marxism*, p. 64; Collins, "Marxism."

theless have enough in common for us to group them together in a single intellectual tradition.[9]

Generally Tory radicals expressed their views through a medievalist historiography.[10] The Middle Ages represented a time of harmony and order when people were "merrie" and devout. The stout yeomen of medieval England were attached to the land or an established trade and so economically independent; the yeomen were a free and vigorous people who, guided by an enlightened aristocracy, provided the backbone of an upright nation. Tory radicals narrated the destruction of medieval communities through the decline of church, aristocracy, and organic social ties. The Acts of Enclosure broke people's tie to the land, producing a more transient population. More recently, the Industrial and French Revolutions had destroyed the old world without providing a new sense of direction or a new social order.[11] Industrialism and democracy created an anarchic society operating according to the laws of mammon and of doing as one pleased. Tory radicals rejected utilitarianism and classical political economy, arguing that relations between social classes should be personal and that society should be founded on a recognition of reciprocal duties. Industrialism had eroded the historic ties binding social groups. A new commercial class ignored the obligations once honored by the landed aristocracy. Uprooted workers were cut adrift from a stable social order, lacked spiritual satisfaction, and, in desperation, might overthrow society. Southey explained that "the great evil is the state of the poor, which ... exposes us to the horrors of a bellum servile [civil war], and sooner or later, if not remedied, will end in one."[12] Disraeli believed that "the relations of the working class of England to its privileged orders are relations of enmity and therefore of peril."[13]

Medievalism was by no means the sole preserve of Tory radicals. A broad medievalism rose out of romanticism. The romantics denounced industrial society for destroying harmony and creating a society governed

---

[9] On other radical Tories, see C. Driver, *Tory Radical: The Life of Richard Oastler* (Oxford: Oxford University Press, 1946); and S. Weaver, *John Fielden and the Politics of Popular Radicalism* (Oxford: Oxford University Press, 1987). For discussions of Tory themes within socialism, see Howell, *British Workers*, pp. 373–88; and M. Pugh, "The Rise of Labour and the Political Culture of Conservatism, 1890–1945," *History* 87 (2002): 514–37.

[10] T. Carlyle, *The Works of Thomas Carlyle* (London: Chapman and Hall, 1896–99), vol. 13: *Past and Present*; and W. Cobbett, *History of the Protestant Reformation in England and Ireland* (London: James Duffy, 1868).

[11] E. Burke, *Reflections on the Revolution in France* (Harmondsworth, UK: Penguin, 1970); and Carlyle, *Works*, vols. 2–4: *The French Revolution*.

[12] R. Southey, *Letters of Robert Southey*, ed. M. Fitzgerald (London: World's Classics, 1901), p. 273.

[13] B. Disraeli, *Sybil* (Harmondsworth, UK: Penguin, 1954), p. 222.

by greed and selfishness, and the romantics influenced many socialists, most notably William Morris.[14] So, we can better explain Hyndman's beliefs by distinguishing the Tory radicalism on which he drew from broader romantic and medievalist traditions. Tory radicals expressed fears of political anarchy and appealed for statesmanship to guide an active state.

Tory radicals were preoccupied with warding off an anarchy they associated with the French Revolution. The main Tory theme in their thought was probably the idea that the French Revolution dramatically illustrated the danger of a violent revolution unconstrained by historic social responsibilities and organic social bonds. Burke had assumed that social harmony existed and so defended the unreformed constitution of the eighteenth century. Later conservatives often highlighted the discordant features of British society and so demanded novel reforms to prevent the rush to anarchy. This demand for novel reforms is the main radical theme in the thought of some Tories. Coleridge proposed a clerisy to prevent the masses from turning to Jacobinism and the aristocracy from renouncing the responsibilities that go with privilege.[15] Other romantics disliked the anarchy of the marketplace and its dehumanizing effect, but they did not generally criticize industrialism for creating a revolutionary mob that could upturn society. Similarly, even when Hyndman's fellow socialists drew on romanticism, they did not issue heartfelt warnings of an anarchic uprising.

British traditions and statesmanship offered Tory radicals a hope for avoiding anarchy. Tory radicals evoked an English tradition of peaceful politics. Carlyle wrote, "These Chartisms, Radicalisms, Reform Bill, Tithe Bill, and infinite other discrepancy, and acrid argument and jargon that there is yet to be, are *our* French Revolution: God grant that we, with our better methods, may be able to transact it by argument alone."[16] Peaceful reform had to eradicate the ills of industrialism and commercialism. It depended on the restoration of the historic alliance between aristocracy and people. Disraeli's novel *Sybil* symbolizes just such an alliance in the marriage of Egremont, the enlightened aristocrat, and Sybil, the daughter of the people.[17] The other members of the Young England group debated whether the current aristocracy would suffice or whether a new one was needed; Lord John Manners held the former view, George Smythe the latter. Tory radicals also called for aristocratic

[14] For an indication of the extent to which British socialists were inspired by the romantic tradition and particularly by Carlyle and Ruskin, see W. Stead, "The Labour Party and the Books That Helped to Make It," *Review of Reviews* 33 (1906): 568–92.

[15] S. Coleridge, *On the Constitution of the Church and State* (London: Hurst, 1830).

[16] Carlyle, *Works*, vol. 29: *Critical and Miscellaneous Essays*, pp. 149–50.

[17] Disraeli attempted a historical justification for this view in *A Vindication of the English Constitution* (London: Saunders and Otley, 1835).

statesmen to pilot the nation through the troubled waters that lay ahead. Disraeli wrote, "If it indeed be necessary that changes should take place in this country, let them be effected by those who ought to be the leaders in all political and social changes."[18] Such calls for statesmen rested on the belief that aristocrats were natural leaders, whereas the masses alone were blind and directionless. Carlyle explained that "the working classes cannot any longer go on without government, without being actually guided and governed."[19]

A romantic celebration of autonomy and freedom generally inspired not a call for Tory statesmen but hostility toward all authority, as, for example, in Morris. However, the romantic emphasis on the creative and imaginative individual could overlap with statesmanship. The overlap appears most prominently in Carlyle's writings on the hero.[20] Yet even here there are important differences. Carlyle's heroes are loners whose leadership qualities come from their personal character. Tory statesmen are aristocrats whose leadership role reflects an idealized vision of the aristocracy as natural guardians of the national interest and the established social order.

Tory radicals usually conceived of the statesman as representative of a harmonious state or nation. The nation-state embodied the collective wisdom of the historical community, providing the setting in which its citizens could have a good life. So, Tory radicals rejected liberal ideals of limited government. They argued that people needed guidance from the state. The government should promote moral social relationships so as to restore a harmonious society and promote the physical and spiritual health of its citizens. The members of Young England wanted to re-create the social harmony of the Middle Ages through a prominent role for the monarchy, an aristocracy that would serve the Crown and lead the people, a revitalized church, an improvement in the welfare of the people, and a policy of conciliation in Ireland.[21]

Many romantics shared the Tory concern with developing a harmonious alternative to the fragmenting and dehumanizing effects of commercialism. Nonetheless, the individualist strain in romanticism meant that, unless they were Tories, the romantics typically believed individuals should question social norms and values, even coming close to an anarchic opposition to all restrictions. They were less likely to pay homage to the nation than to universal cosmopolitan ideals. Certainly,

---

[18] Cited in W. Moneypenny and G. Buckle, *The Life of Benjamin Disraeli, Earl of Beaconsfield* (London: John Murray, 1929), vol. 1, p. 917.

[19] Carlyle, *Works*, vol. 29, p. 155.

[20] Ibid., vol. 5: *Heroes and Hero Worship*.

[21] R. Faber, *Young England* (London: Faber and Faber, 1987).

romantic socialists, such as Morris and Edward Carpenter, had a less statist vision than did Tory radicals; they even looked forward to a time when there would be no need for government.[22] Of no leading British socialist other than Hyndman could Max Beer have written that he was "a patriot burning with zeal to see all his countrymen, the scions of a great race, well-housed and warlike, having a stake in their worldwide Empire, the boundaries of which they should be prepared to defend and to extend."[23]

FROM TORYISM TO MARXISM

Hyndman was born in 1842 to an upper-class family, both sides of which were staunch Tories connected with the West Indies.[24] His father was "a member of the Conservative Club, and a supporter of the Tory Party."[25] Hyndman's education followed what he described as "the ordinary beaten track of the public school or the tutor, the University, the Church, or the Bar."[26] In his own case this track followed a series of private tutors, a spell at Cambridge, where he proved to be a formidable cricketer, and entry to the Bar, though he had no intention of practicing the law. He then toured Italy and, there when Garibaldi burst upon the scene, acquired a job as correspondent for the *Pall Mall Gazette*.

When Hyndman returned to Britain, he began to enter politics as a radical Tory. He first ventured into the slums of the East End at the instigation of his friend Raymond Lluellyn, who later became a Conservative Member of Parliament (MP). His early political writings were on the conservative topic of empire; he argued that the current administration of the colonies was defective, the empire was in danger of falling apart, and the solution lay with a self-governing Commonwealth in which the colonies had parliamentary representation.[27] Then, in 1880, Henry Munro Butler-

---

[22] W. Morris, *The Collected Works of William Morris*, intro. M. Morris (London: Longmans, 1910–15), vol. 16: *News from Nowhere*; and E. Carpenter, "Forecast of the Coming Century," in *Forecasts of the Coming Century*, ed. E. Carpenter (Manchester: Labour, 1897).

[23] M. Beer, *A History of British Socialism* (London: George Bell, 1929), p. 230.

[24] For biographical details, see Tsuzuki, *Hyndman*. Also see H. Hyndman, *The Record of an Adventurous Life* (London: Macmillan, 1911); H. Hyndman, *Further Reminiscences* (London: Macmillan, 1912); and R. Hyndman, *Last Years of H. M. Hyndman* (London: Grant Richards, 1923).

[25] H. Hyndman, *Record*, p. 7.

[26] Ibid., p. 97.

[27] H. Hyndman, *The Indian Famine* (London: E. Stanford, 1877) and "The Bankruptcy of India," *Nineteenth Century* 9 (1881): 443–62.

Johnstone, the Conservative MP for Canterbury, lent Hyndman a French copy of *Capital*. Marx's book made an immediate impression. Hyndman wrote: "I have learned more from its perusal, I think, than from any other book I ever read."[28] *Capital* seemed to him to reflect the concerns of Tory radicalism. He thought that Marx had laid bare the process by which commercialism destroyed traditional ties and created a disinherited working class with anarchic tendencies. But he still saw socialism as a threat, not a goal, describing the German socialists as "fanatics" and speaking more generally of the "demon of socialism."[29]

As a Tory radical, Hyndman adopted a medievalist historiography, feared impending anarchy, sought to avoid anarchy by means of aristocratic statesmanship, and upheld a national vision. After reading *Capital*, he wrote an article titled "The Dawn of a Revolutionary Epoch," which did not consider history but expressed all the other leading themes of Tory radicalism.

Hyndman warned his readers that the social conditions created by the Industrial Revolution were storing up future troubles. British towns exhibited "all the elements of the fiercest and, under certain conditions, of the most uncontrollable democracy the world has ever seen."[30] Here, like other Tory radicals, Hyndman associated democracy with apocalyptic conceptions of socialism, communism, anarchism, and nihilism. Violent revolution loomed as a dangerous threat: "When we reflect for a moment upon the disproportion of numbers, can we fail to be struck with the danger that might come upon all if some eloquent, fervent enthusiast, stirred by the injustices and inequalities around him, were to appeal to the multitude to redress their social wrongs by violence?"[31] Hyndman, almost alone among British socialists, warned his countrymen of the danger of a mob he feared was becoming revolutionary.

Despite these fears, Hyndman, like so many Tory radicals, took heart from the calming influence of Britain's political inheritance.

> Our long political history has not passed for nothing. The working classes, it is true, feel their own power more and more; but so long as they think they can see their way to what they want through constitutional means, they have no mind to try the subversionary doctrines of the Continental agitators.[32]

---

[28] Cited in Tsuzuki, *Hyndman*, p. 33.

[29] H. Hyndman, "The Dawn of a Revolutionary Epoch," *Nineteenth Century* 9 (1881): 5, and *The Text Book of Democracy: England for All* (London: E. Allen, 1881), p. 86.

[30] H. Hyndman, "Dawn," 14.

[31] Ibid.

[32] Ibid.

Hyndman's hope depended, however, on the restoration of an alliance between the aristocracy and the people. He wrote, "Granting that the English people are not democratic in the Continental sense, admitting that they do respect their 'natural leaders,' and are ready to follow them politically and socially in orderly fashion, this presupposes that the upper classes are ready to lead."[33] Hyndman identified the natural leaders with the upper classes. He claimed that true statesmanship consisted in providing aristocratic leadership, not simply Bismarck's strategy of repressing revolt.

> His [Bismarck's] marvelous success in consolidating Germany has blinded men's eyes to his incapacity for any real statesmanship in the wider sense. In place of helping the mass of the population to a better position, instead of teaching the upper classes and the royal family that the only hope of safety for his country in these days is to make common cause with the people, and lighten the burdens which grind them down, he has thought only of violence and aggrandisement.[34]

Characteristic themes of Tory radicalism appear yet again in Hyndman's vision of social reconciliation through a renewed nation and state action. The rich must recognize the duties of possession, enter more fully into the lives of the people, and introduce order to the disruptive commercial system. The necessary reforms will entail some state control but not the removal of property rights.

> The principle of State management ... is making way at the same time that notions which extend to dealing with all property for the benefit of the mass ... are gaining strength and coherence. The former system may be peacefully and perhaps beneficially worked out; the latter must involve anarchy and bloodshed.[35]

As a Tory radical, Hyndman turned to Disraeli to discuss the policy that he believed "could alone save this country and the empire from disastrous collapse."[36] He told Disraeli that "the only hope of rapid improvement ... lay with the Conservative Party"; but Disraeli replied that the Conservative Party was dominated by vested interests and could not undertake the action that Hyndman proposed.[37] Hyndman therefore decided to form a new party. Aided by two other Tory radicals, Butler-Johnstone and Morrison Davidson, he gathered together representatives

---

[33] Ibid., 15.
[34] Ibid., 6.
[35] Ibid., 17.
[36] H. Hyndman, *Record*, p. 237.
[37] Ibid., p. 241.

of the metropolitan Radical Clubs and the Irish community to organize the meetings that founded the Democratic Federation (DF). Hyndman gave the delegates at the founding conference of the DF a copy of his new work, *England for All*.[38] This work summarized Marx's economics before outlining a program of Tory Democracy.

The inaugural meeting of the DF brought Tory and popular radicals together with some liberal radicals. A month later, in July 1881, the DF published its program, which consisted mainly of the Chartist demands that had not yet been met alongside a call for land nationalization.[39] By the end of 1881, most of the liberal radicals had left the DF. They were replaced by a group of upper-class Tory socialists. Henry Champion was an ex-artillery officer.[40] Robert Frost was his school friend from Malborough. James Joynes had just left his teaching job at Eton. They were members of the Land Reform Union, who had begun to edit *The Christian Socialist*, inspired by the legacy of F. D. Maurice and Charles Kingsley. These Tory radicals encouraged Hyndman and the popular radicals to accept the label "socialist." It was a couple of years later, in 1883, that the DF finally changed its name to Social Democratic Federation and adopted a new, avowedly socialist program written by Hyndman and Morris.[41]

An Orthodox Marxist

Many scholars argue that by 1883 Hyndman was an out-and-out Marxist. Yet, while Hyndman did adopt Marxism, the then orthodox form of Marxism proved compatible with his continuing to voice many of the main themes of Tory radicalism.

In the 1880s Marxism appeared as a positivist science founded on an objectified dialectic. Marx spoke of the death of philosophy and called his own theories scientific without saying precisely what he meant. When he died, his theories were available mainly through *The Communist Manifesto* and the first volume of *Capital*, where the subjective side of the dialectic is left implicit or, as some commentators would have it, superseded by a more positivist theory. Then Engels propelled Marxism into an overtly positivist direction. Arguably, Marx's dialectic focused on

[38] H. Hyndman, *England for All*.

[39] *Radical*, 16 July 1881.

[40] J. Barnes, "Gentleman Crusader: Henry Hyde Champion in the Early Socialist Movement," *History Workshop* 60 (2005): 116–38.

[41] The Democratic Federation, *Socialism Made Plain: Being the Social and Political Manifesto of the Democratic Federation* (London: W. Reeves, 1883). Also see H. Hyndman and W. Morris, *A Summary of the Principles of Socialism* (London: Modern, 1884).

the opposition of subject and object, and so it applied only where we find consciousness playing a role, that is, in human history but not the natural sciences. Engels took a different view. He adopted a rigid dialectic that went beyond the domain of consciousness to become a formal process operating throughout nature. He denied the role of the conscious subject and turned the dialectic into a series of objective truths. In doing so, he implied that the dialectic applies to all matter, that all of reality necessarily follows the laws of the dialectic, and that the dialectic governs history irrespective of human agency.[42]

Hyndman's Marxism embraced scientism and a rigid dialectic. He had a positivist model of science as the discovery of objective laws through the accurate collection of empirical facts. Marxism was a science because it fitted this model.

> The elaborate diagnosis which will to-day enable a first rate pathologist to state precisely the course of physical, and through physical of mental disease in a manner surprising even to the educated, is due to as carefully recorded observations as those which have guided the astronomer to his irrefragable conclusion. Rigid accuracy, so far as possible, in the tabulation of facts, guided all the while by scientific imagination, has taken the place of the slip-shod guess-work of old time led astray by theological crazes. The same with the study of the movements and relations of mankind in civilized society to-day.[43]

Hyndman saw the dialectic as the formal and positivist laws of Engels. He thought that to prove scientifically his Marxist theory of history, he needed only to demonstrate empirically that the dialectic applied to nature, which he did by reference to an ear of corn: "There is the seed which you sow, this is split up or differentiated in the earth, and then it reappears in the ear again, but on a higher plane."[44]

This scientism informed Hyndman's analysis of human nature. His conception of people as producers served as an axiomatic, objective, and scientific fact. It contrasts sharply with Marx's arguments that people distinguish themselves from animals by producing their means of subsistence and that people constantly interact with reality so as to both change the world and re-create their own nature. Similarly, Hyndman portrayed human needs as fixed products of the individual's objective material be-

---

[42] F. Engels, *Anti-Dühring* (Moscow: Progress Publishing, 1947) and *Dialectics of Nature* (Moscow: Progress Publishing, 1972).

[43] H. Hyndman, *The Historical Basis of Socialism in England* (London: Kegan Paul, 1883), p. 434.

[44] H. Hyndman, *The Economics of Socialism* (London: Twentieth Century, 1896), p. 3.

ing and, reflecting his mechanical materialism, as overwhelmingly concerned with physical welfare. His view contrasts with the suggestion that needs are partly subjective and dependent on society's understanding of the minimum acceptable standard of living.

The scientism of orthodox Marxism created a kind of ethical vacuum. Marxism seemed independent of any particular moral standpoint. In the 1880s and 1890s orthodox Marxists often implied that Marxism was a positive science that separated facts from values. Even when Karl Kautsky argued that social democracy needed a moral ideal, he added that "this ideal has no place in scientific socialism ... in a man like Marx, for example, the presence of a moral ideal occasionally breaks through into his scientific investigation, but he is continually aiming, and rightly, to banish it."[45] Revisionist Marxists tried to fill the ethical vacuum in Marxism by combining it with neo-Kantianism, as did Eduard Bernstein, or even with a positivist ethic, as did Bax.[46]

Hyndman inserted his Tory radicalism into this ethical vacuum. He too believed that Marxism concerned what "is," not what "ought to be." His Marxism did not entail any particular ethic, so he could combine it with his Tory radicalism. Hyndman's ethic began with a patriotism verging on chauvinism and racism: "In America, in Australia, all the world over, the Anglo-Saxon blood is still second to none."[47] He wanted to maintain Britain's proud history of leading the world in political reform: "I hope to see England lead as the successful pioneer in the realization of this great ideal of economic and social emancipation."[48] He thought that involving the working class would stimulate their patriotism. Feeding and housing them would make them strong. The result would be a population upon which to build a truly majestic empire, an empire that could secure peace and justice throughout the world.

The scientism of orthodox Marxism also encouraged a widespread acceptance of a theory of economic breakdown. Marx referred both to the tendency of the rate of profit to fall and to the underconsumption that

---

[45] K. Kautsky, *Selected Political Writings*, ed. P. Goode (London: Macmillan, 1983), p. 43.

[46] E. Bernstein, "Kant against Cant," in *Evolutionary Socialism*, trans. E. Harvey (London: Independent Labour Party, 1909).

[47] H. Hyndman, *The Coming Revolution in England* (London: W. Reeves, 1884), p. 31.

[48] H. Hyndman, *The Future of Democracy* (London: Allen and Unwin, 1915), p. 217. Also see H. Hyndman, "The English Workers as They Are," *Contemporary Review* 52 (1887): 136: "Let us hope that a full and timely recognition of the just demands of the people ... will enable England to take that lead in the peaceful reorganization of society for which she is fitted by the state of her economical development and the political freedom which, on the whole, her inhabitants enjoy."

would come with overproduction, but he did not say exactly what would cause capitalism to collapse. Here the orthodox view of Marxism as a positive science suggested that the dialectic governed history irrespective of human agency, so the collapse of capitalism was an inevitable economic fact established by the objective laws of the dialectic. Certainly the Erfurt Program embraced a sort of breakdown theory, and even Kautsky, who denied that Marx had a breakdown theory, believed that cyclical depressions were inevitable and would become increasingly serious and that mechanization would necessarily raise the level of production above society's capacity for consumption.[49]

Hyndman accepted the theory of economic breakdown. He argued that capitalism involved a fundamental antagonism between social production and individual appropriation. Capitalism would collapse because of the combined impact of the "circulation of commodities" and "industrial crises."[50] The circulation of commodities explained the growth of monopolies and trusts, both of which reflected the increasingly social nature of capitalist production. Hyndman argued that to continue to exist, capitalists must constantly sell their commodities so as to obtain the money necessary to start the process again; to sell their products, they must compete with their fellow capitalists; and to compete successfully, undercutting their competitors while maintaining profits, they must lower costs by increasing the scale of production. Thus, there was an inevitable tendency toward monopoly. He wrote, "This law of capitalist existence, that each producer must increase his scale of production or fall by the wayside, means, in practice, that only the biggest are fit to survive," and "the process goes on and on until competition reaches its logical term in combination and monopoly."[51]

Hyndman's analysis of the recurrent industrial crises that afflicted capitalism took the form of a short story. The story lacked theoretical precision but seemed to identify two causes. One cause of industrial crises was the overenthusiasm that grips people during periods of growth. Firms expand production and sell in more and more dubious markets. Foreign advisers change their tone (Hyndman did not explain why), and people discover that some of the demand was pure speculation and some the purchase of British goods with British-loaned capital. The other cause of industrial crises was the impact of mechanization on wages and profits. Growing demand and production lead to falling unemployment and

---

[49] K. Kautsky, *The Economic Doctrines of Karl Marx* (London: Black, 1925).

[50] "Circulation of Commodities" and "Industrial Crises" are chapter headings in H. Hyndman, *Economics*.

[51] H. Hyndman, *Economics*, p. 137.

rising wages. The rise in wages encourages manufacturers "to try to get the better of their neighbours by introducing improved machinery," and this mechanization leads to increased production "at a lower price with fewer hands."[52] Consequently, the market becomes "glutted" and unemployment rises. These problems are then exacerbated both because manufacturers with an advantage attempt to maintain their profits by putting more goods on the market at lower prices and because increasing unemployment means that fewer people earn money with which to buy goods. The ensuing depression generates radical ideas and acts as the motive force for social change: "The same economic pressure which produces the discontent and grievances leads to combination; the lot of workers is so bad as a whole that they are beginning to think that no change could be for the worse; ideas are gradually spreading among them which would lead them to strive for a complete overthrow."[53]

Orthodox Marxism relied on a scientism apparent in the theory of an inevitable economic breakdown. As a result, Marxism often lacked any well-defined politics. Marx himself neither wrote a coherent theory of the state nor considered the difficulties of socialist organization such as the relationship between leaders and followers. Yet, the main source of orthodox Marxism's lack of a clear politics was its reliance on a theory of economic breakdown. This theory often led to a policy of inaction and isolation. Inaction followed from the belief that the collapse of capitalism was inevitable, so there was little anybody could do either to hasten it or to prevent it. Isolation followed from the belief that capitalism was bound to collapse irrespective of human agency, so there was little point in forming pacts for mere political advancement.

Once again Hyndman inserted his Tory radicalism into the vacuum. His breakdown theory implied that there was nothing a dedicated Marxist could do to bring the revolution about, just as there was nothing that a committed capitalist could do to prevent the revolution. Thus, he criticized Lenin for seizing power with minority support and maintaining power by terror. The Bolshevik Revolution could not be a properly socialist revolution because Russia had not passed through the capitalist stage of economic development, and "the process of historic evolution, slow or fast, cannot be overleapt by the most relentless fanatic."[54] As we will see, Hyndman's own politics generally consisted of a call for Tory statesmanship to ensure that the inevitable reform would be peaceful and result in a harmonious nation.

[52] Ibid., p. 155.
[53] H. Hyndman, *Coming Revolution*, p. 31.
[54] H. Hyndman, *The Evolution of Revolution* (London: Grant Richards, 1920), p. 384.

A Tory Statesman

Hyndman's orthodox Marxism left spaces in which he could insert Tory radicalism. Hyndman's scientism facilitated his fusion of Marxism with the medievalist historiography of Tory radicalism. His *Historical Basis of Socialism in England* owed as much to William Cobbett as it did to Marx. The Middle Ages were a time when the people owned the land that they farmed or the tools with which they plied their trade. The yeoman sustained the vigorous nation that had secured the democratic freedoms that we enjoy today. This idyll disappeared when the people's link to the land was undermined by the dissolution of the monasteries and the acts of enclosure. The spread of industrialism and capitalism then brought Britain to the brink of anarchy. Here Hyndman appealed to Marx, arguing that Marx's great contribution to socialist thought was his scientific analysis of capitalist development, and this analysis proved that capitalism was hurtling headlong toward indiscriminate destruction. Marx had demonstrated just how well grounded was the Tory radicals' fear that capitalism had created a disinherited working class that would overthrow society.

According to Hyndman, Marx's economic science proved that capitalism would collapse. Socialism was inevitable. The only remaining question was whether or not the revolution would be peaceful. As Hyndman explained, "All that we want may be obtained in a peaceful manner; though, peaceful or not, the transformation of society will come about."[55] Indeed, because the revolution was inevitable, the role of the politician was not to bring it about so much as to ensure it would be as peaceful and constructive as possible. Hyndman claimed that Britain was on the brink of anarchy. Progress toward socialism was inevitable; the difficult and important task was to maintain peace and stability while making progress. When he wrote "The Dawn of a Revolutionary Epoch" after having read *Capital*, his message concentrated on the need for stability during a period of potentially violent and anarchic upheavals. The same message dominated his later, more overtly Marxist writings. As he wrote, "How to anticipate this downfall, and to ward off the danger of an intermediate period of anarchy, should be the thought and work of economists and statesmen in every country."[56]

---

[55] H. Hyndman, *Social Democracy: The Basis of Its Principles and the Cause of Its Success* (London: Twentieth Century Press, 1904), p. 23.

[56] H. Hyndman, *Economics*, p. 247. Compare H. Hyndman, "Social Democrat or Socialist?" *Social-Democrat* 1 (1897): 231. There he describes a social democrat as somebody who accepts the class struggle and uses political means to introduce the revolution "as far as possible peacefully."

Tory radicalism continued to infuse Hyndman's analysis of the road to peaceful reform. He believed that the British had a national affinity for peaceful politics:

> Patriotism is part of our heritage: self-restraint necessarily comes from the exercise of political power. Even the poorest are ready to accept the assurance of real reform, rather than listen to those who urge them to resort in desperation to violent change.[57]

Yet, the rise of industrial capitalism had left the people devoid of suitable leadership. Without leadership, the workers were blind; the "working men" were "hopelessly incompetent in their own class interests."[58] Equally, the aristocracy had lost its "natural" sense of direction: "Tory 'leaders' are quite afraid to lead."[59] Britain thus needed statesmen to warn the nation of the dangers that confronted it, provide a lead to the nation, and wait until a crisis enabled the statesmen themselves to come to the fore. Hyndman saw himself as just such a statesman.

> People don't believe things are really as bad or dangerous as they are, either in this country or elsewhere. ... I do not believe I shall ever come to the front, except in a desperate crisis, when other men chuck the job up as too difficult & too dangerous. ... The money-grubbing middle class has to be crushed into impotence, the mass of the people have to be roused & the aristocrats have to be rendered harmless before a single serious reconstructive measure can be carried peacefully. ... Rather a large undertaking this, I fear, & one which very, very few will deliberately enter upon. And yet if we don't enter upon it, and that soon, the approaching terrible troubles to our Empire will find us quite unprepared and wholly incompetent to deal with them.[60]

Hyndman wanted statesmen to ensure that socialism would arise peacefully. His socialist vision then fused his Marxism with the Tory radicals' vision of a harmonious nation guided by the state. He argued that the state acted as an instrument of repression only because of its class composition. For example, Parliament had passed the acts of enclosure because it consisted "exclusively of landowners."[61] Now the growth of democracy would result in a time "when all will be able to recognize that its [the state's] friendly influence is needed to prevent serious trouble, and

---

[57] H. Hyndman, *England for All*, pp. 5–6.

[58] G. Brown, ed., "Documents: Correspondence from H. M. Hyndman to Mrs. Cobden Sanderson, 1900–1921," *Labour History Bulletin* 22 (1971): 14.

[59] C. Holmes, ed., "Documents: H. M. Hyndman and R. D. Blumfield Correspondence, 1913," *Labour History Bulletin* 24 (1972): 28.

[60] G. Brown, ed., "Documents," 13.

[61] H. Hyndman, *England for All*, p. 17.

lead the way to a happier period."[62] Even Hyndman's specific proposals resembled those of Young England. He opposed moves to commit the DF to the abolition of the monarchy, called for an improvement in the people's welfare through palliatives such as decent housing, and encouraged the DF to focus on government misrule in Ireland.

So, Hyndman's Marxist and other socialist critics misunderstand his politics. Their respective portraits of him as a reformist parliamentarian or rhetorical revolutionary ignore his debt to Tory radicalism. Hyndman's Marxist critics interpret him as a reformist parliamentarian. No doubt Marx often looked to a more revolutionary transformation. Nonetheless, the Marxist interpretation ignores both the element of truth in the interpretation of Hyndman as a rhetorical revolutionary and the fact that Hyndman's parliamentarianism was not the core of his political strategy but a facet of his Tory radicalism. As we have seen, Hyndman's parliamentarianism arose from his fusion of orthodox Marxism and Tory radicalism. Orthodox Marxism indicated that revolution was inevitable, and Tory radicalism implied that what mattered was thus not whether revolution would happen but how it would happen. Again, orthodox Marxism seemed compatible with disparate ethics, and Tory radicalism then emphasized the value of statesmen using the state to promote social reconciliation.

Hyndman's other socialist critics interpret him as a rhetorical revolutionary. No doubt Hyndman constantly proclaimed the necessity of violence if radical reforms were not introduced peacefully. In one public debate, he announced, "I strive for a revolution—peaceful if possible, forceful if need be."[63] Nevertheless the interpretation of Hyndman as a rhetorical revolutionary ignores his parliamentarianism and fails to present his revolutionary rhetoric as a product of his Tory radicalism. As a Tory radical, Hyndman tried to warn the nation of forthcoming dangers. His revolutionary rhetoric was intended less to galvanize the workers than to induce the ruling classes to accept the statesmanlike action that he believed was necessary to avoid bloodshed. Even in his most militant moods, his revolutionary rhetoric aimed not at social revolution but at a widespread crisis that would enable statesmen such as himself to come to the fore and introduce bloodless change.

Clearly, Hyndman was neither a straightforward parliamentary reformist nor a straightforward firebrand revolutionary. His political strategy consisted of the idea that he, as a Tory statesman, might ensure that inevitable change was peaceful. He believed that a bloodless revolution could be brought about only through "the agency of the state as the

---

[62] Ibid., p. 31.

[63] H. Hyndman, *Socialism vs Smithism* (London: Modern Press, 1883), p. 13.

organized power of the people."[64] Thus, because the British state was undemocratic and class based, political reform along Chartist lines was an immediate necessity. The state had to become democratic. The workers had to be given the power to introduce change without bloodshed. Democratization required more than the vote; the American experience showed that the suffrage was inadequate unless combined with reforms such as the payment of election expenses, equal electoral districts, and free compulsory education.[65] Hyndman's strategy was, therefore, to pursue parliamentary action in order to obtain political reform and thereby promote a peaceful transition to socialism.

HYNDMAN AND THE SOCIAL DEMOCRATIC FEDERATION

The guiding thread of Hyndman's political activity was his belief that socialists should use parliamentary action to introduce the reforms necessary to ensure a peaceful transition to socialism. Within the SDF, this strategy led him to defend the merits of political action. Within the socialist movement, it led him to advocate socialist unity as a basis of effective parliamentary candidatures. And within the labor movement, it led him to oppose the dilution of socialism through compromises with the trade unions.

In the SDF Hyndman consistently defended the importance of political action as a means to obtain political reform and to promote peaceful revolution. Hyndman's critics explain the many splits in the SDF by reference to his personality; the Marxists blame his authoritarianism and jingoism; other socialists blame his lack of tact.[66] Yet, the splits also reflected clear differences over political strategy. In the first split Hyndman defended parliamentary action against those who favored education aimed at future revolution. The SDF initially adopted a parliamentary strategy. But in 1884 its annual conference voted against political action, adopting a modified version of the program of the Labour Emancipation League. Then, on 27 December 1884, a motion of no confidence in Hyndman was passed by ten votes to eight. Morris and the majority resigned and formed the Socialist League. Hyndman and his followers were left in charge of the SDF. They called an extraordinary conference at which, in the words of a contemporary newspaper report, Hyndman argued:

> With a political programme we develop into a party; if we keep clear of politics we simply become a clique. We wish to prove that we are as

---

[64] H. Hyndman, *Economics*, p. 248.
[65] H. Hyndman, *Social Democracy*, p. 23.
[66] See, respectively, E. Thompson, *Morris*, and Tsuzuki, *Hyndman*.

advanced as any party in the country. He [Hyndman] did not think we should gain much by political action, but we should educate the people.[67]

The conference then passed two motions in support of Hyndman's political strategy. The first reinstated the old program of the SDF with its demand for political reforms as a way of securing social reforms. The other declared that the SDF would "take political action in whatever way circumstances may suggest."[68] Further splits soon followed. One came when the SDF accepted money from the Conservative Party to finance candidates in the 1885 general election. The members who opposed political action if it were financed by the Conservatives left to form the short-lived Socialist Union or to join the Fabian Society. The next disagreement concerned the comparative effectiveness of political and industrial action and the extent to which socialists should tailor their demands to the immediate struggles of trade unionism. Socialists such as John Burns and Tom Mann left to focus on unions and syndicalist organizations.[69] Yet another split followed in the early 1890s when a band of impossibilists influenced by James Connolly were expelled by people, such as Hyndman, who favored political action.

Within the socialist movement, Hyndman's political strategy led him to seek socialist unity as a basis for effective political action. He believed that a united party was necessary for successful parliamentary action, but that a united party could do good only if it were genuinely socialist. Throughout the 1890s, the SDF seemed willing to combine with the ILP to form a united socialist party. Yet the ILP leadership opposed unity because they feared that an alliance would alienate their trade-union supporters. In 1897 a vote among the members of the ILP and the SDF revealed a huge majority in favor of unity. The SDF began preparations for a federal relationship, but the ILP leaders refused to acknowledge the result, arguing that only a third of their members had voted. The ILP leadership launched a blistering attack on the sectarianism of the SDF, thereby securing a vote against unity at their 1898 annual conference. Later the SDF withdrew from the Labour Representation Committee (LRC) because, unlike the ILP, it would not dilute its socialism to appease the unions. Repentant SDF members later recalled that "in its earlier years, the S.D.F. had made the same grave error of detaching itself from the Labour Movement, but it at least had the excuse that it did so

---

[67] *Justice*, 11 April 1885.

[68] Ibid.

[69] Burns and Mann had already developed their own strategies on behalf of the SDF in the provinces. See J. Owen, "Dissident Missionaries? Re-narrating the Political Strategy of the Social Democratic Federation, 1884–1887," *Labour History Review* 73 (2008): 187–207.

because the Labour Representation Committee of that time, concerned to secure the adhesion of the Trade Unions, declined to avow a Socialist objective."[70] In a final attempt to establish socialist unity, the SDF called for a British Socialist Party (BSP), but despite the involvement of some socialists from the ILP, the Clarion, and elsewhere, the BSP was effectively just the SDF under a new name.

Finally, Hyndman's belief in promoting socialism through parliamentary action led him to support cooperation with trade unions only for that end. In the early 1880s Hyndman held that the iron law of wages meant that unions were ineffective if widespread and detrimental to unskilled workers if restricted to skilled workers. Yet, by the end of the decade, he had rejected the iron law of wages for a more Marxist theory of surplus value and so had become friendlier to the unions. In 1888 *Justice* called for the formation of unions among the unskilled. By 1899 Hyndman himself was advocating collaboration between Marxists and trade unions.[71] Even then, however, his main concern remained socialist unity, not cooperation with the unions. As one of his colleagues recalled, Hyndman "supported trade unions and strikes, but only as auxiliaries to a considered general economic and political scheme."[72] The source of Hyndman's attitude to the trade unions was, in other words, his political strategy. He wanted socialist unity to reform Parliament, not labor unity to improve the welfare of the workers. Thus, even when he rejected the iron law of wages, he still argued that because the unions were liberal, they would not promote the peaceful introduction of socialism. They could not have a role in his political strategy until they became socialist. Because Hyndman believed that the role of socialists was to encourage peaceful change, he concentrated on political, not economic or industrial, reform.

CONCLUSION

Hyndman and the SDF thus focused on political action and political reform to promote a peaceful transition to socialism. The SDF continually entered candidates for elections despite constant defeats and large expenses. In 1892 it sponsored two candidates without success. In 1895 Hyndman stood at Burnley but, like the other three SDF candidates,

---

[70] H. Lee and E. Archbold, *Social-Democracy in Britain* (London: Social Democratic Federation, 1935), p. 266. That Hyndman rejected the LRC for this reason is apparent from H. Hyndman, *Reminiscences*, pp. 259–72.

[71] The critics' misunderstanding is a consequence of their failure to distinguish between Hyndman's early theory of surplus values in *England for All* and his later more Marxist theory in *Economics*. Hyndman's changing policy toward trade unions is traced in Tsuzuki, *Hyndman*.

[72] F. Gould, *Hyndman: Prophet of Socialism* (London: Allen and Unwin, 1928), p. 157.

failed to get elected. In 1900 all three of the SDF candidates received the endorsement of the LRC but still lost. In 1906 the SDF entered nine candidates, again without success, although Will Thorne was elected as a Labour candidate backed by the LRC and the Gasworkers' Union. The elections of 1910 were a fiasco. In the first, all of the SDF candidates came last; in the second, only Hyndman stood, and he came last. Throughout this time, the SDF also continually tried to build a broader socialist alliance so as to improve its electoral prospects. In 1908 Hyndman wrote to Holbrook Jackson, "I (and we of the S.D.F.) have always been ready for nearly 28 years to cooperate with anyone who wished to bring about the formation of a thorough-going Socialist Party in Great Britain." Yet, a properly socialist party did not mean diluting the socialist message to appease the trade unions. So Hyndman continued by lamenting the fact that "now a Socialist Party in the combined sense is opposed by the I.L.P. in favour of the Parliamentary Labour Party."[73]

The SDF undertook more revolutionary agitation only during the mass unrest of the mid-1880s. At that time the SDF concentrated on gaining support by leading industrial strikes and social demonstrations. The climax came with Black Monday, 8 February 1886, when Burns addressed a crowd attending a Fair Trade League rally of the unemployed and drew a substantial section away to an SDF meeting on the north side of Trafalgar Square. This section of the crowd marched down Pall Mall, where they smashed windows, and along Piccadilly, where they looted shops. At Hyde Park the SDF's leaders advised the crowd to disperse, as the time for revolution had not yet come. Even then, in 1886, Hyndman's strategy remained much the same as ever. He still wanted political reform to secure a peaceful revolution. The only change lay in the means to political reform. Parliamentary action was temporarily of secondary importance because the SDF had "more chance of getting revolutionary political change through vehement social agitation."[74]

[73] Hyndman to Holbrook Jackson, 17 July 1908, Hyndman Collection, Harry Ransom Center, Austin, Texas.
[74] *Justice*, 1 January 1887.

CHAPTER FIVE

William Morris

HISTORIANS HAVE DISMISSED Ernest Belfort Bax as irrelevant and denounced Henry Mayers Hyndman as domineering, but they have generally idealized William Morris. Morris is everyone's favorite British socialist. Every socialist camp has tried to claim him as one of its own, with a fierce debate raging for much of the twentieth century over whether or not he was a Marxist.

Early commentators insisted Morris was an ethical socialist. John Bruce Glasier remembered Morris telling a meeting, "To speak quite frankly, I do not know what Marx's theory of value is, and I'm dammed if I want to know"; "I have tried to understand Marx's theory, but political economy is not my line, and much of it appears to me to be dreary rubbish."[1] And Morris had written, "Whereas I thoroughly enjoyed the historical part of *Capital*, I suffered agonies of confusion of the brain over reading the pure economics."[2] The evidence suggested that Morris had never grasped the economic foundations of Marxism; he was a socialist solely for moral reasons.

From the 1950s until recently, a number of historians placed Morris firmly in the Marxist tradition. Robin Page Arnot led the way, dismissing Morris's own words by saying that the first chapters of *Capital* were notoriously difficult, and Morris had confessed only to having difficulties with them, not failing to understand them.[3] Historians discovered considerable evidence that Morris was familiar with Karl Marx's economics. Morris read *Capital* in French in 1883, and again in English in 1887. He kept both editions in his library, and they were well thumbed. Moreover, Morris coauthored with Bax a series of articles that provide

A version of this chapter appeared as "William Morris: The Modern Self, Art, and Politics," *History of European Ideas* 24 (1998), 175–194. Published by Elsevier Science Ltd.

[1] J. Glasier, *William Morris and the Early Days of the Socialist Movement* (London: Longmans, 1921), p. 32.

[2] W. Morris, *The Collected Works of William Morris*, intro. M. Morris (London: Longmans, 1910–15), vol. 23: *Signs of Change: Lectures on Socialism*, p. 278.

[3] R. Arnot, *William Morris: The Man and the Myth, Including the Letters of William Morris to J. L. Mahon and Dr. John Glasse* (London: Lawrence and Wishart, 1964). Also see P. Meier, *William Morris: The Marxist Dreamer*, 2. vols. (Sussex, UK: Harvester, 1978); and, of course, E. Thompson, *William Morris: Romantic to Revolutionary* (London: Lawrence and Wishart, 1955).

one of the most accurate contemporary summaries of the first volume of *Capital*.[4] In the first edition of E. P. Thompson's classic study, Morris came across not only as a Marxist but also as a Marxist who struggled with the problems his practice posed him until at last he reached the Grail of Leninism.[5]

However, the new evidence was nearly as problematic as the old. To have read *Capital* is not to have understood it. And the articles could have been the work of Bax, with little help from Morris. Indeed, Morris wrote in his diary, "Tuesday to Bax at Croydon where we did our first article on Marx: or rather he did it: I don't think I should ever make an economist even of the most elementary kind."[6] More importantly, the accounts of Morris as a Marxist seemed to do scant justice to the utopian elements in his thought. His writings reveal a man much more concerned to imagine a new way of life than to analyze the economic logic of capitalism. By the late twentieth century, a new crop of scholars were locating Morris alongside anarcho-communists and left libertarians such as Peter Kropotkin.[7]

Let us change tack for a moment. Does it matter whether or not Morris was a Marxist? In one sense, the nature of Morris's politics is an important matter. Morris has long been an icon of British socialists, inspiring thinkers and politicians as diverse as Clement Attlee, G.D.H. Cole, Ramsay MacDonald, and R. H. Tawney. To study the origins and limitations of his politics is one way of approaching the origins and limitations of British socialism. In another sense, however, the ideological label we pin on Morris does not seem very important. Ideologies are not mutually exclusive, reified entities. They are overlapping traditions with ill-defined boundaries. Whether or not we describe Morris as a Marxist depends on how we define Marxism as much as on how we view Morris, and to conclude Morris was a Marxist would not rule out his also being either an ethical socialist or an anarchist.

---

[4] The articles were published in *Commonweal* throughout 1887 and republished as W. Morris and E. Bax, *Socialism: Its Growth and Outcome* (London: Swan Sonnenschein, 1893).

[5] Thompson renounced the Leninist pieties of the first edition in the revised edition. Future references in this chapter are to the following revised edition: E. Thompson, *William Morris: Romantic to Revolutionary* (London: Merlin, 1977).

[6] W. Morris, *Socialist Diary*, ed. F. Boos (London: Journeyman, 1982), p. 32.

[7] F. Boos and W. Boos, "The Utopian Communism of William Morris," *History of Political Thought* 7 (1986): 489–510; D. Goodway, *Anarchist Seeds Sown beneath the Snow: Left-Libertarian Thought and British Writers from William Morris to Colin Ward* (Liverpool: Liverpool University Press, 2006); J. Hulse, *Revolutionists in London: A Study of Five Unorthodox Socialists* (Oxford: Clarendon Press, 1970); R. Kinna, "William Morris and Anti-Parliamentarianism," *History of Political Thought* 15 (1994): 593–613; and F. MacCarthy, *William Morris: A Life for Our Time* (London: Faber and Faber, 1994).

Far too many interpretations of Morris are distorted by their authors' concern to claim him for their preferred ideology. A focus on fitting him into a reified account of any one ideology can neglect his debt to broader traditions such as romanticism and Protestantism. This chapter aims to improve our grasp of Morris's socialism by relating him to such traditions.

ROMANTICISM AND PROTESTANTISM

The young Morris lived in an intellectual world defined by romanticism. He devoured the medieval histories of Walter Scott when he was four or five. At school in Marlborough, he reveled in the surrounding country-side. At university in Oxford, he became an aesthete, admired medieval architecture, and wrote romantic pieces. The prose he wrote at Oxford, like his later poetry, exhibits the characteristic debts of third-generation romantics: medievalism, gothic fiction, folklore, Scott's novels, and John Ruskin's aesthetics. His prose romances are Pre-Raphaelite works full of dreaminess, a delight in sensory details, subjectivity, and a deliberate simplicity.[8]

Morris's commitment to romanticism in his presocialist days is well known. What matters is its content. Like most romantics, Morris longed for good art, and he identified good art with natural harmony. According to Morris, art was the highest expression of the human spirit. He wrote that "art is a very serious thing" and that people like him "love art most" because it "is to us as the bread we eat, and the air we breathe."[9] Art gives meaning to human life. Without art "the progress of civilisation" would be "as causeless as the turning of a wheel that makes nothing."[10] Romantics lauded art because it embodied the imagination of the creative individual. Morris desperately wanted to fortify imagination and creativity against the mechanical and regimented society he found about him. Artists embodied to an exceptional degree the capacities that ennoble humanity.

The role of artists is to produce good art through their creative imagination. Like many romantics, Morris then defined good art as that which creates the effect of a natural harmony. He elegized and idealized nature. His poems often invest nature with personality, finding in it human

---

[8] Morris, *Works*, vol. 1: *The Defence of Guenevere: The Hollow Land*, pp. 149–325. His study "'Men and Women' by Robert Browning" defends Pre-Raphaelite concerns. See Morris, *Works*, vol. 1, pp. 326–48.

[9] Morris, *Works*, vol. 22: *Hopes for Art: Lectures on Art and Industry*, pp. 29–31.

[10] Ibid., p. 31.

emotions and a moral message. As he himself recognized, the romantic movement in literature inspired "a feeling for the romance of external nature."[11] Naturalness is a prerequisite of good art. Something is beautiful, Morris explained, "if it is in accord with Nature, and helps her: ugly if it is discordant with nature, and thwarts her: it cannot be indifferent."[12] He did not want art "to imitate nature" precisely; rather, he wanted artists to create "forms and intricacies" that look "natural" by, for example, evoking patterns of vegetation and thereby bringing us into a harmonious relationship with nature.

Like many romantics, Morris believed that good art could unite the individual with nature and also with society, history, and even God. Art should fuse everything into a harmonious whole. The churches of northern France are "the most beautiful ... of all the buildings that the earth has ever borne" precisely because their builders had produced works exhibiting such harmony. Morris wrote:

> Ah, do I not love them [the builders] with just cause who certainly loved me, thinking of me sometimes between strokes of their chisels? And for this love of all men that they had, and moreover for the great love of God which they certainly had too; for this, and for this work of theirs, the upraising of the great Cathedral front, with its beating heart of thoughts of men wrought into the leaves and flowers of the fair earth, wrought into the faces of good men and true, fighters against the wrong, of angels who upheld them, of God who rules all things.[13]

Morris's debt to Ruskin, his place among the Pre-Raphaelites, and his concern with a natural and simple beauty all appear in his golden rule that you should "have nothing in your houses that you do not know to be useful or believe to be beautiful."[14]

Morris believed art was the highest expression of the human spirit, and good art required naturalness and harmony. These beliefs were general features of much romanticism. Yet, Morris rejected the high romantic belief in the individual genius of the poet and the autonomy of art. He emphasized the place of art in the everyday world, arguing that everyone had the capacity to create art and that art should have an integral place in people's daily activities.

This concern to sanctify the everyday worlds of work and home owes much to Protestantism. Although Morris described puritanism and clas-

---

[11] Ibid., p. 59.
[12] Ibid., p. 4.
[13] Ibid., vol. 1, p. 349.
[14] Ibid., vol. 23, p. 77.

sicism as the "things which I hate most in the world," he had in mind the cold austerity of puritan ethics, rather than the more general Protestant focus on the central ethical importance of daily activities.[15] Morris's evangelical family brought him up in what he described as "rich establishment puritanism," and in his youth he had thought of a career in the church.[16] Only later, after he lost his faith, did he, along with Edward Burne-Jones, pledge himself to art. Art would replace religion as the centerpiece of people's daily lives. Art would direct hearts and minds to lofty affairs.

Morris's experience of the "Firm" entrenched his conviction that art should sanctify daily life.[17] The Firm was initially called Morris, Marshall, Faulkner and Company, but later became just Morris and Company. It concentrated primarily on interior design. Morris's involvement led him to conceive of himself less as an artist or poet in the high romantic image than as a craftsman engaged in the "lesser arts" and with an eye on profit. The focus of his activity shifted from poetry and architecture to patterns and designs. He increasingly wrote of the importance of laborers' being craftsmen and of art dominating the domestic setting of our leisure. His main concern became "the crafts of house-building, painting, joinery and carpentry, smith's work, pottery and glass-making, weaving, and many others"—"that great body of art, by means of which men have at all times more or less striven to beautify the familiar matters of everyday life."[18]

For Morris, the decorative arts were as much art as were the high arts. He thought that anything people made was a work of art expressing the human spirit. In his view, "Everything made by man's hands has a form, which must be either beautiful or ugly."[19] This broad concept of art made art integral to everyday life at work and at home. For a start, most people spent much of their working lives producing art. If people were producing aesthetically pleasing art, they would enjoy their labor and so the main part of their lives. Morris argued, "The chief duty of the civilized world to-day is to set about making labour happy for all," that is, to promote good art.[20] In addition, most people spent much of their time outside of work using products made by others. If people were using

[15] W. Morris, *The Letters of William Morris to His Family and Friends*, ed. P. Henderson (London: Longmans, 1950), p. 247. When possible I have referred to letters as they appear in the more recent and comprehensive edition edited by N. Kelvin. However, to avoid any confusion, all references to a letter specify the relevant editor.

[16] Ibid., p. 184.

[17] P. Stansky, *Redesigning the World: William Morris, the 1880s, and the Arts and Crafts Movement* (Princeton, NJ: Princeton University Press, 1985).

[18] Morris, *Works*, vol. 22, p. 4.

[19] Ibid.

[20] Ibid., p. 43.

aesthetically pleasing art, they would enjoy their leisure and so the other main part of their lives. Morris argued, "Without these [decorative] arts our rest would be vacant and uninteresting."[21] The decorative arts could fulfill people's daily lives: "To give people pleasure in the things, they must perforce *use*, that is one great office of decoration; to give people pleasure in things they must perforce *make*, that is the other use of it."[22] Implicit in Morris's aim was the need to make art truly popular. People had to be artists and connoisseurs, producing art with their labor and using art in their leisure time. Besides, "if she [art] is ever to be strong enough to help mankind once more, she must gather strength in simple places," not just in "rich men's houses."[23]

Morris described Ruskin as his "master" in social theory, and his presocialist lectures indicate the strength of the debt.[24] Morris followed Ruskin in promulgating ideals of naturalness and harmony, in defining art broadly to include everyday objects, and, crucially, in using the sociology of art to critique contemporary society.[25] Morris used Ruskin's sociology to bring a social dimension to his evaluation of works of art. He equated good art with the nature of the labor that went into it, saying, "Real art is the expression by man of his pleasure in labour."[26] Good art depended on a society in which people could express their creativity and so enjoy their work. Bad art reflected a society that stifled the workers' individuality, preventing them from enjoying their labor.

This sociology of art led Morris to a medievalist historiography akin to the one we discussed in the last chapter as characteristic of Tory radicals as well as romantics. The Middle Ages were a time of harmony, vigor, and beauty. People were bound together by strong communal ties. They led simple, happy lives surrounded by useful and aesthetically pleasing objects. The rude simplicity of the Middle Ages inspired good art, most notably, for Morris, the churches of northern France and the Icelandic Sagas. In contrast, the immorality and unhappiness of contemporary society appeared in the paucity of modern art.

Morris wanted to promote good art by rediscovering the aesthetic values of naturalness and harmony in everyday life, and in particular by rebuilding society in accord with principles of simplicity and honesty.

---

[21] Ibid., p. 5.

[22] Ibid.

[23] Ibid., p. 113.

[24] *Justice*, 16 June 1884.

[25] J. Ruskin, "The Nature of Gothic," in *The Works of John Ruskin*, ed. E. Cook and A. Wedderburn (London: G. Allen, 1903–12), vol. 10: *The Stones of Venice—II: The Sea Stories*, pp. 180–269.

[26] Morris, *Works*, vol. 22, p. 42.

Simplicity was the human corollary of the romantics' praise of nature: people should live naturally. Honesty entailed a reversal of current commercial practices: workers should not produce slovenly goods, factory owners should pay fair wages, and consumers should not seek unreasonably low prices. Morris, like Ruskin, called for a moral economy based on the "careful and eager giving his due to every man," rather than the utilitarian values of the countinghouse.[27] He thought that a new society of happiness could rise like a phoenix from a new morality of simplicity and honesty, a morality that acknowledged the humanity, worth, and creativity of the producer. He wrote:

> If we were only to come to our right minds, and could see the necessity for making labour sweet to all men . . . then indeed I believe we should sow the seeds of a happiness which the world has not yet known . . . and with that seed would be sown also the seed of real art, the expression of man's happiness in his labour—an art made by the people, and for the people, as a happiness to the maker and the user.[28]

So, Morris's early writings on the plight of modern art reveal his romantic ideal of good art as based on naturalness and harmony, his Protestant concern to sanctify daily activity, and his Ruskinian indictment of economic liberalism as inimical to good art. Initially, however, his hostility to economic liberalism did not spill over into hostility to political liberalism. On the contrary, Morris played a prominent role in the Eastern Question Association, serving as treasurer of the committee that convened its national conference and as a member of the subcommittee that drafted the manifesto for the conference. The Eastern Question Association was a Liberal-inspired group formed to fight the jingoism of the Conservative government of Benjamin Disraeli. Morris committed himself to the Liberals with their alternative foreign policy. Yet, when William Gladstone became prime minister in 1880, his Liberal government repressed the Irish and bombarded Alexandria. Morris was horrified. He despaired of liberalism, writing, "The action and want of action of the new Liberal Parliament, especially the Coercion Bill and the Stockjobber's Egyptian War, quite destroyed any hope I might have had of any good being done by alliance with the Radical party."[29] In January 1883 Bax persuaded

---

[27] Ibid., pp. 47–48. For Ruskin's moral economy, see J. Ruskin, "Unto This Last," in *Works*, vol. 17: *Unto This Last, Munera Pulveris, Time and Tide, and Other Writings on Political Economy, 1860–1873*, pp. 15–114.

[28] Morris, *Works*, vol. 22, p. 46.

[29] W. Morris, *The Collected Letters of William Morris*, ed. N. Kelvin (Princeton, NJ: Princeton University, 1984–87), vol. 2, pt. A: *1881–84*, p. 230.

Morris to join the Democratic Federation.[30] In November 1883, during a talk at University College, Oxford, Morris announced his conversion to socialism.[31] Ruskin was in the chair.

The Marxist

Morris, following Ruskin, had long argued that art reflects the conditions of labor in society. The arts "are connected with all history and are clear teachers of it."[32] Now Morris, following Marx, also argued that different social systems represent different solutions to the necessity of obtaining subsistence from nature by labor. In both cases, something like the economic base explained something like a social superstructure. Nonetheless, there are differences between a Marxist social theory and a Ruskinian concern with good art and the social conditions necessary for its production. We can understand Morris's socialism by seeing how he brought them together.

Even Morris's broad definition of art did not really include social and political relations. His socialism consisted, above all else, of a belief that conditions of labor determine not only the nature of art and so the quality of individual lives, but also the character of social and political relationships. Morris thus began to insist on the fact of class struggle. The conditions of labor divided civil society into classes that had opposing interests. Earlier Morris had talked of the need "to bridge the gap between the classes."[33] Now he argued that "the workman's real master is not his immediate employer but his *class*."[34] Morris's new belief in the class struggle brought with it a commitment to Marx's social theory. History consisted of the struggle of classes to advance their interests. Even Morris's tone echoed that of Marx: "The middle class had freed commerce from her fetters of privilege, and had freed thought from her fetters of theology, at least partially; but it had not freed, nor attempted to free, labour from its fetters."[35] Morris's new belief in the class struggle even dampened his enthusiasm for medieval society. Beneath medieval society's "rough plenty, its sauntering life, its cool acceptance of rudeness and violence, there was going on a keen struggle of classes which carried with it the hope of progress."[36]

---

[30] G. Shaw, "The New Politics," Shaw Papers, British Library, London, BM:50683.

[31] The talk was Morris's "Art under Plutocracy," in *Works*, vol. 23, pp. 164–91.

[32] Morris, *Works*, vol. 22, p. 8.

[33] Ibid., vol. 23, p. 162.

[34] Ibid., p. 224.

[35] Ibid., p. 66.

[36] Ibid., p. 62.

A powerful belief in the class struggle led Morris to condemn the state as an instrument of class oppression. People were producers, not citizens; the notion of a common nationality was illusory. Parliament was a committee of the upper classes that presented a facade of democracy while oppressing the working class. After one incident, Morris argued that the violent repression of protesters had revealed the true nature of the state, with the police and judges enforcing the interests of property and flagrantly violating the supposed rights of the common people. He wrote, "The greatest humbug which Sunday's events have laid bare is the protection afforded by the law to the humblest citizen."[37] More generally, Morris argued that the capitalist state merely allowed the workers to participate in their own slavery. The nature of the state and the reality of the class struggle were hidden by the operation of ideology. Ideology—especially the Christianity of the churches—protected the interests of private property. The capitalist is "furnished with what he can use as a mask under the name of morals and religion."[38]

Morris's commitment to the idea of the class struggle is unproblematic. The same cannot be said of his economic analysis of capitalism. On the one hand, he clearly tried to come to terms with *Capital*, and the articles he wrote with Bax really do show an impressive grasp of Marx's ideas. On the other hand, even if Glasier's story of Morris's easy dismissal of economic theory is an invention, nobody who reads widely in Morris's socialist writings can fail to recognize how much he prefers to depict a communal way of life rather than trying to unravel any economic logic to capitalism. Moreover, the articles he wrote on his own are far less impressive than those he wrote with Bax. Indeed, at the same time as he published the articles with Bax, he wrote two lectures by himself in which he outlined a theory of surplus value based on the twin pillars of the capitalists' monopoly of the means of production and an iron law of wages. He titled one lecture "Monopoly; or, How Labour Is Robbed." In the other lecture he explained:

> The capitalists, by means of their monopoly of the means of production, compel the worker to work for less than his due share of the wealth which he produces—that is, for less than he produces. He must work, he will die else, and as they are in the possession of the raw material, he must agree to the terms they enforce.[39]

This theory of surplus value differs from Marx's in *Capital*. Marx argued that labor power had greater use value than exchange value. The differ-

[37] *Commonweal*, 19 November 1887.
[38] Morris, *Works*, vol. 23, p. 231.
[39] Ibid., p. 223.

ence was the source of surplus value. No doubt the historical fact that the proletariat were a landless class helped to explain why labor power had become a commodity for sale in the market. But for Marx, capitalists necessarily acquired surplus value when they purchased labor power irrespective of any supposed law of wages or monopoly of the means of production. Given that Morris said his economic theory derived less from reading Marx than from "conversation with such friends as Bax and Hyndman and Scheu," perhaps we should not be surprised that his theory of surplus value incorporated the Lassallean perspective of the latter two.[40]

So, Morris's Marxist sociology owed at least as much to his sociology of art as to his grasp of Marx's economic theory. His socialism consisted mainly in his belief that class struggle was the force driving the dialectical movement of history, and his belief in class struggle just took the place of his earlier Ruskinian belief that the history of art reflected the changing conditions of labor. Morris now argued that in the feudal era craftsmen related to their products as artists, but they did so in a class-ridden society. The bourgeoisie had destroyed the political power of the landed aristocracy, only to build a capitalist society that denied the artistic nature of labor. Whereas medieval cities such as Oxford and Rouen were full of beautiful buildings, an attractive building in a modern suburb was a surprise.[41] Contemporary art was in such dire straights that students of design had to study artifacts from the past, rather than modern goods. The dire plight of art reflected the nature of labor under capitalism. Capitalist production for profit destroyed the relationship between craftsmen and their products. Craftsmen were replaced by wage slaves. The growth of factories compelled workers to labor for long hours at monotonous tasks. Industrialization turned them into adjuncts of machines, preventing them from expressing their individual spirit. Commercialization forced them to make commodities that catered to the whims of the wealthy instead of satisfying genuine needs. Workers were thus denied the self-respect that came from doing useful work. Capitalism was an immoral economy premised on a ceaseless search for profit at the expense of human values. Finally, a communist society would enable craftsmen once more to relate to their products as did artists, but it would do so without the constraints and antagonisms of social class. Art would thus serve riches, not wealth—"the means of living a decent life," not "the means for exercising dominion over other people."[42] Art and fellowship would flourish as never before.

---

[40] Ibid., p. 278.

[41] Morris had admired Rouen. See Morris, *Letters*, ed. Kelvin, vol. 1: *1848–1880*, pp. 19–22.

[42] Morris, *Works*, vol. 23, p. 143.

Morris's Marxism also reflected his earlier thought in more minor ways. Most obviously, much of the appeal of socialism was aesthetic. Morris could not "conceive of anyone who loves beauty, that is to say the crown of a full and noble life, being able to face it unless he has full faith in the religion of socialism."[43] In addition, the pattern of the dialectic harked back to a romantic belief in an organic cycle in human affairs. Before he became a socialist, he wrote of the growth of art that "like all growth, it was good and fruitful for awhile; like all fruitful growth, it grew into decay; like all decay of what was once fruitful, it will grow into something new."[44] Finally, Marx's concept of class echoed his earlier concern with people as artistic producers. It grouped people together according to their relationship to the means of production.

What does our analysis of Morris's socialism imply about the suitability of the ideological labels commentators have pinned on him? It seems reasonable to call him a Marxist. He considered himself a Marxist. He joined Marxist organizations. And his views on capitalism and class show the influence of Marx. Because traditions and ideologies overlap, we might want to call Morris an anarchist or an ethical socialist as well as a Marxist. Still, there are good reasons why we may be wary of these labels. He explicitly denied he was an anarchist, battled against the anarchists in the Socialist League, and granted the need for some kind of social authority, maybe even some kind of coercion.[45] Similarly, although Morris inspired ethical socialists, it is anachronistic to call him an ethical socialist. The ethical socialist movement arose in the provinces during the 1890s, whereas Morris was active mainly in London in the 1880s.

Although it seems reasonable to describe Morris as a Marxist, we should be careful about assimilating him to Marxist orthodoxies. Arnot overstated the case when he argued that Morris's socialism rested on economics, not a "historical, ethical 'and literary' basis."[46] Against Thompson as well as Arnot, we should insist that Morris's economic theory was not Marx's; Morris's socialism rested on the class struggle and a concern for good art, not on economic theory; and Morris's socialism drew heavily on Ruskin's aesthetic ideals and sociology of art. Morris even defined socialism in terms of these ideals, not an economic theory.

[43] W. Morris, *William Morris: Artist, Writer, Socialist*, ed. M. Morris, with an account of William Morris by Bernard Shaw (Oxford: Blackwell, 1936), vol. 1: *Morris as a Writer*, p. 240.

[44] Morris, *Works*, vol. 22, p. 9.

[45] Morris argued against the anarchists: "If individuals are not to coerce others, there must somewhere be an authority which is prepared to coerce them not to coerce." He explained, "I am not pleading for any form of arbitrary or unreasonable authority, but for a *public conscience* as a rule of action: and by all means let us have the least possible exercise of authority." See Morris, *William Morris*, vol. 2: *Morris as a Socialist*, pp. 314 and 316.

[46] Arnot, *Morris*, p. 11.

What I mean by socialism is a condition of society in which there should be neither rich nor poor, neither master nor master's man, neither idle nor overworked, neither brain-sick brain workers, nor heart-sick hand workers, in a word, in which all men would be living in equality of condition, and would manage their affairs unwastefully, and with the full consciousness that harm to one would mean harm to all.[47]

The Utopian

Attempts to establish Morris's Marxist credentials obscure the utopian and purist nature of his socialism. Morris did not move from being a romantic to being a revolutionary, as Thompson suggests. On the contrary, he remained a romantic, and, moreover, his romantic and Protestant concerns led him to a purist form of socialism, not a revolutionary one. Morris came to think that collective ownership of the means of production was essential to end exploitation. Nonetheless, his dominant concern remained the place of art in everyday life. Romanticism and Protestantism defined his utopian vision and political strategy.

Morris's socialist ideal echoed his romantic and Protestant concern to bring art into everyday life. He wanted everyone to feel about their daily work as do artists, since he believed that creativity is a "need of man's soul."[48] He also wanted everyone to enjoy art in their domestic lives; being surrounded by beautiful objects was also a need of the soul. These ideals defined his political strategy, leading him to disparage the struggle for higher wages and even public ownership of the means of production on the grounds that they would do little to end the true slavery of the working class. He was a purist, denouncing almost all forms of political action because they dirtied the hands of those who undertook them.

According to Morris, daily life consisted of two dominant moods: energy and idleness. Our aim should be happiness in both moods, and art brings just such happiness. Morris wrote that "the aim of art is to increase the happiness of men, by giving them beauty and interest of incident to amuse their leisure, and prevent them wearying even of rest, and by giving them hope and bodily pleasure in their work; or, shortly, to make man's work happy and his rest fruitful."[49]

---

[47] Morris, *Works*, vol. 23, p. 277.
[48] Ibid., p. 203.
[49] Ibid., p. 84.

In the mood of idleness, happiness comes from enjoying and using works of art. This happiness is simple and natural, as exemplified by an evening in Morris's utopia:

> The wine was of the best; the hall was redolent of rich summer flowers; and after supper we not only had music . . . but, at last we got to telling stories, and sat there listening, with no other light but that of the summer moon streaming through the beautiful traceries of the windows, as if we belonged to time long passed, when books were scarce and the art of reading somewhat rare.[50]

People needed a decent environment in which to enjoy art during their leisure and thereby satisfy the mood of idleness. The population of Morris's utopia moved back to the countryside, where they lived in simple communal dwellings. They took great care to preserve natural beauty. One of the first things a visitor noticed was the cleanness of the Thames.[51]

In the mood of energy, happiness comes from producing art. Morris's broad view of art included all labor. To be artists, people did not have to create particular products. They just had to feel a particular way about the products that they created. Specific conditions of labor promoted the required feeling, but the feeling, not the conditions of labor, was what mattered. Workers should have varied tasks so that they did not feel compelled. They should be able to stamp their individuality on each product so that they felt the hope of creation. And they should produce goods that fulfilled genuine needs so that they felt self-respect.[52] It was vital to make work enjoyable because people needed to work in order to exercise their energies. The population of Morris's utopian society feared a shortage of work.[53] People needed "honourable and fitting work" in order to satisfy the mood of energy.[54]

Because Morris allowed for the needs of both consumers and producers, there arose the question of what should happen if consumers had legitimate desires that could be satisfied only if producers acted in a way that undermined their status as artists. Morris believed that such conflicts would be rare because machinery would alleviate heavy and monotonous work. However, if a conflict did occur, the decision would balance the nature of the work against the social value of the product. If the work were particularly degrading or the product not essential, society would have to forgo the product.

---

[50] Ibid., vol. 16: *News From Nowhere*, p. 140.
[51] Ibid., p. 6.
[52] Ibid., vol. 23, pp. 164–91.
[53] Ibid., vol. 16, pp. 91–92.
[54] Ibid., vol. 23, p. 194.

Morris's vision of a communist society emphasized the fulfillment of everyday life through the naturalness and harmony of good art. His Rus-kinian social theory then led him to relate this vision to a transformation in industrial relations. Art would become the watchword of the factory of the future. The market value of commodities would be insignificant com-pared with the quality of labor. Workers would resemble the craftsmen of old. They would create beautiful artifacts imprinted with their own personalities. They would take satisfaction from their work and from the knowledge that others gained pleasure from using their creations. Collective ownership of the means of production mattered less as a way of eliminating surplus value than as a way of promoting an industrial system devoted to art. The slavery of the workers would end less because exploitation vanished than because art flourished.

> The attractive work of our factory, that which it was pleasant in itself to do, would be of the nature of art; therefore all slavery of work ceases under such a system, for whatever is burdensome about the factory would be taken turn and turn about, and so distributed would cease to be a burden, would be in fact a kind of rest from the more exciting or artistic work.[55]

This belief in craftsmanship did not lead Morris to reject mechanization outright. He just wanted people to judge the worth of machines accord-ing to whether they made labor more pleasant, not whether they made production cheaper. In his communist society, "Machines of the most in-genious and best approved kinds will be used when necessary, but will be used simply to save human labour."[56] Once everybody became a crafts-man, they would judge the worth of the work of others and of machines in terms of beauty and use value, rather than profit and exchange value. The mutual exchange of useful products would replace the competitive market.

For Morris, good art depended on a transformation in social life as well as in industrial conditions. His sociology of art suggested that good art required an honest and simple social life akin to that of the Middle Ages. People had to recognize that "fellowship is heaven, and lack of fellowship is hell: fellowship is life, and lack of fellowship is death."[57] Morris liked "to think of barbarism once more flooding the world, and real feelings and passions, however rudimentary, taking the place of our wretched hypocrisies."[58] His utopia was a society of neighbors in which

---

[55] Morris, *William Morris*, vol. 2, p. 135.
[56] Ibid., p. 134.
[57] Morris, *Works*, vol. 16, p. 230.
[58] Morris, *Letters*, ed. Kelvin, vol. 2, pt. B: *1885–88*, p. 436.

people would assist each other gladly, taking pleasure in being of service. People would live simple lives, finding happiness in natural acts such as eating, loving, and sleeping. They would eat in large communal dining halls before sitting around retelling heroic stories. Children would learn by play with an emphasis on swimming and carpentry, and they would spend the summer camping out in the woods. At harvest time, everyone would carouse in the fields.

A neglect of Morris's particular debt to romanticism and Protestantism has obscured crucial continuities in his utopian ideals. Romantic themes persist in his concern to promote good art based on naturalness and harmony. Protestant themes persist in his attempts to sanctify daily life by entrenching art in work and leisure—the moods of energy and idleness. A Ruskinian sociology of art persists in his belief that good art depends on a society based on fellowship and a moral economy. Even when Morris called for collective ownership of the means of production, he did so principally because he believed it was necessary for good art to flourish in everyday settings.

THE PURIST

Morris's debt to romanticism and Protestantism led him to a purist approach to political action, not a revolutionary one. In Morris's view, socialism depended on art's having a new role in daily life, so a change in everyday attitudes and activities was more important than either a change in institutions or the acquisition of political power. He told his fellow socialists, "The religion of Socialism calls upon us to be better than other people since we owe ourselves to the society which we have accepted as the hope of the future."[59] He warned them of "the error of moving earth & sea to fill the ballot boxes with Socialist votes which will not represent Socialist *men*."[60]

All of Morris's arguments against parliamentary action drew on his concern to transform daily life in accord with a new spirit of art. For a start, Morris believed that parliamentary action was unlikely to do the socialist cause much good. Parliamentary action could secure only material ends; it could not turn workers into artists. Socialist members of Parliament might point out concessions with which the ruling class could prolong the slavery of workers, but they could not promote good art in daily life. In addition, Morris believed that parliamentary action might damage the socialist cause. He feared that if socialists entered Parlia-

---

[59] *Commonweal*, 28 August 1886.
[60] Morris, *Letters*, ed. Kelvin, vol. 2, pt. B, p. 693.

ment, they would draw attention away from the fundamental need to transform people's daily activities and attitudes. He argued that "the real business of Socialists is to impress on the workers that they are a class, whereas they ought to be Society; if we mix ourselves up with Parliament we shall confuse and dull this fact in people's minds instead of making it clear and intensifying it."[61] Besides, parliamentary action would corrupt the socialists who engaged in it.

> I really feel sickened at the idea of all the intrigue and degradation of concession which would be necessary to us as a parliamentary party: nor do I see any necessity for a revolutionary party doing any "dirty work" at all, or soiling ourselves with anything which would unfit us for being due citizens of the new order of things.[62]

Morris's moral and aesthetic ideals led him to question not only parliamentary action but also palliatives and trade unions. He argued that if capitalism's "wrongs and anomalies were so capable of palliation that people generally were not only contented, but were capable of developing their human faculties duly under it, and that we were on the road to progress without a great change, I for one would not ask anyone to meddle with it."[63] He denounced palliatives because even if they promoted material well-being, they would not transform the place of art in daily life. Palliatives could not turn workers into artists or bring good art into the home. Similarly, Morris often dismissed trade unions because they struggled for better wages and conditions of work, rather than a mode of being capable of sustaining good art.

> The position of the Trades Unions, as anything but benefit societies, has become an impossible one; the long and short of what they say to the masters is this: We are not going to interfere with your management of our affairs except so far as we can reduce your salary as our managers. We acknowledge that we are machines and that you are the hands that guide us; but we will pay as little as we can help for your guidance.[64]

As Morris rejected parliamentarianism, palliatives, and strikes, he had little option but to propose a policy of abstention. He advocated refusing to participate in bourgeois institutions, arguing, "The true weapon of the workers as against Parliament is not the ballot-box but the *boycott*."[65] The boycott would provide the pure example necessary to inspire a new

---

[61] *Commonweal*, July 1885.

[62] Morris, *Letters*, ed. Kelvin, vol. 2, pt. B, p. 598.

[63] Morris, *Works*, vol. 23, p. 229.

[64] Morris, *William Morris*, vol. 2, p. 443.

[65] *Commonweal*, 7 June 1890. For his "Policy of Abstention," see Morris, *William Morris*, vol. 2, pp. 434–52.

type of person. At least for now socialists should form a party of principle. They should content themselves with an educative propaganda: "Our business I repeat is the making of socialists."[66] Action must wait because "until we have that mass of opinion, action for a general change that will benefit the whole people is impossible."[67]

In his book *News from Nowhere*, Morris described the political action that he thought would follow the successful education of the workers.[68] The existence of an educated population that was aware of the ills of capitalism and that gave minimal obedience to existing authority would compel the state to adopt a policy of either force or fraud. At first the monopolists would try a policy of fraud, introducing state socialism in an attempt to buy the workers off. This fraud would fail because the workers would be educated to recognize it for what it was. So the monopolists would turn to force. The workers would respond by combining in one great federation. When the economy next suffered a cyclical depression, the workers would insist on taking control of the natural resources of the nation. Then there would be a civil war. The workers would emerge victorious and go on to establish communism.

Morris's account of the transition to socialism may appear here to include a revolutionary strategy. Nonetheless, there are three closely related reasons why we might suspect it expresses his basic rejection of politics. First, Morris believed the revolution had to represent the transformation of everyday life through the rise of a new spirit of art. He wrote:

> I want a real revolution, a real change in Society: Society a great organic mass of well-regulated forces used for the bringing-about [of] a happy life for all. And the means for attaining it are simple enough; education in Socialism, and organization for the time when the crisis shall force action upon us: nothing else will do us any good at present: the revolution cannot be a mechanical one, though the last act of it may be civil war, or it will end in reaction after all.[69]

Second, revolutionary action presupposed a prior change in everyday attitudes. In particular, there was to be no action until the workers were educated. The revolution thus receded constantly from view. Morris began "with the distinct aim of making Socialists by educating them, and of organizing them to deal with politics in the end," so the revolution always could be postponed on the grounds that the time for it had not yet arrived.[70] Third, Morris's concept of a future revolution can seem, there-

---

[66] Morris, *William Morris*, vol. 2, p. 518.
[67] *Commonweal*, 15 November 1890.
[68] Morris, *Works*, vol. 16, pp. 103–30.
[69] Morris, *Letters*, ed. Kelvin, vol. 2, pt. B, p. 368.
[70] Ibid., p. 369.

fore, to be less a call for political action than a symbol for the vastness of the change he desired. The revolution marked the tragedy needed to ensure a complete break with the present. "The world was being brought to its second birth; how could that take place without a tragedy?"[71]

Historians might acknowledge a purist strand to Morris's actions only to deny that this purism was integral to his socialism. Thompson argues, for example, that Morris became disillusioned with politics only as a negative reaction to Hyndman's opportunism.[72] Thompson then goes on to suggest that once Morris left the Social Democratic Federation (SDF), his struggles against anarchists in the Socialist League led him to embrace revolutionary political action. In contrast, I suggest that Morris's anti-parliamentarianism derived from his aesthetic and moral ideals. His experience of Hyndman's "opportunism" might have strengthened his dislike of the compromises necessitated by political action, but the dislike was already there. When he first joined the SDF, he wrote, "The aim of socialists should be the founding of a religion, towards which end compromise is no use."[73] Soon after, when the SDF adopted a new program, he wrote that it "is better than the old one, and is not parliamentary."[74] Morris reacted negatively to parliamentary action, palliatives, and trade unions because of his emphasis on creating a new spirit of art in daily life.

The only remaining question is whether or not Morris's experiences in the Socialist League led him to reject purism for a revolutionary strategy. As we saw in the last chapter, Morris headed the majority that, in December 1884, broke with the SDF to form the Socialist League. The founders of the Socialist League included two main factions; the anarchists rejected the SDF's parliamentarianism, whereas the circle based around Friedrich Engels and the Marx family objected only to Hyndman's Tory moralism. The League was unstable. In January 1885 Edward Aveling, Marx's son-in-law, proposed that the League try to build a Socialist Labour Party by working with trade unions and participating in local elections. The anarchists opposed him. A temporary compromise was reached that precluded current action in favor of a policy of education.[75] Then, in May 1887, the League's third annual conference passed an explicitly purist and anti-parliamentary resolution: "The primary duty of the Socialist party is to educate the people in the principles of Socialism, and to organise them to overthrow the capitalist system: this Conference endorses the policy

[71] Morris, *Works*, vol. 16, p. 132.

[72] E. Thompson, *Morris*, pp. 763–816.

[73] Morris, *Letters*, ed. Kelvin, vol. 2, pt. A, p. 219.

[74] Ibid., pp. 312–13.

[75] The Socialist League, *The Manifesto of the Socialist League* (London: Socialist League, 1885).

of abstention from parliamentary action hitherto pursued by the League, and sees no reason for altering it."[76]

At the next annual conference the Marx family circle who dominated the Bloomsbury branch proposed a motion that would allow individual branches to choose whether or not to run candidates in elections. Morris had tried to avoid a split, but when forced to act, he now proposed a purist anti-parliamentary amendment. The amendment was passed, and the Bloomsbury branch withdrew from the League.

By 1887 the League consisted therefore mainly of Morris and his friends, the anarchists of the Labour Emancipation League, and anarchist exiles from Europe such as Gustave Brocher, Andreas Scheu, and Sebastian Trunk. Morris favored purism. But the anarchists supported various forms of violent action. Joseph Lane and others from the Labour Emancipation League generally called for a bloody revolution while rejecting individual acts of violence.[77] Yet, even individual "propaganda by the deed" attracted a group of anarchists who had joined the League in 1886, including Thomas Cantwell, Fred and Henry Charles, David Nicoll, Henry Samuels, and John Taylor. In 1890 the anarchists ousted Morris as editor of the League's newspaper, *Commonweal*. Later that year Morris and his friends left to form the independent Hammersmith Socialist Society.

It is true that Morris's struggles with anarchists in the League led him to take a slightly less hostile view of palliatives and other stepping-stones toward socialism. During the May Day celebrations of 1894 and 1895, he even spoke from the platform of the SDF. Nonetheless, the Hammersmith Society renounced both parliamentarianism and the social revolutionary stance of the anarchists in favor of a purist policy of education.[78] The Society's funds were to be used only to educate people in socialism by peaceful means, including lectures, publications, and street meetings. At the very most, therefore, Morris seems to have glimpsed some of the difficulties confronting his purism while continuing to feel that he personally could not take any stance other than a purist one. He said the League had failed because "you cannot keep a body together without giving it something to do in the present," but he still concluded, "Socialism is spreading, I suppose, on the only lines on which it could spread, and

---

[76] *Commonweal*, 4 June 1887.

[77] J. Lane, *Anti-Statist Communist Manifesto* (London: International Revolutionary, 1887).

[78] Hammersmith Socialist Society, *Statement of Principles* (London: Hammersmith Socialist Society, 1893). Also see the minutes of the Hammersmith Socialist Society, William Morris Papers, British Library, London, BM:45891-3.

the League is moribund simply because we are outside those limits, as I for one must always be."[79]

Morris came to believe only that unsuccessful attempts at parliamentarianism and state socialism would necessarily proceed the moment the workers turned to his ideals and strategy. He did not change the content of his ideals or his strategy. On the contrary, his farewell article in *Commonweal* clearly stated his continuing belief in purism.

> There are two tendencies in this matter of methods: on the one hand is our old acquaintance palliation [parliamentarianism] . . . on the other is the method of partial, necessarily futile, inconsequent revolt [anarchism]. . . . With both of these methods I disagree; and that the more because the palliatives have to be clamoured for and the riots carried out by men who do not know what Socialism is, and have no idea what their next step is to be, if contrary to all calculation they should happen to be successful. Therefore, at the best our masters would be our masters still, because there would be nothing to take their place. . . . The authorities might be a little shaken perhaps, a little more inclined to yield something to the clamours of their slaves, but there would be slaves still, *as all men must be who are not prepared to manage their own business themselves.*[80]

The strength of Morris's purism had led him to reject both parliamentary action and revolutionary action. He became convinced socialists would try such action. But at no time did he renounce his strategy of abstention. Arguably, he found himself in the wilderness of the Hammersmith Society precisely because he could not endorse any feasible political strategy.

CONCLUSION

Historians have ignored or underplayed Morris's purism in part because they have concentrated on placing him in fixed ideological categories rather than tracing the broader traditions that influenced him, notably romanticism and Protestantism. Ironically, Morris's debt to these broader traditions and his purism help explain why he has become everyone's favorite socialist. For a start, Morris's utopian vision satisfies longings widespread in modern culture. He satisfies a romantic longing for harmony with oneself, one's fellow human beings, and nature. And he satisfies a Protestant longing to sanctify everyday work and domesticity. In addition, Morris's purism means that socialists can avow his utopia without

---

[79] Morris, *Letters*, ed. Henderson, pp. 231–32.
[80] Morris, *William Morris*, vol. 2, p. 516.

embracing any contentious political strategy. Ethical socialists can applaud his emphasis on a new moral spirit without worrying about how to create it. Marxists can celebrate his avowal of communism without worrying about the haziness of his account of how and when it is to be established. Anarchists can exult in his opposition to the state and parliamentary action without worrying about the structure of the organization through which the change is to be made.

Morris is the great dreamer of the British Left. During the depression of the 1930s, Barbara Castle, the future Labour Party politician, tramped across the Yorkshire moors, overlooking the ugly, polluted industrial towns of the valleys. Her despair was dispelled when she read Morris's poem "The Message of the March Wind," with its evocation of fellowship—the old inn and roaring fire with a fiddler playing and people dancing. Morris wanted to improve the world, to make it simpler, more enjoyable, beautiful, fulfilling, and just. His socialist utopia educates our aspirations; it gives us a glimpse of a better world. We should be grateful, but our gratitude need not blind us to either his purism or the importance of political action.

CHAPTER SIX

The Social Democratic Federation

HISTORIANS OFTEN NARRATE the early years of British Marxism as a titanic struggle between Henry Mayers Hyndman and William Morris, with other walk-on parts being played by the likes of Edward Aveling (Karl Marx's son-in-law), Ernest Belfort Bax, and even Friedrich Engels. The plot is tragic; the good Morris gets sidelined, the villainous Hyndman dominates, and his authoritarianism and jingoism antagonize the workers, thus strangling the Marxist movement at birth. For a long time, the members of early Marxist organizations played a remarkably small role in the story. Their scripted lines came from the old historiography: they were class-conscious workers who, following the legacy of the Chartists, recognized the social causes of social evils and set out to eradicate those evils through political action.[1] But they fluffed their lines and followed Hyndman into the wilderness instead of forging a powerful Marxist organization.

A new historiography has made these old scripts and plots seem implausible. Historians increasingly challenge the idea that the first half of the nineteenth century saw the emergence of a uniform industrial and capitalist economy, let alone a class-conscious working class. Economic and social historians have shifted their emphasis from the rise of an industrial proletariat to the persistence of skilled artisans.[2] Social and intellectual historians have revealed continuities from the traditions of popular radicalism through Chartism and even into various movements of the 1860s and 1870s.[3]

A version of this chapter appeared as "The British Social Democratic Federation 1880–1885: From O'Brienism to Marxism," *International Review of Social History* 37 (1992), 207–229. Published by Cambridge University Press.

[1] F. Engels, *The Condition of the Working Class in England* (Harmondsworth, UK: Penguin, 1987).

[2] R. Samuel, "The Workshop of the World: Steam Power and Hand Technology in Mid-Victorian Britain," *History Workshop* 3 (1977): 6–72.

[3] G. Stedman Jones, "Rethinking Chartism," in *Languages of Class: Studies in English Working Class History, 1832–1982* (Cambridge: Cambridge University Press, 1983), pp. 90–178. Also see G. Claeys, *Citizens and Saints: Politics and Anti-politics in Early British Socialism* (Cambridge: Cambridge University Press, 1989), and M. Finn, *After Chartism: Class and Nation in English Radical Politics, 1848–1874* (Cambridge: Cambridge University Press, 1993).

The erosion of the old historiography raises questions about the ordinary members of early Marxist organizations, especially the Social Democratic Federation (SDF). One question is, how did their beliefs change from the popular radicalism of the Chartists, with its emphasis on political solutions, to a Marxism that included calls for the collective ownership of the means of production? Another question is, why did they remain in the SDF rather than follow Morris into the Socialist League? This chapter tries to answer such questions. The early members of the SDF were often artisans and popular radicals. They were followers of James Bronterre O'Brien from London's radical clubs. Their socialism continued to echo themes from O'Brienism. These themes overlapped at key points with the political theory Hyndman had forged against the background of Tory radicalism.[4]

JAMES BRONTERRE O'BRIEN (1804–64)

James Bronterre O'Brien was an Irishman who settled in England and became the "schoolmaster of the Chartists."[5] O'Brien concentrated on the undemocratic nature of the British political system. He argued that social evils had political causes. The ruling classes had a monopoly of the legislative process, and this monopoly enabled them to introduce the oppressive laws under which the few robbed the many. O'Brien told the workers that "it is because you are unrepresented that you have no property," and that "wages-slavery is wholly and solely the work of tyrannical laws which one set of men impose upon another by fraud and force."[6]

For O'Brien, social problems may have had political causes, but they were still among the main problems of his day. The worst social problems included the private ownership of land and the current systems of currency and exchange: "Unquestionably land-usurpers and money-changers . . . must *in foco conscienta* be distinguished from all other sinners," since "we know of no great social evil in civilized life that is not clearly traceable, directly or indirectly, to these two classes."[7] O'Brien believed

---

[4] Historians generally describe the SDF as dogmatic and revolutionary. See H. Collins, "The Marxism of the Social Democratic Federation," in *Essays in Labour History, 1886–1923*, ed. A. Briggs and J. Saville (London: Macmillan, 1971); S. Pierson, *Marxism and the Origins of British Socialism* (Ithaca, NY: Cornell University, 1973); and W. Wolfe, *From Radicalism to Socialism* (New Haven, CT: Yale University Press, 1975).

[5] A. Plummer, *Bronterre: A Political Biography of Bronterre O'Brien, 1804–1864* (London: Allen and Unwin, 1971).

[6] *National Reformer*, 3 October 1846; J. O'Brien, *The Rise, Progress, and Phases of Human Slavery* (London: W. Reeves, 1885), p. 94.

[7] O'Brien, *Rise*, p. 128.

that God had given the land to all people, but a small section of the population had used unjust laws to appropriate the land for themselves. Moreover, because the amount of land is fixed, the private appropriation of the land denied people without property the chance to produce their own subsistence; it forced them to work for the landowners. O'Brien concluded that the moment you allow the few to monopolize the land, "your community is divided into tyrants and slaves—into knaves who will work for nobody, and into drudges who will have to work for anybody or everybody but themselves."[8] The private ownership of land divides society into opposing classes. It underlies all other social problems.

O'Brien also denounced money lords for cheating society through contemporary systems of currency and exchange. Because the currency rested on commodities (gold and silver), the money lords who monopolized these precious metals effectively monopolized the currency. The money lords "leave us without any instruments of exchange at all, but what may be convertible, upon their own fraudulent terms, into those two favoured metals."[9] Moreover, the money lords used their parliamentary power to manipulate for their personal advantage the money supply and the national debt. For example, as chancellor and as prime minister, Robert Peel had promoted laissez-faire, thereby increasing foreign competition and thus reducing the value of commodities. Peel also tightened the money supply, which raised the value of money in comparison with commodities, and so again reduced the value of commodities. This decline in the value of commodities swelled fixed money obligations, such as debts and taxes. As a result, both profits and wages declined, "for the more the producers (employers and employed) have to give out of the common stock to pay taxes and the interest of public and private debts, the less there must be left for themselves."[10] Only the money lords benefited from Peel's policies. They alone possessed monetary assets, such as fixed interest stocks, the value of which increased relative to commodities.

Land and finance were the enemies of capital as well as labor. Indeed, O'Brien denounced capitalists only because they sometimes acted as money lords or as middlemen. Like money lords, capitalists issued debt for their own gain at the expense of the workers: "The mercantile middle-classes are everywhere organising chartered companies to give themselves perpetual vested interests in the labour of the working-classes, and mortgage the latter to posterity through public loans and State indebtedness."[11]

[8] Ibid., p. 127.
[9] Ibid., p. 135.
[10] Ibid., p. 122.
[11] Ibid., p. 144.

Again, O'Brien complained of "middlemen who . . . get their living by buying your [the workingman's] labour at one price and selling it . . . at another."[12] Although O'Brien denounced capitalists for sometimes behaving like money lords, he nonetheless argued that they were able to do so only because the people had no access to land. If people are excluded from land, they fall prey to middlemen. O'Brien believed that "the monopoly of the land in private hands is a palpable invasion of the rights of the excluded parties, rendering them more or less the slaves of landlords and capitalists."[13]

The fundamental oppositions in O'Brien's writings were those of popular radicalism. He pitted rulers against people, and idlers against workers. The ruling class used a monopoly of political power to defraud the people. The result was a social split between idlers and workers, for the rulers used their political power to obtain "incomes" that were "purely and wholly the *creation of law*, and not of their own labour."[14] Thus, the unequal distribution of political power created "an unnatural division of society into classes, *viz.*, those who labour and produce as well as consume, and those who consume only."[15]

O'Brien's proposals for reform reflected his analysis of the problems of contemporary society. Because the unrepresentative political system underlay current social evils, "we must first have political equality."[16] O'Brien called above all else for the implementation of the Charter, the six points of which were universal suffrage, annual parliaments, no property qualifications for Members of Parliament (MPs), payment of MPs, voting by a secret ballot, and equal electoral districts. The political reforms of the Charter, especially manhood suffrage, would create a representative democracy. The people would obtain the legislative power that they needed to eradicate poverty and slavery. So, "manhood suffrage must be the cry and watchword . . . to get honest laws passed upon Land, Credit, Currency, and Exchange."[17] Sometimes O'Brien seemed to put social reform before political reform, as when he said that "a reform of parliament can effect little good except in so far as it may conduce to a reform in the construction of society."[18] However, even if his primary goal was social reform, the key means remained political reform. As he

---

[12] *Poor Man's Guardian*, 15 December 1832.

[13] O'Brien, *Rise*, p. 101.

[14] Ibid., p. 113.

[15] J. O'Brien, "Bronterre's Second Letter to the People of England," *Political Letters and Pamphlets*, 12 February 1831.

[16] *National Reformer*, 7 January 1837.

[17] *National Reform League Tract No. 5*, November 1855.

[18] "Proceedings of 2nd Co-operative Congress." Cited by Plummer, *Bronterre*, p. 38.

explained, "The end I have in view is social equality for each and all, to obtain this we must first have political equality."[19]

According to O'Brien, the people would use political power to tackle social ills through land and currency reform. Land nationalization was the most important piece of legislation required of a reformed parliament. Indeed, "No reform that will not give the people the means of acquiring property by honest industry—which will not enable them to be independent of wages-slavery—which will not enable them to live in houses of their own, and allow them free access to the soil of their country, is worth their serious attention."[20] Land nationalization would enable people to work the land so they could provide for their own livelihood. It would free them from the tyranny of the landlords and capitalists. The many would no longer have to work for the few. Similarly, currency reform would end the tyranny of the money lords. O'Brien believed that the money lords were able to rob the people because gold and silver were both commodities and the basis of the currency. He thus proposed a paper currency "based on real consumable wealth" and, in particular, on labor or just possibly corn.[21] If a currency were based on labor, its value would not fluctuate with the availability of precious metals, so there would be a proper equilibrium between production and consumption. A person who produced goods worth £x would be given currency worth £x with which to buy consumables. There would be no way for money lords to make money yield yet more money. O'Brien even proposed a system of direct exchange and state stores to eliminate parasitic middlemen. At no time did he demand collective ownership of the means of production.

LONDON CLUBLAND (1864–81)

When O'Brien died, he left behind a group of followers, many of whom later joined the SDF. Charles Murray supervised the arrangements for O'Brien's funeral, and in 1884 the SDF's newspaper, *Justice*, advertised his lecture titled "Personal Recollections of Bronterre O'Brien."[22] His

---

[19] *National Reformer*, 7 January 1837.

[20] O'Brien, *Rise*, p. 127.

[21] Ibid., p. 102.

[22] Plummer, *Bronterre*, p. 269; *Justice*, 15 November 1884. For confirmation that Charles Murray was an O'Brienite when he joined the SDF, see H. Hyndman, *The Record of an Adventurous Life* (London: Macmillan, 1912), p. 246; and H. Lee and E. Archbold, *Social-Democracy in Britain* (London: Social Democratic Federation, 1935), p. 245. For an early expression of his beliefs, see C. Murray, *A Letter to Mr. George Jacob Holyoake* (London: Pavey, 1854).

brother, James Murray, was a chief mourner at O'Brien's funeral, and in 1883 he sat on the SDF's executive committee.[23] George Harris wrote to Victor Hugo asking him to give a speech at O'Brien's funeral, and Harris later gave a lecture to the Marylebone branch of the SDF titled "Socialism vs. Liberalism."[24] Hyndman recalled walking back from an SDF meeting with two more of O'Brien's followers, William Morgan and Richard Butler.[25] And there was William Townshend, whom Max Beer found selling books and as ready as ever to talk politics and praise O'Brien.[26]

Most of these O'Brienites were skilled artisans. Butler was a compositor, Harris was a tailor, and the Murray brothers, Morgan, and Townshend were shoemakers. These trades remained skill intensive during the 1860s and 1870s. Mass production made little headway, and industrialization was patchy. Employers often stuck with hand labor both because it was flexible and because mechanization was expensive. New techniques of production generally created new skills even as they eroded old ones. Moreover, the O'Brienites were Londoners. They were employed in the bespoke trades of the West End. These bespoke trades were altered by industrialization and by a market economy, but they still consisted largely of skilled craftsmen who worked individually or in small groups. Workers were increasingly employed by others for wages, but they were rarely machine operatives. The O'Brienites are probably representative of the rest of the SDF's membership. Membership averaged a mere 580 during the 1880s, and of these, fewer than 100 lived outside London.[27] Charles Booth's magnificent survey, conducted in the early 1880s, found that the tailors and shoemakers of the West End of London preserved the customs of their crafts and were sympathetic to republicanism and socialism.[28] So, the working lives of the members of the SDF remained fairly stable throughout the mid-Victorian era. However, the 1880s, and especially the 1890s, brought upheaval. Londoners experienced drastic changes in the local labor market. Prominent industries migrated, including shoemaking and shipping, which moved respectively to towns such as Northampton and Gravesend. The bespoke trades of the O'Brienites entered a time of

[23] *Reynolds's*, 8 January 1865. As a member of the DF's executive, James Murray was a signatory to the Democratic Federation, *Socialism Made Plain: Being the Social and Political Manifesto of the Democratic Federation* (London: W. Reeves, 1883).

[24] Plummer, *Bronterre*, p. 268; *Christian Socialist*, September 1883.

[25] H. Hyndman, *Record*, p. 254.

[26] M. Beer, *Fifty Years of International Socialism* (London: Allen and Unwin, 1935), pp. 13–14.

[27] P. Watmough, "The Membership of the Social Democratic Federation, 1885–1902," *Labour History Bulletin* 34 (1977): 35–40.

[28] C. Booth, *Life and Labour of the People of London*, series 1: *Poverty*, vol. 4 (London: Macmillan, 1902–3), p. 141.

de-skilling and mechanization, with, for example, mechanical typesetting increasingly replacing the skilled work of hand-setting compositors.

The O'Brienites were not idle in the time between Chartism and the making of the socialist movement in the 1880s. They were obviously actively involved in the National Reform League (NRL), which O'Brien had founded in 1849. However, they were also active in other radical organizations. Harris and Charles Murray were among the British representatives at the meeting that inspired the formation of the International Working Men's Association. Later they served on the International's general council, as did George Milner and Townshend.[29] The Holborn branch of the NRL arranged the 1869 Bell Inn Conference, which founded the Land and Labour League.[30] Finally, O'Brienites were active in the republican movement of the early 1870s. Indeed, they were widespread among the relatively few republicans who defended the Paris Commune of 1871. James Murray was one of the organizers of the pro-Commune rally in Hyde Park.[31]

Despite Marx's undeniable intellectual power, he had little impact on the beliefs of the O'Brienites. The O'Brienites typically conceived of the International as a way of advancing political and social reform against landlords and money lords. Charles Murray spoke of "just laws on land, credit, currency, and exchange" as "identical with those on which the international was based."[32] Even in the twentieth century, Townshend thought that O'Brien could have defended their corner. He told Beer, "I wish Bronterre O'Brien had lived a few years longer, he would have been the man to argue currency matters out with Marx."[33] Marx himself recognized that, despite their usefulness, the O'Brienites disagreed with him. He wrote that the "O'Brienites, in spite of their follies, constitute an often necessary counterweight to trade unionists," since "they are more revolutionary, firmer on the land question, and not susceptible to bourgeois bribery."[34]

Many of the O'Brienites' radical organizations collapsed in the early 1870s. The International and the Land and Labour League faded away. The republican movement disintegrated after the Commune. Worst of all from the O'Brienites point of view, the Reform League disbanded after

---

[29] H. Collins and C. Abramsky, *Karl Marx and the British Labour Movement* (London: Macmillan, 1965).

[30] R. Harrison, *Before the Socialists* (London: Routledge and Kegan Paul, 1965), pp. 210–50.

[31] *Justice*, 9 March 1889.

[32] *International Herald*, 1 June 1877.

[33] Beer, *Fifty Years*, p. 14.

[34] K. Marx and F. Engels, *Letters to the Americans, 1848–1895* (New York: International, 1953), p. 89.

the passing of the 1867 Reform Bill, even though the bill did not introduce manhood suffrage. In 1874 Morgan led the O'Brienites in founding the Manhood Suffrage League (MSL) to fill the gap left by the collapse of all these radical organizations.[35] The formation of the MSL was part of a shift in the broad pattern of radical politics. As the big umbrella organizations weakened, so radical workingmen retreated into local clubs. For example, the Stratford Dialectical and Radical Club broke with the local branch of the National Secular Society because local members wanted to engage with political issues and not limit themselves to antitheological work. These local London clubs combined fun, education, and politics. Club members might meet in a pub to hear a talk on the poetry of Shelley and end up discussing his politics. Tom Mann, later an active member of the SDF, recalled how his Shakespeare Mutual Improvement Society rented a room at the Devonshire Club in Chiswick.[36]

The O'Brienites concentrated on the MSL, but their influence extended to many London clubs. Members of the MSL often joined other clubs: Mr. Pottle belonged to the MSL, the West Central Democratic Club, and the Clerkenwell Patriotic Club.[37] Members of the MSL often gave talks at other clubs, as did Charles Murray at the Rose Street Club.[38] Indeed, while some club members already held radical views, others learned their radicalism from the O'Brienites before going on to join the Marxist groups of the 1880s. Clubland figures who later joined the SDF included the poet John Leno of the MSL; Edwin Dunn, who was the secretary of the Marylebone Democratic Association and who denounced political economy at the Claremont Eclectic Debating Society; Tom Lemon, who instigated the break between the Stratford Dialectical and Radical Club and the National Secular Society; Mr. Lord, who was president of the English section of the Rose Street Club; John Williams, also of the Rose Street Club; and James Macdonald of the Marylebone Democratic Association, who said he was converted to socialism by the O'Brienites.[39] The prominence of the O'Brienites in the London clubs explains why Frank Kitz, who graduated from the clubs to various Marxist and anarchist

[35] On the London clubs, see H. Mayhew, *Report Concerning the Trade and Hours of Closing Usual among the Unlicensed Victualling Establishments at Certain So-Called "Working Men's Clubs"* (London: Judd and Co., n.d.); T. Oakey, *A Basketful of Memories* (London: J. Dent, 1930); and for a discussion, see S. Shipley, "Club Life and Socialism in Mid-Victorian England," *History Workshop Pamphlet* 5 (1971).

[36] T. Mann, *Memoirs* (London: Labour Publishing, 1923), pp. 11–20.

[37] See *International Herald*, 12 October 1872; and A. Rothstein, *A House on Clerkenwell Green* (London: Marx Memorial Library, 1983). The Clerkenwell Patriotic Club was founded by Tom Mottershed, who had sat on the General Council of the International.

[38] *The Republican*, April 1880.

[39] J. Leno, *Drury Lane Lyrics* (London: J. Leno, 1868); *Labour Standard*, 11 February 1882; Shipley, *Club Life*, pp. 41–43; *Justice*, 21 July 1894 and 11 July 1896.

groups, later said that the members of the MSL "were the chief actors in bringing about the revival of socialism."[40]

It was, however, Hyndman who provided the main impetus for the formation of the SDF. Once Benjamin Disraeli told him the Conservative Party could not lead the action needed to prevent revolution, he began to think of building a new party. Hyndman approached the Rose Street Club in search of support, and on 30 October 1881, he gave a lecture to the MSL titled "The Tyranny of Capital in America and England."[41] Indeed, Hyndman and his Tory friends arranged the inaugural conference of the Democratic Federation (DF) only after they "had gathered around us enough of the Radical Clubs and Irish communities."[42] Dunn of the Marylebone Club sent out the invitations.

Many radical clubs left the DF in late 1881 when it issued a manifesto attacking "the hollowness and hypocrisy of capitalist Radicalism."[43] Yet the O'Brienites remained part of the nascent Marxist organization. Indeed, Hyndman wrote in a letter that "the Liberal wirepullers, specially paid for that purpose, are at work taking the Clubs from us . . . for my part I have thrown in my lot with the Federation. . . . Charles Murray and all the old '48 men are heartily with us."[44] The membership of the DF consisted largely of the O'Brienites and a few other popular radicals from the London clubs.

The Democratic Federation (1881–83)

O'Brienism dominated discussions among the founders of the new organization. The preliminary meetings concentrated on issues of political representation.[45] The first meeting passed the motion that "the present system of electing members of parliament has resulted in 'the exclusion of any representative of the majority of the people.'"[46] Dunn acted as a

[40] Kitz wrote an autobiography in *Freedom*, January–July 1912. The reference is to *Freedom*, February 1912.

[41] *Justice*, 21 July 1894, and *National Reformer*, 30 October 1881.

[42] H. Hyndman, *Record*, p. 247.

[43] *Justice*, 4 August 1884.

[44] Mill-Taylor correspondence, cited by Tsuzuki, *Hyndman*, p. 47. Tsuzuki claims that "all" the clubs left the DF, but they did not. His source—*Justice*, 9 August 1884—is an unreliable self-assessment. Indeed, Tsuzuki himself rightly disparages the claim in the same article that the DF was a committed socialist organization from the moment it was founded.

[45] I have found the following reports of the preliminary meetings in 1881: the first meeting, *Radical*, 5 March 1881, and *Echo*, 3 March 1881; the second meeting, *Daily News*, 7 March 1881, and *Radical*, 12 March 1881; the third meeting, *Observer*, 20 March 1881, and *Daily News*, 21 March 1881.

[46] *Radical*, 5 March 1881.

spokesman for the workingmen who attended the preliminary meetings. His letter to the *Radical* shows that he thought that political imbalances caused social ills.

> We live in an age when every class is united, and is duly represented in Parliament, save that of the majority of the nation. The landholders are united and bound by one common interest; they govern of course the House of Lords, and have many representatives in the Commons. . . . So with the other classes, all are organised, and use their organisation to subdue and keep in subjugation the labouring masses of the people. Such being the case it cannot be wondered at that our laws are framed and our taxes arranged so that the people bear the burden.[47]

Like O'Brien, Dunn juxtaposed the ruling classes with the people and argued that the cause of the people's plight lay in their lack of parliamentary representation.

The preliminary meetings adopted reforms that echoed O'Brien's theories. The first meeting accepted a provisional program of purely political reforms. Political concerns dominated to such an extent that there was no mention of any social measure until the third meeting, when Mr. Finlayson proposed that they accept nationalization of the land.[48] The delegates did not ignore social questions. On the contrary, they wanted a movement "having for its object the promotion and settlement of the various social and political questions of the day."[49] But they believed that the way to solve social problems was by political reforms.

Similar beliefs dominated the inaugural conference of the DF.[50] Hyndman's opening address firmly established the political purport of the meeting. He said that "the conference had been called together because there was so little general harmony between Democratic and Radical organisations in this country, the consequence of which was that motion after motion was passed through the House of Commons contrary to the feelings of both parties."[51] The meeting would begin by considering the question of the franchise, because "the voting in this country was confined to too few."[52] After Hyndman's speech, the delegates adopted a series of resolutions, all of which called for political reforms apart from

---

[47] Ibid., 12 March 1881. On Dunn's role, see *Daily News*, 7 March 1881, and *Radical*, 12 March 1881.

[48] *Daily News*, 21 March 1881.

[49] Ibid., 7 March 1881.

[50] I have found the following accounts of the inaugural conference: *Daily News*, 9 June 1881; *Echo*, 9 June 1881; *Pall Mall Gazette*, 9 June 1881; *St James's Gazette*, 9 June 1881; *The Times*, 9 June 1881; and *Reynolds's*, 12 June 1881.

[51] *Daily News*, 9 June 1881.

[52] Ibid.

one, which demanded nationalization of the land. Finally, Justin McCarthy argued that the Irish problem stemmed from an unjust distribution of political power that made possible social exploitation. He said that "the Liberal Party had in his opinion gone to shipwreck, as those formerly belonging to it had lately been going in for all the old, discreditable, abominable weapons of coercion and oppression to enable alien landlords to squeeze rack rents out of an oppressed peasantry."[53] Once again the solution was political: "What Irishmen most wanted was a domestic Parliament."[54]

The declared object of the DF was to unite "Democrats and workers throughout Great Britain and Ireland" and thereby advance the reforms laid out in its program.[55] The DF's program opened with the demands of the Charter that had not yet been met: adult suffrage, triennial parliaments, equal electoral districts, and payment of MPs. There then followed several other political measures: corrupt practices to be made illegal, the abolition of the House of Lords, legislative independence for Ireland, and national and federal parliaments throughout the Commonwealth. The final demand was O'Brien's main social reform: land nationalization.

Hyndman hoped the DF would get the support of all radicals. The O'Brienites pushed him faster than he wanted to go. They propelled the DF to the extreme edge of popular radicalism. They talked of the struggle between labor and capital and of the need for a social revolution. Nonetheless, their social theory remained that of O'Brien. They distinguished the people, or working classes, from the rulers, or idle classes. They saw political power as the crucial prop of economic oppression. And they gave the land monopoly a special place among social evils. The struggle might be between labor and capital, but all social evils could still be ended by giving the workers access to land and so making it unnecessary for workers to become wage slaves.

The beliefs of the O'Brienites at this time are clear from the proceedings of the 1882 annual conference of the DF. When Mr. Jones proposed "that the establishment of a British Republic be added to the programme," Robert Banner cautioned the meeting against being led away with the idea that "Republicanism was always synonymous with liberty."[56] Banner here rejected the O'Brienites' belief that exploitation arose out of the political system. He was a Scottish socialist influenced by the anti-parliamentarianism of Andreas Scheu. Herbert Burrows also opposed the

---

[53] Ibid.

[54] Ibid.

[55] *Radical*, 16 July 1881.

[56] Ibid., 3 June 1882. It was not until 1884 that Edward Carpenter's donation enabled the DF to publish *Justice*. Information on the early history of the DF depends on other newspapers, of which the *Radical* is the most useful.

motion but on different grounds. He had turned to socialism from the secularist movement, and he argued that although he was a republican, the public would not accept republicanism. He thus moved an amendment that covered the monarchy without explicitly mentioning it: the DF should demand the "abolition of the House of Lords and all hereditary legislators codies."[57]

Charles Murray expressed the views of the O'Brienites when he seconded Burrows's amendment. He said:

> The real cause of the evils from which the masses suffered was not the monarchy, but the fact that they were in the hands of capitalists. What they wanted was a social revolution, and believing that the programme of the association was well calculated to advance that social revolution, he seconded the amendment.[58]

If we read current meanings back into Charles Murray's words, we might conclude that he was a socialist. However, if we look closely, we find that he was merely extending his O'Brienism. Capitalists might have replaced landlords as the main enemy, but capitalist oppression still depended on political power and the monopoly of the land. The clue to Murray's O'Brienism is his last sentence: the DF's program contained nothing but political measures and land nationalization, and yet this program would "advance" the social revolution against the capitalist. He still gave no indication of believing in the need for collective ownership of the means of production.

Banner made his views clear in an article titled "Social Revolution, Not Political Reform." He argued that political reforms were useless: "Parliamentary government is a mockery, and the cry for the franchise a sham." He continued by suggesting that land nationalization would favor only the capitalist: "Nationalisation of the Land alone will not benefit the toilers but the non-toilers, for it will increase the capital at their disposal, and will give them a greater command over all commodities in the market."[59] It seemed that only an expropriation of the capitalist would suffice.

The O'Brienites disagreed. When Morgan gave a lecture to the MSL titled "The Programme of the Democratic Federation," he located the DF squarely in the radical tradition, arguing that "there never was a conference of more genuine Radicals" than its inaugural conference.[60] Unlike Banner, Morgan applauded the DF's political stance. In his opinion, "The political part of the programme meant a thorough reform of the House of

---

[57] *Radical*, 3 June 1882.
[58] Ibid.
[59] Ibid., 29 April 1882.
[60] Ibid., 25 June 1881; and for the lecture's title, see Ibid., 18 June 1881.

Commons, and it was useless to expect any radical reform from a House that was composed of landlords, capitalists, contractors, employers of labour, and speculators."[61] The O'Brienites believed in the efficacy not only of parliamentary reform but also of land nationalization. Edmund Jones argued that the land question was "the most important of all human considerations," and Morgan claimed that "the unanimous vote in favour of the nationalisation of the land showed that the delegates were sound upon the land question, and it only required a few more such conferences to be held over the country to make it the question of the day."[62] Finally, Lord's talk titled "Irish Land and British Labour" shows that the O'Brienites still saw the ills of capitalism as consequences of political oppression and the denial of land rights. The capitalist just continued the system of monopolization begun by the landlord. Lord "drew a comparison between the position of the Irish tenant, who depended upon the landlord for permission to cultivate the land, and the British workman, who depended upon the capitalist for leave to work."[63] The capitalists took a tribute as monopolists and middlemen. Lord placed them alongside the landlords and money lords.

> The annual wealth produced by the workers was £950,000,000 sterling, while the producers received in wages only £250,000,000. The balance of £700,000,000 was appropriated by landlords, profitmongers, and capitalists.[64]

Although the O'Brienites wanted a social revolution, they still believed that they could get a social revolution by political reforms and land nationalization. In their view, the program of the DF would result in social revolution. They differed from Banner not on the importance of social change but on the means by which to attain social change. Banner demanded the expropriation of the capitalist. The O'Brienites demanded political reform and land nationalization.

The Growth of Socialism (1883–84)

In the winter of 1882 the DF held a series of conferences on "stepping stones," such as the eight-hour day and public work for the unemployed.[65] In 1883 Hyndman and Morris wrote a manifesto for the DF calling for

[61] Ibid., 25 June 1881.
[62] Ibid., 25 March 1882 and 25 June 1881.
[63] Ibid., 2 April 1881.
[64] Ibid.
[65] *Justice*, 9 August 1884.

the immediate adoption of the stepping-stones and declaring the DF a socialist organization.[66] In 1884 the DF changed its name to the Social Democratic Federation, and it adopted a new program calling for "the production of wealth to be regulated by society in the common interest" and "the means of production, distribution and exchange to be declared and treated as collective or common property."[67]

By the end of 1884 the O'Brienites believed in the need to collectivize the means of production. They had moved away from O'Brienism toward socialism. They placed more emphasis on the struggle between wage earners and wage payers. They were more equivocal about the idea that social evils originated in a corrupt political system, often talking instead of the social causes of social evils. And they demanded collectivization. Nonetheless, their socialism merely attached aspects of orthodox Marxism to their earlier beliefs. The change was not a sudden conversion to a "true" socialism; it was a subtle shift in a language of popular radicalism.

The continuity in the O'Brienites' beliefs can be striking. A good example is James Murray's article titled "Our Duty towards the Slaves of the Soil." He spoke on behalf of the people, not the proletariat, and agrued that the source of all exploitation was the rulers' monopoly of political power, not the buying and selling of labor.

> Socialists must take in hand the task of making plain to the tillers of the soil, that their poverty, as also the poverty of all useful men, has a common origin. That the remedy for all is the same. That the sufferings of the people are the outcome of criminal legislation in the interests of the exploiting classes.[68]

Moreover, the land monopoly remained a historical condition of capitalist exploitation. With agriculture "crushed and cowed, the bulwark of defence was gone that stood in the way of the subjugation of all."[69]

Generally, however, the O'Brienites shifted their beliefs to advocate abolition of the private ownership of the means of production. They moved toward a concept of class based on the wage relationship. One wrote that the socialist revolution "will abolish all distinctions of class, or difference between wage-payers and wage-earners, and will render the workers their own employers."[70] The O'Brienites came to think that social evils were somewhat independent of political causes; *Justice* told the

---

[66] Democratic Federation, *Socialism Made Plain.*
[67] *Justice*, 25 October 1884.
[68] Ibid., 30 August 1884.
[69] Ibid.
[70] Ibid., 10 May 1884.

workers that "their bad food, bad housing, bad education, bad clothing, are all directly due to the social oppression from which they suffer."[71] And they thus concluded that "social changes need social action."[72] Moreover, they argued that capitalist exploitation was separate from the land monopoly, so to end wage slavery, socialists had to nationalize the means of production as well as the land.

Although the O'Brienites' beliefs shifted, there were also important continuities. The talk was of the wage earners, not the people, but the wage earners were still juxtaposed with idle monopolists. Capitalists were just put alongside the landlords and money lords. *Justice* was to "preach discontent to the wage-earning classes, and call upon them to show a bold front to the landlords and capitalists."[73] The capitalists were an independent evil set against the workers, but their ability to exploit people depended on a monopoly—their exclusive ownership of the means of production.

> The landlords monopolise the land, and the capitalists the machinery. . . . How does the capitalist act? He extorts from those labourers who are excluded from the land a share of all that they produce, under threat of withholding from them the implement of production.[74]

The O'Brienites recognized the capitalists as an exploiting class, but the means of exploitation remained a monopoly.

The O'Brienites did not distinguish use value from exchange value, let alone adopt Marx's theory of surplus value. They argued that capitalist exploitation was the result of monopoly. The worker takes four hours a day to produce commodities the value of which is equivalent to the worker's subsistence. But the capitalists use their monopoly of machinery to force the worker to labor for ten hours a day. They allow the worker to labor the necessary four only if the worker also labors for six more hours. The worker must accept this arrangement or starve. So the worker labors for six extra hours, creating surplus value that the capitalist appropriates. As Harry Quelch explained, "It is by overwork that the surplus value is created upon which the idlers live."[75] The capitalists may obtain surplus value only by purchasing labor, but they do so because their monopoly of machinery and an iron law of wages mean they can buy labor for subsistence wages. It is the capitalists' monopoly of machinery that forces workers "to sell their labour for a bare subsistence wage."[76]

[71] Ibid., 29 March 1884.
[72] Ibid.
[73] Ibid.
[74] Ibid.
[75] Ibid., 31 May 1884.
[76] Ibid., 19 January 1884.

For the O'Brienites, the struggle was against a series of monopolies, not capitalism as a distinct mode of production. Society was a natural institution that had been corrupted by monopolies. Capitalist exploitation might be independent of political injustices and the land monopoly, but, likewise, political ills and the land monopoly were somewhat independent of capitalist exploitation. The state acted in the interests of the monopolists only because it was an unrepresentative imposition upon a natural social order. So, radicals could reasonably aim to eliminate monopolies one at a time. They could successfully reform the state and nationalize the land before then turning to the capitalists' monopoly of machinery.

It is important to recognize that the socialism of the O'Brienites overlapped with that of Hyndman at a number of crucial points. Their popular radicalism, like his Tory radicalism, drew on the older ideas of the Country Party. He could plausibly link his socialist ideal to a radical tradition that culminated in O'Brien.

> Is there nothing inspiring in such an ideal . . . ? There is to me. That for which generations have striven vainly is now possible to us. . . . Tyler and Ball, and Cade and Kelt, Vane and Blake and Harrison, Priestly and Cartwright, Spence and Owen, Vincent, Ernest Jones, and Bronterre O'Brien—a noble band indeed! . . . How do courtly fuglemen and ennobled sycophants look by the side of these? A great democratic English Republic has ever been the dream of the noblest of our race. . . . To bring about such a Republic is the cause for which we Socialists agitate to-day.[77]

Moreover, Hyndman and the O'Brienites believed in broadly similar political strategies. They all thought that the SDF should try to create a democratic state that the workers could then use to solve social problems. The membership accepted Hyndman's leadership because his strategy was their strategy.

UNDERSTANDING THE SOCIAL DEMOCRATIC FEDERATION

After the O'Brienites adopted socialism, they supported Hyndman's political strategy. Their position became clear at a special meeting of the DF held at Anderton's Hotel in January 1884. Hyndman opened the proceedings by explaining how the workers were exploited and why nationalization of the means of production was needed. In the meeting they had to decide how to reach this socialist goal. Hyndman himself argued here

[77] Ibid., 14 June 1884.

that the DF should "take advantage of the growing influence of the State, so that it might be dominated and used by the workers instead of by the middle, capitalist and landlord classes."[78]

James Murray supported Hyndman. He proposed a resolution: "This meeting of Socialists demands universal suffrage, proportional representation and payment of members as a means of obtaining reduction of the hours of labour, socialisation of the means of production, and the organisation of Society."[79] This resolution expressed the new socialist outlook of the O'Brienites. It demanded collective ownership of the means of production while implying that political evils were independent of social evils. Capitalists and landlords dominated the political system, but their doing so was not a necessary feature of a capitalist society. Radicals might reform the political system without first reforming the social system. The reformed political system might then be an instrument with which to reform the social system. Political reform by itself would not create socialism, but it would provide a tool for doing so. A democratic state would give political power to the workers, and the workers could then use political power to nationalize the land and the means of production. Political reform was a prelude to social reform.

> Abolition of the House of Lords, Universal Suffrage, Payment of the Expenses of Elections out of the Rates, and Payment of Members— these measures would, for the first time in our history, place supreme political power in the hands of the mass of the people. . . . But, Fellow-Citizens, what will you do with the suffrage when you get it? . . . It has but one use, to enable the workers, as a class, to take possession of the power of the State so as to use that power for social purposes.[80]

Political measures were not a complete cure, but they were the means to a complete cure. Many members of the DF still embraced O'Brien's political strategy. They thought that the immediate need was for political reforms, which, once introduced, would enable the workers to initiate social reforms. The difference was that the social reforms required of a democratic parliament now included nationalization of the means of production as well as the land.

Two groups in the DF disagreed with Hyndman and the O'Brienites. The first group completely rejected politics, trusting "more to social agitation."[81] Mr. Setternick proposed an alternative to James Murray's resolution, saying that "in the opinion of this meeting . . . the working

[78] Ibid., 19 January 1884.
[79] Ibid.
[80] Ibid., 12 July 1884.
[81] Ibid.

classes of this or any other country cannot depend any longer upon parliamentary representation to better the condition of the wage-slaves."[82] Charles Murray immediately opposed Setternick's resolution. The O'Brienites could not accept Setternick's statement because they believed that although political reform was not all that was necessary, it was both part of what was necessary and a means of promoting the other reforms that were necessary. Aveling spoke for the second group that disagreed with Hyndman and the O'Brienites. He neither rejected political action nor believed that political reform would facilitate social reform. Instead, he argued that participation in political movements was a way of building working-class support for social reforms. The point was not to obtain political ends as a means to social ends, but to take part in political movements as a way of promoting social movements.

In the first half of 1884, Hyndman and the O'Brienites retained the upper hand. The program of the DF concluded with a call for political reforms as a preliminary to social palliatives.

The Democratic Federation, as a means by which these [social palliatives] are to be attained, calls for—

1. Adult Suffrage.
2. Annual Parliaments.
3. Proportional Representation.
4. Payment of members, and Official Expenses of Elections, out of the Rates.[83]

However, as we saw in the previous two chapters, at the end of 1884, the Marx family circle and the anti-parliamentarians passed a vote of no confidence in Hyndman and left the SDF to form the Socialist League. The remaining members of the SDF reinstated the old parliamentary program. The SDF then consisted mainly of the O'Brienites and a few Tory radicals, including Hyndman and also Henry Champion, Robert Frost, and Mrs. Hicks.

Once we understand what tied the members of the SDF to Hyndman, we can make better sense of this early split in the SDF. Hyndman's dictatorial and chauvinistic attitude may have played a part in the split. But if Hyndman's unpleasantness was the cause of the split, we should expect the members to have followed Morris. Historians thus struggle to explain why they did not do so. E. P. Thompson even argued that the members did not understand the dispute: "The fact is that to the membership the whole thing appeared as a mystery."[84] But the membership

---

[82] Ibid.
[83] Ibid., 5 April 1884.
[84] E. Thompson, *Morris*, p. 364.

must have known about Hyndman's personality, must have read some of his journalistic writings, must have listened to some of his speeches, and must have heard some of the numerous warnings against him. The fact is surely that the members of the SDF stuck by Hyndman because, like him, but unlike the Socialist League, they wanted political reforms to create a democratic state that might then end capitalist exploitation. The split between the SDF and the Socialist League involved a dispute over political strategy. But this dispute was not, as Chushichi Tsuzuki suggests, about whether or not to contest parliamentary elections.[85] The Socialist League attracted not only anti-parliamentarians such as Banner, but also people, such as Aveling, who believed that participation in movements for political reform could build support for social reform. Similarly, Hyndman's supporters wanted to contest elections not only to raise support for socialism, but also because they believed that political reform was an important first step toward social reform.

The SDF continued to stand by the commitments that distinguished it from the Socialist League. Whereas the Socialist League promoted a decentralized or even a nongovernmental utopia, the SDF promoted radical democracy—a parliamentary system based on universal suffrage, with popular control of Parliament being strengthened by measures such as annual elections, referenda, a principle of delegation, abolition of the House of Lords, and the introduction of an elected civil service. Similarly, whereas the Socialist League advocated education for an often unspecified future action, the SDF wanted immediate political action to secure various stepping-stones on the way to a socialist society. Even when the SDF was associated with revolutionary rhetoric and mob violence in the mid-1880s, it remained firmly committed to parliamentary action as a means of securing piecemeal reforms and a peaceful transition to socialism. Its official manifesto declared,

> As means for the peaceable attainment of these [social] objects the Social Democratic Federation advocates: Adult Suffrage, Annual Parliaments, Proportional Representation, Payment of Members and Official Expenses of Elections out of the Rates, Abolition of the House of Lords and Hereditary Authorities, Disestablishment and Disendowment of all State Churches.[86]

Although the SDF continued to defend a political theory indebted to popular radicalism, by the late 1880s the main alternative was no longer the purism of Morris and the Socialist League, but the parliamentary strategy and faith in representative democracy of the Fabians. Against

---

[85] Tsuzuki, *Hyndman*, pp. 60–67.
[86] The manifesto was printed in *Justice* regularly throughout the mid- and late 1880s.

The Social Democratic Federation • 125

the Fabians, the SDF affirmed the importance of seeking a radical restructuring of the British state. The dispute focused on the importance of the referendum. *Justice* argued that "a declaration against the referendum is a declaration against democracy," for it shows that the "Fabian clique wishes to impose on the mass of Englishmen legislation which they either do not understand, or understanding do not accept."[87] Before long the SDF had to engage in similar disputes with the Independent Labour Party (ILP). For example, when Keir Hardie dismissed the political emphasis of the SDF as evidence that it espoused mere radicalism, *Justice* replied that "the SDF is no less a political than a revolutionary body" because "the political machinery [suitably reformed] may be a means to secure economic freedom."[88] Whereas the SDF called for dramatic political reforms to turn the British state into a proper democracy, the Fabians and the ILP generally believed that the British state was more or less democratic and insisted that the vital task was to work through Parliament to improve the conditions of the workers. The SDF's commitment to radical democracy pushed it to the margins of British socialism.

CONCLUSION

The members of the SDF came initially from the radical London clubs. Many were followers of O'Brien, and their socialism continued to echo themes from his brand of popular radicalism. In particular, his emphasis on the importance of political reform helps explain why the members remained with Hyndman in the SDF instead of joining rival organizations such as the Socialist League.

More generally, early British Marxists turned to socialism against the background of the traditions of secularism and popular and Tory radicalism. These traditions were broadly hostile to the evangelicalism and classical political economy that dominated the nineteenth century. They inspired various critics of capitalism, and, during the 1880s, some of these critics turned to Marxism.

The preceding chapters pointed intermittently to the relationship of early British Marxism to secularism. Bax was an avowed atheist who vehemently opposed religion, especially Christianity. The O'Brienites were generally secularists who had participated in various radical political movements linked to the National Secular Society. Hyndman showed some fashionable interest in Eastern religions, but he was a secular agnostic who debated Charles Bradlaugh on the merits of socialism without

[87] *Justice*, 27 March 1897.
[88] Ibid., 21 October 1893.

any reference to religion. Before and after that debate, several prominent secularists joined the SDF, including Aveling, John Burns, and Herbert Burrows. Indeed, the National Secular Society was, along with the radical clubs, the main source of recruits for the Marxist movement. Few Marxists held religious beliefs. The principal exceptions were the Christian socialists, notably Champion, Frost, and James Joynes. But even their Christian faith seems to have remained largely separate from their politics after they joined the SDF. They appeared then primarily as Tory radicals committed to social reform and willing to denounce the "evil influence" of church leaders.[89]

A debt to secularism influenced the content of British Marxism. Most Marxists were scientific rationalists. They believed Charles Darwin had finally proved the truth of scientific materialism against appeals to the supernatural and religion. They interpreted Marx as contributing to the same materialist science. Marxists such as Aveling argued that Christianity and capitalism were the great dragons of the time and that Darwin and Marx were their slayers. Even Bax, as an avowed idealist, believed that Marxism lacked any metaphysics or ethics. Generally, the early Marxists presented Marxism as an economic and historical science revealing laws of exchange and development.

The content of British Marxism also reflected a debt to particular radicalisms. The preceding chapters have shown how Bax drew on republican radicalism, Hyndman on Tory radicalism, and the O'Brienites on popular radicalism. Early British Marxists often infused Marx's economic theory with radical themes. They often ignored Marx's distinction between use and exchange value and thus his analysis of exploitation as arising from the treatment of labor power as a commodity. Instead, they associated exploitation with monopolies of land and machinery, arguing that it was because the capitalists had a monopoly of the means of production that they could pay the workers less than the true value of their labor. Many Marxists even continued to treat the monopoly of the land as the main social ill on the grounds that it drove workers into the hands of the capitalists. The nationalization of the land often retained pride of place among their demands right through the 1880s and even the early 1890s. Moreover, early British Marxists often saw social ills as resting in part on political ones. They continued to call for political reforms as a prelude to social ones. Few thought a social revolution had to precede any political change. Most believed that the creation of a truly democratic parliament would enable the workers to introduce social reforms. Marxism provided them with an economic analysis, but the politics remained that of their radicalism.

[89] Ibid., 2 May 1885.

Morris now appears as an outlier among early British Marxists. His background was in Protestantism, liberal radicalism, and especially romanticism, rather than popular radicalism and secularism. His romanticism continued to influence his antistatist vision and his purist political strategy. Morris's nongovernmental socialism pushed him to the margins of the Marxist movement, leaving him more or less alone in the Hammersmith Socialist Society. Equally, however, his romanticism and nongovernmental leanings soon attracted the attention of the early ethical socialists. In part 2, we will turn to the Fabians and their debt to liberalism. Then in part 3, we will see how various ethical socialists drew on romanticism and other traditions in ways that led some of them to adopt more nongovernmental visions.

PART TWO

The Fabians

CHAPTER SEVEN

Theories of Rent

THE BRITISH SOCIALIST MOVEMENT emerged as people from diverse traditions grappled with the crisis of faith and the collapse of classical political
economy. We have now seen how a few Tory radicals and republicans
came together with popular radicals and continental exiles from the London clubs to form Marxist organizations, most importantly the Social
Democratic Federation. Soon after, a few liberal radicals began to join
the socialist movement. Historically, liberal radicals generally believed
in classical political economy and the implausibility of socialist schemes.
Then, as classical political economy fell apart, liberal radicals adopted
neoclassical, marginal, and positivist economic theories, and some of
them used these theories to defend socialist ideas. At least as importantly,
liberal radicals were generally Christians and often evangelicals. The crisis of faith led many of them to adopt an evolutionary and ethical positivism that inspired a widespread enthusiasm for humanitarian reform and
sometimes for socialism.

Liberal radicalism and an evolutionary and ethical positivism fed into
a type of socialism quite different from the Marxism that arose out of republican radicalism and secularism. Part 2 explores pathways from liberal
radicalism and ethical positivism to Fabian socialism. The Fabians, like
the Marxists, were few in number, especially in the 1880s and 1890s. The
Fabian Society initially resembled a discussion group in which middle-
class progressives grappled with changing economic theories and moral
concerns. These discussions eventually resulted in a distinctive theory
of socialism based on liberal rather than Marxist economic theory. This
chapter studies the background to Fabianism, challenging the idea that
it was a single theory based on a shared theory of rent. Chapters 8 and 9
discuss in more detail the two most important Fabian theorists. George
Bernard Shaw illustrates how the Fabians rejected Marxist economics,
looking instead to the new economic theories arising from the collapse
of classical economics. Sidney Webb shows the importance of an ethical
and evolutionary positivism for many Fabians and how—even more than
theories of rent—it inspired Fabian schemes for socialism. Chapter 10 ex-

A version of this chapter appeared as "Fabianism and the Theory of Rent," *History of
Political Thought* 10 (1989), 313–327. Published by Imprint Academic.

amines the Fabians' political strategies, demonstrating how their varied economic theories led them to advocate different strategies.

Thus this chapter examines the Fabians' rejection of Marxist economics for theories arising in the wake of the collapse of classical economics. Far too many historians have caricatured the Fabians as bureaucratic elitists who were inspired by utilitarianism and classical political economy.[1] Even when historians look more seriously at the beliefs of the Fabians, they generally argue that the Fabians adopted a reformist socialism based on a shared theory of rent derived from the classical liberalism of David Ricardo.[2] In their view, this theory of rent blurred the distinction between classes, making it possible, first, to equate socialism not with ending capitalism but with taxation of unearned increment for the benefit of society and, second, to reject a revolutionary politics in favor of parliamentary gradualism and the permeation of bourgeois parties. However, the leading Fabians actually held different economic theories. They owed less to utilitarianism and classical political economy than to ethical positivism and neoclassical and marginal economic theories. Insofar as there is a distinctive Fabian socialism, it derives not from a shared theory of rent but from a shared endeavor by ethical positivists and liberal radicals to respond to the crisis of faith and especially the collapse of classical economics.

THE EARLY FABIANS

Most of the leading Marxists were secularists, barely troubled by the crisis of faith. The main exceptions were the Christian socialists, such as H. H. Champion, Robert Frost, and James Joynes. While these Christian socialists got involved in the Social Democratic Federation, they also explored more personal and spiritual forms of transformation. They were part of a group that coalesced around a wandering scholar, Thomas Davidson, when he visited London in 1883. Most of the members of this group

---

[1] See, most famously, E. Hobsbawm, "The Fabians Reconsidered," in *Labouring Men* (London: Weidenfeld and Nicolson, 1964).

[2] I. Britain, *Fabianism and Culture* (Cambridge: Cambridge University Press, 1982), p. 76; E. Durbin, "Fabian Socialism and Economic Science," in *Fabian Essays in Socialist Thought*, ed. B. Pimlott (London: Heinemann, 1984), pp. 41–43; G. Foote, *The Labour Party's Political Thought* (London: Croom Helm, 1986), pp. 26–27; A. McBriar, *Fabian Socialism and English Politics, 1884–1918* (Cambridge: Cambridge University Press, 1962); N. MacKenzie and J. MacKenzie, *The First Fabians* (London: Weidenfeld and Nicolson, 1979), p. 112; S. Pierson, *Marxism and the Origins of British Socialism* (Ithaca, NY: Cornell University Press, 1973), pp. 119–23; and D. Ricci, "Fabian Socialism: A Theory of Rent as Exploitation," *Journal of British Studies* 9 (1969): 105–21.

were looking for a new faith in tune with modern science and oriented toward humanity. At their second formal meeting, Davidson suggested they call themselves the Fellowship of the New Life and declare their aim to be the reconstruction of society in accordance with the highest moral possibilities. At the next meeting, Champion proposed a resolution that condemned the competitive economic system. Others objected that this resolution broke with the spiritual basis of the group. On 4 July 1884 those who favored social reforms formed the Fabian Society.

The founders of the Fabian Society combined the ethical and spiritual concerns of the Fellowship with an interest in land nationalization and, in some cases, Marxism. Champion, Joynes, and Frost were involved with the *Christian Socialist*, the Land Reform Union, and the Social Democratic Federation (SDF). Edward Pease and Frank Podmore had turned to spiritualism in the belief that it offered a scientific approach to religious questions, and they were attracted to the land reform proposals of Henry George. Pease was a fringe participant in activities of the SDF, as were the Tory radicals and journalists Hubert Bland and Frederick Keddell.

Although the Fabians knew they wanted to address social issues, they were more interested in discussion than in action. The basis of the Fabian Society was Champion's resolution that "the members of the Society assert that the Competitive system assures the happiness and comfort of the few at the expense of the suffering of the many and that society must be reconstituted in such a manner as to secure the general welfare and happiness."[3] Yet, when Podmore introduced the other resolutions founding the Society, they advocated self-education as a prelude to practical action.

That with the view of learning what practical measures to take in this direction [of social reform] the Society should:

(a) Hold meetings for discussion, the reading of papers, hearing of reports, etc.
(b) Delegate some of its members to attend meetings held on social subjects, debates at Workmen's Clubs, etc., in order that such members may in the first place report to the Society on the proceedings, and in the second place put forward, as occasion serves, the views of the Society.
(c) Take measures in other ways, as, for example, by the collection of articles from current literature, to obtain information on all contemporary social movements and social needs.[4]

[3] E. Pease, *The History of the Fabian Society* (London: A. Fifield, 1916), p. 32.
[4] Ibid., p. 34.

The Fabians were formulating their views. Meetings involved lectures and reports of lectures on land reform and other schemes of social reconstruction, including currency reform, Marxism, utopian socialism, and anarchism.[5]

Initially, Fabian sympathies fell mainly on land reform movements and British Marxism. Like the SDF, the Fabians spent part of 1884 to 1886 defining their position in relation to anarchism. Champion, Frost, and Joynes soon ceased to play much of a role. Yet Bland, Pease, and Podmore remained, and they were joined by Shaw, another land reformer from the fringes of the SDF. Against them stood Charlotte Wilson, an avowed anarcho-communist, who joined the Fabians' executive committee in December 1884 and who now had the support of the members of the Socialist League who attended Fabian meetings. In 1886 the Fabians published a tract, "What Socialism Is," which contained sections on both collectivism and anarchism without seeking to adjudicate between the two.[6] As Shaw recalled, "The question was, how many followers had our one ascertained Anarchist, Mrs. Wilson, among the silent Fabians?"[7] The Fabians addressed this question at a meeting open to all socialists on 17 September 1886. Bland proposed a possibilist motion calling for a political party. William Morris proposed an impossibilist alternative, calling for an emphasis on education and denouncing party organization and parliamentary action as false steps. The meeting passed Bland's motion by 47 votes to 19 and rejected Morris's by 40 votes to 27. Thereafter the Fabians formed a parliamentary league that began as a separate organization but soon became a political committee of the main Society. Most of the anarchists had only ever been members of the Socialist League. Wilson herself resigned from the executive committee in April 1887. It was only then, in June 1887, that the Fabians finally adopted as the basis of membership the emphatic statement that began: "The Fabian Society consists of Socialists."

By 1887 the Fabians had rejected anarchism and increasingly distanced themselves from Marxism. Their clear break with Marxism owed much to the growing presence in the Fabian Society of Sydney Olivier, Graham Wallas, and Sidney Webb. These Fabians echoed the humanitarian reformism and liberal radicalism that had left Pease, Podmore, and Shaw on the margins of the SDF. And, together with Shaw, they quickly came to dominate the Society. Pease recalled:

[5] Fabian Society Minute Book, 1884, Fabian Papers, British Library of Political and Economic Science (BLPES), London.

[6] C. Wilson et al., "What Socialism Is," *Fabian Tract* 4 (1886).

[7] G. Shaw, "The Fabian Society: What It Has Done and How It Has Done It," *Fabian Tract* 41 (1892): p. 12.

For several years, and those perhaps the most important in the history of the Society, the period in fact of its adolescence, the Society was governed by the seven essayists, and chiefly by four or five of them. ... Sidney Webb, Bernard Shaw, Graham Wallas, and Sydney Olivier worked and thought together in intellectual partnership. ... For many years there were probably few evenings of the week and few holidays which two or more of them did not spend together.[8]

During those years, they forged Fabianism through discussions of economic theory in the meetings of Wilson's Hampstead Historic Circle and Henry Beeton's Economic Circle.

RENT AFTER RICARDO

The leading Fabians—Olivier, Shaw, Wallas, and Webb—were involved in the broader debates about how to rethink economics after the collapse of classical economics, especially the classical theory of distribution. Large parts of these debates concerned different concepts of land rent and related economic surpluses.

Classical political economy included theories of economic surpluses such as rent. Most famously, Ricardo based a theory of rent on the labor theory of value. He argued that rent arose from advantages of soil and location. These advantages meant that people obtained different incomes for similar labor so that some people received a surplus, or rent. Ricardo described rent as a surplus because it came from the "original and indestructible powers of the soil," not labor. There was no true market in land. Land was a natural monopoly and variable in quality.[9] Landowners received as rent a surplus based on the quality of their land. Other classical political economists extended Ricardo's theory. John Stuart Mill showed that Ricardo's theory applied to all natural sources of wealth with variable productivity.[10]

[8] Pease, *History*, p. 64. Wallas first raised the possibility of what evolved into the *Fabian Essays* by saying that he, Olivier, Shaw, and Webb "are the only four people in England who are agreed about anything." See Graham Wallas to Sidney Webb, n.d. (May 1888?), with replies from Olivier, Shaw, and Webb, Wallas Papers, BLPES.

[9] D. Ricardo, *Works and Correspondence*, ed. P. Sraffa (Cambridge: Cambridge University Press, 1951), vol. 1: *On the Principles of Political Economy and Taxation*, pp. 11–20, 67, and 69–70.

[10] J. Mill, "The Principles of Political Economy," in *The Collected Works of John Stuart Mill* (Toronto: University of Toronto Press, 1963–91), vols. 2 and 3: *The Principles of Political Economy*. Ricardo had recognized this with respect to mines. See Ricardo, *Works*, vol. 1, pp. 85–87.

After the collapse of the classical theory of distribution, economists developed various analyses of rent and related surpluses. The most dramatic response to the crisis of classical political economy was the Marginal Revolution. Adam Smith had rejected a utility theory of value because of the paradox that air is useful and free whereas diamonds are comparatively useless and yet expensive.[11] W. S. Jevons explained this paradox by distinguishing between total utility and final degree of utility. He argued that water has a low value, "because we usually have so much of it that its final degree of utility is low."[12] Jevons thus defended a marginal utility theory of value according to which "the ratio of exchange of any two commodities will be the reciprocal of the ratio of the final degrees of utility of the quantities of commodity available for consumption after the exchange is completed."[13]

Yet economists disagreed about the relationship of Jevons's theory to classical political economy. Neoclassical economists such as Alfred Marshall wanted to combine Jevons's theory of value with classical economics. Marginalists such as P. H. Wicksteed wanted to extend Jevons's concept of marginal utility from exchange to production and distribution.[14] Neoclassical economics and marginalism inspired analyses of rent very different from one another and from that of Ricardo. Moreover, although Marshall and Wicksteed published their main books only after the Fabians had reached their theories of rent, the Fabians were, as we will see, not only familiar with their ideas but influenced by them.[15]

Marshall's synthesis of Jevons and classical economics relies on his "scissors" theory of value. Value is a product of the scissors of supply and demand, where demand is conceived in terms of marginal utility, and supply in terms of the cost of production or marginal effort and sacrifice. Marshall argued that which blade—supply or demand—does the cutting depends on the timescale considered. In the short term, market value dominates so that demand fixes price. In the long term, however, the flexibility of supply means supply responds to market value and short-term demand, so the actual cost of production or actual value ultimately fixes price. Marshall even argued that in the long term supply is itself a cause

[11] A. Smith, *The Wealth of Nations*, ed. E. Cannan (London: Methuen, 1961), pp. 32–33.

[12] W. Jevons, *The Theory of Political Economy*, ed. R. Collison Black (Harmondsworth, UK: Penguin, 1970), p. 111.

[13] Ibid., p. 139.

[14] P. Flatau, "Jevons's One Great Disciple: Wicksteed and the Jevonian Revolution in the Second Generation," *History of Economics Review* 40 (2004): 69–107.

[15] For evidence that Marshall and Wicksteed were forming their views in the early 1880s, see, respectively, J. Keynes, "Alfred Marshall," *Economic Journal* 34 (1924): 311–72; and L. Robbins, *The Evolution of Modern Economic Theory and Other Papers on the History of Economic Thought* (London: Macmillan, 1970), pp. 190–92.

of demand, "for if the supply is increased, the thing will be applied to uses for which it is less needed, and in which it is less efficient."[16]

So, Marshall distinguished between market and actual value as well as between total and marginal utility. These distinctions inform his analyses of economic surpluses. A consumer's surplus arises because the consumer gets the total utility of a commodity, even though he pays a price fixed by the utility of the last increment of that commodity. Thus, "those parts of his purchases for which he would gladly have paid a higher price rather than go without them, yield him a surplus of satisfaction."[17] A producer's surplus arises because the price of a factor of production is determined by supply and demand at its margin; a surplus goes to those elements of the factor of the production that are not at the margin. For example, the capitalist acquires a surplus "through being remunerated for all his saving, that is waiting, at the same rate as for that part which he is only just induced to undergo by the reward to be got for it."[18]

Marshall's analysis of the producer's surplus applies to all factors of production, including capital and labor as well as land. A producer's surplus arises simply because the law of diminishing returns means that the economy uses elements of a factor of production that are of varying quality: the difference between the elements of a factor of production that are and are not at the margin creates a producer's surplus. Nonetheless, Marshall still distinguished land from other factors of production. He argued that the supply of land is fixed, so it cannot respond to demand even in the long term. Rent—the producer's surplus associated with land—is therefore not required in order to maintain an adequate supply of land.

> The more nearly it is true that the earnings of any agent of production are required to keep up the supply of it, the more closely will its supply so vary that the share which it is able to draw from the national dividend conforms to the cost of maintaining the supply: and in any old country land stands in an exceptional position, because its earnings are not affected by this cause.[19]

Yet, Marshall admitted that his distinction between land and other factors of production, and so his distinction between rent and other producers' surpluses, was far from absolute. The supply of land is permanently fixed, so it yields rent. But the supply of other objects, such as mines and factory machinery, is often fixed for short periods, so they too yield quasi-rents.

[16] A. Marshall, *Principles of Economics*, ed. C. Guillebaud (London: Macmillan, 1961), p. 526.
[17] Ibid., p. 830.
[18] Ibid., p. 831.
[19] Ibid., p. 832.

The marginalists rejected Marshall's analysis of supply and demand, and so his theory of rent. Wicksteed evoked the margin as a tool of equilibrium analysis, rather than a source of economic surpluses. He argued that the marginal utility of a commodity fixes its value and price. The concept of time plays little role in his theory; there is no time lag, and there is no distinction between market and actual value. The market reaches general, not partial, equilibrium.

> If we can exchange things for each other or choose between them on certain terms, then we can increase our supply of the more valued thing at the expense of the other, thereby lowering the marginal significance of one and raising that of the other, till their significance coincides with the terms on which they are obtainable as alternatives. When this point is reached there is equilibrium; and successful administration of resources consists in maintaining such equilibrium.[20]

So, unless rent reflects market failure, it must be part of the general equilibrium reached by the market. Rent must be a part of the correct price of the relevant article. As Wicksteed explained, "The Ricardian law of rent is nothing whatever but a statement that the better article commands an advanced price in proportion to its betterness."[21] There is no economic difference between paying rent for better rather than worse land and paying a greater price for a better rather than worse instance of another commodity. Monopolies may inflate prices. But the difference between more and less expensive instances of any given commodity arises because the former is better than the latter. People pay for the greater value of superior articles. Wicksteed thus concluded that any distinction between land rent and other payments for superior articles must rest on a moral argument, not an economic one. Economically all such payments are the same, but "it is open to any one to examine or to dispute the ethical or social claim of any factor of production to a share, in accordance with its marginal significance."[22]

WEBB: A NEOCLASSICAL THEORY

Most of the leading Fabians moved toward socialism while discussing economics in the mid-1880s. When Webb joined the Hampstead Circle, he challenged Marxist economics by drawing initially on Mill but increasingly on Marshall and neoclassical economics. Shaw recalled how at the

---

[20] P. Wicksteed, *The Common Sense of Political Economy, and Selected Papers and Reviews on Economic Theory*, ed. L. Robbins (London: Routledge, 1935), p. 37.

[21] Ibid., p. 569.

[22] Ibid., p. 573.

Hampstead meetings, "F. Y. Edgeworth as a Jevonian, and Sidney Webb as a Stuart Millite, fought Marxian value theory tooth and nail."[23] Then, during the late 1880s, Webb developed a theory of rent by extending the work of Francis Walker. At just that time Marshall was drawing on Walker's analysis to develop a theory of distribution. By 1889 Webb was writing to Marshall that they agreed "absolutely in economics," and to Beatrice Webb, "I do feel a sort of reverence for Marshall as 'our leader' in Economics and I always uphold him as such."[24]

Webb's theory of rent first appeared as a response to Walker.[25] In 1887 Walker published an article that explained profits in terms of the ability of employers. He argued that ability merited reward, but he also noticed that if ability was used in conjunction with a fixed amount of capital, then—like land—it produced a differential surplus, which he called a "rent of ability."[26] Webb's response was a discussion of the place of the theory of rent in the kind of neoclassical theories being developed by Walker and Marshall.

So, like the neoclassical economists, Webb did not treat the margin as the source of value but, rather, as the site at which the operation of supply and demand determines value and price. He argued that the market is characterized by "equal returns to the last increment" but that the nature of these returns is determined by supply and demand.[27] This emphasis on supply and demand at the margin led Webb, like Marshall, to pay attention to time. Webb distinguished between "current rates" and the "normal rate to which variations in the current rate ... tend to conform over a long period."[28] Finally, Webb, again like Marshall, argued that the distinction between a commodity's normal value and its marginal value generates surpluses. Instances of a commodity are produced under the "most diverse conditions, varying indefinitely in advantage," and yet they sell for one price. Those produced with advantages thus obtain a surplus, "which is the cause alike of rent, interest, and rent of ability."[29]

Webb's analysis of rent is part of a neoclassical theory of a producer's surplus. Like all producers' surpluses, rent arises from the law of dimin-

[23] G. Shaw, "Bluffing the Value Theory," *To-day* 11 (1889): 129.

[24] S. Webb and B. Webb, *The Letters of Sidney and Beatrice Webb*, ed. N. MacKenzie, vol. 1: *Apprentices, 1873–1892* (Cambridge: Cambridge University Press, 1978), pp. 124 and 229.

[25] S. Webb, "Rate of Interest and Laws of Distribution," *Quarterly Journal of Economics* 2 (1888): 188–208.

[26] F. Walker, "The Source of Business Profit," *Quarterly Journal of Economics* 1 (1887): 265–88.

[27] S. Webb, "Rate of Interest and Laws of Distribution," 194. Compare A. Marshall, *Principles*, p. xvi.

[28] S. Webb, "Rate of Interest and Laws of Distribution," 192.

[29] Ibid., 193.

ishing returns. Workers apply their labor to the land that yields most, but "the law of diminishing return prevents them all crowding, like flies on a honey-pot, to the best site."[30] What might distinguish land rent from other producers' surpluses is the fixed supply of land. Certainly, Marshall argued that the fixed supply of land prevented it from responding to demand even in the long term. And as soon as Webb considered rent, he too associated it with a fixed supply of the relevant factor of production.

> As regards the extra produce over that at the margin of cultivation, which is due to greater advantages of site, there is no difficulty. President Walker has himself demonstrated how all the various differences fall under the head of "economic rent." He will be prepared to include in this term all advantages permanently fixed to any "immovable," and doubtless to extend it to those derived from unchangeable and durable forms of capital, such as ships and some heavy machinery.[31]

Clearly Webb accepted the neoclassical analysis of rent as a type of producers' surplus that arises because of the fixed supply of a factor of production. His argument was that this analysis covers interest as well as land rent. Capital shares the features of land that produce rent. The supply of capital is fixed. Interest cannot be justified as necessary to maintain a supply of capital.

Neoclassical economists such as Marshall and Walker suggested that the supply of capital was variable, so interest was necessary to maintain it. Webb offered three linked arguments to the contrary. First, he denied that the supply of capital depended much on the provision and rate of interest. At the very beginning of his article, he wrote:

> It is by no means admitted that the accumulation of capital depends solely or even mainly upon the rate of interest. Economists have always laid stress upon the other motives for thrift, which led, for instance, the French peasant up to 1871 and the Maltese cottager up to 1886 to hoard metallic currency without the inducement of interest at all.[32]

Later in the article, Webb defined economic interest in neoclassical terms as the excess produce over economic wages that is due to capital rather than to land or ability. When he then went on to consider the nature of interest, he immediately repeated his claim that interest was not necessary to maintain the supply of capital: "Unless it can be proved this [interest] is the only motive of accumulation (which it is not), it is clear that it

---

[30] Ibid., 194.
[31] Ibid., 201.
[32] Ibid., 191.

cannot be assumed that the supply of capital is actually regulated by the return to be obtained from its use."[33]

Webb argued, second, that interest arises not from the need to ensure a supply of capital but because of time lags inherent in the market. These time lags temporarily fix the supply of capital, thereby giving rise to interest. Interest is a result of "opportunity and chance."

> The constantly changing conditions of the industrial community make the economic position of every member of it vary from day to day. Mere priority and proximity are constantly found to be as effective guards of *temporary* monopoly as a patent or favourable site. The profits of business depend largely upon seizing those frequently recurring separate advantages; and though this may be claimed as an element of business ability, it is so much a matter of chance that many of these "windfalls" must be put down as adventitious advantages of the possession of capital, in a certain form, at a particular point of time and space. This "rent of opportunity" forms a considerable part of "economic interest."[34]

Because interest is due to a temporary monopoly, it is directly analogous to land rent. It is, therefore, at this point in his article that Webb defined interest by a "law of rent." To argue that interest is a product of a fixed supply is to argue that interest is, in neoclassical terms, rent.

Finally, Webb dismissed the other possible neoclassical distinction between land rent and interest. He argued that the law of diminishing return applies to capital just as much as to land. The capitalist, "like the farmer with his land, finds that, after a certain not invariable point, an addition of capital ceases to enable the labor employed to obtain a proportionally increased return."[35] Just as we do not grow all of our corn in the most fertile field, so we do not spin all of our cotton in the most productive mill.

Webb's theory of rent was then complete. It did not require a further moral claim about capital being unearned.[36] Neoclassical theory bases rent on the law of diminishing returns and the surplus returns to advantageous sites. If the surplus returns occur because of a fixed supply, they are not necessary to maintain the supply of the relevant factor of production. They are not part of actual value. They are a product of a monopoly or time lag. Webb's argument that interest is not paid to ensure an adequate supply of capital is in itself an indictment of interest. It implies that interest

---

[33] Ibid., 203.
[34] Ibid.
[35] Ibid., 204.
[36] Contrast McBriar, *Fabian Socialism*, pp. 37–44.

is neither a reward for human effort nor necessary for the efficient function of society, but rather an unearned result of a temporary monopoly.

So, Webb argued that given neoclassical assumptions, interest was analogous to rent. He challenged claims that diminishing return and fixed supply apply only to land, not capital. Indeed, when he read Marshall's *Principles of Economics*, he picked just these claims for criticism. He wrote to Beatrice:

> He [Marshall] has failed to rid himself quite of the erroneous old notion that Land differs from other forms of capital, and the faulty contrast between Increasing and Decreasing Return is a corollary. He has taken from me what he calls "Quasi-Rent," but not my further point of both Land and Capital being equally under both I. [Increasing] and D. [Diminishing] return.[37]

Yet Webb's disagreements with Marshall about the relationship of interest to land rent occurred against the background of shared neoclassical assumptions. In another letter, Webb expressed anxiety about a book he had promised to write, claiming that Marshall "has largely cut the ground from under my feet, and said much that I meant to say."[38]

SHAW: A MARGINALIST THEORY

Whereas Webb's theory of rent drew on neoclassical theory, Shaw relied on marginalism. As we will see in the next chapter, Shaw entered the Fabian Society as something of a Marxist, subscribing to the labor theory of value but rejecting the idea that the proletariat was a revolutionary actor. Then, in 1884 and 1885, a controversy broke over the nature of value. Wicksteed attacked Marx's labor theory of value from a marginalist perspective. Shaw entered the fray as Marx's white knight, but found himself convinced by Wicksteed's rejoinder. Shaw recalled:

> I put myself into Mr. Wicksteed's hands and became a convinced Jevonian, fascinated by the subtlety of Jevons's theory and the exquisiteness with which it adapted itself to all the cases which had driven previous economists, including Marx, to take refuge in clumsy distinctions between use value, exchange value, labour value, supply and demand value, and the rest of the muddlements of the time.[39]

---

[37] Webb and Webb, *Letters*, vol. 1, p. 171. The same concerns underlay Webb's dialogue with Walker. See S. Webb, "The Rate of Interest," *Quarterly Journal of Economics* 2 (1888): 469–72.

[38] Webb and Webb, *Letters*, vol. 1, p. 175.

[39] The debate originally appeared in the pages of *To-day*. It is reproduced in Wicksteed, *Common Sense*, pp. 705–33.

Shaw then began to discuss economics with Wicksteed at the fortnightly meetings of Beeton's Economic Circle.

Shaw adopted marginalism. For a start, Shaw defined value in terms of marginal utility, not the cost of production at the margin of cultivation. He wrote, "Exchange value is fixed by the utility, not of the most useful, but of the least useful part of the stock."[40] This marginal utility determines the value of all commodities of a given type. There is no contrast between a commodity produced at the margin and other similar commodities that acquire a surplus by virtue of not being produced at the margin. Shaw thus suggested that the market is in equilibrium. Commodities that "are scarce, and therefore relatively high in value, tempt us to produce them until the increase of the supply reduces their value to a point at which there is no more profit to be made out of them than out of other commodities."[41] Shaw thus adopted a static analysis. Although he often presented his economic ideas in a speculative narrative, he did not recognize time lag in the market.

Because Shaw relied on marginalism, he could not have adopted Webb's theory of rent. Shaw's rejection of time lags made Webb's concept of a temporary monopoly meaningless, and the minimal role Shaw gave to "real costs" precluded his building on the idea of a producer's surplus. Instead, Shaw had to develop a separate theory of rent based on the marginalism of Jevons and Wicksteed.

Wicksteed and other marginalists argued that rent arises simply because in any functioning market better articles will command higher prices than worse articles of the same type. Shaw agreed. So, for example, Shaw described "rent of ability" as a payment for individual superiority. A rent of ability goes to talented individuals who make land more profitable.

> What if the Proletarian can contrive—invent—anticipate a new want—turn the land to some hitherto undreamt-of use—wrest £1,500 a year from the soil and site that only yielded £1,000 before? If he can do this, he can pay the full £1,000 rent, and have an income of £500 left for himself. This is his profit—the rent of his ability—the excess of its produce over the ordinary stupidity.[42]

This marginalist theory of rent gave Shaw ways of denouncing particular varieties of rent. First, as Wicksteed suggested, Shaw could make a moral argument challenging the right of a factor of production to a share in accordance with its marginal significance. Second, Shaw could argue that

---

[40] G. Shaw, "Economic," in *Fabian Essays*, ed. G. Shaw, intro. A. Briggs (London: Allen and Unwin, 1962), p. 46. Also see G. Shaw, "Concerning Interest," *Our Corner* 10 (1887): 162–75 and 193–207.

[41] G. Shaw, "Economic," pp. 48-49.

[42] Ibid., pp. 41-42.

a particular payment was a product of a monopoly, and so not part of a functioning market.

Shaw used both arguments to condemn land rent. He argued, first, that land rent is unearned. Man is "mocked by Earth his step-mother," who makes rewards for labor a lottery.

> The wise and patient workman strikes his spade in here, and with heavy toil can discover nothing but a poor quality of barley, some potatoes, and plentiful nettles, with a few dock leaves to cure his stings. The foolish spendthrift on the one side of the hedge, gazing idly at the sand glittering in the sun, suddenly realizes that the earth is offering him gold—is dancing it before his listless eyes lest it should escape him.[43]

The idea that rent is an unearned product of chance dominates Shaw's critique of land rent and interest. He constantly returns to this idea, using all his literary skill to divorce land rent and later interest from effort and merit. His argument builds on his appeal to natural advantages that are distributed irrespective of personal worth.

Shaw argued, second, that land rent is a product of a monopoly. Land is a natural monopoly and essential for production. Thus, landowners can charge for access to the land. There is "a payment for the privilege of using land at all."[44] The absence of freely available land forces the workers to sell themselves. Next, Shaw followed the marginalists in defining the value of factors of production, including labor, as their marginal utility. He claimed that there is so much labor available that the utility of its last increment is zero. Laborers "are valueless, and can be had for nothing."[45] The landowner pays subsistence wages because that is the marginal utility of labor. A monopoly enables landlords to live on the labor of others, to whom they pay mere subsistence wages.

Shaw's critique of capitalism involved extending these two arguments from land and rent to capital and interest. He argued that interest is the product of rent and therefore of "lottery" and market failure. Capital is merely stored land rent. The existence of a labor market enables capitalists to purchase laborers for any purpose. The surplus generated by land rent gives capitalists the necessary purchasing power. So, for a railway,

> all that is necessary is to provide subsistence for a sufficient number of labourers to construct it. If, for example, the railway requires the labour of a thousand men for five years, the cost to the proprietors of the site is the subsistence of a thousand men for five years. This subsistence

---

[43] Ibid., p. 35.

[44] Ibid., p. 42.

[45] Ibid., p. 51.

is technically called capital. It is provided by the proprietors not consuming the whole excess over wages of the produce of the labour of their other wage workers, but setting aside enough for the subsistence of the railway makers.[46]

The link between land rent and capital is disguised by the scale on which capital operates. Railways cannot be undertaken by the individual landlord on his land using his surplus. Railways require the creation of joint stock companies. Nonetheless, in Shaw's opinion, interest is a product of applying land rent back to land. Interest is "obtained by special adaptations of land to production by the application of capital," which is just stored land rent.[47] Thus, if land rent is wrong, so is capital, and if capital is wrong, so is interest. Capital is land rent, so "shareholder and landlord live alike on the produce extracted from their property by the labour of the proletariat."[48]

POSITIVIST ALTERNATIVES

In the late 1880s, the Fabians forged several theories of rent that gave their socialism an economic basis notably different from Marxism. When *Fabian Essays* was published in 1889, theories of rent still dominated Fabian socialism. Shaw published his theory in *Fabian Essays*. Webb had published his main article on rent the previous year. Other Fabians had also published on the topic, notably Olivier, with his "Capital and Land" in *Fabian Tract* 7. Yet, after 1890, rent played an increasingly minor role in Fabian socialism. One way to approach the declining importance of neoclassical and marginalist theories of rent is to highlight the positivist alternatives that other leading Fabians offered. Few Fabians showed much interest in the type of abstract economic theories that attracted Shaw and Webb. Shaw suggested that "activity in that department [abstract economics] was confined to Webb and myself."[49] The other Fabians, most notably Olivier and Wallas, drew instead on positivism and the moral and historical approaches to political economy that it inspired.

Olivier: A Moral Theory

Historians have paid too much attention to the Fabians' abstract theories of rent, neglecting the importance within the Society of a positivist ethic and even a positivist political economy. Olivier's father was an evangeli-

---

[46] Ibid., p. 52.
[47] Ibid., p. 59.
[48] Ibid., p. 53.
[49] G. Shaw, "On the History of Fabian Economics," in *History*, by Pease, p. 262.

cal priest. When Olivier was at the University of Oxford, he decided that Christianity was incompatible with the theory of evolution. This decision caused personal anguish and family tension. Olivier himself retained the evangelical sense of duty, transferring it from God to humanity. Indeed, he continued to defend a Christian upbringing on the grounds that it instilled sound moral sense in children.[50] Olivier also grew up as a liberal radical. At Oxford his tutor was Thomas Case, who continued to promote utilitarian radicalism rather than the fashionable idealism. As Olivier focused on a moralistic concern with social duty, so his own liberal radicalism shifted toward a kind of reformist humanitarianism. After leaving Oxford, he worked voluntarily in the Settlement Movement, helped manage the *Christian Socialist*, attended positivist meetings, and formed an Auguste Comte reading group with Wallas and Sidney Webb. He moderated his praise of Mill with criticism for ignoring the social nature of morality and assuming that an efficient economy depended on individualistic motives.[51]

Olivier flirted with the Marxism of the SDF, but it was Comte and positivism that appealed to him most. Positivism inspired historical and moral alternatives to the abstract—and, to its critics, deductive—method of classical economics. Olivier argued that Marx's error was a preference for "abstraction" over empirical science; Marxism ignored the substance of economic life, so it "does not take us very far towards a full appreciation of the laws according to which the actual exchange values in commodities in modern societies are determined."[52] And Olivier argued that the labor theory of value was immoral; it implied that individuals create goods, thereby encouraging individualist demands.[53] Olivier wanted a moral economics to inspire a "larger socialism" based more on social duty. He insisted that "the complete Socialist criticism of our economy is not that it is capitalistic, but that it is individualistic."[54] Socialism consisted primarily not in new relations of production but in eliminating selfishness. Socialists should concentrate on creating new habits of mind, for "nothing can supplant the individualistic motives for exertion save the new social religion, nothing appease the conflict of rights, save the study and the following of duties."[55]

---

[50] S. Olivier, *Sydney Olivier: Letters and Selected Writings*, ed. M. Olivier (London: Allen and Unwin, 1948), p. 67.

[51] S. Olivier, "John Stuart Mill and Socialism," *To-day* 2 (1884): 490–504.

[52] Olivier, *Letters*, p. 52.

[53] S. Olivier, "Perverse Socialism," *To-day* 6 (1886): 110–11.

[54] Ibid., 112.

[55] Ibid., 114.

Earlier historians have argued that there is a single Fabian theory of rent, that Webb's outline of it is incomplete, and that Olivier's tract, "Capital and Land," provides the missing piece. They suggest that Ricardo's analysis of land rent joins the claim that land gets a differential return with a moral argument that the excess is undeserved; that Webb argued that capital gets a differential return, but not that the excess is underserved; and that Olivier provided a moral dimension to Webb's argument.[56] In contrast, I argued earlier that Webb's theory is complete; it does not need a moral supplement. Olivier's tract is not part of a single Fabian theory of rent. It expresses his personal economic beliefs, which draw on moral economics.

Olivier's tract explicitly addresses the land nationalizers' argument that "capital, unlike land, is created by labor, and is therefore a proper subject of private ownership, while land is not."[57] His interest is less in economic analysis than in ethics. Nonetheless, he provides a somewhat confused account of the source of interest. He argues that interest is paid to capital not because of the labor of the capitalist but for two other reasons. First, capital gets interest because it is "subject to monopoly"; capitalists charge workers for access to the means of production.[58] Second, capital claims interest as a toll equal to the difference between the value of the product of the enterprise in which it is embodied and the value of the product of the least efficient enterprise producing similar goods. Nonetheless, Olivier continues, this extra value is a product not of the skill and energy of capitalists but of natural and social advantages. For example, "The New River Company's Water shares are worth a king's ransom, not because Sir Hugh Myddleton's venture was costly, but because London has become great."[59] Olivier also suggests that insofar as capital is not a product of natural and social advantages, it is just stored land rent derived from others' labor.

Wallas: A Historical Theory

While Olivier emphasized moral economics, Wallas was developing a historical approach also associated with positivism.[60] Olivier and Wallas had strikingly similar backgrounds. Wallas's father was an evangelical clergyman in Devon. Wallas was a bit of a religious prig at school. He lost

---

[56] McBriar, *Fabian Socialism*, p. 38.

[57] S. Olivier, "Capital and Land," *Fabian Tract* 7 (1888): 3.

[58] Ibid., 15.

[59] Ibid., 6.

[60] Wallas had a brief interest in the abstract economics of Ricardo and Jevons. See G. Wallas to E. Pease, 4 February 1916, Wallas Papers.

his faith when he learned about evolutionary biology at Oxford. He later recalled a lecture by T. H. Green:

> The lecture was an argument for human immortality, based on the statement that since we only knew of the existence of our bodies from the testimony of our conscious mind, there is no *a priori* reason for believing that the dissolution of the body affects the continued existence of the conscious mind. Green asked for questions: I, being fresh from reading Darwin, asked him whether his argument applied to the conscious mind of a dog, and Green answered that he was not interested in dogs.[61]

Like Olivier, Wallas was tutored by Case, and he found Case's fusion of Aristotelianism and utilitarianism far more compelling than Green and the rising tide of idealism. Yet, his transfer of the evangelical sense of duty to society led him away from Case and Mill and toward Comte. He became a socialist as he read books Olivier sent him and as he discussed Comte with Olivier and Webb.

Wallas blended reformist humanitarianism with a positivist approach to political economy. Like Olivier, he wanted to craft a larger socialism based on social duty and concrete studies of social possibilities. Wallas's first published article was titled "Personal Duty under the Present System."[62] It asked what middle-class socialists could do to improve society. The answer was to promote a sense of duty such that people would use their advantages for the common good. Another of Wallas's early articles discussed Aristotle to draw attention to the importance of an empirical and historical social science, rather than an abstract and deductive one. Plato stands in for a deductive style of reasoning that "is always anxious to show what good or bad effects must follow from any political or social expedient." Aristotle represents a contrasting scientific attitude that "prefers, if possible, to see what effects have followed in the cases where that expedient has been tried."[63] Wallas wanted social scientists to make extensive use of history as a source of empirical data on what effects follow from what causes.

This positivist approach to political economy led Wallas to explain rent in terms of concrete social contexts, not an abstract theory. He described rent as a consequence of the legal institution of private property. If people privately own an object that they are not using, they naturally

---

[61] G. Wallas, "L. T. Hobhouse," in *Men and Ideas* (London: Allen and Unwin, 1940).

[62] G. Wallas, "Personal Duty under the Present System," *Practical Socialist* (1886): 118–20 and 124–25.

[63] G. Wallas, "Aristotle on Wealth and Property," *To-day* 10 (1888): 16.

try to make money by letting it out to others. If they are prevented from doing so, they will have no incentive for seeing that it is used, so it will be wasted. As Wallas explained, "If you allow a selfish man to own a picture by Raphael, he will lock it up in his own room unless you let him charge something for the privilege of looking at it."[64]

Throughout the 1880s Wallas expressed dissatisfaction with abstract economics. He argued that the whole value controversy was pointless. In his opinion, value was an "ambiguous and unscientific" term, covering a multitude of meanings; it should be replaced by more specific terms, including "ratio of exchange," "final utility," and "labour cost."[65] He wanted Beeton's circle to adopt a similar sociological approach.[66] And he illustrated this empirical and historical approach to social theory in his lectures on the Chartists.[67] The lectures electrified the other Fabians. They created a current away from abstract economic theory, toward a more positivist approach. Shaw recalled:

> The departure [from abstract economic theory] was made by Graham Wallas, who, abandoning the deductive construction of intellectual theorems, made an exhaustive study of the Chartist movement. It is greatly to be regretted that these lectures were not effectively published. Their delivery wrought a tremendous disillusion as to the novelty of our ideas and methods of propaganda; much new gospel suddenly appeared to us as stale failure. ... The necessity for mastering the history of our own movement and falling into our ordered place in it became apparent; and it was in this new frame of mind that the monumental series of works by the Webbs came into existence.[68]

Beatrice Webb, like Wallas, was already developing a positive sociology. And, by the end of the 1880s, Sidney Webb too had shifted his attention from abstract economics to historical accounts of social and economic organizations.

CONCLUSION

All the leading Fabians spent a large part of the late 1880s studying, discussing, and writing on economic issues. Yet, their economic thinking

---

[64] G. Wallas, "Property under Socialism," in *Fabian Essays*, ed. G. Shaw, p. 173.

[65] G. Wallas, "An Economic Eirenicon," *To-day* 11 (1889): 80–86.

[66] G. Shaw, *Collected Letters, 1874–1897*, ed. D. Laurence (London: Reinhardt, 1965), p. 237.

[67] G. Wallas, "The Chartist Movement," *Our Corner* 12 (1888): 111–18 and 129–40.

[68] G. Shaw, "Fabian Economics," pp. 262–63.

was more fluid and varied than it appeared within the old historiography. The leading Fabians were liberal radicals, so, unsurprisingly, they generally began with at least some interest in land reform. Olivier and especially Shaw also flirted with Marxism. The debates among the leading Fabians then left all of them convinced of the need to look beyond not only Marx but also the classical tradition of political economy to which Marx belonged. All of the leading Fabians responded to the dilemma of the collapse of classical economics by attempting to defend socialism using analyses of rent that were based on new economic theories. Yet, they drew on different economic theories to defend different analyses of rent; Shaw drew on marginalism, Webb on neoclassical theory, Olivier on ethical positivism, and Wallas on historical economics.

The leading Fabians did not share a single theory of rent. We should be skeptical, therefore, of the old historiographical argument that a shared theory of rent provided the basis of a Fabian socialism that was committed to permeation, gradualism, and state capitalism. This argument applies best to Webb's theory of rent, but as we will see in chapter 9, even he was rapidly moving toward positivist sociology. More importantly, the old historiography fails to capture the distinctive nature of Shaw's theory of rent, which, as we will see in chapters 8 and 10, led to a vision and political strategy notably different from that of Webb. Finally, the old historiography neglects the distinctiveness of Olivier's and Wallas's political theories. Olivier's moral economics fed into a political program of educating and uplifting the population. He believed that socialism should be built ethically through solidarity, not conflict, and through the performance of duties, not the demand for rights. He opposed both the class hatred implied by a new workers' party and the competitive individualism of the Liberal Party. Wallas's concern with institutions and their impact on behavior led him to view social change as a gradual historical process based on the educative effect of good institutions. Socialism depended initially on democracy, for democratic participation educated the citizens, equipping them to work socialist institutions. Thereafter, socialists gradually extended social control over some of the means of production and perhaps later some of the means of consumption.[69]

No single economic theory inspired Fabianism. The leading Fabians adopted different approaches to economic theory, different analyses of rent, and different political strategies and visions. Clearly, therefore, we need to rethink the old historiography of Fabianism. The next three chapters do so. The leading Fabians were liberal radicals and reformist humanitarians. Some Fabians briefly adhered to Marxist ideas. The next

---

[69] G. Wallas, "Property under Socialism," in *Fabian Essays*, ed. G. Shaw.

chapter describes Shaw's involvement with Marxism. Once the Fabians rejected Marxism, they adopted various economic theories, all of which flourished following the collapse of classical economics. Many Fabians had little interest in abstract economic theory. Others became increasingly interested in positivist sociology. Chapter 9 will discuss Webb's growing use of sociological alternatives to abstract economic theories. Insofar as there is a distinctive Fabian socialism, historians might identify it with themes deriving from a liberal radicalism, especially reformist humanitarianism, and modified in response to the dilemma of the collapse of classical economics.

CHAPTER EIGHT

George Bernard Shaw

MANY OF THE EARLIEST members of the Fabian Society had been on the fringe of the Marxist Social Democratic Federation (SDF). Many had Christian backgrounds. They responded to the crisis of faith in part with a reformist humanitarian zeal focused on ameliorating the conditions of the poor. This humanitarianism included sympathy for programs of economic and social reform, mainly land nationalization but also Marxism. Some of the early Fabians combined their reformist humanitarianism with a loosely Tory inheritance. The main examples were H. H. Champion, Robert Frost, and James Joynes. They soon drifted away from the Fabians. The other early Fabians typically combined their reformist humanitarianism with a background in a tradition of liberal radicalism. Examples included Edward Pease, Frank Podmore, and George Bernard Shaw. They were soon joined by others, including Sydney Olivier, Graham Wallas, and Sidney Webb. Typically these Fabians crafted their socialist ideas in response to the collapse of classical economics. They then rejected Marxist economics for neoclassical, marginalist, and positivist alternatives.

The Fabians' break with Marxism appears most clearly in the case of Shaw. All of Shaw's biographers recognize the importance of Marxism for his intellectual development in the 1880s. In 1911 Archibald Henderson wrote of Karl Marx's *Capital* that no book "influenced Shaw so much."[1] Hesketh Pearson later wrote that *Capital* "changed his [Shaw's] outlook, directed his energy, influenced his art, gave him a religion, and, as he claimed, made a man of him."[2] Most recently, Michael Holroyd has written, "It seemed to him [Shaw] that Marx was 'a giant and a genius,' who was to change the world more fundamentally than Jesus or Mahomet."[3] These biographers echo Shaw, who wrote that his last novel was "pure Marx" and that "Marx made me a socialist."[4]

A version of this chapter appeared as "The Marxism of George Bernard Shaw 1883–1889," *History of Political Thought* 13 (1992), 299–318. Published by Imprint Academic.

[1] A. Henderson, *George Bernard Shaw: His Life and Work* (London: Hurst and Blackett, 1911), p. 90.

[2] H. Pearson, *George Bernard Shaw: A Full Length Portrait* (New York: Harper, 1942), pp. 51–52.

[3] M. Holroyd, *Bernard Shaw*, vol. 1: *1856–1898: The Search for Love* (London: Chatto and Windus, 1988), p. 130.

[4] G. Shaw, *Sixteen Self Sketches* (London: Constable, 1949), pp. 81 and 50.

However, although Shaw's biographers agree on the significance of his debt to Marxism, those historians who have studied Shaw's ideas in the 1880s downplay his Marxism.[5] Louis Crompton contrasts Marxists, who were hostile to the clergy, with Shaw, who "after his early manhood was never a rationalist or secularist."[6] Crompton concludes that Shaw was, at most, "willing to adopt Marxism as a tentative creed" and to admire Marx as a denouncer of injustice.[7] Similarly, Willard Wolfe recognizes that Shaw viewed himself as a Marxist, only then to dismiss this view by adding that "it was a curious and very limited interpretation of Marx— scarcely 'Marxist' at all from the point of view of the S.D.F."[8] Wolfe prefers to describe Shaw as an anarchist who followed a "libertarian path" to socialism.

There is a gap between Shaw's biographers, who assert the importance of his Marxism, and intellectual historians, who deny it. This chapter attempts to close that gap and thereby improve our understanding of the process by which the Fabians drew on liberal economic theories to challenge Marxism and develop alternative socialist theories. Shaw was a Marxist until he turned to marginalism, and even thereafter his version of Fabianism retained themes from his Marxism.

LIBERAL RADICALISM

When Shaw first arrived in London, he led a bohemian lifestyle as a penniless writer. He spent his days reading or writing in the British Museum and his evenings in lecture halls and debating societies, listening and talking to liberal radicals, deists, and secularists. Liberal radicalism overlapped with the popular radicalism exemplified by the O'Brienites. Yet, throughout the first half of the nineteenth century, there were significant differences between the two. One difference was social class; whereas the popular radicals were generally artisans, liberal radicals were more likely to be clerks and professionals.

[5] The only exception used to be P. Hummert, *Bernard Shaw's Marxian Romance* (Lincoln: University of Nebraska Press, 1973). Hummert neglects the Marxism of Shaw's era, searches for evidence of pure Marxism, and, most astonishingly of all, finds it; he turns Shaw's competitive free-trade utopia into cooperative communism. A recently published book provides a better study of the recurring tension between Marxism and liberalism in Shaw's thought. See J. Alexander, *Shaw's Controversial Socialism* (Gainesville: University of Florida Press, 2009).

[6] L. Crompton, introduction to *The Road to Equality: Ten Unpublished Lectures, 1884–1918*, by G. Shaw (Boston: Beacon Press, 1971), p. xxvi.

[7] Ibid., p. xxviii.

[8] W. Wolfe, *From Radicalism to Socialism* (New Haven, CT: Yale University Press, 1975), p. 121.

Popular and liberal radicals also generally held somewhat different beliefs. So, for example, Jeremy Bentham had been keen to distinguish his liberal radicalism from the more popular version of Thomas Spence.[9] Bentham replaced militant secularism and the language of rights with administrative rationalism and the language of utility. Whereas a language of rights encouraged popular radicals to make absolute claims, a language of utility helped liberal radicals to look more benignly on gradual agendas that responded to shifting social contexts. For example, whereas Chartists and other popular radicals insisted on a principle of universal male suffrage, liberal radicals, including J. S. Mill, often equivocated, suggesting that "one man one vote" might be damaging unless people were educated sufficiently.[10] Sometimes liberal radicals tried to evaluate the utility of reforms by drawing on classical political economy to assess their impact. Liberal radicals treated economic laws as more natural than did popular radicals, paying less attention to the effects of political power. They saw monopolies as products of natural facts, such as the fixed and variable quality of land, as much as of a corrupt use of power. Many of them accepted a Malthusian view of poverty as a more or less inexorable result of the pressure of population on economic resources. Finally, liberal radicals were thus less interested than popular radicals in curing social ills through political reform. Political reform would not overcome the natural laws of political economy. Political reform was an end in itself and a means to good government. Liberal radicals promoted rational institutional and administrative improvements that would enable government to function more effectively.

The differences between liberal and popular radicalism were still apparent when Shaw arrived in London. Yet, many advanced liberal radicals had broken with the utilitarianism of Bentham. Mill had foreshadowed the break. He set out as a Benthamite prodigy but tasted the forbidden fruits of Samuel Taylor Coleridge and August Comte with their challenge to rationalistic and deductive approaches to human life.[11] Mill suggested that Bentham had moved too quickly from the general laws of human nature to actual behavior in a way that failed to allow adequately for the impact of history, institutions, and entrenched practices. He rethought

[9] J. Bentham, "Radicalism Not Dangerous," in *The Works of Jeremy Bentham*, ed. J. Bowring (Edinburgh: Tait, 1833–43), vol. 3: *Usury, Political Economy, Equity, Parliamentary Reform*.

[10] J. Mill, "Considerations on Representative Government," in *The Collected Works of John Stuart Mill* (Toronto: University of Toronto Press, 1963–91), vol. 19: *Essays on Politics and Society*, pp. 470–79.

[11] J. Mill, "Coleridge" and "Auguste Comte and Positivism," in *Collected Works*, vol. 10: *Essays on Ethics, Religion and Society*, pp. 117–63 and 261–368.

the tone of his youthful liberal utilitarianism in order to build "the foundation of these [his early opinions] more deeply and strongly."[12]

Moving the foundations altered the shape of the building. Liberal radicals became increasingly concerned with ethical positivism, altruism, and social duty rather than personal utility. Shaw joined both the London Dialectical Society and its younger offshoot, the Zetetical Society. The Dialectical Society had been formed in the late 1860s specifically to provide a forum in which to discuss Mill's work. The Zetetical Society was formed in 1878 to "search for truth in all matters affecting the interest of the human race."[13] Shaw described its views as "individualistic, atheistic, Malthusian, evolutionary, Ingersollian, Darwinian, Herbert Spencerian."[14] These views reflect the new liberal radicalism that emerged in the 1870s following the impact of evolutionary theory. If Mill accepted most of the philosophy of liberal radicalism while modifying its anti-interventionist social theory, Spencer transformed its philosophy only to defend the ideal of the minimal state. Liberal radicals, including the members of the Zetetical Society, started to fuse the evolutionary philosophy of Spencer with either secularism or ethical positivism. Shaw was a secularist; he dubbed himself an infidel, lectured for the National Secular Society, and distributed copies of *The Fruits of Philosophy* during the trial of Annie Besant and Charles Bradlaugh. Later he recalled how he shocked the staid members of the Shelley Society by proclaiming, at their first open meeting, that, like Shelley, he was "a socialist, an Atheist, and a Vegetarian."[15]

Several other members of the Zetetical Society found secularism less congenial than ethical positivism. They modified Mill and Comte to focus on social duty as part of an activist and reformist humanitarianism. Many found the squalor of urban society emotionally and morally shocking. Social surveys and novels alike began to document the extent of poverty and its corrosive and demoralizing effects on individual lives. Some liberal radicals felt a duty to go among the poor, educate them, and improve them and their conditions. Yet, liberal radicals were often unsure about what to do. They may have been full of reformist zeal, but many remained attached to forms of classical political economy that suggested poverty was more or less inexorable.

---

[12] J. Mill, "An Autobiography," in *Collected Works*, vol. 1: *Autobiography and Literary Essays*, p. 175.

[13] Zetetical Society, Abridged Prospectus, Passfield Papers, BLPES, London, PP:VI:4.

[14] G. Shaw to A. Henderson, 17 January 1905. Cited in Henderson, *George Bernard Shaw*, p. 136. Robert Ingersoll (1833–99) was an American lawyer, writer, and lecturer famous for his attacks on Christianity.

[15] G. Shaw, *Bernard Shaw: Collected Letters*, ed. D. Laurence, vol. 1: *1874–1897* (London: Reinhardt, 1965), p. 145.

The reformist humanitarianism of the liberal radicals led most commonly to an interest in the possibility of land reform. As we saw in the last chapter, classical political economists such as Ricardo taught that landlords got their wealth not because of their merit or their importance for the economy but simply because of natural properties of land. Radical liberals proposed numerous solutions to the land problem all through the nineteenth century. For example, Mill founded the Land Tenure Reform Association in 1870 with the aim of promoting legislation to make the buying and selling of land easier, thereby creating an admittedly imperfect market that might erode the landlords' monopoly. Mill had preferred land nationalization to tenure reform but had dismissed it as politically impossible. Alfred Wallace disagreed, and in 1880 he formed the Land Nationalisation Society. In 1883 the founders of the Land Reform Union split with the Land Nationalisation Society over the issue of compensation for landlords. The Land Reform Union immediately contacted the American land reformer Henry George, offering to guarantee his expenses if he returned to Britain.

On 5 September 1882, Shaw had heard George speak at Memorial Hall in Farringdon Street. Shaw brought a copy of George's *Progress and Poverty* and became involved with the Land Reform Union, which also included Champion, Joynes, and Frost. Like these Christian socialists, Shaw became caught up in the debate between land nationalizers and Marxists. In 1883 he went to a meeting of the SDF at which he accused the Marxists of neglecting the real issue of land reform. When Henry Mayers Hyndman then scoffed at Shaw's economic naïveté, Shaw went off and read the first volume of *Capital* and returned "to announce my complete conversion by it." [16]

Shaw had become a Marxist. He became a candidate member of the SDF, spoke at its rallies, and attended a meeting of its executive. Hubert Bland too was hanging around the edges of the SDF. In May 1884 he told Shaw about the new Fabian Society and then sent Shaw a copy of the first Fabian tract, along with an invitation to the next Fabian meeting.[17] Shaw went to the meeting on 16 May 1884, enrolled in the Fabian Society on 5 September 1884, and was elected to the Society's executive on 2 January 1885.

Marxism and Economics

At the time Shaw joined the Fabians, he called himself a Marxist. His grasp of Marxism resembled that of his contemporaries, including Ernest

---

[16] G. Shaw, *Sixteen*, p. 58.
[17] Bland to Shaw, 5 May 1884, Shaw Papers, British Library, London, BM:50510.

Belfort Bax, Hyndman, William Morris, and members of the SDF. As we saw in part 1, although these early British Marxists disagreed about the question of political action, they generally thought of Marx primarily as a scientific economist and a historian who showed the importance of class struggle. As Hyndman explained, Marx had transformed socialism from "Utopian schemes" into "a distinct scientific, historical theory, based upon political economy and the evolution of society, taking into account the progress due to class struggles."[18] Most British Marxists also shared certain economic ideas. They ignored Marx's distinction between use and exchange value. They argued that there was only one type of value, and it depended on the labor embodied in any given commodity. Surplus value existed because the workers had to work or else they would starve, the workers could not work without access to the means of production, and the capitalists' monopoly of the means of production enabled them to charge the workers for access to the means of production. The amount that the capitalists could charge the workers was determined by an iron law of wages according to which competition among the workers drove wages down to subsistence level.

When Shaw called himself a Marxist, he meant that he subscribed to the economic and social theory of the early British Marxists. Shaw believed in the labor theory of value and a Lassallean iron law of wages, and he argued that exploitation was a result of monopolies that also led to class struggles. He later recalled how "in 1885 we used to prate about Marx's theory of value and Lassalle's Iron Law of Wages as if it were still 1870."[19]

Unlike Marxists indebted to romanticism or Tory radicalism, Shaw's Marxism was not embedded in a historiography that disparaged modern competitive, market societies. Instead, he began with abstract economic theory, arguing that markets were a necessary consequence of human nature.[20] Individual self-interest led people to specialize in order to produce more. This specialization entailed a division of labor and so a system of production for exchange in which the market acted as an exchange mechanism. Human nature also determined how the market operated. People tried to satisfy their desires for minimal cost by buying things as cheaply as possible and selling things as dearly as possible. Markets thus involved competition with buyers competing for commodities and vendors competing for customers. According to Shaw, however, competition and markets were neither good nor bad in themselves; what mattered was the social context.

---

[18] H. Hyndman, *Socialism and Slavery* (London: Modern Press, 1884), p. 3.

[19] G. Shaw, "The Fabian Society: What It Has Done and How It Has Done It," *Fabian Tract* 41 (1892): 15.

[20] G. Shaw, "Competition," BM:50700-46. BM:50700 consists of a series of cards on which Shaw kept lecture notes.

As a Marxist, Shaw held a labor theory of value. If "it has taken twenty hours to produce a sovereign," "a table worth a sovereign is a table which, from first to last, it has taken twenty hours to produce."[21] Shaw argued that if society allowed free rein to competition, the market would force prices down to the cost of production, which, according to his labor theory of value, equaled the labor embodied in a commodity. However, the contemporary social context gave some groups a monopoly. It was the ability of these groups to avoid competition that caused inequality and poverty. In contemporary society, the worker "possesses nothing but his labor force, and that is useless to him without materials to employ it on."[22] Although nature supplied these materials in the form of land and minerals, "the landlord has intercepted the supply, and has sold to the capitalist what he cannot use in his own way."[23] Monopolies enabled landlords and capitalists to exploit workers.

Shaw fleshed out his theory of exploitation using the example of a monopolist who wants to build a railway.

> He [the monopolist] will deal with five hundred food producers first, saying nothing whatever to them about the railway, but merely stipulating that, on condition of his permitting them to use his land (which they absolutely must do, or else starve) they should produce in addition to their own subsistence, subsistence for five hundred other men besides himself, and hand that stock of food over to him as rent. This done the five hundred others are absolutely at his mercy, as he has their food in his possession. So he makes his own terms with them; and these terms are, that when the railway is made they shall continue to work just as hard as before, and that the increase in production which will result from the greater economy of the railway system shall go into his pocket. When the railway is finished the workers are no better off and he is enormously richer.[24]

Here the land monopoly enabled landlords to charge agricultural workers for access to the land, forced industrial workers to agree to the terms of the monopolist, and enabled the monopolist to acquire the capital with which to pay the industrial workers. An iron law of wages then determined how much the monopolist could charge the workers.[25] As Shaw explained, the workers must eat, so they must sell their labor "in

[21] G. Shaw, *Letters*, vol. 1, p. 82.

[22] Ibid., p. 83.

[23] Ibid.

[24] G. Shaw, "That the Socialist Movement Is Only the Assertion of Our Lost Honesty," BM:50702.

[25] The iron law of wages fitted well with his secularist Malthusianism. See G. Shaw, "Socialism and Malthusianism," BM:50700-14.

the market as a commodity," and competition between workers meant the value of their labor was the cost of producing their labor, that is, their subsistence.[26]

During the mid-1880s Shaw's analysis of exploitation led him to accept the class struggle as understood by contemporary Marxists. His economic theory showed that landlords and capitalists directly exploited the workers by underpaying them. The interests of the workers were directly opposed to the interests of the monopolists. Like many early British Marxists, Shaw thus understood the class struggle as one between workers and monopolists. Many of his Marxist contemporaries attacked capitalists only for being monopolists, suggesting capitalists were useful if they worked. An article in *Justice* explained, "Those who organise labour are always worthy of their hire," so "it is only the absolutely idle who are simply the enemies of the workers."[27] The class struggle between workers and monopolists here corresponds broadly to one between workers and idlers, and even one between useful workers on one hand and idlers and useless workers on the other.

Like many early British Marxists, Shaw believed that because all surplus value derived from monopoly, the workers could end exploitation by destroying monopolies. Yet, whereas Marxists indebted to Tory radicalism or romanticism also called for an end to industrial and commercial society, he wanted only to eliminate monopoly so as, in his view, to enable competition to work positively.[28] Shaw envisaged a free-trade utopia. In his view, once the land was nationalized and the workers were given free access to the means of production, then competition would work beneficially. He argued that "when England is made the property of its inhabitants collectively, England becomes socialistic," because "artificial inequality will vanish then before real freedom of contract; freedom of competition, or unhampered emulation, will keep us moving ahead; and Free Trade will fulfil its promises at last."[29]

Even Shaw's faith in competition and his free-trade utopia echoed the ideas of some British Marxists, notably the old O'Brienites and other popular radicals. Many Marxists believed that surplus value was a result of an artificial monopoly placed on top of a natural exchange process: they did not conceive of surplus value as integral to any system in which, for example, labor is bought and sold. Thus, they often argued that if socialists removed the artificial monopolies of the landlords and capitalists, the exchange process would function in a natural and beneficial manner.

---

[26] G. Shaw, *Letters*, vol. 1, p. 85.
[27] *Justice*, 29 March 1884.
[28] G. Shaw, "Exchange: Fair and Unfair," BM:50700-10.
[29] G. Shaw, *An Unsocial Socialist* (London: Constable, 1930), p. 216.

They looked to a time when there would be no monopolies, a time when workers would have free access to the land and to the tools of their trade. They wanted to free the workers from the clutches of the monopolists, rather than to eliminate competition or markets.

The most unusual feature of Shaw's Marxism was not his faith in competition or his free trade utopia, but his interest in the effects of competition on capitalists. He argued that competition among the capitalists forced them to lower prices in order to obtain customers. Just as capitalists "only secure profit by obtaining from their workmen more products than they paid them for," so they "only tempt customers by offering a share of the unpaid-for part of the products as a reduction in price."[30] Competition forced capitalists to sell goods for less than their true value. Thus, the capitalists did not pocket all surplus value. Some surplus value went to consumers as lower prices.

So, in the mid-1880s, Shaw's social and economic thought echoed that of most early British Marxists. He shared their belief in a class struggle rooted in economic relationships. And he shared their labor theory of value, iron law of wages, and critique of monopoly as the cause of exploitation; like many of them, he suggested that the land monopoly was the root cause of all other social ills. Shaw's Marxism differed from that of Hyndman and Morris mainly because he rejected their historiographies, with their debts to Tory radicalism and romanticism, in favor of a more liberal outlook. The difference was not about the class struggle or abstract economic theory. Marxists such as Hyndman and Morris opposed competition on the grounds that it was immoral, a threat to social stability, or a source of alienation and shoddy workmanship. Shaw adhered to a more liberal belief in the beneficial role of competition and markets in efficiently supplying human wants.

Marxism and Politics

The main confusions about Shaw's beliefs in the mid-1880s arguably concern politics more than economics. Some intellectual historians fail to recognize Shaw as a Marxist because they do not locate him appropriately in the context of the Marxism of his contemporaries; they appear instead to compare his beliefs with their preconception of what Marxists should believe. But even more contextual accounts can downplay Shaw's

---

[30] Ibid., p. 191. Shaw first outlined this theory in a published letter entitled "Who Is the Thief?" *Justice*, 15 March 1884. One commentator has dismissed the letter as not serious—see Hummert, *Shaw's Marxian Romance*, p. 27—but Shaw repeated the views of the published letter in a private one; see G. Shaw, *Letters*, vol. 1, pp. 82–86.

Marxism on the grounds that his political ideas closely resemble anarchism and anti-parliamentarianism. One source of this confusion is that, as we saw in part 1, the economic theory of the early British Marxists was compatible with a wide range of ethical and political beliefs. To clear up the confusion, we might locate Shaw's views of anarchism, the state, parliamentary action, and revolution in the context of both his Marxism and the various ideals and strategies of his fellow socialists.

Let us begin with Shaw's relationship to anarchism. The main evidence for describing Shaw as an individualist anarchist is his 1885 article titled "What's in a Name (How an Anarchist Might Put It)." This article describes democratic government as being as much an infringement on personal liberty as czarism. Shaw wondered, "What objection would he [the czar] be open to that does not apply to popular government just as strongly?" He concluded, "The sole valid protest against Czardom, individual or collective, is that of the Anarchist, who would call no man Master."[31] However, Shaw subsequently denied that the article expressed his views. On the one hand, the guarded nature of the article's title suggests that, as Shaw claimed, his intention was "to show Mrs. Wilson my idea of the line that an anarchist paper should take in England."[32] On the other hand, Shaw said that "there is nothing in [the article] that I object to commit myself publicly to," and, moreover, he used bits of the article in another lecture.[33] The evidence of the article is inconclusive.

Historians should focus not on a single article but on all of Shaw's writings during the mid-1880s. Shaw often stimulated discussion by taking a particular view to an apparently logical conclusion, and it would be foolish to argue he always held the extreme positions thus reached. Wolfe examines Shaw's contemporary writings and concludes that Shaw was not an anarchist in that he did not want to abolish the state as a political institution, but he was an anarchist in that his economic ideal was economic individualism functioning without capitalism.[34] Now, as we have seen, Shaw believed that eliminating the monopolies of land and capital would liberate a natural exchange process. Of course, if we want, we can describe Shaw's vision of a natural exchange process as an anarchist utopia. However, we should still remember that many British Marxists shared his vision. Even if we call Shaw an anarchist, we should not follow Wolfe in trying to distinguish this anarchism from contemporary Marxism.

---

[31] G. Shaw, "What's in a Name (How an Anarchist Might Put It)," *Anarchist*, March 1885.

[32] G. Shaw, *Letters*, vol. 1, pp. 109–10.

[33] Ibid., p. 110; G. Shaw, "Retrospect, Circumspect, Prospect," BM:50700-34.

[34] Wolfe, *Radicalism*, p. 137.

A similar confusion surrounds Shaw's view of the role of the state. Shaw saw the state "doing the work itself—competing with private enterprise."[35] His logic was simple. He did not want the state to own all of the means of production because that would make the state a new monopolist. But he did want the state to control some industry because that would break the monopolies of the landlords and the capitalists. The state should provide free access to the means of production, but if individuals wished to purchase some of the means of production, they should be free to do so. If the state owned some of the means of production, private capitalists would be unable to exploit the workers; if they tried to do so, the workers would move to state-owned enterprises, which would give them free access to the means of production. Here because Shaw believed that exploitation was due to monopolies, not the buying and selling of labor, he could argue that the introduction of the state as a competitor would end monopoly control of the means of production and so end exploitation. There was no need to collectivize all private property.

Shaw's belief in the state as an economic competitor distinguished him from almost every contemporary anarchist. Moreover, his vision of the state once again fitted well with contemporary Marxist theories. We have already seen how Shaw's vision of the state drew on his Marxist economic theory. And we should recall that many members of the SDF held a very similar vision for very similar reasons. They too believed that if there were no private monopolies and if the workers had free access to the means of production, then exploitation would no longer be possible. Few of them wanted to abolish all private ownership of the means of production. On the contrary, until 1884 the SDF was demanding nationalization only of land and related capital enterprises such as mines and railways. Many contemporary Marxists still believed that land nationalization would end exploitation by destroying the private monopoly of the means of production. It is true that by 1885 Hyndman was talking of bringing all the means of production under state control.[36] But Hyndman's position was unusual and contested even in the SDF. Indeed, Shaw's article "What's in a Name (How an Anarchist Might Put It)" should probably be seen as an attack on Hyndman's turn to a more thoroughgoing collectivism. Shaw was doing exactly what Mrs. Wilson had suggested when she asked him to write the article; he was "attacking our common enemy, the collectivists."[37]

---

[35] G. Shaw, "Competition." Compare G. Shaw, "A Fabian Manifesto," *Fabian Tract* 2 (1884).

[36] H. Hyndman, *Socialism and Slavery.*

[37] Mrs. Wilson to Shaw, 10 December 1884, BM:50510.

We can now consider Shaw's political strategy. Wolfe again assimilates Shaw to the anarchistic anti-parliamentarianism of the Socialist League. Wolfe reminds us that it was Robert Banner, one of the founders of the Socialist League, who introduced Shaw to *Capital*. He also claims that "for several years thereafter Shaw continued to derive his most important ideas from Scheu," who was another leading figure in the Socialist League.[38] More generally, Wolfe argues that Shaw desired a clean sweep to end capitalism, and this desire made him "a natural ally of William Morris and his fellow members of the revolutionary wing of English Marxism."[39] We have seen that Shaw did not share the anarcho-communist vision of Morris and Scheu. But what was Shaw's political strategy? Did he reject parliamentary action for social revolution?

There is no real evidence that Shaw rejected parliamentary action. He and many other Fabians remained on the fringes of the SDF while it favored contesting elections. Indeed, Shaw himself recalled that the early Fabians finally broke with the SDF, not in the dispute that led to the formation of the Socialist League, but over the Tory Gold scandal. The Tory Gold scandal arose when Hunter Watts, the treasurer of the SDF, revealed that the SDF had funded the three candidates it entered in the general election of 1885 using money that had come from agents of the Conservative Party.[40] Shaw and the other Fabians thought that the SDF should not have accepted money from the Tories because doing so was tactically naive, but they did not oppose all electoral action. Shaw argued that although "the idea that taking Tory money is worse than taking Liberal money is clearly a Liberal party idea and not a Social-Democratic one," the action of the SDF had weakened the position of the socialists because it had alienated "London radicalism" and revealed the weakness of British socialism.[41]

Insofar as Shaw opposed parliamentary action, he did so for tactical reasons, not as a matter of principle. Shaw believed that people currently overestimated the strength of the socialists, and so made concessions to them that they would not make if electoral action revealed the true weakness of the socialists. At the time of the Tory Gold scandal, he argued:

Out of our wonderful show of 50–70–80 or a hundred thousand men at Dod St. [where socialists had led a campaign for free speech], the polling has proved that not a hundred were Socialists. The Federation are convicted of offering to sell their fictitious numbers to the highest

---

[38] Wolfe, *Radicalism*, p. 121.
[39] Ibid., p. 131.
[40] *Pall Mall Gazette*, 4 December 1885.
[41] G. Shaw, "Fabian Society," p. 6.

bidder (in money, not reforms). The League have no feeling in the matter except one of gratified spite at the disgrace of their rivals. All England is satisfied that we are a paltry handful of blackguards.[42]

The SDF had chosen the wrong moment to contest an election. But parliamentary action was perfectly acceptable in principle. Indeed, as we saw in the last chapter, within a year of the Tory Gold scandal, the Fabians had voted against Mrs. Wilson and her anarchist supporters from the Socialist League and then gone on to found the Fabian Parliamentary League.

If Shaw was no anti-parliamentarian, he was also no revolutionary. Indeed, his main disagreement with the SDF was on exactly this point. He was so far from the Socialist League's belief in social revolution that he did not even think the workers could be galvanized to form a socialist party. Indeed, Shaw left the SDF not because he rejected Marxist economics or the class struggle, but because he did not believe that the proletariat was a revolutionary class. He complained that the workers are "more conventional, prejudiced, and 'bourgeois' than the middle-class."[43] In Shaw's Marxist novel, the hero finds his niche reading blue books and patiently presenting the socialist case to his own class, not proselytizing among the workers.[44] In 1885 Shaw himself appealed to middle-class socialists to participate in the socialist movement in order to prevent it from degenerating into "a mob of desperate sufferers."[45]

Shaw was a Marxist from 1883 until about 1886. He shared the contemporary understanding of Marxist economic and social theory. Moreover, his political strategy and vision closely resemble those of many members of the SDF. Far from being an anarchist, Shaw favored parliamentary action with the goal of nationalizing land and other key resources, thereby eliminating monopolies and so exploitation. Shaw's most obvious disagreements with his fellow Marxists reflect his debt to a tradition of liberal radicalism, rather than Tory radicalism, romanticism, or even popular radicalism. Not only did he have a positive view of market competition, he also denied that the workers were a revolutionary class that would or could establish socialism.

---

[42] Letter of 14 December 1885, Scheu Papers, International Institute of Social History, Amsterdam. Cited by C. Tsuzuki, *H. M. Hyndman and British Socialism* (Oxford: Oxford University Press, 1961), p. 71.

[43] G. Shaw, "George Bernard Shaw," in *Forecasts of the Coming Century*, ed. E. Carpenter (Manchester, UK: Labour Press, 1897), p. 160.

[44] G. Shaw, *Unsocial Socialist*.

[45] *Christian Socialist*, April 1885.

SECULARISM AND GEORGISM

A proper grasp of the content of Shaw's Marxism can help to clear up confusions about his relationship in the mid-1880s to secularism and to Georgism (the economic ideas of Henry George).

Earlier we noticed how Shaw, like many Marxists, had been involved in the secularist movement. Clearly, by the twentieth century, Shaw had adopted a mystical vitalism indebted to Henri Bergson's theory of creative evolution. What remains less clear is the relationship of Shaw's changing metaphysical beliefs to contemporary secularism and Marxism. Crompton distinguishes sharply between Shaw's secularism and creative evolutionism, and then identifies Shaw's socialism with his evolutionism in contrast to the secularism of many Marxists. In Crompton's view, Shaw "believed that ultimately social instincts, to be vital and courageous, must rest, not on logic or self-interest, but on religious convictions," and this appeal to religion divided him from the early British Marxists.[46]

However, there is no real sign of Shaw's moving away from secularism during the 1880s. Contrary to Crompton's opinion, Shaw consistently based his socialism on economic analysis and an appeal to self-interest. In one lecture, he argued explicitly that socialism was more efficient than capitalism, but not more virtuous, since it too rested on self-interest.[47] In another, he told his audience that socialism would arise out of self-interest, and that given half a chance the workers would exploit the capitalists just as much as the capitalists now exploited the workers.[48] As late as 1890, he wrote a letter to a fellow Fabian explaining as follows:

> If you tell me that selfishness is a bad principle, I admit that it is so qua principle (not qua selfishness); but if you go on to say that the working classes are going to take over the land and capital of the country in a spirit of pure self sacrifice, or for any other reason than that it will benefit themselves, then I lacerate the very soul of Wood by my derisive laughter.[49]

Throughout the 1880s Shaw relied on economic analysis rather than mystical religious appeals.

Shaw's appeals to self-interest extended his secularist assault on the accepted values of the middle and upper classes. He used the place of self-

---

[46] Crompton, introduction to *Road to Equality*, p. xxvii.

[47] G. Shaw, "The Attitude of Socialists towards Other Bodies," BM:50700-5.

[48] G. Shaw, "The New Politics," BM:50685.

[49] G. Shaw, *Letters*, vol. 1, p. 269. Compare G. Shaw, "Socialism and Human Nature," BM:50683.

interest in economic theory to create paradoxes and to shock bourgeois moral sensibilities. His extravagant appeals to self-interest enabled him to avoid appealing to ethical principles, and so to challenge the moralism of the Victorian middle and upper classes. In all these ways, his economic theory reflected his aesthetics. He championed the new art of Henrik Ibsen, Richard Wagner, and James Whistler precisely because he thought that they too challenged the easy platitudes of the Victorians.[50] Far from believing socialism had to rest on religious convictions, Shaw was a secularist iconoclast opposed to any principle qua principle.

Iconoclasm was a prominent theme in contemporary secularism, with Bradlaugh signing his newspaper articles "iconoclast." Shaw's iconoclasm was common among the middle-class secularists who joined the early Marxists. The Avelings, Bax, and, to some extent, the Blands all shared Shaw's commitment to a new art that challenged Victorian religious and moral pieties. As we saw in chapter 3, Bax was a secularist and Marxist who, to the bemusement of Friedrich Engels, directed his most scathing barbs at the moral hypocrisy of the capitalist hearth. Shaw and Bax formed a close friendship based on iconoclasm and aesthetics as much as politics. It was Bax who first found Shaw employment as a music critic in the early 1880s. Shaw then wrote in a preface to *Major Barbara* of his debt to Bax as "a ruthless critic of current morality" and, as late as 1926, added that he and Bax "would have been hanged long ago if our brave bourgeoisie had had the least notion of our opinion of it."[51] An iconoclastic attachment to new art also brought Shaw and the Avelings together within the British Ibsenite movement. Edward Aveling wrote a scathing review of the first bastardized performance of Ibsen's *A Doll's House*. Later Shaw played the part of Krogstad in an early reading of the original version of *A Doll's House*, in which Eleanor Marx-Aveling played Nora.[52] For these secularist Marxists, iconoclasm and aesthetics were linked to the socialist struggle because capitalism was bound up with the dominance of the false icons and moral hypocrisy of Victorian society. According to Shaw, for example, "Virtue, morals, ethics, are all a noxious result of private property."[53]

---

[50] G. Shaw, *The Quintessence of Ibsenism* (London: Walter Scott, 1891), *The Perfect Wagnerite* (London: Richards, 1898), and *The Sanity of Art* (London: New Age Press, 1908).

[51] G. Shaw, *John Bull's Other Island; How He Lied to Her Husband; and Major Barbara* (London: Constable, 1931), p. 206; and *Daily Herald*, 29 November 1926.

[52] E. Aveling, "'Nora,' and 'Breaking a Butterfly,'" *To-day* 1 (1884): 473–80. Shaw later used Aveling as a model for Dubedat in G. Shaw, *The Doctor's Dilemma* (Harmondsworth, UK: Penguin, 1946).

[53] G. Shaw, *Letters*, vol. 1, p. 266.

A proper recognition of Shaw's secularist iconoclasm might suggest that he was unlikely to have found much appeal in George's Christian moralism. Yet, Wolfe argues that Shaw followed George in deriving socialism "as an ethical corollary" of "classical Liberal assumptions," and that this ethical socialism, which "was alien to the S.D.F.," "remained the permanent foundation of his [Shaw's] social faith."[54] Shaw did indeed share a number of assumptions with classical economics, as did all the other early British Marxists and Marx himself. But Shaw did not accept George's economic theory, let alone his ethics. On the contrary, we have seen that as soon as Shaw read *Capital*, he left the land nationalizers and joined the fringes of the Marxist movement. His new economic theory corresponded very closely to that of the SDF, and it did not require a strong ethical foundation. His economic theory implied that monopolists obtained surplus value because they possessed a monopoly. Like many contemporary Marxists, his only important ethical claim was that this state of affairs was wrong because people should get the value they themselves create. He argued that "if six hours useful labour exchanges for six hours labour, ten hours for ten, and so forth without regard to the degree of skill involved, the result is socialism."[55]

Shaw's Marxism superseded his Georgism. His economic theory was that of contemporary British Marxists, and it coincided with that of George only where theirs did so. His ethics similarly echoed ideas common among contemporary Marxists. He had no time for the moralism of John Ruskin, let alone the overt Christianity of George. On the contrary, Shaw relied on a labor theory of value with its implicit idea that people should get the fruits of their own labor. He presented socialism as an economic theory rooted in assumptions about self-interested behavior, competition, and the market. In doing so, he made a pyrotechnic spectacle of his opposition to bourgeois morality, including bourgeois claims that socialism rested on a nobler concept of the self or a higher cooperative ideal. Like several other Marxists, he still pursued a secularist battle against every symptom of Victorian religion and morality.

Forging Fabianism

From 1883 to about 1886, Shaw's views closely resembled those of the Marxists. It was during the period from 1886 to 1889 that he and the other Fabians developed alternatives to contemporary Marxism. As we saw in the last chapter, Shaw himself rejected Marx for W. S. Jevons and

[54] Wolfe, *Radicalism*, p. 122.
[55] G. Shaw, "That the Socialist Movement."

adopted a marginalist theory of rent. Yet here too historians are confused about Shaw's intellectual development, partly because they do not locate him in the context of contemporary Marxism and partly because they do not distinguish his marginalism from neoclassical theory.

Confusion surrounds the relationship of Shaw's theory of rent to Georgism, anarchism, Marxism, and collectivism. Wolfe argues that George taught Shaw the importance of the differential theory of rent, and it led him to break with anarchism.[56] Yet, if Shaw adopted his theory of rent from George, with whose work he had been acquainted since 1882, why did he not adopt it, and criticize anarchists for neglecting it, until 1887? This question arises only because Wolfe mistakenly regards Shaw as a Georgist in the early and mid-1880s. If we accept that Shaw was a Marxist, we can answer simply that Shaw did not criticize the anarchists for ignoring rent because his Marxist economics did not include a theory of rent. Shaw himself recalled that during the early 1880s, "in spite of Henry George, no socialist seemed to have any working knowledge of the theory of economic rent."[57]

Moreover, Shaw was never an anarchist. He supported parliamentary action, and even his free-trade utopia included a role for the state. When he adopted a theory of rent, it merely reinforced his existing arguments against the anarchists. It was only after Shaw and the Fabians had broken decisively with Wilson and the anarchists that Shaw defined anarchism as "a doctrine ... having for its economic basis an invincible ignorance of the law of rent."[58] It was only in 1887 that Shaw first invoked rent as an unearned increment that does not derive from monopoly and so cannot be returned to the worker simply by abolishing all monopolies.

Shaw adopted a theory of rent not from George but from the marginalism of Jevons and P. H. Wicksteed. Yet confusion arises here over the relationship of his marginalism to Marxism. Once Wolfe denies that Shaw was a Marxist, he argues that Shaw's "chief reason for accepting Jevons's theory ... was probably that it gave him a new stick with which to beat the English Marxists."[59] However, Shaw ceased to be a Marxist when, and only when, he became a marginalist. As we saw in the last chapter, Shaw was a Marxist right until he and Wicksteed debated the theory of value, at which time Wicksteed converted him to a marginalist perspective. Shaw himself recalled that "when Philip Wicksteed, converted by Jevons, attacked the famous value theory of Marx ... I had to defend it because nobody better was available," but "when I had thoroughly

---

[56] Wolfe, *Radicalism*, pp. 142 and 285.
[57] G. Shaw, "Fabian Society," p. 15.
[58] G. Shaw, "A Word for War," *To-day* 8 (1887): 84.
[59] Wolfe, *Radicalism*, p. 288.

mastered what was left valid of Capitalist political economy I found that ... as to abstract value theory Marx was wrong and Wicksteed right."[60] Again, he explained that "the canker of infidelity in me" against Marx "had first taken the form of refusing to pooh-pooh Wicksteed as an idiotically perverse bourgeois."[61] All the available evidence supports Shaw's version of events. Before 1887 Shaw had never criticized Marx's theory of value. In May 1887 he wrote an article that expressed his disagreement with Marx's theory of value.[62] In August 1887 he wrote a critical review of *Capital*.[63] Shaw ceased to be a Marxist only sometime between the middle of 1885 and the beginning of 1887, and he did so only because Wicksteed convinced him that Jevons's theory of value was right and Marx's theory of value was wrong.

After 1887 Shaw believed in a marginalist theory of land rent.[64] Take two plots of land, A in a fertile region close to the market and B on poor-quality soil far from the market. Assume the annual profit from A to be ten thousand pounds. B will yield less even if an identical amount of labor is expended on it, for it is less fertile and the cost of transporting its produce to the market is greater. So assume that the annual profit from B is five thousand pounds. The owners of the two plots of land could do a deal. The owner of B could work A, paying the owner of A five thousand pounds of the annual profit and keeping the other five thousand. Then the owner of B would have as much wealth as before and yet gain the advantages of living close to the town. And the owner of A would become an idle landlord living on the rent paid by the owner of B. Land rent is a consequence of the variable fertility of land, not a monopoly.

Shaw's marginalist theory of land rent did not entirely displace his Marxism. If his theory of rent was to support socialism, he had to combine it with a critique of capital and interest, and his critique of interest still relied on contemporary Marxism with its analysis of the effects of monopoly and an iron law of wages. First, Shaw argued that land is a natural monopoly, and that the absence of available land forces the workers to sell their labor. Next, as a marginalist, he argued that the workers sell their labor for its marginal utility, which is just their subsistence. Finally,

---

[60] G. Shaw, *Sixteen*, p. 81.

[61] G. Shaw, "Bluffing the Value Theory," *To-day* 11 (1889): 129.

[62] G. Shaw, "Marx and Modern Socialism," *Pall Mall Gazette*, 7 May 1887. Hyndman replied in *Pall Mall Gazette*, 11 May 1887. Shaw wrote a final rejoinder in *Pall Mall Gazette*, 12 May 1887.

[63] G. Shaw, "Karl Marx and *Das Kapital*," *National Reformer*, 7, 14, and 21 August 1887.

[64] G. Shaw, "Concerning Interest," *Our Corner* 10 (1887): 162–75 and 193–207; "The Hyndman-George Debate," *International Review* 2 (1889): 50–57; and "Economic," in *Fabian Essays*, ed. G. Shaw, intro. A. Briggs (London: Allen and Unwin, 1962).

he argued that monopoly and this iron law of wages are what make possible capitalist exploitation. Capitalists who have a monopoly of capital can hire workers for subsistence wages.

As late as 1890 Shaw still analyzed most surplus value in the same way as did many contemporary Marxists. He explained that the "excess of the product of labour over its price is treated as a single category with impressive effect by Karl Marx."[65] He had jettisoned the labor theory of value for marginalism, only then to provide a marginalist defense of the contemporary Marxist theory of surplus value. In Shaw's opinion, Marx's theory of value contained a contradiction, but a marginal utility theory of value could still support the Marxist analysis of exploitation: "Wicksteed, detecting the contradiction, rejects the theory and replaces it, without essential damage to Marx's superstructure, by a more modern analysis of value."[66]

Nonetheless, Shaw's theory of rent did prompt him to turn away from his free-trade utopia toward a collectivist one. Wolfe argues that Shaw became a collectivist because he adopted the Jevonian idea that "the pressure of public demand against the margin of supply, rather than the labor of individuals or classes, was the chief factor in determining such economic values."[67] But Wolfe confuses Jevons's marginal theory of value with the neoclassical scissors theory of Alfred Marshall. It was the neoclassical theorists, not the marginalists, who identified value with the interaction of supply and demand at the margin of cultivation. As a marginalist, Shaw rejected this neoclassical theory of value. Instead, Shaw, like Jevons and Wicksteed, identified value with the utility of the final increment of any good.

Shaw's collectivism followed specifically from his marginalist theory of land rent. He still believed that most surplus value arose because monopolists used their monopoly to exploit the workers; monopolists charged the workers for access to the means of production, and the excess of labor then drove wages down to subsistence levels. He still believed that such exploitation could be resolved simply by eliminating monopolies. However, land rent now posed a different problem for Shaw. Land rent arose not because monopolists charged people for access but because of natural advantages of fertility and location. The problem of land rent could not be resolved simply by eliminating monopolies. Land rent existed because better land was better than worse land. It would remain even if socialists eradicated all monopolies. Thus, Shaw now concluded that a socialist state would have not only to compete with the monopolists but

[65] G. Shaw, "Economic," p. 59.
[66] G. Shaw, "Bluffing," p. 132.
[67] Wolfe, Radicalism, p. 289.

also to collect land rent and use it for the benefit of the whole community. Shaw adopted collectivism because he believed that land rent was a natural and ineradicable surplus.

CONCLUSION

Shaw was a Marxist from 1883 until Wicksteed convinced him of the truth of the Jevonian theory of value. Further, Shaw continued to hold many of his Marxist beliefs even after turning to marginalism and so perhaps remained, as he claimed, "as much a Marxist as ever."[68] The continuing influence of Marx on Shaw distinguishes his economic theory—and, as we will see in chapter 10, his political strategy—from that of the other leading Fabians, notably Wallas and Webb. Likewise, Shaw's iconoclastic attacks on bourgeois morality differed from the ethical positivism of Olivier as well as of Wallas and Webb. After reading his paper on Ibsen to the Fabians, he wrote, "I have opened fire from the depths of my innermost soul against the confounded ideals of Truth, Duty, Self-Sacrifice, Virtue, Reason."[69]

Equally, Shaw's engagement with Marxism echoes that of some other Fabians, including most obviously Besant and Bland but also Pease, Podmore, and even Olivier. Most early Fabians were liberal radicals and humanitarians who joined movements for land reform and flirted with the Marxism of the SDF. Their radicalism made them sympathetic toward the economic theory and some of the social reforms advocated by contemporary Marxists, but their liberalism and their humanitarian ethic made them suspicious of the more dogmatic and revolutionary aspects of Marxism. In 1884 the Fabians thus commended the SDF for its "good and useful work" while condemning the rhetorical "phrases" of Hyndman.[70]

The Fabians broke with Marxism in the late 1880s as they became influenced by alternative economic theories and, as we shall see in the next chapter, as Wallas and especially Webb became increasingly influential in the Society. By 1888 there was a growing consensus among the Fabians that socialism drew on alternative economic theories—positivism, neoclassical, and marginalism—with their analyses of rent and concrete historical circumstances. Members of the Fabian Executive Committee then decided to spend the autumn giving a series of lectures titled "The Basis and Principles of Socialism." The Executive Committee consisted of

---

[68] G. Shaw, *Sixteen*, p. 81.
[69] G. Shaw, *Letters*, vol. 1, p. 254.
[70] Fabian Society Minute Book, 1884, Fabian Papers, BLPES.

Besant, Bland, William Clarke (a radical liberal journalist), Olivier, Shaw, Wallas, and Webb. Revised versions of their lectures were published later in 1889 as *Fabian Essays in Socialism,* edited by Shaw.[71] The essays were a spectacular success, beyond all conceivable expectations. The first one thousand copies sold out in a month. By 1900 there were American, Dutch, German, and Norwegian editions.

Arguably, *Fabian Essays* was the high point of Fabian theory. When historians write about Fabian socialism, they usually refer to what they take to be the shared themes of the essays. The essays represented an attempt to define a broad and practical form of socialism without relying on Marxist economics. They began by identifying theoretical bases of socialism, then went on to consider the organization of society under socialism, and concluded with discussions of the political action needed to create socialism. The whole volume is a prodigious achievement. Nonetheless, it is a mistake to assume that the essays express one shared socialist theory. The prestige of Marxism with its basis in abstract economic theory often beguiles historians into treating Fabianism as similarly based on an abstract economic theory found in Shaw's essay with its discussion of rent. Yet, the Fabians still held varying economic theories, and overall the essays owe less to abstract economic theory than to positivist sociology. The next chapter explores Webb's role in promoting a positivist focus on institutions.

[71] For a detailed study of the *Essays,* see C. Hill, *Understanding the Fabian Essays in Socialism* (Lewiston, UK: Edwin Mellen, 1996).

CHAPTER NINE

Sidney Webb

HISTORIANS OFTEN DESCRIBE the Fabians as straightforward descendants of the utilitarian liberal radicalism of the early nineteenth century. However, the liberal inheritance of the Fabians is more complex than that. Most Fabians had Christian, and often evangelical, backgrounds. Many responded to the crisis of faith by adopting reformist humanitarianism. Tory and Liberal strands of reformist humanitarianism certainly inspired the founders of the Fabian Society, including H. H. Champion, Edward Pease, and Frank Podmore. Humanitarianism prompted the Fabians to explore land reform, Georgism, and even Marxism. Most of the Tory radicals left the Fabians. Their place was taken by liberal humanitarians, including Sydney Olivier, Graham Wallas, and Sidney Webb. In the mid-1880s, these Fabians joined George Bernard Shaw in responding to the collapse of classical economics by using neoclassical, marginalist, and positivist theories to justify a range of reform proposals. They broke with Marxism and crafted a distinctive Fabian socialism. The last chapter looked at Shaw to clarify their break with Marxism. This chapter looks at Webb to clarify the debt of their socialist ideas to liberal reformist humanitarianism, and especially ethical and evolutionary positivism.

Webb is a favorite example for those historians who want to emphasize the continuity between Fabianism and utilitarian radicalism. Brian Crowley describes Webb as a "utilitarian socialist planner" who followed J. S. Mill to socialism.[1] The Fabian Society similarly is portrayed as an organization that rejected revolutionary socialism for a practical gradualist ethos. Its advocates suggest that it developed a practical socialism suitable for British soil. Its critics complain that it undermined the innate creativity of the more working-class socialists. The advocates and critics agree that Webb and the Fabians developed a bureaucratic and statist

A version of this chapter appeared as "Sidney Webb: Utilitarianism, Positivism, and Social Democracy," *Journal of Modern History* 74 (2002), 217–252. Published by The University of Chicago Press.

[1] B. Crowley, *The Self, the Individual, and the Community: Liberalism in the Political Thought of F. A. Hayek and Sidney and Beatrice Webb* (Oxford: Clarendon Press, 1987), p. 1. Also see E. Barker, *Political Thought in England, 1848–1914* (Oxford: Oxford University Press, 1928), pp. 213–17; G. Cole, *British Working Class Politics, 1832–1914* (London: Routledge, 1941), pp. 122–23; and M. Mack, "The Fabians and Utilitarianism," *Journal of the History of Ideas* 16 (1955): 76–88.

social democracy. A slightly modified version of this view recognizes that Webb owed a debt to positivism, but it then equates his positivism with a rationalism that is, in turn, assimilated to utilitarianism. Here too Webb comes across as dismissive of the moralistic concern with altruism and duty that was common among other socialists. He is again said to have led the Fabians in adopting "a form of utilitarianism," and so a type of socialism that was "limited to practical efforts to modify the existing industrial order."[2] More generally, innumerable portraits depict Webb as a soulless machine whose only interest was utilitarian reforms and the political machinations necessary to get them adopted.[3]

Strangely, intellectual historians who study Webb's political thought almost never explore his early and largely unpublished manuscripts. Yet these manuscripts show that Webb belongs not in a tradition of utilitarian radicalism but in an intellectual milieu peculiar to the late Victorian era. Webb was an ethical positivist in a sense that was common then but had almost no precursors in the early Victorian era and retained few adherents by the 1930s. Webb became a socialist for moral reasons reflecting the humanitarian drift of the 1870s. He defined his socialism in terms of an evolutionary philosophy popular among his contemporaries. His socialism took a collectivist turn when he rejected the concrete-deductive method of Mill for positivist economics with its historical and institutional concerns. In short, Webb broke with earlier strands of liberal radicalism due to the crisis of faith and the collapse of classical economics. Webb was a reformist humanitarian whose ethical and evolutionary positivism continued to dominate his socialism.

ETHICAL AND EVOLUTIONARY POSITIVISM

Webb was born in London in 1859 to a lower-middle-class family.[4] His father appears to have lacked any formal qualifications and to have worked as a bookkeeper and business adviser. His father was definitely

---

[2] S. Pierson, *British Socialists: The Journey from Fantasy to Politics* (Cambridge, MA: Harvard University Press, 1979), pp. 31–32.

[3] The most amusing example is the satire by H. G. Wells, *The New Machiavelli* (London: Bodley Head, 1911). Recent studies challenge the caricature; see R. Harrison, *The Life and Times of Sidney and Beatrice Webb, 1858–1905: The Formative Years* (Basingstoke, UK: Palgrave, 2001); and Kevin Morgan, *The Webbs and Soviet Communism* (London: Lawrence and Wishart, 2002).

[4] A largely neglected source of information is his brother's notes. See C. Webb, "Notes on Sidney Webb," in Tawney Papers, BLPES, London. Otherwise most of the information comes from B. Webb, *Our Partnership* (Cambridge: Cambridge University Press, 1975), pp. 1–11; and M. Cole, ed., *The Webbs and Their Work* (London: F. Muller, 1949), pp. 3–26. For a discussion, see Harrison, *Life and Times of Sidney and Beatrice Webb*.

a liberal radical who sat on the local vestry, and he is rumored to have backed Mill in the constituency of Westminster during the 1865 general election. Webb's mother was a hairdresser with evangelical leanings. She took her children to church every Sunday, scouring London for a low-church preacher suitably free of the taint of ritualism. Webb himself left school at the age of about fifteen. He began work as a junior clerk in a brokerage firm, but before long, he entered the civil service, where he progressed rapidly, excelling in examination after examination. By 1884 he had progressed as far as was possible by merit to become a first-division clerk in the Colonial Office. During the mid-1880s, he also qualified as a barrister, though he accepted only one brief.

All through Webb's life, his ideas developed as much through personal discussions, correspondence, and organized societies as through reading. During his twenties, he participated in many discussion groups, debating societies, and mock parliaments in London. He gave numerous lectures, beginning with groups of his fellow students at colleges of further education, continuing with the Zetetical and other debating societies, and then the formal courses he taught at institutions such as the City of London College.

The early lectures indicate Webb's youthful religious, ethical, and philosophical concerns as he rejected his mother's evangelicalism for an ethical positivism.[5] The first extant lecture is titled "The Existence of Evil."[6] Here Webb described Christianity as inconsistent with belief in a material world that is governed by the unchanging laws uncovered by science. Science teaches us that not even God can alter the laws of nature. Moreover, Webb continued, God is omnipotent by definition, so science makes the existence of God impossible. Science contradicts religion. Yet, Webb remained reluctant to abandon all religious faith. He defended a belief in God on the grounds that "any religion is better than no religion," since people need faith to prompt them to do their duty and aim for lofty goals. Christianity still had value for Webb, not because it was true but because he feared that morality would wither in a secular world.

Numerous Victorian evangelicals shifted their attention from God to humanity. The second extant lecture by Webb, "On Serving God," clearly discarded Christianity for reformist humanitarianism and the service of humanity.[7] Webb argued that praise of God was valuable only if it promoted human welfare, but a religion designed solely to enhance human

---

[5] Many of these lectures are preserved in the Passfield Papers, BLPES. Although the recorded dates are often estimates, many of those discussed here are confirmed by Zetetical Society, "Programme for the Autumn and Winter Terms, 1881–82," Shaw Collection, HRC, University of Texas at Austin.

[6] S. Webb, "The Existence of Evil," Passfield Papers, PP:VI:1 (n.d.).

[7] S. Webb, "On Serving God," PP:VI:1 (n.d.).

life in this world was not a religion at all. Again, Webb accepted that Christians often believed "the service of God on earth" consisted "in serving man," and, because he allowed that our reasons for promoting human welfare were unimportant so long as we did so, he would not quarrel with people who claimed they tended to humanity in order to minister to God. Nonetheless, he thought that a humanitarian religion was "only an allegorical way of stating utilitarian principles."

Although here Webb seems to appeal to a utilitarian ethic, utilitarianism is a slippery theory. On one level, the identification of the morally good with that which promotes general happiness appears almost as a necessary but vacuous truth, since we can subsume most other moral doctrines under the umbrella concept of happiness. On another level, as soon as anyone gives any positive content to the umbrella concept of happiness, utilitarianism becomes contentious. Like several of his contemporaries, Webb played on the ambiguous nature of utilitarianism. He sometimes appealed to it as a principle, but he always did so with a notion of happiness that made him scarcely a utilitarian at all. For Webb, individuals have a duty to act for the social good, not their own happiness. It is just that a "happy life" happens to come from "absorption of self in some pursuit, leaving the pleasures to be picked up along the way."[8] Personal duty and social service effectively swamp the idea of happiness. The result resembles ethical positivism far more closely than it does utilitarian radicalism. No wonder that Webb began criticizing utilitarianism for encouraging selfishness. He believed that "utilitarianism became the Protestantism of Sociology, and 'how to make for self and family the best of both worlds' was assumed to be the duty, as it certainly was the aim, of every practical Englishman."[9]

Several of Webb's contemporaries poured ethical positivism into the utilitarian bottle. As we saw in chapter 3, several varieties of positivism acquired at least some Victorian followers. A few Victorians adhered to Auguste Comte's liturgical religion, and a few more adopted a republican positivism that sought to integrate the working class into a political vision of liberty, equality, and fraternity. Many more responded to the crisis of faith with a positivist ethic of social duty buttressed by an evolutionary philosophy. Webb adopted the latter ethical positivism, as did many other leading Fabians, including Annie Besant as well as Pease, Olivier, and Wallas.[10] For example, although Webb adopted a positivist ethic and soci-

---

[8] S. Webb, "The Ethics of Existence," PP:VI:3 (1880–81).

[9] S. Webb, "The Historic Basis of Socialism," in *Fabian Essays*, ed. G. Shaw, intro. A. Briggs (London: Allen and Unwin, 1962), p. 77.

[10] A. Besant, *The True Basis of Morality* (London: Freethought, n.d.); E. Pease, "Ethics and Socialism," *Practical Socialist* 1 (1886): 16–19; G. Wallas, "Personal Duty under the Present System," *Practical Socialist* 1 (1886): 118–20 and 124–25; and the extracted letters

ology, he complained that Comte unfortunately "enveloped" these things "in a dense mass of other doctrines which have impeded their progress."[11]

The crisis of faith led many liberal radicals more or less self-consciously to break with their predecessors and turn instead to evolutionary philosophy, ethical positivism, and sociology. Webb's own absorption in ethical positivism appeared in his ensuing lectures to the Zetetical Society. They were titled "The New Learning of the Nineteenth Century: Its Influence on Philosophy," "The Ethics of Existence," "Heredity as a Factor in Psychology and Ethics," and "Lecture on the Works of George Eliot." Webb now explicitly identified his moral beliefs with those expressed by Eliot's positivist hymn "Oh May I Join the Choir Invisible."[12] He devoted a whole lecture to praising Eliot's novels for their portrayal of the ideal of social service.[13] Like many ethical positivists, he continued to express his opinions in biblical language.

> The world to a great extent commits its evil by want of thought and is blameable only for its ignorance. But some are unhappy enough to see, and they must beware lest they sin against light. What shall they do to be saved?[14]

Again, like many ethical positivists, Webb answered this question in a way that still echoed the evangelical concern with personal duty and social service. He argued that individuals were the products of the community that educated them and gave them meaning. The individual rightly conceived is "a manufactured article, a store of value, an investment of the world's capital," and so should act as a "trustee" holding his "skill and energy" on behalf of "the world."[15]

So, Webb rejected Christianity because it clashed with science and particularly evolution. He argued that biology had revolutionized knowledge as much as had the new learning of the Renaissance.[16] Georges Cuvier began with zoology and botany; J. W. von Goethe started biology; and these sciences had culminated in the Darwinian theory of evolution, which Herbert Spencer had since shown to apply to the study of society.

Webb associated knowledge with modern science and especially evolutionary theory. Evolution established the existence of an external, ma-

---

in M. Olivier, "Memoir," in *Sydney Olivier: Letters and Selected Writings*, ed. M. Olivier (London: Allen and Unwin, 1948), pp. 60–67.

[11] S. Webb, "The Economic Function of the Middle Classes," PP:VI:20 (1885).

[12] S. Webb, "Ethics of Existence."

[13] S. Webb, "George Eliot's Works," PP:VI:6 (1882).

[14] S. Webb, "The Way Out," PP:VI:19 (1884–85).

[15] S. Webb, "Ethics of Existence."

[16] S. Webb, "The New Learning of the Nineteenth Century and Its Influence on Philosophy," PP:VI:2 (1880).

terial world. For a start, evolution undermines philosophical idealism; it proves the world existed prior to the human mind, so the mind cannot have created the world. Besides, Webb added, every effect has a cause, so if we experience an effect of which we do not know the cause, we still must admit it has a cause, and since we do not know this cause, it "is not itself in relation to our mind," so we must admit the existence of an "external world."[17] In addition, evolutionary theory removes the grounds of transcendental idealism. Webb understood Kant to have argued that our belief that two and two equals four was so strong that it could not possibly have come from our experience of the external world. But, he countered, evolution solves Kant's problem by suggesting that we know that two and two is four because of the accumulated experience of the whole human race, not our individual experience.[18]

For Webb, the existence of the external material world established the need for empirical studies. Earlier British radicals often prided themselves on their empiricism, but they based their empiricism on the individualistic and associationist psychologies of John Locke and David Hartley.[19] Evolutionary philosophy now prompted many liberal radicals to shift their attention to social psychology or sociology.[20] Webb even argued that the philosophical radicals had little impact on the world precisely because they tried to implement ideal abstractions.[21] Reform should be based on the scientific knowledge provided by the new learning; if it were not, it would fail. Webb promoted an evolutionary sociology according to which history reveals natural laws that govern the life history of social organisms. Human societies, like species, evolve, becoming increasingly integrated through cooperation and constantly shedding limbs that have ceased to fulfill any function.

Evolution had supplanted the individualistic psychologies of Locke and the utilitarians as the basis of scientific inquiry. For Webb, J. S. Mill thus stood as the last great "pre-scientific" thinker.[22] Only Mill's logic and political economy remained, at least for the moment, undisturbed by the new learning. Webb recognized that other approaches to political economy seemed to fit better with his evolutionary philosophy. Yet, in 1885

---

[17] Ibid.

[18] S. Webb, "Heredity as a Factor in Psychology and Ethics," PP:VI:5 (1882).

[19] We saw in chapter 8 that Mill foreshadowed a general break with Bentham. For Mill's particular disquiet about associational psychology as an educational principle, see J. Mill, "An Autobiography," in *The Collected Works of John Stuart Mill* (Toronto: University of Toronto Press, 1963–91), vol. 1: *Autobiography and Literary Essays*, pp. 141–43.

[20] J. Burrow, *Evolution and Society: A Study in Victorian Social Theory* (Cambridge: Cambridge University Press, 1966), pp. 179–227.

[21] S. Webb, "Heredity."

[22] S. Webb, "New Learning."

he dismissed these various alternatives. The "empirical" method of daily observation advocated by Cliffe Leslie "has as yet produced no body of knowledge worthy of the name of a science." The "historical" method of Thorold Rogers does not cover economics, but rather represents "a portion of the great domain of history." And the "sociological" method of Comte, although promising, has not produced results to "match those of political economy." Webb thus concluded, "The only useful method of political economy remains the ... concrete-deductive method of Ricardo, Mill and Cairnes" and "with slight modifications of Prof. Marshall and Prof. Walker."[23]

THE MORALIZATION OF THE CAPITALIST

Webb's milieu was the new learning; he responded to the crisis of faith by rejecting evangelicalism and religion generally for ethical positivism and evolutionary sociology. Webb and Shaw first met in October 1880, and by 1882 they were serving together on the Zetetical Society's committee. Shaw introduced Webb to the nascent Fabian Society. Webb read a paper titled "The Way Out" to the Fabians on 20 March 1885. On 1 May 1885 he joined the Society.[24] However, Webb did not sympathize with land nationalization and Marxism, which then dominated the Fabian Society. When Shaw asked him to join the Land Reform Union, Webb explained that he was a land reformer, not a land nationalizer, but that he would join, as land nationalization was "not an article of faith."[25] Likewise, in 1884 he said, "I am, I am sorry to say, no believer in state socialism."[26] It was only after he had joined the Fabians that he declared he was a socialist. At that time, he identified anarchism, collectivism, and positivism as three different types of socialism, expressing obvious sympathy for the last.[27]

To understand Webb's socialism, we have to follow his explorations in abstract economic theory during the mid-1880s. There is no evidence that Webb wrote about economic theory until after his lecture on George Eliot dated 1882. Thereafter, he wrote on little else until 1890. He gave several series of lectures at the Working Men's College: "Political Economy" in 1883–84, "The Economic History of Society in England" in 1884–85,

[23] S. Webb, "On Economic Method," PP:VI:25 (1885?).

[24] S. Webb, "Way Out."

[25] S. Webb, *The Letters of Sidney and Beatrice Webb*, 3 vols. (Cambridge: Cambridge University Press, 1978), vol. 1: *Apprenticeships, 1873–1892*, p. 80.

[26] *Church Reformer*, March 1884.

[27] S. Webb, "What Socialism Means: A Call to the Unconverted," *Practical Socialist* 1 (1886): 89–93.

and "The Distribution of Wealth" and "Low Wages" in 1885–86. The following year he began lecturing at City of London College: "The Production of Wealth" in 1886–87, "The Outlines of Political Economy" in 1887–88, and "Capital" and "The Fundamental Principles of Economics, Illustrated by American Examples" in 1888–89.

For most of the 1880s Webb continued to believe that the concrete-deductive method of Mill remained valid for political economy. His evolutionary philosophy inspired an interest in empirical sociology that left him somewhat dissatisfied with the concrete deductive method. But he did not believe fully in positivist, historical, and sociological approaches to political economy. Instead, he adopted a neoclassical approach. Like Alfred Marshall, he acknowledged the need to adjust pure theory to account for particular circumstances, while nonetheless sticking primarily to abstract theory. As we saw in chapter 7, Webb treated Marshall, even more than Mill, as his guide to political economy, basing his socialism on arguments made in accord with Marshall's neoclassical theory.

Webb accepted Marshall's analysis of value as being defined by the operation of supply and demand at the margin of production. Each factor of production received payment in proportion to its marginal cost of production. Because every increment of the relevant factor of production got the same payment, the increments that were not at the margin received a surplus. The surplus went to the owners of advantageous land, labor, and capital. For example, because all land was paid at the rate necessary to bring the last increment of land under cultivation, more fertile land generated rent for the landowner. Marshall, Frank Walker, and other neoclassical theorists argued, however, that interest, unlike rent, was necessary to maintain the required supply of capital. Webb rejected this idea. He equated interest with land rent by arguing that the supply of capital is fixed. Far from regulating the supply of capital, interest is paid mainly because time lags in the market temporarily fix the supply of capital. Similarly, he described the extra wages paid to skilled workers as a "rent of ability," arguing it was a result of the supply of their skill temporarily being fixed.

Although Webb's abstract economic theory led him to socialism, his socialism echoed his ethical positivism. Land rent, interest, and the rent of ability derived from a fixed supply of a factor of production. They were paid to individuals with advantageous positions. Yet, Webb argued that these advantageous positions existed because of society, not individuals. The workings of the social organism created temporary monopolies of capital and skilled labor. Thus, because society created these rents, no individual had a right to them. Rent and interest should be used to benefit the society that created them, not an individual who just happened to occupy an advantageous position. Even "the skilled labourer is exactly in the position of the landlord or the capitalist; he is a trustee who possesses social force: his brain does not belong to himself but to society at large, and he is bound to use it to the full extent—to use it for all, not for himself."[28] In this way, Webb's economic theory fitted in neatly alongside his ethical positivism with its calls for personal duty and social service. People in an advantageous situation had a duty to use the benefits they thus obtained so as to promote the good of society. Only social service could justify the wealth associated with rent, interest, and the rent of ability. As Webb explained to his middle-class audience, we should live frugally and use our wealth to benefit society as a whole, for "we are the cause of the misery of the poor by consumption of more than our share of the produce."[29]

Webb argued that rents are social products that necessarily will appear in any economy. Like Shaw, he concluded that anarchism simply was not viable, since rents can neither be eradicated nor returned to individual producers. Webb wanted rents to be used for social purposes, arguing that "interest, or rent, consumed without adequate service rendered is simply robbery."[30] Yet, Webb continued, the social use of rents might arise from the moralization of capitalists just as easily as from collectivism. If capitalists rendered service in proportion to the interest they received, the interest would become a social resource. What matters is that the monopolists not use their wealth for personal consumption, for the balance between what they receive and what they consume "is almost of necessity devoted to purposes of public utility, even if it be only reinvested in production."[31]

According to Webb, socialism could arise from either the moralization of the capitalist or collectivism. He offered several reasons to favor the moralization of the capitalist. For a start, he echoed Comte's faith in elites. Collectivism would put rent in the hands of the state, which represented the average citizen, and so would use rent only for purposes approved by the majority. Moralization would give a greater say to those "thinkers who are at the head of the column of progress."[32] In addition, Webb argued that moralization would be easier. Collectivism required great advances in the morality and education of the masses. Moralization required only a slight extension of current behavior, since monopolists already reinvested more than they consumed. Finally, Webb argued that individualist motivations helped to ensure efficient production, so the system of production should be left in private hands even as reforms were made to the system of distribution. He wanted to retain private property

[28] S. Webb, "The Economics of a Positivist Community," *Practical Socialist* 1 (1886): 39.
[29] S. Webb, "The Need of Capital," PP:VI:28 (1886).
[30] S. Webb, "Way Out."
[31] Ibid.
[32] Ibid.

on the grounds that it remained the best "system of wealth production," and although this system "involves great inequality of *wealth*," "it *does not* involve great inequality in the consumption of wealth."[33]

When Webb joined the Fabian Society, he was not a socialist. Even when he first declared he was a socialist, he fused Marshall with Comte to propose that the means of production remain the private property of monopolists but with the monopolists using their wealth for the social good. His early socialism fused neoclassical economic theory with ethical positivism.

> Socialism is founded upon no new system of political economy, nor upon any new statistics. It is mainly the emphatic assertion of two leading principles. We recognise, first, as the central truth of modern society, the interdependence of all. No man works alone; by division of labour and mutual exchange all are sharing in each other's toil. ... We claim, in the second place, to be but applying the doctrines of the economists in insisting on the ethical right of the joint workers, and the workers alone, to the whole produce of their labour, without any deduction for the monopolists.[34]

So defined, socialism requires nothing more than moralization. Webb wanted to "leave administration mainly as it is at present, in private hands but under some government regulations; equal personal consumption, and by workers only, being realised chiefly by an advance in personal morality."[35] Webb even suggested that equating socialism with collectivism was as narrow-minded as equating Christianity with Methodism. Throughout the mid-1880s, Webb defended his positivist socialism in critical studies of leading alternatives, including anarchism, Marxism, cooperation, and land reform.[36]

Positivist Economics

During the mid-1880s, Webb fused neoclassical theory and ethical positivism. Then, after 1888, he increasingly turned away from neoclassical economics and toward the historical and institutional concerns of

---

[33] S. Webb, "Economic Function."

[34] S. Webb, "What Socialism Means," p. 91.

[35] Ibid., p. 92.

[36] See, respectively, S. Webb, "Considerations on Anarchism," PP:VI:18 (1884–85); "Rent, Interest and Wages: Being a Criticism of Karl Marx and a Statement of Economic Theory," PP:VII:4 (1886); "Economic Limitations of Cooperation," *Co-operative News*, 12 January 1889; and "Henry George and Socialism," *Church Reformer*, January 1889 and March 1889.

positivist economists. His growing interest in promoting positivist ideals through social organizations led him to renounce the idea of moralizing the capitalist and instead to champion collectivism.

In 1886 Webb believed that the "universally approved" concrete-deductive method provided the starting point for economics, but that this method relied on an oversimplified model of human nature, so economists later had to make a "correction for actuality."[37] He told his students at the Working Men's College that although political economy begins with "self-interest," it "must have regard for history," so it "must correct for real life."[38] Webb's attempts to correct for real life inspired him to begin studying historical sociology. He became interested in social organizations and their impact on the operation of the laws of political economy. There is almost no evidence of his pursuing any such interest before 1888.[39] His earlier writings began with the philosophical implications of evolution and ended by considering how to reform society in line with neoclassical economics and ethical positivism. After 1888 he switched his attention to positivist economics and social organization. He even defined socialism as a "principle of social organisation" in a paper titled "Rome: A Sermon in Sociology" and subtitled "A Lecture upon the Development of the Social Ideal in European History." This paper contained long passages that he repeated word for word in his contribution to the famous *Fabian Essays*.[40]

Webb's interest in positivist economics and social organization provided the context in which he moved from the moralization of the capitalist to collectivism. By 1888, Webb gave content to his socialism by drawing on evolutionary sociology, not concrete-deductive economics. He began to describe socialism as "a statement of the principles of social organisa-

[37] S. Webb, "Rent, Interest and Wages."

[38] S. Webb, "Notes for Lectures on Political Economy," PP:VI:23.

[39] Webb provided a historical analysis of economics in a series of lectures preserved in the Passfield Papers. See S. Webb, "Feudalism," PP:VI:10; "The Growth of Industrialism," PP:VI:11; and "The Reformation," PP:VI:12. The tentative date given for these lectures is 1883, since they are taken to be a lecture series he gave at the Working Men's College in 1883–84. However, the leaflet announcing Webb's lectures at the college lists the headings of the various lectures, and none corresponds to the lectures preserved in the Passfield Papers. See "Working Men's College Session, 1883–4: Political Economy; Leaflet Announcing a Series of Eight Lectures by Sidney Webb," PP:VI:8. Moreover, a covering note in the Passfield Papers draws attention to a letter from Webb to James Baldwin, 10 June 1889, in which he writes that he read the first two lectures to the Literary and Philosophical Society. The covering note then adds: "As the letter was presented to the Collection when Section VI was already completed, it was thought unwise, in the absence of precise data, to shift 10–12 forward—perhaps erroneously—to yet another presumed date."

[40] S. Webb, "Rome: A Sermon in Sociology," PP:VI:34 (1887–88?). The paper was published as S. Webb, "Rome: A Sermon in Sociology," *Our Corner* 12 (1888): 53–60 and 79–89.

tion" derived from "positive knowledge of sociological development."[41] Socialism is just the efficient organization of society, and empirical sociology teaches us how to organize society efficiently. J. K. Ingram—a historical economist and positivist—even become Webb's archetypal socialist.[42] Like Comte, Webb argued that economic centralization, the concentration of capital, and mass production brought gains in efficiency by reducing costs and eliminating wasteful competition. In particular, Webb applied evolutionary theory to history. He concluded that societies, like organisms, become ever more efficient as they grow in complexity and as they adopt integrated and cooperative forms of organization. He even quoted from the biologist T. H. Huxley, saying that evolution consists in the "substitution of consciously regulated co-ordination among the units of each organism, for blind anarchic competition."[43]

So, Webb started to identify socialism, defined as the efficient organization of society, with cooperative and coordinated organization and thus with state activity. Capitalism was an unscientific form of social organization.[44] It was inefficient as a way of maximizing production, let alone welfare. For a start, the declining marginal utility of incomes implied that the rich attained relatively little welfare or happiness from large parts of their income; the same amount would give far greater welfare and happiness to the poor. In addition, the poor could not create "effective demand," so the capitalist economy ended up producing commodities to meet the whims of the rich rather than the basic needs of the poor. Finally, because capitalism thus failed to meet the basic needs of the poor, it undermined their efficiency and so impaired the whole process of production.

For Webb, the moralization of the capitalist would no longer suffice to realize socialism. Moralization would not necessarily increase social integration or limit competition. Socialism involved collectivism. Only an extension of state institutions and state activity would bring the requisite increases in social efficiency and social solidarity. Socialism depended on "the gradual public organisation of labour for all public purposes, and the elimination of the private capitalist and middle-man."[45] It required legal and institutional reforms, and it would be built using statutory and administrative tools, not moral exhortation.

---

[41] S. Webb, "The Economic Basis of Socialism and Its Political Programme," PP:VI:33 (1887).

[42] S. Webb, *Socialism in England* (Baltimore: American Economic Association, 1889), pp. 47–49.

[43] S. Webb, "Historic Basis," p. 92.

[44] S. Webb, "The Difficulties of Individualism," *Fabian Tract* 69 (1896).

[45] S. Webb, "Historic Basis," p. 87.

Generally, Webb associated collectivism with two main requirements. The first requirement was for the state to take as tax the rents of land, capital, and ability and use them for public purposes. This requirement followed from Webb's neoclassical economic theory. The state played the role he had ascribed earlier to the moralized capitalist. Under socialism, the state would enforce the social duties that went with wealth. Taxation would preclude the possibility of the wealthy using their rents for selfish ends. The revenue raised by taxation would fund the provision of public goods such as education, libraries, museums, and parks. Webb's second requirement for collectivism was that the state should regulate industry so as to establish an integrated, cooperative, and thus efficient form of organization. This requirement followed from Webb's new interest in positivist economics and, in particular, his use of evolutionary sociology to link efficiency to cooperation and coordination. The state would play a more active role as social organizations adopted increasingly complex patterns.

Webb's ethical positivism and evolutionary sociology facilitated his combining his collectivism with other contemporary strands of thought. One such strand was social Darwinism.[46] Webb believed that the principle of natural selection taught that more efficient societies thrived. For example, the Prussians beat the French in the war of 1871 because they were better organized. Sometimes Webb adopted a national focus, arguing that only socialism could ensure the survival and prosperity of Britain in the struggle for survival. At other times, he took a more general view, arguing that because evolutionary sociology taught us that socialism was an efficient form of social organization, the more socialist a society was, the more it would thrive over time.

Social Darwinism suggested to Webb that socialism was inevitable. Socialism thus appeared as an empirical version of a Hegelian world-historic idea. For Webb, all of modern thought led more or less inexorably to socialism: "Through Comte and John Stuart Mill, Darwin and Herbert Spencer, the conception of the social organism has at last penetrated to the minds, though not yet to the books, even of our professors of Political Economy."[47] Socialism was emerging everywhere without people's realizing it. Webb depicted "both great parties drifting vaguely before a nameless undercurrent which they fail utterly to recognise or understand."[48] Society was already saturated with numerous examples of practical state socialism, ranging from the Post Office and public educa-

---

[46] See in particular S. Webb, "Twentieth Century Politics: A Policy of National Efficiency," *Fabian Tract* 108 (1901).

[47] S. Webb, "Historic Basis," p. 78.

[48] Ibid., p. 64.

tion to the Factory Acts and a ferry across the Thames.[49] People might not recognize these interventions as socialism, but that is what they were; after all, Webb now defined socialism to include any extension of state intervention.

The positivist background to Webb's collectivism helps to explain two of its best-known features: gradualism and permeation. Webb defined socialism in terms of coordination, cooperation, and efficiency, all of which were bound together in the natural process of social evolution. This natural process unfolded with each incremental advance in state intervention or state action. Socialism had begun to develop as soon as people first cooperated within society. It continued to expand in organized action. And it would reach higher stages as people became increasingly conscious of the laws governing social evolution. There would never come a moment when we could say "Now socialism is established" because it was not a distinct form of social organization but only the fuller recognition of principles informing all social organization. Webb believed that the Fabians could further the socialist cause by gradually extending municipal enterprise, that is, by gas and water collectivism. They might even create socialism through vestry elections; that is, elections to the parochial church councils that, at the time, were responsible not only for some ecclesiastical affairs but also for some lay matters, generally including the administration of the poor law.

> Select good candidates whom you can depend upon to provide a proper sanitary staff, large enough to cope with the new work which the Public Health Acts require. Insist on the payment of Trade Union wages to all men in Vestry employ. See that the Vestry has the dust collected by its own men, and no longer employs contractors who make the bigger profit the more they neglect their duty. Discourage false economy by preventing the Vestry from employing unfair printers, or purchasing goods from sweaters, who, by low wages and long hours are filling the work-houses and increasing the poor rates. Demand proper baths and wash-houses.[50]

Webb saw no need for a radical break with capitalism or a sudden shift in the underlying constitution of social life. Socialism would evolve gradually.

Webb's strategy of permeation also appears in a new light once we recognize the positivist background to his socialism. For a start, the idea of permeating other political parties clearly resembles that of moralizing the capitalist. The Fabians could act as positivist experts, providing infor-

---

[49] Webb gave seven pages of examples. Ibid., pp. 78–84.

[50] Fabian Society (drafted by S. Webb), "Manifesto to Progressive Londoners on the Vestry Elections" (1893), Shaw Collection, HRC.

mation and policies to diverse politicians. In addition, Webb's evolutionary sociology suggested that socialist policies represented the outcome of scientific knowledge of the requirements of an industrial economy. Politicians of all parties might recognize the rationality of the relevant policies. If they did not, the inexorable process of evolution would overtake them anyway. Socialism was the outcome of positivist science—part of a necessary process of social evolution—that in some respects could remain apart from concrete political struggles for power and office. Webb at times even suggested that "the avowed Socialist party in England will probably remain a comparatively small disintegrating and educational force, never itself exercising political power, but supplying ideas and principles of social reconstruction to each of the great political parties in turn as the changing results of English politics bring them alternatively into office."[51]

So, Webb's collectivism rose out of his interest in positivist economics. At first, he combined this interest with a continuing commitment to abstract economic theorizing.[52] Later his courtship and marriage to Beatrice encouraged him to leave behind his interest in neoclassical economics and to concentrate almost entirely on sociological and historical approaches to society. Beatrice Webb (née Potter) also drew heavily on the new learning with its evolutionary and ethical positivism. She was tutored by Spencer and continued to believe in his evolutionary sociology long after she rejected his political views. She reviewed her early life in her diaries from the perspective of one of Eliot's heroines. Her work for Charles Booth convinced her of the importance of empirical studies of social practices and institutions as alternatives to abstract political economics.[53] By the time Beatrice met Sidney, she had applied an evolutionary sociology in her study of the cooperative movement.[54] Soon after,

[51] S. Webb, *Socialism in England*, p. 20.

[52] In 1889, after writing the paper on Rome, Webb lectured to Section F of the British Association, vigorously defending the idea of a science of economics divorced from questions of "particular social arrangements." See S. Webb, "On the Relation between Wages and the Remainder of the Economic Product," PP:VI:41 (1889).

[53] B. Webb, *My Apprenticeship* (London: Longmans, 1926). Historians have located Beatrice as well as Sidney in a direct line of descent from Bentham, thus ignoring her ethical positivism and evolutionary sociology. See S. Letwin, *The Pursuit of Certainty* (Cambridge: Cambridge University Press, 1965). Yet, Beatrice explicitly described how she and Sidney broke with utilitarianism. She acknowledged early utilitarian influences, and she identified broad areas of agreement, notably "that human action must be judged by its results." But she added that she and Sidney insisted that such results must include a "noble character" and "sense of conduct," so they "altogether reject[ed] the 'happiness of the greatest number' as a definition of our own end." B. Webb, *Our Partnership* (Cambridge: Cambridge University Press, 1975), p. 210. I skip over the differences between Beatrice's and Sidney's socialist thought, but for useful discussions see Harrison, *Life and Times of Sidney and Beatrice Webb*; and Kevin Morgan, *Webbs and Soviet Communism*.

[54] B. Webb, *The Co-operative Movement in Great Britain* (London: Swan Sonnenschein, 1891).

she persuaded Sidney to give up his plan to write a book about economic theory. She made it something of a condition of their marriage that he devote himself to studies of a more positivist and sociological character.[55] By then, moreover, as we have seen, he had begun to concentrate on the detailed application of collectivist principles to the institutions and problems of modern society; he had begun to contrast the concrete-deductive method with a new sociological method that could uncover "natural" laws.[56] Together the Webbs then embarked on their massive studies of trade unions and local government.[57]

Bureaucracy and Elitism

The Webbs relied on a positivist evolutionary sociology to direct the detailed historical studies of institutions that they hoped would then guide collectivist social reforms. Many historians describe Fabianism and especially the collectivism of the Webbs as the ideology of a new class of technocrats. Carl Levy, for example, argues that Fabian socialism "combine[d] an appeal for 'social service' with schemes that substituted for traditional elites and capitalist entrepreneurs a stratum of managers and experts." The Fabians "aimed firstly, to create effective collectivist forms of capital accumulation in mature industrial capitalist states, and secondly to bring into being 'healthy' productivist bourgeoisies and their disciplined 'proletarian negators.'"[58] Yet, portraits of the Webbs as bureaucratic elitists rather miss the mark. Although Webb's ethical positivism informed a strong rhetorical and moral emphasis on the role of the state and independent experts, his actual proposals do not translate this rhetoric into excessively bureaucratic and elitist institutions.

Clearly Webb rejected what he saw as the untrammeled individualism of the free market. As we have seen, moreover, his theory of rent precluded anything akin to the withering away of the state. While he expected political conflict to decline so that the role of the state would shift from the government of persons to the administration of things, he thought that the role of the state in administering the unearned increment was likely to increase. Nonetheless, we should not be too quick to

---

[55] Webb and Webb, *Letters*, vol. 1, p. 178.

[56] S. Webb, "History of Economic Theory," PP:VI:64.

[57] S. Webb and B. Webb, *The History of Trade Unionism* (London: Longmans, 1894) and *English Local Government from the Revolution to the Municipal Corporations Act*, 8 vols. (London: Longmans, 1906–29). And on their sociological approach, see their preface to *Industrial Democracy* (London: Longmans, 1920).

[58] C. Levy, "Conclusion: Historiography and the New Class," in *Socialism and the Intelligentsia, 1880–1914*, ed. C. Levy (London: Routledge, 1987), p. 275.

equate a growing administrative role for the state with a technocratic bureaucracy.

Sometimes Webb appeared to suggest that collectivism involved a bureaucratic state invading every aspect of daily life. He argued that "it is of comparatively little importance in the long run that individuals should develop to the utmost if the life of the community in which they live is not thereby served."[59] The individual seemed to be subordinated to a soulless machine.

> The perfect and fitting development of each individual is not necessarily the utmost and highest cultivation of his own personality, but the filling, in the best possible way, of his humble function in the great social machine. We must abandon the self-conceit of imagining that we are independent units, and bend our jealous minds, absorbed in their own cultivation, to this subjection to the higher end, the Common Weal.[60]

Because individual fulfillment derived from performing a social function, society ended up determining what the individual should do, rather than individual choices defining the nature of society.

Although Webb sometimes wrote as if he favored extensive state intervention in every aspect of social and economic life, his concrete proposals remain surprisingly modest. Webb suggested that the role of the state would grow, but he did not envisage the extensive bureaucracy and state control one might expect given his collectivist ethic. To the contrary, for Webb, socialism depended mainly on, first, the taxation of the unearned increment to finance the provision of public goods such as museums and parks and, second, the extension of municipal enterprise. Local government was the main arena of socialist activity. Webb wanted municipalities to provide services and, perhaps, control some industries. Generally, he envisaged municipal services and industries competing with one another and with private enterprises. He implied here that the greater efficiency of socialist organization virtually guaranteed they would compete effectively with private firms. Well might the Webbs protest that "the Socialist State, far from being a centralized and coercive bureaucracy, presents itself to us as a highly diversified and extremely numerous set of social groupings in which, as we ourselves see it, governmental coercion, as distinguished from National and Municipal Housekeeping, is destined to play an ever dwindling part."[61]

---

[59] S. Webb, "Difficulties of Individualism," p. 16.
[60] S. Webb, "Historic Basis," p. 90.
[61] S. Webb and B. Webb, "What Is Socialism," *New Statesman*, 21 June 1913.

We can reconcile the strength of Webb's collectivist ethic with his relatively modest proposals by recognizing his continuing attachment to ethical positivism. Even before Webb adopted collectivism, he subordinated the individual to society. In the mid-1880s, he argued as follows:

> The sphere covered by definite ethical rules of conduct constantly increases in extent. ... We now believe that in any given circumstances, one course, if only we knew *which*, would produce more social happiness than any other course. ... There are no purely self-regarding acts. Every act, even the seemingly most "morally indifferent" affects the universe for good or for evil, everlastingly, irreparably. There is no forgiveness of sins. ... [Thus] if society knew all, society would naturally and properly, supervise all.[62]

After he adopted collectivism in about 1887, he defined it in ethical terms as just such a "subordination of personal interest to the general good."[63] His strong collectivist ethic restated ethical positivism with its emphasis on social duty.

> We are not isolated units free to choose our work: but parts of a whole, the well-being of which *may* be inimical to our fullest development or greatest effectiveness. ... I think George Eliot meant to say this in Maggie Tulliver. We have no *right* to live our own lives. What shall it profit a man to save his own soul, if thereby even one jot less good is done in the world?[64]

The strength of Webb's collectivist ethic derives, therefore, not from his socialism or his positivist sociology but from the altruism and social duty that were so common among Victorians and especially the ethical positivists.

Again, Webb continued to locate his strong collectivist ethic within the kind of evolutionary narrative that his generation associated with the new learning. He argued that early societies had little functional differentiation or specialization, so the actions of one individual did not have much effect on others. But, in contrast, contemporary societies have evolved into complex organisms based on a division of labor such that there are no self-regarding actions. A profound interdependence dramatically extends the arena in which people now need to consider their social duty. Because all actions have social consequences, individuals can

---

[62] S. Webb, "Considerations on Anarchism."
[63] S. Webb, *Socialism in England*, p. 12.
[64] Webb and Webb, *Letters*, vol. 1, p. 158. The reference is to G. Eliot, *The Mill on the Floss*.

never just do as they please. Today people should constantly subjugate their personal desires to the requirements of the organic whole. Webb's analysis of the complexity of modern society thus combined with his emphasis on social duty to inspire a strong moral collectivism. He did not subordinate the individual to society because he equated socialism with a centralized, bureaucratic, and coercive state. He did so because he continued to believe in themes derived from his evolutionary and ethical positivism.

The Webbs' positivism also informed their view of the role of expertise. At times the Webbs appeared to suggest that collectivism would involve moving away from democracy toward rule by administrative and managerial elites. They clearly believed in experts as a source of neutral, rational, and compelling advice. In their view, much of the activity of government could be left to the "disinterested professional expert who invents, discovers, inspects, audits, costs, tests or measures."[65] Experts could discover facts about society and its requirements. Professional administrators could draw on this social science as an indispensable guide to efficient and effective policies. Sometimes the Webbs' praise of these elites appeared to dismiss democracy. Elections seemed to be mere token gestures designed to secure a vague sense of popular consent for the policies the experts designed.

However, although the Webbs occasionally wrote as if technocratic elites might replace democracy, their proposals remained modest. They constantly stressed the interrelationship of democracy and socialism. Socialism was an inevitable product of democracy. And democracy was integral to socialism. Indeed, the Webbs' pioneering histories consistently highlighted the creative and democratic capacity of the working class. They wrote that trade unions "offer the century-long experience of a thousand self-governing working class communities."[66] For the Webbs, democracy was a prerequisite of good government. Experts and other civil servants could provide advice and even implement policies, but decision making had to remain the provenance of elected representatives.

When the Webbs praised scientific expertise, they were generally contrasting the rational coordination that they believed would characterize socialism with the industrial anarchy that they associated with capitalism. Experts would help overcome the chaos of an industrial system in which the major decisions arose out of a series of arbitrary judgments by numerous unconnected industrial autocrats. Yet, the Webbs did not

---

[65] S. Webb and B. Webb, *A Constitution for the Socialist Commonwealth of Great Britain*, ed. S. Beer (Cambridge: Cambridge University Press, 1975), p. 198.

[66] Webb and Webb, *History of Trade Unionism*, pp. 475–76.

intend thereby to limit the claims of parliamentary democracy. On the contrary, they argued that the expert "will have no power of command, and no right to insist on his suggestions being adopted"; "his function is exhausted when his report is made."[67] Authority and the power to command would remain exclusively with elected bodies. As the Webbs often explained, "The ultimate decision on policy rests in no other hands than those of the citizens themselves."[68]

The Webbs defended the authority of representative institutions over the executive and civil service. They also wanted to extend the scope of representative institutions throughout society. When R. B. Haldane defined democracy as the rule of an assembly of representatives who, once elected, are free to decide the general will, Sidney objected to the dangers of any such concentration of power and sovereignty. He highlighted the importance of institutional pluralism in deciding the general will. He pointed out that "already we have several elections concurrently, Parish, District, Borough and County Councils; Trade Unions or Professional Associations and Co-operative Societies; as well as Parliament."[69] In their *Constitution for the Socialist Commonwealth* (1920), the Webbs advocated extending democracy from the state to economic and social institutions, appealing, for example, to democracies of consumers and of producers as well as to the need for workers to participate in all areas of industrial management.[70] Earlier, in their *Industrial Democracy* (1897), they had evoked new professional representatives who might maintain a more "intimate and reciprocal" relationship with their electors, thereby bringing "the ordinary man into active political citizenship" and increasing "the real authority of the people over the representative assembly, and of the representative assembly over the permanent civil service."[71] The Webbs wanted to open the public sphere to working men and women, and they constantly made proposals to deepen and extend the role of representative institutions.

We can reconcile the Webbs' faith in experts with their commitment to democracy by referring to their evolutionary sociology. For a start, the Webbs argued that as society evolved, the process of functional differentiation would sharpen the distinction between elected representatives and expert advisers. Government would combine popular control with administrative efficiency. Expert advisers would deal only in facts that

---

[67] Webb and Webb, *Constitution*, p. 198.
[68] Webb and Webb, *Industrial Democracy*, p. 848.
[69] Webb and Webb, *Letters*, vol. 3: *Pilgrimage, 1912–1947*, p. 152.
[70] Webb and Webb, *Constitution*, pp. 164–67.
[71] Webb and Webb, *Industrial Democracy*, pp. 70–71.

all rational individuals could agree on. In addition, the Webbs argued that the rise of evolutionary theory dramatically increased the range of such facts and their role in determining actions. Knowledge of social evolution meant that politicians would have to make fewer choices. Experts could reveal as a fact what course of action was best, given that society was evolving into distinct functional units that were held together by cooperation and coordination. Rational individuals of all political parties would agree with the facts. As Sidney explained, "The importance of complete consciousness of the social tendencies of the age lies in the fact that its existence and comprehensiveness often determine the expediency of our particular action."[72] The Webbs did not favor technocratic elites as an alternative to democracy. Rather, their evolutionary sociology suggested that expertise could play an ever greater role in representative democracy.

CONCLUSION

"Two typewriters clicking as one" has proved to be a popular image of the Webbs. Its popularity derives in part from the closeness of their collaboration, but even more from the suggestion of a mechanical mode of being based on a severe efficiency and a repression of emotion, aesthetics, and other areas of judgment. The old historiography portrays Sidney in particular as crudely rationalistic and bureaucratic. To some, he represents an extension of the utilitarian mind-set. To others, he illustrates the rise of a new class of professional and technocratic administrators. However, these portraits of Webb are wildly inaccurate. Webb was not a crude advocate of a rationalistic and technocratic state; nor was he a utilitarian. He was an ethical and evolutionary positivist whose later socialism was still dominated by a historical sociology that articulated the functional differentiation and development of social institutions.

Few scholars have explored Webb's early and largely unpublished writings. These manuscripts show that he drew on a new learning associated with Comte, Darwin, and Spencer. His socialism emerged out of a liberal radical milieu dominated by ethical positivism and evolutionary sociology. It was a positivist ethic that led him to socialism. And it was an evolutionary sociology that prompted him to adopt collectivism as an expression of his ethical ideal. His collectivist ethic certainly provided him with a rhetorical stick with which to beat laissez-faire and individualism; he insisted that the good of society would not arise

---

[72] S. Webb, "Historic Basis," p. 82.

magically out of individuals pursuing their private advantage. Nonetheless, Webb's strongly collectivist ethic did not translate directly into a bureaucratic and elitist state taking control of ever-greater spheres of social and economic life. Generally, Webb looked only to progressive taxation to fund public goods, and to local government enterprises to compete with private firms.

CHAPTER TEN

Permeation and Independent Labor

HISTORIANS HAVE LONG DEBATED the extent to which the Fabians acted as John the Baptist to the Labour Party. Initially, most historians accepted the Fabians' account of themselves as the single most important group in getting socialism a foothold on British soil. In this view, the Fabians forged a gradualist constitutionalist tradition of socialism that gave rise to the Labour Party by way of the Independent Labour Party (ILP).[1] Then, during the latter half of the twentieth century, most historians dismissed the Fabians as largely inconsequential. Eric Hobsbawm and Alan McBriar led those who argued that the ILP took its strategy from labor Marxists such as H.H. Champion, with the Fabians having little impact on the rise of a popular socialist movement or on the Labour Party.[2] These revisionists condemned the Fabians as elitist and irrelevant. The Fabians were elitist because they ignored the grassroots of working-class politics in favor of the high politics of the day. They were irrelevant because the Labour Party arose from the interaction between the ILP and the trade unions, both of which had been ignored, or even opposed, by the permeation-besotted Fabians. The Fabians were bypassed by the rise of a new class-based politics associated with Marxism and, of course, the working class itself.

A version of this chapter appeared as "Fabianism, Permeation and Independent Labour," *Historical Journal* 39 (1996), 179–196. Published by Cambridge University Press.

[1] See G. Shaw, "The Fabian Society: What It Has Done and How It Has Done It," *Fabian Tract* 41 (1892). Also see M. Cole, *The Story of Fabian Socialism* (London: Heinemann, 1961); A. Freemantle, *This Little Brand of Prophets* (London: G. Allen, 1960); J. Milburn, "The Fabian Society and the British Labour Party," *Western Political Quarterly* (1958): 319–40; E. Pease, *The History of the Fabian Society* (London: A. Fifield, 1916); P. Pugh, *Educate, Agitate, Organise* (London: Methuen, 1984); and D. Ricci, "Fabian Socialism: A Theory of Rent as Exploitation," *Journal of British Studies* 9 (1969): 105–21.

[2] See E. Hobsbawm, "The Fabians Reconsidered," in *Labouring Men* (London: Weidenfeld and Nicolson, 1964); and A. McBriar, *Fabian Socialism and English Politics* (Cambridge: Cambridge University, 1962). The revisionists' view of the labor Marxists derives from H. Pelling, "H. H. Champion: Pioneer of Labour Representation," *Cambridge Journal* 6 (1953): 222–38. Also see G. Foote, *The Labour Party's Political Thought* (London: Croom Helm, 1986); S. Pierson, *Marxism and the Origins of British Socialism* (Ithaca, NY: Cornell University Press, 1973); and, to a lesser extent, P. Thompson, *Socialists, Liberals and Labour, 1885–1914* (Oxford: Clarendon Press, 1965).

The debate over the impact of the Fabians is one in which both sides capture part of the truth. Equally, both go awry. The problem is that both sides in the debate treat Fabianism as a monolithic and stable political strategy, and more particularly they treat the Fabians as liberal radicals who consistently and uniformly committed themselves to a high politics in which they provided expert ideas to other constitutional parties. The two sides disagree only about whether or not these ideas were important for the creation of the Labour Party. The positive view concentrates on the continuities between liberal radicalism and the Labour Party and presents the Fabians as the main bridge between the two. The negative view concentrates on the place of working-class identities, interests, and organizations in the formation of the Labour Party, thereby dismissing the Fabians' high politics and liberal inheritance.

Yet, in previous chapters, we found that Fabianism was neither monolithic nor stable. Fabianism was often in flux, especially in the crucial years of the 1880s and the early 1890s leading up to the formation of the ILP in 1893. The early Fabians were involved with the Fellowship of the New Life and Christian socialism as well as land reform and Marxism. Most had responded to the crisis of faith with a reformist humanitarianism that left them rather dissatisfied with the scientism and secularism of the Social Democratic Federation. But they did not have a clear alternative social or economic theory. It was only in the mid- to late 1880s that leading Fabians drew on alternative economic theories to provide novel defenses of socialism. Even then, moreover, Fabianism accommodated various conflicting theories. Different Fabians provided varied defenses of socialism by drawing on marginalist, neoclassical, and positivist economic theories.

This chapter explores the Fabians' fluid and diverse political strategies. It begins by distinguishing two main varieties of permeation, one associated with George Bernard Shaw and the other with Sidney Webb. Thereafter the chapter explores the rise and shifting fortunes of these two political strategies within the Fabian Society as a whole, looking especially at their role in defining the Society's attitude to the formation and growth of the ILP.

Varieties of Permeation

Contemporaries were well aware of the diverse political strategies found among the Fabians. As late as 1887, Brailsford Bright, who was a Fabian, identified three competing outlooks.

British Socialists may, at present, be divided into three sections, namely: (1) The Social Democrats of the Federation, and certain members of the Fabian and Christian Socialist Societies, and others who wish to remain an entirely distinct party. ... (2) Those Fabians and others who prefer to make use of the existing Radical party, forming an "Extreme Left" wing thereof. ... (3) Those who hold aloof from all existing parties without forming any political party or groups of their own, but would support any party, or any individual candidate or member of Parliament, who, for the time being, seemed to be promoting the growth of Socialism.[3]

Historians typically place Hubert Bland in the first category but fail to distinguish the second and third categories. Yet the Fabians debated the merits of the second and third categories long after they broke with Marxism. Shaw generally advocated a strategy akin to Bright's second category. Webb led those who countered with one akin to Bright's third category.

Shaw's and Webb's different political strategies derived from their respective economic theories. Shaw's marginalist theory of rent continued to overlap with Marxist theories, such as those of the O'Brienites in the Social Democratic Federation (SDF). Surplus value consisted of, first, an economic rent due to natural advantages of fertility and location and, second, monopoly payments made for the privilege of using the means of production at all. Like many Marxists, he argued that monopolies enabled capitalists and landlords to charge workers for access to the means of production.[4] Capitalists, qua monopolists, exploited the workers. Shaw's economic theory thus suggested that there was a class struggle between workers and monopolists. According to Shaw, socialism made explicit the radicals' implicit idea of an irreconcilable clash of interests between these warring classes.

Early Fabians such as Bland and Shaw did not break with the SDF because they rejected the idea of class struggle. They believed in the class struggle. They just did not believe that the workers were revolutionary.[5]

[3] J. Brailsford Bright, "English Possibilists," *Practical Socialist* 2 (1887): 10.

[4] Most contemporary socialists interpreted Marx as having made similar arguments. See H. Hyndman, *The Text Book of Democracy: England for All* (London: G. Allen, 1881), pp. 39–50; W. Morris, "Monopoly; or, How Labour Is Robbed," in *The Collected Works of William Morris*, introd. M. Morris (London: Longmans, 1910–15), vol. 23: *Signs of Change: Lectures on Socialism*, pp. 238–54; S. Olivier, "Perverse Socialism," *To-day* 6 (1886): 47–55 and 109–14; and S. Webb, "Rent, Interest and Wages: Being a Criticism of Karl Marx and a Statement of Economic Theory," Passfield Papers, BLPES, London, PP:VII:4.

[5] See the autobiographical accounts in H. Bland, *Essays by Hubert Bland*, ed. E. Nesbit (London: Goschen, 1914); and G. Shaw, *Sixteen Self Sketches* (London: Constable, 1949).

Bland explained that "the revolt of the empty stomach ends at the baker's shop."[6] Shaw believed that although one might expect current injustices to lead the workers to rise up to set things to right, "an army of light is no more to be gathered from the human product of nineteenth-century civilisation than grapes are to be gathered from thistles."[7]

Bland and Shaw advocated a parliamentary road to socialism, rather than a revolutionary one. Yet, they argued that the class struggle implied socialists could not expect any help from the owners of property. The Liberal Party was useless because it represented the monopolists, whose interests were diametrically opposed to those of the workers. A new party was thus essential. Bland called for "the formation of a definitely Socialist party."[8] Shaw told the editor of the *Scots Observer*, "I thirst for the blood of the Liberal Party; and if ever your sham fight with them becomes a real one, you may come to me for a lead."[9] Bland, Shaw, and several other early Fabians wanted a new socialist party. Shaw asked that a Fabian manifesto "emphatically repudiate the Liberal Party and denounce Gladstone in express terms"; he argued that we should "proclaim ourselves, not an advanced guard of the Liberal party, but definitely Social-Democratic."[10]

Shaw wanted a new socialist party to fight the monopolists of the Liberal and Conservative parties. Yet, when the SDF entered candidates in the general election of 1885, they got little support. Shaw then concluded that a new party was not currently feasible. Most workers were radicals but not socialists. Socialists initially would have to concentrate their energies on building the support they needed to sustain a future political party. Where, though, were socialists to find this support? Shaw looked to the extreme radicals. He argued that radicals and socialists were natural allies because the radicals implicitly recognized the class struggle. Indeed, he believed that the Liberal Party would split and the radicals would join the socialists. Liberals and radicals were not natural allies. They could cohabit momentarily only because of their mutual support for home rule for Ireland. Once the issue of home rule disappeared, the liberals and radicals would go their separate ways. Shaw advised a liberal friend of his to "read the Star & watch the struggle between *our* Social Democratic

[6] H. Bland, "The Socialist Party in Relation to Politics," *Practical Socialist* 1 (1886): 156.

[7] G. Shaw, "Transition," in *Fabian Essays*, ed. G. Shaw, intro. A. Briggs (London: Allen and Unwin, 1962), p. 235.

[8] H. Bland, "The Outlook," Ibid., p. 253. Also see Bland, "Socialist Party" and "The Need of a New Departure," *To-day* 8 (1887): 131–41.

[9] G. Shaw, *Collected Letters*, ed. D. Laurence, 4 vols. (London: Reinhardt, 1965–88), vol. 1: *1874–1897*, p. 252.

[10] Ibid., p. 276.

editor [Massingham] & *your* Home Rule Liberal editor [O'Connor]." He asked the friend, "When you have grasped the situation, will you join Goschen & [will] Hartington join us?" And he told the friend, "Home Rule is not eternal, and when it is settled, the *via media* vanishes."[11]

According to Shaw, radicalism had an innate trajectory toward a new socialist party. The class struggle pitched the radical workers against the monopolists controlling the Liberal Party, and the dynamics of this struggle would drive the radicals to socialism. Shaw wanted the Fabians to declare themselves "prepared to act with the Radical party as far as that party pursues its historic mission of overthrowing Capitalist Liberalism in the interest of the working classes, but utterly hostile to it as far as it is only the tail of the National Liberal Federation."[12] Clearly Shaw did not foresee the Liberal Party's being driven to socialism by the wire-pulling of the Fabians. Instead, he believed that the class struggle would produce a split within the Liberal Party. After this split, there would be two parties, one of which would consist of the monopolists and the other would unite the workers. The Liberals would combine with the Tories in a party of reaction. The radicals would combine with the socialists in a "real Party of Progress."[13]

The question facing Shaw was how best to bring out the implicit conflict between workers and monopolists. How could socialists lure the radicals away from the Liberal Party and into the socialist camp? Initially, Shaw adopted the SDF's strategy of zealous propaganda and outdoor demonstrations. In the late 1880s Shaw began to advocate what he called permeation. He wanted socialists to join radical organizations and work within them to turn the radicals into socialists. For example, he advised the North Kensington branch of the SDF to pursue a Fabian policy and "throw in their lot with the Radicals," because "socialism must be established, if it is to come at all, by the whole working class of the country."[14] Socialists should cooperate with the radicals in order to gain the support of the workers, not to influence the Liberals. Socialists could work with radicals, since most radicals were workers who opposed monopoly. But socialists could not work with Liberals, since most Liberals were monopolists who defended private property.

Shaw's aim of luring the radicals away from the Liberals stands in contrast to Webb's version of permeation. Webb believed that economic surpluses, such as land rent and interest, derived entirely from advantages

[11] Ibid., p. 235.
[12] Ibid., p. 276. Compare G. Shaw, "The Attitude of Socialists towards Other Bodies," Shaw Papers, British Library, London, BM:50700-5.
[13] *Star*, 1 April 1889.
[14] G. Shaw, *Letters*, vol. 1, pp. 350–51.

of fertility, location, and circumstances. He objected to the surpluses going to individuals on the grounds that these advantages were not necessary to attract capital and they were a result not of personal effort or ability but of social forces. In his view, all surplus value was social value rather than a tribute taken from the worker. There was no class war and therefore no need for a new party. Indeed, when Webb first declared he was a socialist, he advocated the moralization of the capitalist. Only in the late 1880s did he begin to advocate collectivism, defining socialism as the efficient organization of society as prescribed by empirical sociology. Webb believed that socialism was based on rational knowledge of social evolution. Socialism could rise from experts' appealing to the rationality of the policy-making elite. The "intelligence of the natural leaders of the community" would lead them to accept the need for socialism.[15] Webb wanted to win over the minds of opinion makers, not the votes of radicals. He told Edward Pease that "nothing in England is done without the consent of a small intellectual yet practical class in London not 2000 in number."[16]

Webb's version of permeation began with the idea of Fabian experts showing politicians what policies were necessary for an efficient society. The Fabians would be backroom boys coming up with the bright ideas that rational politicians would adopt as a matter of course. In principle, the target of this permeation was a cross-party elite, since Conservatives too would recognize the impartial merits of socialist policies. In practice, however, Webb considered Liberals more open than Conservatives to Fabian expertise. He foresaw the Liberals adopting a progressive program, getting elected, and then introducing socialist legislation, with the Fabians providing them with suitable policies. Webb saw the Fabian Society as an intellectual advisory group—a Jeeves to the Liberal Party's Bertie Wooster. The problem was that the Liberal elite did not always stick to the script. Webb told Beatrice Potter (before they got married) that "it is difficult to know how to treat the Liberal leaders" because "they are generally such poor creatures, and so hopelessly 'out of it'"; "I wish their education could be taken in hand in some way that would save the Fabian Society from becoming more and more conceited."[17] By the end of the 1880s, Webb became so concerned that the Liberal elite were not listening to the Fabians' advice that he extended his strategy of permeation

[15] S. Webb, *English Progress towards Social Democracy* (London: Modern, 1888), p. 15. For an example of his use of facts to appeal to common reason, see S. Webb, "Facts for Socialists," *Fabian Tract 5* (1887).

[16] S. Webb and B. Webb, *The Letters of Sidney and Beatrice Webb*, ed. N. MacKenzie, 3 vols. (Cambridge: Cambridge University, 1978), vol. 1: *Apprenticeships, 1873–1892*, p. 102.

[17] Ibid., p. 132.

to include joining local Liberal associations and using them as platforms from which to gain the ears of the Liberal elite.

Generally, Webb opposed independent socialist candidates for Parliament. He believed that independent action was unnecessary because the existing parties could be shown the impartial advantages of socialism and thus led to introduce suitable legislation. He also believed that independent action was impolitic because it would antagonize the local Liberal associations through which socialists could best influence the Liberal elite. Unlike Shaw, Webb did not want to split the Liberal Party, luring the radicals over to a new socialist party. Instead, he argued that the existing Liberal Party was quite capable of establishing socialism. He spoke of his hopes of the Liberals, not the radicals, saying, "I feel no doubt that we shall be able to drive the official Liberals on into a very sea of Socialism."[18]

THE FABIAN SOCIETY IN THE 1880s

When permeation rose in the Fabian Society, it could mean either pulling the radicals into a new party, as it did for Shaw, or using local Liberal groups to influence Liberal elites, as it did for Webb. Most of the early Fabians favored Shaw's strategy. They were less interested in foisting socialist policies onto a recalcitrant Liberal Party than in forging a new party of radicals and socialists that would advance the interests of the workers. It was only after the Fabians had broken with Marxism and anarchism that Webb began to propose his alternative idea of permeation.

As we have seen, the founding Fabians were a mixture of radicals involved with land reform on the fringes of the SDF. The first executive committee of the Society consisted of Bland, Frank Podmore, and Frederick Keddell, a Marxist who soon left to commit himself entirely to the SDF. The second executive consisted of Bland, Alice Hoatson (who was Bland's lover), Pease, Shaw, and Charlotte Wilson.[19] Most of these Fabians thought that radicalism led inexorably to socialism, since both were based on hostility to monopolies and the class-based exploitation to which they gave rise. Shaw had no difficulty getting the other Fabians to agree in 1884 to his publishing a tract on behalf of the Society in which he insisted that everybody should labor to provide for his or her wants, that monopolies of land and capital caused poverty and divided society into warring classes, and that the solution to these problems lay in land

[18] Ibid., p. 220.
[19] For a list of executive members, see Pease, *History*, appendix 3. Also see Minutes of the Executive Committee, Fabian Papers, BLEPS.

nationalization and state competition with private enterprise.[20] When Annie Besant joined the Fabians in 1885, she too talked of socialism as the logical outcome of radicalism and so of the need to wean the radicals away from the Liberal Party.[21]

The early Fabians wanted a new party that would combine socialists and radicals. They worked mainly with the Marxists of the SDF to attract radicals to the socialist cause. For a start, they joined in the Marxists' outdoor propaganda. Besant was a much practiced stump orator who spoke from both SDF and Fabian platforms. Shaw joined the SDF in the struggle to prevent the police from closing the speakers' corner at Dod Street. In addition, the early Fabians spent numerous evenings proselytizing to secularists and other radicals. Besant had been a vice president of the National Secular Society, and, as a socialist, she now held public debates with prominent secularists and spoke at local secularist branches and radical clubs.[22] Shaw gave sixty-six public lectures in one year alone. As one of his biographers writes, "Every Sunday he spoke, usually in the London area, sometimes against the blaring of brass bands, often at workmen's clubs and coffee houses, to secular societies and radical associations, expounding and arguing from squalid platforms in dens full of tobacco smoke, to a little knot of members."[23] The goal of this propaganda and proselytizing remained a new party uniting radicals and socialists. In 1886 the Fabians organized a conference of radicals and socialists, including members of the SDF, at South Place Chapel, to discuss a "common basis on which Radicals, Socialists, and Social Reformers of all kinds can cooperate for practical work in and out of parliament."[24]

At first Fabian opposition to the attempt to forge a new party came from Wilson and her anarchism. The early Fabians and the SDF had to defend their strategy against Wilson and the Socialist League. As we saw in chapter 7, the Fabians decisively rejected anarchism at an open meeting in 1886. Afterward, they formed the Fabian Parliamentary League. The original Council of the League included Ashman, Besant, Bland, T. Bolas, Brailsford Bright, Sydney Olivier, and Shaw, almost all of whom seem to have favored a new socialist party. The League's manifesto called on British socialists to follow the lead of those Continental socialists who had made electoral progress in local and national government. In

[20] G. Shaw, "A Manifesto," *Fabian Tract* 2 (1884).

[21] A. Besant, *Radicalism and Socialism* (London: Freethought, 1887); and *Link*, 7 April 1888.

[22] A. Besant and G. Foote, *Is Socialism Sound?* (London: Freethought, 1887).

[23] M. Holroyd, *Bernard Shaw* (Harmondsworth, UK: Penguin, 1988–94), vol. 1: *1856–1898: The Search for Love*, pp. 192–93.

[24] "Fabian Notes," *Our Corner* 7 (1886): 189. On the proceedings, also see A. Besant, "The Fabian Conference," *To-day* 6 (1886): 8–14.

local elections the League would even run candidates where it was strong enough. In general elections the League proposed supporting the candidate who was most sympathetic to socialism "until a fitting opportunity arises for putting forward Socialist candidates to form the nucleus of a Socialist party in Parliament."[25]

When Webb joined the Fabians in May 1885, he found himself opposed to the Society's strategy. He disapproved not only of Wilson's anarchism, but also of the strategy of the other early Fabians. He was less concerned with founding a new party than with promoting socialist policies through the Liberal Party. Initially, Webb's only real ally among the Fabians was Graham Wallas, who joined the Fabian Society in 1886. Like Webb, Wallas rejected the class war and considered the Liberal Party quite capable of introducing socialism through piecemeal legislation. So, while Besant, Bland, Pease, Podmore, Shaw, and the others were trying to draw the radicals away from the Liberals, Webb wrote to Wallas identifying their electoral interests with those of the Liberals and then complaining, "We have gone a tremendous crash in the towns."[26] Wallas and Webb initially opposed the Fabian Parliamentary League on the grounds that an independent party would hamper efforts to provide the Liberals with an efficient socialist program. Webb complained to Pease, "I hardly understand your so heartily supporting the party of action rather than education."[27]

So, in the late 1880s, the Fabians were unevenly split between two rival political strategies. Shaw and the larger "party of action" wanted to build a new party. Webb and the smaller "party of education" hoped to infiltrate the Liberal elite with socialism. The unusual nature of London politics enabled these two parties to agree on a single strategy at the local level. The Local Government Act of 1888 had at long last created a citywide government in the form of the London County Council (LCC). The members of the LCC split into Progressives, who were generally radical reformers, and Moderates, who did not want to go so far so quickly. The Progressive councillors included John Burns of the SDF. They introduced legislation to give council workers an eight-hour day and to write a fair-wages clause into council contracts. All the Fabians were happy to support the Progressives in London politics. Shaw and the party of action saw the Progressives as a local example of radicals and socialists combining in a new party. Wallas and Webb may have wanted to work with the Liberal Party, but as there was no Liberal Party on the LCC, they decided to work with the Progressives. All the Fabians

[25] "Fabian Parliamentary League Manifesto," *Practical Socialist* 2 (1887): 47.

[26] Webb and Webb, *Letters*, vol. 1, pp. 94–95.

[27] Ibid., pp. 101–2.

agreed on working with the Progressives in London. Indeed, when Wallas and Webb joined the council of the Fabian Parliamentary League, they steered it firmly toward local politics and away from national political action. In 1888 Besant wrote a lead article, and Webb wrote a letter, in which they both proposed joint democratic committees to coordinate the votes of radicals and socialists in the election for the London School Board.[28] Thereafter Webb became the Fabians' acknowledged expert on local government, writing numerous tracts outlining and defending a program of municipal reform.[29]

Although the Fabians agreed on a strategy for London, they disagreed on national politics. Whereas Shaw wanted to attract the radicals to a third party, Webb thought that the threat of a third party was useful only as a way of encouraging Liberals to adopt progressive policies. So, when the Liberal Party disappointed the socialists by adopting the Nottingham Programme of 1887, Shaw responded with a "Radical programme" that was meant to pull radicals toward socialism, whereas Webb wrote a pamphlet for private circulation among "leading London Liberals," calling on them to adopt a program that would win the support of radical workingmen.[30]

The late 1880s saw a subtle shift in Shaw's strategy. The mid-1880s had been a time of mass unemployment and social unrest. Besant, Shaw, and others joined rallies and meetings. Trafalgar Square became a center of socialist protest. On 8 November 1887, the police forbade demonstrators to enter the square. The ban exacerbated matters. Few radicals had shown sympathy for the unemployed, but they complained that the ban infringed on the right to free speech. Radicals and socialists arranged a joint rally against coercion in Ireland to culminate in the square in defiance of the ban. The date, 13 November 1887, became known as Bloody Sunday. Four columns of demonstrators set out from different parts of London to reach the square simultaneously. Besant and Shaw marched at the head of the column from the East End. The police baton-charged the demonstrators and broke up the protest before sizable numbers could reach the square. One hundred and fifty people were detained. Three days later a socialist died of injuries sustained on that day. Bloody Sunday led Shaw to reconsider his political strategy. He turned away from vigorous propaganda and toward his version of permeation. He wanted socialists to infiltrate local Liberal organizations so as to convert radicals to the need for a new party.

[28] *Link*, 2 June 1888.

[29] S. Webb, *The London Programme* (London: Swan Sonnenschein, 1891).

[30] G. Shaw, "The True Radical Programme," *Fabian Tract* 6 (1887); S. Webb, *Wanted a Programme: An Appeal to the Liberal Party* (London: Labour, 1888).

At the same time, Webb modified his political strategy. Webb had never shown much interest in political demonstrations. He had spent the mid-1880s making direct approaches to the Liberal elite; he sent his draft of an Eight Hours Bill to Herbert Gladstone, one of the Liberal Party managers, and a Fabian tract on leasehold enfranchisement to every Liberal MP just before a parliamentary debate on that issue.[31] It was in the late 1880s, however, that Webb started to complain about the difficulties of getting the Liberal elite to listen. He began to stress the importance of participating in local Liberal associations as a means of securing the attention of the elite. Just after Bloody Sunday, he wrote to Pease ignoring "the most sensational political event of the year." He concentrated instead on the tactic of working through local Liberal associations to win over Liberal politicians.

> I believe very much in getting hold of the Liberal caucuses. They are just on the turn, without knowing it, and a little push from inside does much to send them in our direction. I hope you take part in the Newcastle one. Champion relates how he talked the matter over with John Morley [the Liberal MP for Newcastle], who was quite friendly and sympathetic with our aims, but said he had not had occasion to look into social matters, and could not do so at present, as his constituents *were not interested in the questions.* Now this is just where the use of political Socialism comes in. If you managed to get resolutions passed at ward meetings etc., as to the necessity of dealing with these things, John Morley would take them up.[32]

After Bloody Sunday, both Shaw and Webb adopted the tactic of joining Liberal groups. However, whereas Webb tried thereby to get Liberal leaders to adopt socialist policies, Shaw hoped to attract the radicals to a new party.

THE FABIANS AND THE ILP

Most of the early Fabians wanted a new party. Webb led a minority who instead concentrated their hopes on Liberal politicians. These different strategies rarely came into conflict during the late 1880s because the socialists were too weak for a new party to be a serious prospect. The Fabians agreed on a single strategy at the local level and went their separate ways at the national level. Besant and Shaw marched on Tra-

---

[31] Webb and Webb, *Letters*, vol. 1, p. 157; S. Webb, "An Eight Hours Bill," *Fabian Tract* 9 (1889), and "The Truth about Leasehold Enfranchisement," *Fabian Tract* 22 (1890).

[32] Webb and Webb, *Letters*, vol. 1, p. 109.

falgar Square. Webb posted draft bills of Parliament to MPs. However, in the early 1890s, socialism expanded rapidly. Much of this expansion occurred with the rise of ethical socialism, which we will explore in later chapters. Yet, the Fabian Society too attracted large numbers of new recruits, partly due to the triumphal publication of *Fabian Essays*, partly because of an extremely successful lecture tour, and partly because of the spread of ethical socialism in the northern counties. The Fabians spread out of London, with new branches appearing in places such as Bradford, Bristol, Manchester, and Sheffield. The London Fabian Society grew from 173 members in 1890 to 640 members in 1893. Membership in the rest of the country grew from about 350 in 1891 to about 1,300 in 1892.[33] The spread of socialism made a new party an increasingly viable prospect.

Typically the new socialists strongly favored a new and independent socialist party. Robert Blatchford, Katherine Conway, Keir Hardie, and Ben Tillett joined the Fabian Society, but they devoted their energy to forming local labor parties with the ultimate aim of creating a national socialist party. For example, the Independent Labour Party in Manchester was founded by Blatchford and John Trevor, both of whom were members of the Fabian Society. While Webb dallied with the Liberals, and while Shaw tried to use Liberal associations to convert radicals to socialism, the new socialists were forming local organizations that constituted the nucleus of the future ILP. Support for a new party reached new levels among the Fabians. When the Society held its first annual conference in February 1892, fifteen local societies sent delegates, who passed a motion declaring that "this meeting, being of the opinion that the best way to forward the Labour cause is by the workers acting independently of both political parties, hails with satisfaction the formation of an independent labour party, and heartily wishes success to the movement."[34]

How did the leading Fabians react to the growing demand for an independent labor party? In brief, Webb opposed such a party, whereas Shaw continued to support the idea of a new party, insisting on certain conditions only because he saw them as essential if an independent party were to prove workable.

Shaw told the first annual conference of the Fabians that the permeation "game is played out," and "the time has come for a new departure."[35]

---

[33] For membership figures, see H. Pelling, *The Origins of the Labour Party, 1880–1900* (Oxford: Clarendon Press, 1965), appendix A.

[34] *Workman's Times*, 13 February 1892. The ILP was not formed until 1893, but even before its formation the word "party" was used to describe the growing movement of labor clubs.

[35] G. Shaw, "Fabian Society," pp. 20 and 19.

In his view, permeation had involved working in Liberal organizations to wean the radicals away from the Liberal leaders, and it had succeeded.

> The Radicals are at last conscious that the leaders are obstructing them; and they say to us, in effect, "Your policy of permeating has been successful: we *are* permeated; and the result is that we find all the money and all the official power of our leaders, who are not permeated and cannot be permeated, arrayed against us. Now show us how to get rid of those leaders or to fight them." [36]

Permeation had worked. For a start, socialist propaganda and education had turned numerous radicals into socialists. Shaw argued that "there are thousands of thoroughly Socialised Radicals to-day who would have resisted Socialism fiercely if it had been forced upon them with taunts, threats, and demands." [37] More importantly, permeation had thereby made visible the class struggle between Liberals and radicals—"property *versus* labour." [38] The result would surely be party realignment. On the one side, when the Liberal leaders realized what was going on, they would not only resist permeation but "close up the ranks of capitalism against the insidious invaders." [39] On the other side, a new party combining socialists and radicals was now a real possibility.

Nonetheless, Shaw warned that there remained the problems of organization and of funding. Certainly, there was enough support for an independent party, but "it is one thing to make people shout and another to make them pay." [40] The workers were capable of funding an independent party, but they might choose not to do so, preferring beer and football to liberty. Shaw believed that "there are unfortunately very few constituencies in which the Working Classes are politically organised enough to take the overwhelming lead in politics which their superiority in numbers has placed within their reach." [41] Any workable socialist strategy had to take account of the lack of political organization among the workers. Moreover, Britain's first-past-the-post electoral system meant that there was a danger that independent candidates would not only fail to get elected but also split the progressive vote, and so enable reactionaries to triumph. Shaw advised the workers to run an independent candidate only where, first, the candidate had a good chance of winning or polling well enough to add respectability to the labor cause or, second, the Liberal and Conservative candidates were equally backward on labor issues.

[36] Ibid., p. 20.
[37] Ibid.
[38] G. Shaw, "The Fabian Election Manifesto," *Fabian Tract* 40 (1892): 5.
[39] G. Shaw, "Fabian Society," p. 19.
[40] G. Shaw, "Fabian Election Manifesto," p. 9.
[41] Ibid., p. 7.

Elsewhere the workers should support the most progressive candidate among those available.

The Fabians adopted Shaw's proposals as their manifesto for the general election of 1892. In Bradford they supported Tillett as a labor candidate because they believed he had a chance to win. In Newcastle they backed a Liberal candidate, John Morley, against a labor candidate on the grounds that the labor cause was hopeless and the candidate would split the progressive vote.[42]

Shaw took a similar view of the growing movement to establish an independent labor party. He argued that the success of permeation had established sufficient support for such a party, but there remained problems of finance. He favored a new party, while proposing that in the absence of a suitable organization, it should remain flexible over its tactics. A new party should vary its tactics locally, running its own candidates in some constituencies and trying to get the Liberals to adopt progressive candidates in others. Indeed, Shaw now defined permeation as much in terms of local flexibility as in terms of luring the radicals away from the Liberals. He equated permeation with "non-centralised local organisation of the Labour Party."[43]

A conference chaired by Hardie to found a national ILP was organized for January 1893 in Bradford. Shaw felt trepidation as the conference drew near. For a start, although he supported the new party, he worried that a national organization would undermine local flexibility. His main concern was the fourth clause of the Manchester ILP, which pledged its members not to vote for any candidate associated with another political party. In addition, Shaw feared that a Tory plot might lie behind the Bradford conference. Burns had become a Liberal politician, and he fueled this fear. Shaw told Burns, "I have been thinking over what you told me, and I think it looks like a formidable Unionist intrigue with Champion at the wires."[44] Many Fabians shared Shaw's suspicion. Champion was already notorious for his part in the 1885 scandal over Tory Gold in the SDF. Moreover, there were rumors that when Hardie stood for the parliamentary seat of Mid-Lanark in 1888, he had been a "tool" of the "Tory intriguer."[45] Nasty questions had been asked about Hardie's funds. Margaret Harkness eased the pressure, saying publicly that she had donated one hundred pounds. Yet, privately she indicated to Beatrice Webb that

---

[42] *Workman's Times*, 27 August 1892.

[43] G. Shaw, *Letters*, vol. 1, p. 377.

[44] Ibid., p. 356; for an indication of what Burns said, see p. 362.

[45] *Justice*, 17 May 1890. Also see Engels to Sorge, 18 January 1893, in K. Marx and F. Engels, *Letters to Americans, 1848–1895*, trans. L. Mins (New York: International Publishers, 1953).

she was just a go-between who had not donated a penny.[46] No wonder, then, that Shaw described Hardie as one of the "ultra-Opportunist ex-candidates who do not object to contest Parliamentary seats in the name of Labour with finances derived from the man in the moon."[47]

The London Fabians sent W. S. De Mattos and Shaw as delegates to the Bradford conference with the provisos that attending the conference did not imply that the Fabian Society would merge into a national labor movement or that it would be bound by any decisions the conference reached. The conference debated the Fabians' credentials before voting to allow them to attend.[48] Shaw was delighted by the proceedings. His fears proved unfounded. The conference refused to have any truck with Champion and rejected the restriction on flexibility embodied in clause four. As Shaw explained, the conference refused "the Tory money move," and when the anti-permeationists "wheeled up their big gun (the 'fourth clause')," the delegates "spiked it at one smack," securing "the freedom of the branches to nobble the Liberals wherever that is obviously the right Labour policy."[49]

Shaw now began to look forward to a time when the Fabians would concentrate on "bringing the Labour party up to the Socialist mark instead of bringing the Radical wing of the Liberal party up to the Independent Labour mark."[50] He thought that the ILP would split the radicals from the Liberals, and then the socialists could turn from the need to establish a new party incorporating the radicals to the task of ensuring that this new party embraced a properly socialist program. In Shaw's view, the only remaining difficulty was financial. Tactical flexibility was necessary only because of organizational weakness. If the ILP had secure funds, it could forget about tactical flexibility and become an effective national party capable of competing in elections to form the government. Shaw made the financial support of the trade unions the litmus test of the viability of independent action.[51] Without the unions' backing, the ILP would be just another socialist sect, a more flexible, and so slightly superior, version of the SDF. To develop into Shaw's cherished new party, the ILP needed the financial backing of the trade unions.

At the 1891 Trades Union Congress (TUC), Hardie had proposed a penny levy on union members to finance a parliamentary fund for

[46] B. Webb, *The Diary of Beatrice Webb*, ed. N. and J. Mackenzie, 4 vols. (London: Virago, 1982–85), vol. 1: *1873–1892*, p. 302.

[47] *Workman's Times*, 28 January 1893.

[48] *Report of the First General Conference of the I.L.P. Held at Bradford on 13 and 14 January 1893* (Glasgow: Labour Literature Society, 1893).

[49] *Workman's Times*, 28 January 1893. Also see G. Shaw, *Letters*, vol. 1, pp. 378–79.

[50] *Workman's Times*, 22 April 1893.

[51] Ibid., 2 December 1893.

labor candidates, but his motion had been defeated by two hundred votes to ninety-three. Now, the 1893 TUC declared for public ownership of the means of production and passed Tillett's motion providing for financial aid to labor candidates in local and parliamentary elections. (Burns helped to ensure that the motion covered workingmen standing as Liberals or Conservatives as well as independent candidates.) In Shaw's mind, this motion clinched the matter. The ILP could obtain the financing, as well as the support, needed to become a national force capable of winning parliamentary seats. He had the new party for which he had long wished.

While Shaw promoted and engaged the ILP, Webb remained noticeably distant, wedded to the Liberal elite. He spent much of 1891 talking to Mr. Fenton about a safe Progressive seat on the LCC, and he even raised with Francis Schnadhorst the possibility of his standing as a Liberal candidate for Parliament in South Islington.[52] Webb and his allies were assiduously courting the ears of Liberal politicians such as H. H. Asquith, Edward Grey, R. B. Haldane, and Lord Rosebery. For example, in 1890 Beatrice Webb spoke to Wallas and Haldane in an attempt to forge links between the Fabians and the Liberal elite. When she visited London in early 1891, she discussed her plans with Wallas and Webb but no other Fabian.[53] Clearly, these three were not thinking of a new party. On the contrary, they actively opposed the enthusiasm of other Fabians for an independent labor party. At the end of 1891, Webb explained to Beatrice that Wallas could not visit her for the weekend because Wallas was needed at a Fabian meeting to "save the society" from the "impatient element" that wants "to throw the whole movement entirely into the Labour Party."[54] Webb spoke publicly against the idea of a labor party at a meeting on 11 December 1891. He reiterated his belief that socialism was about social feeling, not class militancy. He wanted a collectivist party "not restricted to manual workers or any one class ... [and] ... not pursuing its own class interest, but open to all and seeking the welfare of the whole community."[55] Webb found little support among the Fabians. He complained that "Wallas and I are losing influence because we are suspected of too much attachment to the Liberal Party."[56]

Ironically, Webb was growing increasingly disillusioned with the Liberals. He protested that the new Fabians had turned on him, even though "these nine months have not made me more Liberal, but less."[57] Webb

[52] Webb and Webb, *Letters*, vol. 1, pp. 258 and 271.
[53] Ibid., pp. 241, 250, 252–54, and 256.
[54] Ibid., p. 350.
[55] Ibid., p. 355.
[56] Ibid., p. 237.
[57] Ibid., p. 354.

believed that the Liberals were drifting without a suitable program. The Liberal government elected in 1892 incensed him by failing to live up to the promise of the 1889 Newcastle program. A disgruntled Webb told Wallas, "The time has come I think for a strong tract showing up the Liberal Party."[58]

By 1893 Shaw was full of enthusiasm for an independent labor party, and Webb was disillusioned with the Liberals. Together they wrote a Fabian tract, "To Your Tents, O Israel," which attacked the Liberal government for failing to implement the Newcastle Program and called on the workers to abandon the Liberals, form a trade-union party, raise thirty thousand pounds, and finance fifty parliamentary candidates.[59] The Fabians called for an independent working-class party backed by the trade unions. Unfortunately, the financial plan adopted by the 1893 TUC relied exclusively on voluntary subscriptions from individual unions. By 1894 most people realized that the individual unions were not going to respond without more vigorous encouragement. Shaw's hopes were dashed. The leading Fabians tried to return to their various styles of permeation. But "To Your Tents, O Israel" had damaged their relationship with the Liberals. Friendly government ministers and other Liberal politicians felt aggrieved at the dismissal of their efforts to introduce suitable policies.[60] Liberal Fabians, such as H. W. Massingham and D. G. Ritchie, resigned from the Society. As a result, the Fabians found it increasingly difficult to work through the Liberals. Pease recalled, "At this point the policy of simple permeation of the Liberal Party may be said to have come to an end."[61]

For the rest of the century, the Fabians limped on with wounded forms of their respective versions of permeation. Shaw continued to argue that permeation "breaks down at a certain point because the parties in power are neither Socialists nor members of the working class working unconsciously towards Socialism in pursuit of their own interests."[62] He maintained that until a suitable alternative appeared, the Fabians should remain tactically flexible, advancing socialism however circumstances suggested.[63] The Webbs, who got married in 1892, repented of their ear-

---

[58] Ibid., vol. 2: *Partnership, 1892–1912*, p. 9.

[59] G. Shaw and S. Webb, "To Your Tents, O Israel," *Fortnightly Review* 60 (1893): 569–89. For an indication of the importance of the decision of the 1893 TUC to finance parliamentary candidates as a cause of the attack on the Liberal government and the call for a trade-union party, see Fabian Society, "Annual Report for the Year Ended March 1894," Fabian Papers.

[60] B. Webb, *Our Partnership* (Cambridge: Cambridge University Press, 1975), p. 110.

[61] Pease, *History*, p. 117.

[62] G. Shaw, "Typescript Syllabus of 1896," BM:50557.

[63] G. Shaw, "Report on Fabian Policy," *Fabian Tract* 70 (1896).

lier outburst. Beatrice recorded her belief that the attack on the Liberal government had been a mistake.[64] Sidney became a Progressive member of the LCC and, in the national arena, returned to a strategy based on the idea of impartial expertise. Now, however, the Webbs began to provide socialist expertise to the cooperative movement, the trade unions, and eventually the Labour Party.

Conclusion

The contemporary Marxist Ernest Belfort Bax described Fabianism as "the special movement of the government official, just as militarism is the special movement of the soldier and clericalism of the priest."[65] The old historiography often caricatured the leading Fabians, and especially Webb, by reducing their theories and politics to an expression of the interests of a rising professional class of bureaucrats. Even when historians explored the actual ideas of the Fabians, they often wrongly treated them as adhering to a homogeneous outlook based on a theory of rent that allegedly inspired a political strategy of permeating the Liberal Party. In contrast, we have found that the leading Fabians held different and changing economic theories that inspired different and changing political strategies. In this chapter, for example, we came across Fabians who had little interest in permeating existing political elites and who concentrated instead on speaking to radical clubs and at outdoor meetings and on joining marches and demonstrations. Many Fabians were neither wedded to the Liberal Party nor hostile to the ILP; they wanted an independent socialist party, especially if it could obtain proper funding.

Nonetheless, Fabian socialism did have some fairly distinctive and widespread features. It is just that these features are best understood as family resemblances and explained by reference to a tradition of liberal radicalism and the dilemmas posed by the crisis of faith and especially the collapse of classical economics. Most of the Fabians reached their socialist convictions against the background of a liberal radical inheritance as opposed to the Tory and popular radicalisms of their Marxist contemporaries.

For a start, many Fabians remained indebted to liberal radicalism in their focus on practical improvements rather than claims about universal rights. By the 1870s, many liberal radicals had replaced the standard of utility with reformist humanitarianism. The crisis of faith encouraged a generation to transfer the evangelical sense of duty from God to human-

---

[64] B. Webb, *Our Partnership*, p. 110.
[65] *Justice*, 9 March 1901.

ity. The tradition of liberal radicalism shifted dramatically, from utilitarianism and an enthusiasm for enlightened self-interest to ethical positivism and the moralization of society. J. S. Mill acted as a bridge between the liberal radicalism of the early and late nineteenth century, defining freedom as doing what one desired while making qualitative judgments between different types of desire.[66] Ethical positivists then began to conceive of the good life as self-denial, and freedom as individual fulfillment through participating in society with and for others. The Fabians' ethical positivism appeared in their concern with social duty as the motive for practical improvements to help the poor.

Many Fabians also continued to echo earlier liberal radicals in their belief that economic theory showed what was and was not a practical improvement. The collapse of classical economics meant that the Fabians often relied here on marginalism, neoclassical theory, positivist economics, and later a positivist historical sociology. However, they still treated the social sciences as offering conclusive arguments against the possibility of utopias. Anarchism was utopian because rent would remain in private hands unless the state collected it and used it to provide collective goods. Revolutionary socialism was utopian because evolutionary theory and positivist sociology proved change is inevitably gradual, with the new order emerging out of the old without any abrupt change. Socialism consisted of the extension of the collectivist tendencies already found in society. Several leading Fabians also drew on liberal radicalism in their use of social science to fuse the actual and the ideal. Earlier liberal radicals often treated the laws of political economy as both an explanation of the actual and a teacher of morality; economic necessity encouraged hard work, sobriety, and thrift. Several Fabians similarly treated positivist sociology as both a guide to social laws and a teacher of social duty and collective and cooperative action.

Finally, the Fabians looked on political reform not as a way to solve social ills but as administrative measures to facilitate good government. Although they did not share Mill's fear that democracy might erode individual liberty, they rarely promoted greater popular participation in government. Generally, they welcomed the rise of a professional civil service and policy experts. The Fabians concentrated on using and improving the established institutions of representative and responsible government. They argued that socialists had a duty to promote reform by taking part in elections, putting pressure on elected politicians, using the press, and joining parties. And they argued that socialists should promote the effi-

---

[66] J. Mill, "On Liberty," in *The Collected Works of John Stuart Mill* (Toronto: University of Toronto Press, 1963–91), vol. 18: *Essays on Politics and Society*; and J. Mill, "Utilitarianism," in *Collected Works*, vol. 10: *Essays on Ethics, Religion, and Society*.

cient organization of public affairs. Indeed, once the Fabians increasingly began to associate socialism with the deliberate extension of collectivist institutions and policies, they often suggested that socialism just was a more widespread and efficient public administration.

The Fabians were liberal radicals who confronted the Victorian crisis of faith and the collapse of classical economics. Some explored secularism, anarchism, Marxism, and theories of rent. Over time, however, Fabian socialism came to draw most heavily on ethical positivism as a response to the crisis of faith and on evolutionary sociology as a response to the collapse of classical economics. The leading Fabians believed that people had a social duty to promote the common good and to uplift the poor through the gradual and continuous development of collective institutions. By the 1890s, Olivier, Wallas, and the Webbs regularly defined socialism in terms of positivist sociology. The distinctive feature of Fabian socialism had become a focus on institutional and administrative relationships rather than economic ones. The Fabians had little patience with either romantic utopias or revolutionary action. Fabianism involved a gradual and institutional approach to social theory and social reform.

PART THREE

The Ethical Socialists

CHAPTER ELEVEN

Welfarism, Socialism, and Religion

THE MARXISTS AND FABIANS were relatively small groups concentrated mainly in London. Yet, as we saw in the last chapter, the Fabian Society grew remarkably quickly from about 350 members in 1891 to about 1,300 a year later. Many of the new socialists came from the provinces. Even if they joined the Fabian Society, they were rarely active in it. Rather, the new socialists were inspired by an ethical socialism that flourished in local organizations, utopian communities, labor churches, and, later on, the Independent Labour Party. These ethical socialists concentrated more on the moral development of individuals than on economic or social reforms. They believed that socialism was above all else an ethical doctrine about individual fulfillment in and through organic social relations. Community was a necessary setting for individual growth; individuals could realize their potential only through suitable relations to others. Many ethical socialists also believed that the triumph of socialism depended above all else on the development of the moral character of individuals. Socialism would rise out of the transformation of individual lives in accord with a new ethic.

British socialism, in general, emerged as people from diverse traditions grappled with dilemmas such as the collapse of classical economics and the crisis of faith. The Marxists came from the traditions of Tory and popular radicalism and often secularism, so they were little troubled by these dilemmas. The Fabians were generally evangelicals and liberal radicals; the crisis of faith led many to reformist humanitarianism and especially ethical positivism, and the collapse of classical economics led them to socialist theories based on marginalist and neoclassical theories of rent and, most importantly, on positivist approaches to political economy. The ethical socialists were generally Christians who grappled with the crisis of faith. Like many Fabians, they were among those Victorians who, in Beatrice Webb's words, transferred "the emotion of self-sacrificing service from God to man."[1] However, they drew less on liberal radicalism than on romanticism. Their socialism relied less on economic and social analyses than on an immanentist faith that inspired an ethic

---

A version of this chapter appeared as "Welfarism, Socialism and Religion: On T. H. Green and Others," *Review of Politics* 55 (1993), 639–661. Published by Notre Dame Press.
[1] B. Webb, *My Apprenticeship* (Harmondsworth, UK: Penguin, 1938), p. 153.

of fellowship and, at times, experiments in personal regeneration and communal living.

Part 3 explores the varied pathways to this ethical socialism. This chapter traces a broad cultural shift from an age of atonement to an age of immanentism. Immanentism appeared in ethical socialism and also in the work of philosophers such as T. H. Green, who used idealism to defend social-welfare liberalism.[2] Immanentist faiths transformed progressive politics by replacing the evangelical ethic of personal duty with one of social fellowship. Chapter 12 looks in more detail at those immanentists who used American romanticism to define a distinctive ethical socialism based on simple living and fellowship. Chapter 13 studies the experiments in communal living that were inspired by ethical socialism. Chapter 14 explores the labor church movement—the leading organization of ethical socialism prior to the formation of the Independent Labour Party.

This chapter suggests that ethical socialism was a response to the crisis of faith. Numerous historians relate the rise of socialism to a process of secularization. Typically, however, they focus on emotional needs that secularism allegedly left unfulfilled. They explain the rise of socialism by reference to desires and aspirations. Either they pay little attention to the beliefs with which people responded to the specific dilemmas that made up the crisis of faith, or they describe these beliefs as the products of displaced emotions rather than of local reasoning. Some historians refer to socialism as a kind of religious faith in an attempt to dismiss its intellectual seriousness. They imply that socialism is the result not of rational reflection but of a different kind of commitment. Often they seem not to recognize that liberalism and conservatism might be traditions that people can feel passionate about. Other historians make a more interesting claim about the particular emotional bases of the appeal of socialism in late-nineteenth-century Britain. These historians argue that evangelicals based their lives on practical works, and when they lost their faith, they turned to social service as an alternative outlet for the desire to do their duty.[3] These historians also argue that nonconformists based their

---

[2] Although Green has more often been seen as the inspiration for a new liberalism, he has also been seen as the philosopher responsible for socialism, or at least ethical socialism. My aim in this chapter is not to try to place Green within a classification of ideologies but to use him to explore a broad cultural shift that is apparent in progressive liberalism as well as in the rise of socialism. It is worth noting, however, that some ethical socialists clearly drew inspiration from Green; see, for example, P. Chubb, "The Significance of Thomas Hill Green's Philosophical and Religious Teaching," *Journal of Speculative Philosophy* 22 (1888): 1–21.

[3] M. Carter, *T. H. Green and the Development of Ethical Socialism* (Exeter, UK: Imprint Academic, 2003); P. Clarke, *Liberals and Social Democrats* (Cambridge: Cambridge

lives on the idea of the Kingdom of God, and when they lost their faith, the ideal of a socialist commonwealth arose as an alternative outlet for their aspirations.[4]

There are serious problems with attempts to assert a psychological link between secularization and social reformism. Consider the claim that socialism and welfarism were surrogate faiths that offered an emotional release for lapsed Christians. One problem with this claim is that many people who lost their faith did not turn to ethical socialism or liberal welfarism. Most secularists did not become socialists; some joined Marxist and other socialist groups, but most aligned themselves with the individualistic radicalism of Thomas Paine rather than a rising tide of social liberalism or ethical socialism. Charles Bradlaugh, G. W. Foote, and the other leaders of the National Secular Society remained hostile to any hint of state interference.[5] Their example should make us suspicious of the claim that a loss of faith left an emotional vacuum that was filled by social reformism.

Consider the weaker claim that a loss of faith encouraged people to treat their socialism or welfarism as a substitute religion. One problem with this claim is that even when secularists became socialists, their socialism showed little sign of being a substitute for Christianity. Edward Aveling and George Bernard Shaw are obvious examples. As secularists and then socialists, they argued that social ills resulted from ignorance and vested interests. They justified socialism primarily by appealing to economic theories. Aveling argued that Marx had laid bare the economic laws governing capitalist societies. Shaw argued that the law of rent meant that only a socialist society could be just. They treated socialism less as a religion than as a science. Indeed, in the late nineteenth century, they treated talk of a higher religion or nobler morality as cant. Aveling wrote, "He that has wholly abandoned the older creeds is always very careful to use no phrase that in any sense, however remote, implies them."[6] Such examples should make us suspicious of the claim that a loss of faith led people to treat social reformism as a substitute faith.

University Press, 1978); M. Richter, *The Politics of Conscience: T. H. Green and His Age* (London: Weidenfeld and Nicolson, 1964); A. Ulam, *Philosophical Foundations of English Socialism* (Cambridge, MA: Harvard University Press, 1951); and A. Vincent and R. Plant, *Philosophy, Politics and Citizenship* (Oxford: Blackwell, 1984).

[4] S. Pierson, *Marxism and the Origins of British Socialism* (Ithaca, NY: Cornell University Press, 1973); and S. Yeo, "A New Life: The Religion of Socialism in Britain, 1883–1896," *History Workshop* 4 (1977): 5–56.

[5] C. Bradlaugh and H. Hyndman, *Will Socialism Benefit the English People?* (London: Freethought, 1884); A. Besant and G. Foote, *Is Socialism Sound?* (London: Freethought, 1887).

[6] E. Aveling, "An Atheist on Tennyson's 'Despair,'" *Modern Thought* 4 (1882): 7.

Undoubtedly, some socialists and welfarists described their political beliefs as a new faith. The relevant question is, how should we account for the emergence of their new beliefs? There is little reason to assume that a continuation of religious needs and emotions can explain their beliefs, especially given that so many secularists provide clear counterexamples. The relationship of the crisis of faith to the rise of social reformism was less one of emotional continuity than of local reasoning. Ethical socialism and liberal welfarism emerged as part of a broad intellectual response to dilemmas that confronted both Christians and theists alike. Several Victorians responded to the crisis of faith with an immanentism that inspired their social reformism. In short, ethical socialism and liberal welfarism did not provide a new home for old religious emotions so much as emerge as part of a new set of religious beliefs.

IMMANENTISM

The Victorian crisis of faith contained several components. Scientific discoveries, historical criticism, and moral qualms all led people to doubt the literal truth of the Bible. And because biblical literalism was widespread, these doubts often became ones about faith itself. Nonetheless, when people stopped believing in the Bible, they did not necessarily become agnostics, let alone atheists. On the contrary, the vast majority turned to liberal Christianity or theism. The crisis of faith was about a change in the content of people's religious convictions more than a rise in secularism.

All through Victorian society, people grappled with the implications for faith of historical criticism, geology, and especially evolutionary theory. At one end of the social scale, T. H. Green, Charles Gore, and other upper-middle-class Anglicans from all stands of the Church of England wrestled with the theological problems of the day. Green's father and maternal grandfather were Anglican priests. He studied at Rugby School and the University of Oxford before becoming a fellow of Balliol College, Oxford, where he joined his mentor Benjamin Jowett, a prominent Broad Church theologian.[7] Similarly, Gore's parents were the brother of the Earl of Arran and the daughter of the Earl of Bessborough. Gore himself studied at Harrow School and the University of Oxford before becoming the principal of Pusey House, Oxford, named after a leading High Church theologian.[8] Elsewhere on the social scale, William Jupp, John Trevor,

---

[7] R. Nettleship, "Memoir," in *The Works of Thomas Hill Green*, ed. R. Nettleship, 3 vols. (London: Longmans, 1885–88), vol. 3: *Miscellaneous and Memoir*, p. 146.

[8] G. Prestige, *The Life of Charles Gore* (London: Heinemann, 1935).

and other lower-middle-class nonconformists grappled with similar issues in the various theistic and ethical societies that eschewed all dogma. Jupp was raised as a Calvinist. He left school at the age of thirteen and went to work as an errand boy. Later he was among those inspired by Thomas Davidson, who formed the Fellowship of the New Life.[9] Trevor too was raised as a Calvinist. He left school at the age of fifteen to train as an architect. Later he founded the Labour Church movement in the hope of providing the working classes with suitable places of worship and infusing a religious spirit into the socialist movement.[10] Gore, Green, Jupp, and Trevor all suffered religious doubts; they all rejected biblical literalism; they all became immanentists; and they all adopted ethical socialism or liberal welfarism.

Science led the assault on biblical literalism. The ethos of science suggested that nature was too uniform for miracles. Geological discoveries undermined histories based on the Old Testament. The theory of organic evolution by natural selection made a literal reading of Genesis untenable, implying that humans had risen from apes, not fallen from Eden. Science did not disprove the existence of God, but it did contradict the Bible, and many people, such as Leslie Stephen, thought that if they could not accept every word of the Bible, they could not be true Christians.[11] Scientific discoveries led some Victorians to agnosticism and even atheism. It led many more to reject evangelicalism and biblical literalism for a more liberal Christianity or theism. Jupp recalled that evolution implied "immeasurable periods of human development," thereby making "the whole scheme of evangelical theology read like a fiction of the brain."[12] Gore, as a newly ordained priest, concentrated on the need to reconcile faith with science in his first set of lectures at Oxford.

Another challenge to biblical literalism came from historical criticism. Charles Hennell, David Strauss, and others applied historical methods to the Bible. They argued that the Bible did not consist of the historical depositions of eyewitnesses. Many suggested that the Bible was a work of myth. When Victorians such as George Eliot read the writings of these historians, they came to regard the Bible as implausible.[13] Jupp too was distressed to find contradictions in the Bible. Gore was one of the leading Anglican theologians to grapple with such issues. He led the *Lux Mundi* theologians who accepted the demise of the Old Testament while clinging to the truth of the New Testament—a radical compromise that came

[9] W. Jupp, *Wayfarings* (London: Headley Brothers, 1918).

[10] J. Trevor, *My Quest for God* (London: Labour Prophet, 1897).

[11] N. Annan, *Leslie Stephen* (London: MacGibbon and Kee, 1951).

[12] Jupp, *Wayfarings*, p. 40.

[13] B. Willey, *Nineteenth Century Studies* (Harmondsworth, UK: Penguin, 1964), pp. 214–60.

to seem conservative only after the rise of theological modernism.[14] The problem was that because God was omniscient, he should have known that the Old Testament was mythological, but the Gospels clearly imply that as Christ he believed the Old Testament was true. It thus seemed that either God was not omniscient or the Gospels were not true. Gore responded to this problem with his doctrine of kenosis. Gore argued that when God took human form, he emptied himself of divine attributes such as omniscience; as Christ, God possessed only contemporary human knowledge.

Moral qualms about evangelical doctrines also led some Victorian Christians to question their faith. Liberal clerics such as F. D. Maurice denounced the doctrine of the atonement and the concept of eternal damnation. They wondered how a just God could allow an innocent Jesus to suffer in place of those who had sinned. And they wondered how a loving God could condemn people to perpetual Hell without any possibility of forgiveness or mercy. As a child, Trevor asked himself: "How could the saved have any joy in heaven, knowing that the lost were suffering eternal torment?"[15] Later he turned away from Christianity when he decided that the Bible could not be true because God must be moral, and yet a moral God could not have rejected the Jews in the way Saint Paul described in the Letter to the Romans.

Scientific, historical, and moral doubts did not necessarily drive people away from Christianity. Clergymen such as Gore and Maurice sought doctrinal solutions to these doubts or simply abandoned the offending doctrines. Nonetheless, the dilemmas facing contemporary Christianity did result in a definite shift in the mental world of the late Victorians. A new religious liberalism spread rapidly as people thought through the implications of the new knowledge for their faith. The various strands of this religious liberalism shared several themes that reflected the dilemmas confronting faith. To embrace science and history, religious seekers needed to replace the idea of a God who intervened miraculously in the natural world with an evolutionary account of the divine. And to appease contemporary morality, they had to reject the idea of eternal damnation for an account showing that humanity could vanquish evil.

Many Victorians tried to reconcile religious faith with Darwinism and historical criticism by replacing a transcendent God acting spontaneously and miraculously with an immanent God operating slowly through earthly processes. Immanentism appeared in all kinds of religious movements around the turn of the century. It attracted Anglicans such as J. R.

[14] C. Gore, ed., *Lux Mundi* (London: J. Murray, 1890).

[15] J. Trevor, *Labour Prophet Tracts* (London: Labour Prophet, 1896), tract 1: *Theology and the Slums*, p. 1.

Illingworth, nonconformists such as R. J. Campbell, and people founding new religions such as Edward Maitland.[16] Immanentists argued that God dwelled in the world, not beyond it or independently of it. God worked his will through natural processes, not miraculous interventions. God revealed himself in the evolutionary development of the world, not through divine revelations in the Bible. Many immanentists thereby reconciled faith with evolution and historical criticism. Evolution merely showed that God worked through gradual changes brought about by natural means. And historical criticism merely showed that the Bible was a product of a particular stage in this unfolding of the divine.

Victorian and Edwardian immanentism might appear to free religion from all doctrine, for if God resides in the world and reveals himself through the development of the world, then any new belief can be presented as the discovery of a new fact about God, and any old belief can be dismissed as but a stage in the evolutionary movement toward a complete knowledge of God. However, Victorian immanentism actually consisted of a set of characteristic religious doctrines. As Jupp recognized, for many of his generation, religion came to signify "an impassioned sense of the Unity and Order of the world and of our own personal relation thereto; an emotional apprehension of the Universal Life in which all individual lives are included and by which they are sustained; the communion of the human spirit with the Unseen and Eternal; faith in God as the Principle of Unity."[17] Immanentists believed, more particularly, in the existence of an inner reality, the unity of all things, and the purposive nature of evolution.

For a start, immanentists believed that God dwelled within everything. All things contained an inner reality that was at one with God. For example, Jupp defined God as the "inner reality of the whole—the one spirit that includes and pervades all the parts."[18] A belief in an inner reality encouraged some immanentists to elevate feeling and instinct over reason and intellect. In their view, life and emotion came from within the self, and so expressed the divine, whereas tradition and reason were part of an outer life that obstructed people's efforts to reach the divine within. For example, Trevor described the true religious life as a practice to be forged in a workshop, not a lesson to be learned at school: "That which you have learned from life to live by, that is your religion."[19]

[16] J. Illingworth, *Divine Immanence* (London: Macmillan, 1898); R. Campbell, *The New Theology* (London: Chapman and Hall, 1907); and E. Maitland, *The New Gospel of Interpretation* (London: Lamley, 1892).

[17] W. Jupp, *The Religion of Nature and of Human Experience* (London: P. Green, 1906), p. 3.

[18] Ibid., p. 174.

[19] Trevor, *My Quest*, p. 211.

Immanentists believed that because the divine exists in all things, everything forms a single whole. The inner reality of each thing is at one with the inner reality of all other things. As Jupp explained, "There is something in me, that is at one with the law by which the flower unfolds from the seed, and at one with the grace of its form or colour."[20] The belief that the universe was a single spiritual whole encouraged some immanentists to call for a higher individualism. They argued both that individuals must follow their own instincts in their progress toward God and that individuals are intrinsically a part of a wider community.

Finally, immanentists believed that because God revealed himself through the development of the universe, evolution is a progressive process that leads to the self-revelation of the divine. According to Trevor, the future promises "continuous progress towards the great Source of all things."[21] Gore even tried to deduce the existence of God from the fact that evolution exhibits a purposive tendency that makes sense only if one postulates a purposeful mind that controls the whole process. "It seems impossible to account for the progressive evolution of living forms unless some sort of direction, some sort of organic tendency to become this or that, is assumed in nature."[22] This teleological view of evolution differs notably from Charles Darwin's view that mutations encounter the natural environment. Most immanentists ignored the difference or did not recognize it. A few challenged Darwin, arguing that evolutionary theory did not require Darwin's particular mechanism of change, and championing instead a Lamarckian alternative.

Immanentism enabled its adherents not only to reconcile science and religion but also to resolve several contemporary moral dilemmas. Immanentism provided an answer to the question, what would sustain public morality if people no longer believed in the Day of Judgment? Even if Christian dogma failed, morality would thrive because people contain the divine within them and their instincts thus impel them to act morally. Immanentism even suggested that good necessarily would triumph over evil because evolution involves the progressive realization of the divine will. As individuals become increasingly aware of the divine within themselves, they become increasingly moral, until eventually good conquers evil.

Many immanentists divided the development of the good moral consciousness into several discrete stages. These stages appear in human history and are echoed in the development of the individual. Jupp's account

---

[20] *Seed-time*, January 1890.

[21] Trevor, *My Quest*, p. 152.

[22] C. Gore, *The Reconstruction of Belief*, 3 vols. (London: J. Murray, 1921–24), vol. 1: *Belief in God*, p. 60.

reads like an intellectual biography of his generation. Humanity initially emphasized the sense of sin; a sense of having done wrong represents the first stirring of moral awareness. Next, humanity adopted the ideal of a loving God as exemplified by Christ; moral awareness expanded to focus on the good and the ideal. Finally, the gospel of today reveals the divine unity of all; a contemporary moral consciousness tells people, "Be ye reconciled to God, to Nature, to your own hearts and to one another, since all are striving, however feebly, towards the same great goal of goodness and of love."[23]

Immanentists such as Jupp even suggested that they and their contemporaries had a special relationship to history. Now that people properly understood the nature of God, they could transcend the unconscious process of evolution and consciously cooperate in the fulfillment of God's will. Now that people properly understood the unity of all, they could grasp the purposive nature of evolution and act deliberately to advance the ideal. At last people could attain the true freedom that came from a self-conscious union with God. This freedom was the perfect freedom of living in harmony with the divine and cooperating with the spiritual law that governed the universe. When people attained this perfect freedom, they recognized themselves to be outgrowths of a universal self, so they were filled with love and sympathy for others. The dominance of love and sympathy throughout society would produce a spiritual fellowship without any need of authority. Society would come to embody an ethic of human brotherhood and the spiritual ideal of fellowship. As Jupp explained, his generation had adopted the ideal of "an organic social communion" because "as we learn that God is not alien to any of us ... it begins to appear highly absurd that we should be alien or indifferent to one another."[24]

Green's idealism was among the most philosophically sophisticated expressions of Victorian immanentism. Green rejected the dogmas of historical theology in favor of idealist metaphysics. His self-appointed task was to reconcile faith with science so as to provide religion with rational foundations. His idealism meant that he approached this task through logical constructions, but his conclusions parallel those of Jupp, Trevor, and Gore. Green described the idealist concept of the concrete universal as a metaphysical presupposition of all knowledge. He argued that the scientific account of the world as one containing objects and events makes sense only if we postulate the concrete universal as a divine principle that is immanent in mind and nature and, indeed, unites mind

[23] W. Jupp, *The Forgiveness of Sins and the Laws of Reconciliation* (London: P. Green, 1903), p. 50.

[24] Jupp, *Religion*, p. 177.

and nature. Scientists could not explain this concrete universal because, to do so, they would have to presuppose that which they hoped to explain. Green concluded, therefore, that science and religion are discrete domains of knowledge brought together by an immanent spiritual principle. His idealism served as a defense of an immanent God.

> That there is one spiritual self-conscious being, of which all that is real is the activity or expression; that we are related to this spiritual being, not merely as parts of the world which is its expression, but as partakers in some inchoate measure of self-consciousness through which it at once constitutes and distinguishes itself from the world; that this participation is the source of morality and religion; this we may take to be the vital truth which Hegel had to teach.[25]

Green then used his idealism to postulate an inner reality, the unity of all things, and a purposive evolution. Divine consciousness is an inner reality: "God is identical with the self of every man."[26] Everything partakes of the divine, so everything is fundamentally at one. Reality exists only as knowledge, and knowledge presupposes consciousness. Just as individual subjects unify the diversity of the world, so God must unify the diversity of individual subjects. Finally, Green argued that the true self of each individual joined with God in a teleological process.

According to Green, the process of evolution was moving toward the ideals of brotherhood and fellowship. Here too he echoed themes found among other immanentists, including Gore, Jupp, and Trevor. Green's Hegelian view of history as the gradual development of reason suggested that humanity becomes increasingly enlightened as reason unfolds. Humanity has a special place in the historical process because God "uses the animal organism of man ... to form a being formally self-conscious, and thus capable of knowledge, able to conceive a world of which each element is determined by relation to the whole."[27] Indeed, as people grasp God's purpose and the developmental nature of history, so they decide to promote it actively. Green's model reformer sacrificed private superficial pleasures in order to advance the divine purpose. Reformers internalize social ends and act for the common good. They thereby attain the perfect freedom that comes from acting in accord with the higher self, which is at one with the divine. They live a life of religious citizenship informed by an ethic of brotherhood. The good society consists of just such citizens pursuing their moral development through the community.

[25] T. Green, "Review of J. Caird: *Introduction to the Philosophy of Religion,*" in *Works,* vol. 3, p. 146.

[26] T. Green, "Fragment of an Address on Romans x.8, 'The Word Is Nigh Thee,'" *Works,* vol. 3, p. 227.

[27] T. Green, "Lectures on Logic," in *Works,* vol. 2: *Philosophical Works,* sec. 21 (p. 182).

Numerous Victorians rejected biblical literalism for an immanentist faith rather than secularism. It is misleading to describe Green, Jupp, and Trevor as Christians, but they believed in the divine. Gore remained happily in the Church of England, becoming, successively, the bishop of Worcester, Birmingham, and Oxford. His Christianity involved his modifying immanentism to place special importance on Christ. In Gore's view, God reveals himself through an evolutionary process during which it is Christ—as God incarnate—who demonstrates the moral character of God. Although Christ is God, "this supernatural Person is no unnatural phenomenon, but is in very truth the consummation of nature's order, or the rectification of it, so far as sin, which is unnatural, has thrown it into disorder."[28] Gore's Christian faith thus placed less emphasis on the atonement than on the incarnation as part of a progressive evolutionary process leading to a triumph over evil. The redemptive power of Christ, as expressed in the church, enabled humanity to build God's kingdom on earth.[29]

SOCIALISM AND WELFARISM

The historical relationship between the crisis of faith and social reformism rests not on an emotional need but on the rise of an immanentist faith. Immanentist theologies led people to an ethical socialism and a liberal welfarism that were notably different from the liberal and radical traditions that flourished earlier in the nineteenth century. A belief in an immanent God encouraged people to look for the Kingdom of God on earth, not in Heaven. New immanentist theologies encouraged people to join with others in a larger community so as to cooperate with God in the evolution of this world toward a spiritual fellowship. These theologies preached the unity of all and an ethic of brotherhood. All people were fundamentally equal. All people contained the divine. Consequently, the immanentists could not remain indifferent to the fate of their fellows. They looked for the material and moral uplift of the less fortunate. Trevor insisted that "somehow the life of the people must be raised."[30] Jupp recalled that his contemporaries learned to conceive of society "not as a mere complex of conflicting individuals, but as an organic whole, or at least as a fellowship of inter-related, mutually dependent human beings, wherein the claims of the personality of each should be recognised and, under a justly established social order, made one with the needs of the

---

[28] C. Gore, *The Incarnation of the Son of God* (London: J. Murray, 1891), p. 229.
[29] On Christ and the church, see, respectively, Gore, *Reconstruction of Belief*, vol. 2: *Belief in Christ*, and vol. 3: *The Holy Spirit and the Church*.
[30] Trevor, *My Quest*, p. 194.

common life."[31] There was a clear break with the individualism of earlier liberal and radical theorists.

Many immanentists were initially just as hostile to Marxist socialism as they were to classical liberalism. The difficulty lay with the widespread identification of Marxism with materialism. Trevor identified "the grand heresy of socialism" as "the teaching that a man can be made better merely by being more comfortable."[32] Immanentists rejected the Marxists' materialism and focus on economic reform. Instead, they called for a new spiritual life. For example, although Jupp and his circle sympathized with socialism as a cure for economic ills, they considered socialists "too exclusively concerned with a change in the *external conditions* of life, laying little or no stress on the necessity of an inward change … without which economic reforms could avail but little."[33] Similarly, Gore complained that Christ "preached no system of political economy" but sought "a profound ethical change based on changed thoughts about God and about man."[34] The immanentists criticized the Marxists and Fabians for being too materialistic over means as well as ends. They typically dismissed questions of political strategy and legislative programs. Instead, they called for personal righteousness as a living example of a new life. As Trevor wrote, "I knew well that within myself I must first find the regenerating life which was needed to regenerate society."[35]

Immanentists generally opposed both liberalism and Marxism in favor of a spiritual and ethical ideal of fellowship. When immanentists such as Jupp and Trevor became socialists, they did not place any greater emphasis on public ownership or state action. They merely redescribed their immanentist theology and ethic of fellowship as a type of socialism. In becoming socialists, they gave socialism a new slant, and had they not done so, they would not have become socialists. They argued that the labor and socialist movement was based on an ethic of brotherhood, not of class. They called for changes in the system of private property only as secondary expressions of a primary commitment to a spiritual ideal of fellowship. Trevor recalled how he became a socialist only when he recognized the connection between "social reform" and "religious life."[36] Similarly, when immanentists such as Green and Gore expressed support for liberalism, they were generally redescribing liberalism in terms of exactly the kind of theology and ethic that Jupp and Trevor associated with socialism. In defending liberalism, they gave liberalism a new slant,

---

[31] Jupp, *Wayfarings*, p. 69.
[32] Trevor, *My Quest*, p. 208.
[33] Jupp, *Wayfarings*, p. 71.
[34] C. Gore, *Strikes and Lock-Outs: The Way Out* (London: P. King, 1926), p. 12.
[35] Trevor, *My Quest*, p. 174.
[36] Ibid., p. 196.

and had they not done so, they would not have remained liberals. They often saw the labor movement as a class movement based on sectional interests, not the general will. They nearly always advocated some continuation of private property as a secondary aspect of their ideal in which moral citizens' pursued a common good. Green argued that property was necessary to the moral growth of individuals in a community.[37] Gore agreed but thought that private ownership of the means of consumption might suffice.[38]

Ethical socialism and liberal welfarism drew on religious and moral beliefs that flourished in response to the crisis of faith. New immanentist theologies inspired people to believe that God was present within everyone and to associate an awareness of the love and energy of God with a social fellowship. Immanentists believed that the divine unity of all meant that people were bound to their fellows in a spiritual relationship. They thought that the individual was part of a larger whole, and the good of the individual lay in the good of society. They called for a new social ethic to replace individualism. In their view, this social ethic would not endanger individual freedom, but rather promote true freedom. The new social ethic would derive from consciousness of the divine within oneself. Perfect freedom consisted in cooperation with the divine purpose. A spiritual fellowship would enable people to realize their inner selves and so gain perfect freedom through a correct relationship to society. Jupp's ideal was a "unity of social action, wherein the individual may find his fitting place, and do the work that is becoming to himself and rightly related to the whole."[39] This social fellowship was just a higher individualism. As Trevor explained, "The new living individualism ... sees that Individualism must take on a far higher form than that of the Manchester School, and, from a competitive materialist Individualism, must grow into a spiritual co-operative one."[40]

Many moralists believe in positive freedom. What distinguished Victorian and Edwardian immanentists was their stress on the religious underpinnings of the ideal. They wanted a spiritual fellowship or religious citizenship, not just an ethic of social duty. For example, Gore wrote that his ethic differed from that of previous radicals precisely in its "vivid sense of the will of a righteous God."[41] It was this belief in a divine order

[37] T. Green, "Lectures on the Principles of Political Obligation," *Works*, vol. 2, secs. 211–32 (pp. 517–35).

[38] C. Gore, introduction to *Property: Its Duties and Rights*, ed. C. Gore (London: Macmillan, 1913), pp. vii–xx.

[39] Jupp, *Religion*, p. 136.

[40] Trevor, *My Quest*, p. 173.

[41] C. Gore, *Buying up the Opportunity* (London: Society for Promoting Christian Knowledge, 1895), p. 14.

within reality that enabled immanentists to describe their social ethic as a higher individualism. They argued that the presence of God within the world implied an underlying kinship of existence, guaranteeing that if each individual attained perfect freedom, the result would be a harmonious society. As Jupp explained, "All the discords belong to a vast and infinite harmony, into which they are finally resolved."[42]

Green provided probably the most philosophically sophisticated account of a positive concept of freedom. He insisted that "the perfection of human character ... is for man the only object of absolute or intrinsic value."[43] And he distinguished between a lower, feeling self that seeks pleasure and a higher, divine self that seeks self-realization. The lower self aims at an illusory good, since pleasure is inherently transient. The higher self aims at the true good through reason or "consciousness of a possibility of perfection to be realised in and by the subject of the consciousness."[44] The good life is a free life spent seeking the perfect ideal, which is found in God. Indeed, Green wanted people to reenact the life of Christ within their actions; the reformer constantly crucified his selfish desires so as to be born again as a social being who aimed at self-realization through social service. Green provided two arguments for why the attempt to realize the divine requires that we act for the common good. First, a principle of reciprocity means that what is good for one is good for all. Reason reveals that individuals are morally equivalent, so the final good must be the self-realization of all. As Green explained, "The true good is good for all men" because they share "the same nature and capacity."[45] Second, individuals can realize their moral nature only in society. A moral character depends on the sacrifice of pleasure and the cultivation of a concern for others. Individuals realize themselves through devotion to the common good. As Green explained, "Human society" is "the organism in which the capacities of the human soul are unfolded."[46] Green thus identified individual freedom with self-realization through service to society. Individual freedom consists of a virtuous character associated with the sacrifice of pleasure for a life of social service. Green argued that to live for God, we must live "for the brethren," and in doing so we "live freely," that is, "in obedience to a spirit which is our self."[47]

A spiritual fellowship was often almost the only content that the immanentists gave to their ethical socialism and liberal welfarism. They

[42] Jupp, *Religion*, p. 162.

[43] T. Green, *Prolegomena to Ethics*, ed. A. Bradley (Oxford: Clarendon Press, 1884), sec. 247 (pp. 266–67).

[44] T. Green, "On the Different Senses of 'Freedom' as Applied to Will and to the Moral Progress of Man," in *Works*, vol. 2, sec. 21 (p. 326).

[45] Green, *Prolegomena to Ethics*, sec. 244 (p. 262).

[46] Ibid., sec. 273 (p. 295).

[47] Green, *Works*, vol. 3, p. 221.

defined their ideal as the realization of the divine purpose, without bothering much about social institutions or public policies. At times, they suggested that because the ideal entailed union with the divine, everything just would be fine, and if the details of the ideal remained opaque, that was because humanity did not yet fully understand the divine purpose. They implied that we could have details of the ideal only if we had a supernatural revelation of the divine, whereas in fact we come to know the divine only through the evolutionary process, so the ideal will remain a bit vague until it becomes manifest. As Trevor explained, "A creed is impossible for us" because we must rely on "our own natural development towards God."[48] Green too proposed few policies, with the exception of temperance and educational reform. He wrote about the need for a new social morality in the abstract, but he shied away from specific proposals for state interference on the grounds that external reforms could provide only suitable conditions for individuals to transform themselves. He wanted to awaken the divine spirit of reason, morality, and fellowship, not to pin this spirit down in particular institutions. Moreover, Green argued that we could be sure of progress toward the ideal due to the working of the spiritual principle in history. He believed that reason ensures that our "wants and desires" become "an impulse of improvement ('Besserungstrieb'), which forms, enlarges and re-casts societies" toward "an unrealised ideal of a best," that is, "God."[49]

Ethical socialists and liberal welfarists often neglected not only the details of their ideal but also the question of how the ideal might be realized. They addressed questions about political action by appealing to a purposive theory of evolution. In their view, the ideal was the historically inevitable terminus of a teleological process. A new morality necessarily would emerge as people followed the divine spark within themselves. Jupp believed that "the inner harmony which prevails throughout the universe ... is overcoming the ephemeral animosities ... of human will"; "the principle of unity ... is being, as it were, focused on the human race—gathering itself there into a conscious purposive realisation."[50] Trevor found "God in the Labour Movement—working through it, as once he had worked through Christianity, for the further salvation of the world."[51] Green too treated progress toward the ideal as an inevitable corollary of the progressive evolution of the divine; the unfolding of reason led inexorably to "universal human fellowship."[52] Yet, unlike most

---

[48] *Labour Church Record*, January 1899.
[49] T. Green, "Address on 2 Corinthians v. 7, 'Faith,'" in *Works*, vol. 3, pp. 269–70.
[50] Jupp, *Religion*, p. 177.
[51] Trevor, *My Quest*, p. 241.
[52] Green, *Prolegomena to Ethics*, sec. 209 (p. 222).

immanentists, Green suggested that although progress was certain, we might never reach the ideal.

For ethical socialists and liberal welfarists, the ideal would rise inexorably from the divine, so political action was less important than personal transformation. Immanentists concentrated on promoting the ideal of fellowship in their own lives. Jupp wrote of his friends that "while their gospel of freedom and human brotherhood required them to strive for a more just distribution of the results of human labour ... it also seemed to demand of them a *personal righteousness* that should refuse to have part in, or profit by, the competitive system."[53] The ideal was not some set of abstract social principles; it was a living power in the life of the believer. Trevor pleaded, "We have not only to think Socialism, to believe Socialism—we must be Socialists."[54] And Gore argued that "Christ requires us not to do such and such things, but to be such and such people."[55] Immanentists characteristically described the socialist movement not as a political movement that sought power in order to construct a new society, but rather as a religious movement that was based on a spiritual ideal. They condemned most political debate as petty and narrow squabbling. What mattered to them was the spread of a new spiritual ideal within people's lives.

The quest for personal righteousness defined the political strategy as well as the ideal of many immanentists. They believed that to become a socialist or a reformer was to undergo a moral conversion. As more and more people experienced this conversion, they would remake their lives in a way that would create the good society. Many immanentists even implied that the making of socialists and reformers was a sufficient condition for the emergence of an ideal society. They identified their ideal exclusively with a moral consciousness, so the development of a new moral consciousness was equivalent to the rise of their ideal. Socialism consisted of a new faith, so as that faith spread, socialism necessarily would become a reality.

CONCLUSION

This chapter has traced a broad cultural shift from the age of atonement to the age of immanentism. The crisis of faith obviously led some people to secularism. Yet, by far and away the most common response to the cri-

---

[53] Jupp, *Wayfarings*, pp. 83–84.

[54] Trevor, *Tracts*, tract 2: *From Ethics to Religion*, p. 21.

[55] C. Gore, *The Sermon on the Mount: A Practical Exposition* (London: J. Murray, 1896), p. 19.

sis of faith was a change of religious faith from evangelicalism and atonement theology to the immanentism found in, for example, incarnational
theology, pantheistic idealism, and new forms of belief such as theosophy.
The age of immanentism transformed social and economic thought in
the later Victorian and Edwardian eras. It gave rise to new socialist and
welfarist beliefs, which broke with the older individualism, emphasized
community, and ultimately sanctioned state action and social welfare.

Historians have noted the resemblance of Green's policy prescriptions
to those of John Bright and William Gladstone. Some conclude that the
late Victorian age does not represent the moment when socialism and welfarism broke with the heritage of classical liberalism.[56] Yet the conclusion
does not follow. It is true that Green's policy proposals did not require
much extension of state action.[57] Like most other immanentists, he shied
away from policy prescriptions, preferring to emphasize the importance
of a new ethic. Nonetheless, what mattered was precisely the shift from
the individualism of classical liberalism to the more social outlook of this
new ethic. Numerous immanentists—Green, Gore, Jupp, Trevor, and others—promoted an ethic of fellowship and a concern with social welfare.
Whatever Green's policy preferences, his immanentism and idealist ethic
paralleled and inspired other strands of thought that collectively contributed greatly to the rise of socialism and welfarism.

Of course, the growth of a social democratic welfare state had many
sources. It owed much to the shift from the older concern with the poor
as individuals to the newer concern with poverty as a social ill, a shift
inspired primarily by the social investigations of people such as Charles
Booth.[58] Moreover, the immanentists did not always take part in this
shift. Green's concern remained with the individual poor, so his preferred
solutions were temperance and education, not unemployment relief and
pensions. Nonetheless, the growth of a social democratic welfare state
owed as much to a new moral idealism as it did to new concepts of poverty. Besides, the new concepts of poverty arose at least partly because a
new moral idealism inspired people to study the poor and their circumstances. Ironically, for example, Booth began his magisterial survey of the
East End of London because he wanted to show that the moral idealists
had misunderstood, exaggerated, and sensationalized poverty. Imma-

[56] J. Morrow, "Liberalism and British Idealist Political Philosophy," *History of Political
Thought* 5 (1984): 91–108. For examples of the contrary—and more common—view,
see, on socialism, Carter, *Green*; and on liberalism, M. Freeden, *The New Liberalism: An
Ideology of Social Reform* (Oxford: Clarendon Press, 1978).

[57] P. Nicholson, "T. H. Green and State Action: Liquor Legislation," *History of Political
Thought* 6 (1985): 517–50.

[58] J. Harris, *Unemployment and Politics: A Study in English Social Policy, 1886–1914*
(Oxford: Clarendon Press, 1972).

nentism was both a direct moral inspiration for the growth of the welfare state and an indirect inspiration for the policies associated with the welfare state.

Immanentism was in many ways the defining feature of ethical socialism. As we will see in the following chapters, it appears within movements for the simplification of life, anarcho-communalism, and the labor churches. The religiosity of these movements was not simply an emotional hangover from a religious faith that had recently been worn away by modern scientific discoveries. On the contrary, it consisted of the distinctive immanentism by which so many people tried to reconcile faith with science. Henry David Thoreau, Leo Tolstoy, and Ralph Waldo Emerson appealed to the ethical socialists because they echoed this immanentism with its emphases on an inner divinity, personal simplicity, and spiritual fellowship.

CHAPTER TWELVE

American Romanticism and British Socialism

IN 1906 WILLIAM STEAD sent a questionnaire to prominent members of the Labour Party asking what books had influenced them.[1] The most frequently cited authors were Thomas Carlyle and John Ruskin, but Ralph Waldo Emerson and Henry David Thoreau were not far behind. Much has been written about the influence of British romanticism on the British socialist movement, and perhaps the obvious impact of Carlyle and Ruskin has obscured that of Emerson, Thoreau, and Walt Whitman.[2] It may be difficult to assess the influence of the American romantics, since their views closely resemble those of their British counterparts. Nonetheless, we can trace clear lines of influence from American romanticism to British socialism, notably by way of Thomas Davidson and Edward Carpenter. Moreover, some ideas were common among American romantics but not among their British counterparts, and we can also follow these ideas through Davidson and Carpenter into the British socialist movement.

The influence of American romanticism shaped much of British ethical socialism in the 1880s and 1890s. In the last chapter I discussed a broad shift from the age of atonement to the age of immanentism. The immanentists believed that the divine was present within everyone, binding people together in a single unity. Typically, they adopted an ethic of brotherhood that did much to inspire the transformation of nineteenth-century liberalism into the social democracy and welfare state of the twentieth century. Yet, the very breadth of the shift from evangelicalism to immanentism leaves us needing a more specific account of its rise and role within the ethical socialism of the 1890s. This chapter shows that ethical socialists drew on the American romantics as inspiration for a general immanentism and for more specific commitments to a simplified life, a return to nature, experimental schools, and communal living.

A version of this chapter appeared previously as "British Socialism and American Romanticism," *English Historical Review* 110 (1995), 878–901. Published by Oxford University Press.

[1] W. Stead, "The Labour Party and the Books That Helped Make It," *Review of Reviews* 33 (1906): 568–82.

[2] J. Mendilow, *The Romantic Tradition in British Politics* (London: Croom Helm, 1986); and S. Pierson, *Marxism and the Origins of British Socialism* (Ithaca, NY: Cornell University Press, 1973).

As we saw in the last chapter, ethical socialism was typically a vague set of ideas focused on the divine within and on human brotherhood. T. H. Green and a few other able philosophers explored these ideas systematically. Typically, however, ethical socialists were less concerned with intellectual analysis and debate than were the Fabians or even the Marxists. Ethical socialists concentrated their energies on personal experience, moral transformation, and utopian experiments. This chapter and the next two pay slightly less attention to the details of people's beliefs and slightly more to the lives and communities inspired by their beliefs.

AMERICAN ROMANTICISM

Romanticism is a vast and vague movement. Distinctions between its national varieties postulate suggestive and delicate shades, not absolute and strong contrasts. However, if we are to show the specific influence of American romanticism on British socialism, we should try to identify themes that are prominent in the writings of Emerson, Thoreau, and Whitman but less important in the works of Carlyle and Ruskin. American romanticism differed from British romanticism in its relationship to Unitarianism and to frontier individualism. The debt to Unitarianism appeared in a spiritual immanentism, which later reappeared in the idea of socialism as a new religion. The debt to frontier individualism appeared in an ideal of self-sufficiency, which later reappeared in the idea of socialism as a new personal life.

Emerson was the dominant figure among the American romantics. His home in Concord, Massachusetts, acted as a regular meeting place for the Transcendental Club, the name of which referred to Immanuel Kant's use of the word "transcendental" to denote the way we can know things a priori. The American romantics followed their German counterparts in reacting against what they regarded as the narrow rationalism and empiricism of the eighteenth century. Emerson was especially influenced by German philosophers such as Friedrich Schelling. The American and British romantics shared a philosophical outlook indebted to German idealism. When Emerson traveled to Europe in 1832 and 1833, he became friendly with both Carlyle and Samuel Taylor Coleridge.

The American romantics drew heavily on Unitarianism in a way the British did not. Emerson studied theology at Harvard, and he remained a Unitarian minister until 1832. Many other American romantics were Unitarians, including William Ellery Channing and George Ripley. The appeal of Unitarianism in Victorian Britain is evident in the popularity in London (extending far beyond socialists) of preachers such as Moncore Conway, another member of the Transcendental Club. The Unitarians offered a rational and liberal approach to Christianity. They rejected what they thought was an irrational concept of the Trinity, arguing instead for the single personality of God. They also rejected what they thought were the immoral dogmas of eternal punishment, inherited guilt, and vicarious atonement. Unitarianism thus opened the way to the immanentism we examined in the previous chapter; it provided inspiration to those turning away from belief in a transcendent God who stood outside of nature and toward belief in a single spiritual deity that existed within nature. Immanentism was unusual among Unitarians until the close of the nineteenth century. But the Unitarian inheritance of the American romantics still gave them a more immanentist outlook than was common among their British counterparts.

The immanentism of the American romantics appears in their view of God as present throughout the world and as realizing a divine purpose through natural processes. Emerson was a spiritual monist. He believed in an "Over-Soul" that unified a spiritual reality, a divine mind pervading the entire material universe.[3] Everything contained a divine spirit, so everything was united in a single whole, and each thing contained within itself the laws and meaning of the whole universe. It is true that some British romantics came near to deifying nature. Ruskin wrote that "God paints the clouds and shapes the moss-fibres, that men may be happy in seeing Him at His work."[4] Ruskin argued that landscape painting can capture the truth and beauty of nature, thereby reflecting the glory of God. However, although Ruskin suggested little more than nature's spiritual solace, Emerson insisted on a spiritual reality within nature. Whereas British romantics typically believed that nature can inspire the imaginative faculty in humans and even point toward the divine, American romantics typically believed that God and nature were coextensive.

Immanentism encouraged the American romantics to argue that people come to know God through direct intuition of an absolute being, not the miraculous revelation embodied in the Bible or Incarnation. Emerson believed that individuals come into contact with the Over-Soul either by entering a mystical state in which they perceive the divine within themselves or by discovering the divine in the truth, beauty, and wholeness of nature.[5] The Emersonian sublime is a mystical, holistic freedom in which individuals recognize their true spiritual selves; people recognize the Over-Soul in themselves and thus come to see the divine in everything

---

[3] R. Emerson, "Nature," in *The Complete Works of Ralph Waldo Emerson*, ed. E. Emerson (London: George Routledge, 1903–4), vol. 1: *Nature, Addresses, and Lectures*, pp. 1–77; and R. Emerson, "The Over-Soul," in *Works*, vol. 2: *Essays: First Series*, pp. 265–97.

[4] J. Ruskin, *The Works of John Ruskin*, ed. E. Cook and A. Wedderburn (London: G. Allen, 1903–12), vol. 5: *Modern Painters (iii)*, p. 384.

[5] R. Emerson, "An Address," in *Works*, vol. 1: *Nature*, pp. 117–51.

else. It is true that many British romantics stressed the role of the imagination and nature as sources of harmony in a fragmented world, but they typically saw harmony in terms of either the individual or an organic society, without reference to the overt religiosity of Emerson.

American romantics argued that because individuals contain the divine, personal intuitions have moral authority. Emerson believed that people should trust themselves, reject external rules, express their inner nature, and be self-reliant.[6] Thoreau—another member of the Transcendental Club—proclaimed the individual conscience, not the law, as the supreme moral arbiter. He argued that political obligation depends on the moral judgment of the individual, and the best government is that government which does not govern.[7] Similarly, British romantics rejected the formal rules and public codes that had dominated the outlook of the Augustans in favor of a belief in the individual's questioning and testing of values and experiences. Their opposition to Augustan limits sometimes led to hostility to all restrictive codes. Percy Bysshe Shelley and William Wordsworth were attracted to the anarchist views of William Godwin. More generally, almost all of the romantics owed a debt to Jean-Jacques Rousseau, and they were almost unanimous in calling for a natural and wholesome existence based on instinct.

The American romantics were more distinctive in drawing on a type of frontier individualism. British romantics typically looked to the example of the Middle Ages, although they rarely agreed on the details of an ideal community, with, for instance, Coleridge calling for a clerisy and national church to balance the forces of progress with those of stability, and Ruskin trying to revive a moral economy based on craftsmanship and guilds.[8] In contrast, the American romantics succumbed to an idealized picture of American history and democracy.

The idealization of American history appeared in the romantics' suggestion that the ideal was being realized through the action of the divine in history. Here Emerson, Thoreau, and Whitman drew inspiration from Jeffersonian and Jacksonian democratic theory, which restated the eighteenth-century belief in the perfectibility of humankind, a belief that fitted snugly alongside the romantics' immanentism. Just as the democrats described the American polity as part of God's design, so the romantics could take the American ideal as the summit of the immanent working out of the divine will. Again, just as the Jacksonian George Bancroft

---

[6] R. Emerson, "Self-Reliance," in *Works*, vol. 2: *Essays*, pp. 43–90.

[7] H. Thoreau, "Resistance to Civil Government," in *Political Writings*, ed. N. Rosenblum (Cambridge: Cambridge University Press, 1996), pp. 1–22.

[8] S. Coleridge, *On the Constitution of Church and State* (London: Hurst, 1830); and J. Ruskin, "Unto This Last," in *Works*, vol. 17: *Unto This Last, Munera Pulveris, Time and Tide, and Other Writings on Political Economy, 1860–1873*, pp. 15–114.

wrote his famous history of America to show it expressed the will of God, so William Channing spoke of the dawn of a new age in which people would surmount their political difficulties to realize their inner spirit.[9]

An idealization of American democracy appeared in the romantics' commitment to a democratic republic composed of self-sufficient farmers. The American romantics believed in the virtue of a rough-and-ready life spent working the land. Some British romantics called for the simplification of life, rejecting as unnatural the wants that were created by industrial society. Ruskin used the example of Gothic architecture to illustrate how mechanization had replaced skill in the workplace.[10] Nonetheless, while Ruskin wished for a return to the kind of skilled craftsmanship that he thought produced good art, Thoreau wanted people to minimize the number of their possessions. Whereas Ruskin wished workers could exercise their creative impulses free from the regime of machines, Thoreau wanted people to become effectively self-sufficient. And whereas Ruskin established new guilds and revitalized the handmade linen industry of Langdale in the Lake District, Thoreau lived alone in a hut at Walden Pond, Massachusetts, where he tried to "simplify, simplify" and so attain spiritual wealth by living close to nature, reducing his material wants, and satisfying any residual needs by his manual labor.[11]

Some ethical socialists drew heavily on American romantics. They adopted an immanentist theology that expressed a genuine religious conviction, not just a romantic pantheism that invested nature with imaginative appeal. And they adopted a rough-and-ready ideal that looked unfavorably on all possessions, not just commercial products, and that praised self-sufficiency and working the land, rather than the craftsmanship of skilled artisans. However, the distinctions between national variants of romanticism are shades, not absolute contrasts. When we consider the particular examples of Davidson and Carpenter, we will fill out the distinctions by showing how American romanticism influenced the lives and beliefs of specific individuals and the groups and movements to which they belonged. What follows traces a definite line of historical influence, where the evidence for historical influence is both conceptual and biographical. Conceptually, some ideas are common to the American

[9] G. Bancroft, *A History of the United States from the Discovery of the American Continent to the Present Time*, 6 vols. (New York: Appleton, 1885); and W. Channing, *An Address delivered before The Mercantile Library Company of Philadelphia* (Philadelphia: Crissy, 1841).

[10] J. Ruskin, "The Nature of Gothic," in *Works*, vol. 10: *The Stones of Venice—II: The Sea Stories*, pp. 180–269.

[11] J. Ruskin, "General Statement Explaining the Nature and Purposes of St. George's Guild," in *Works*, vol. 30: *The Guild and Museum of St. George*, pp. 45–59; and H. Thoreau, *Walden* (Edinburgh: David Douglas, 1884).

romantics and some British socialists, but not to the British romantics. Biographically, the lives and autobiographical writings of some British socialists establish their debt to the American romantics.

DAVIDSON: FELLOWSHIP OF THE NEW LIFE

> It was on a first visit to Concord that I was told the story ... of how when [Father Taylor] was asked whether he thought Emerson would have to go to hell, he replied that if he did the tide of emigration would likely turn that way.
> —P. Chubb, *On the Religious Frontier*

Thomas Davidson was born in Scotland and educated at Aberdeen before becoming a wandering scholar. He traveled from place to place, learning and teaching with equal enthusiasm, in a life akin to that of Giordano Bruno, the Renaissance pantheist whom he admired.[12] Davidson arrived in America sometime around 1866. In Boston he participated in a philosophical club, the members of which included the educationist and philosopher William Torrey Harris—a friend of Emerson's who did much to introduce German philosophy to America when he founded the Saint Louis School of Idealism. Davidson lectured alongside Emerson at summer schools and taught classics under Harris in the public schools of Missouri. His recollections of his time in the United States suggest that he accepted much of American romanticism, as found in the Boston radicals, but rejected its philosophy, as found in the Saint Louis Hegelians. He said, "I came to America and fell first among Boston Radicals with whom I very cordially sympathised, and then among St. Louis Hegelians with whom I never in any degree sympathised"; "Hegelianism has always seemed to me the wildest of nonsense."[13] Later, in the early 1880s, Davidson moved on to Italy, where he studied the life and thought of Antonio Rosmini-Serbati.[14] When he had joined the philosophical club in Boston, he talked incessantly of Aristotle, but by now, just as Rosmini-Serbati fused Aquinas and G.W.F. Hegel, so he hoped to combine his Aristotelianism with American romanticism. Davidson's Emersonian immanentism implied that "forms" constituted the eternal

---

[12] T. Davidson, "Autobiographical Sketch," ed. A. Lataner, *Journal of the History of Ideas* 18 (1957): 531–36. Also see W. Knight, ed., *Memorials of Thomas Davidson, the Wandering Scholar* (London: Fisher Unwin, 1907).

[13] Davidson, "Autobiographical Sketch," 532.

[14] J. Blau, "Rosmini, Domodossola and Thomas Davidson," *Journal of the History of Ideas* 18 (1957): 522–28.

essence of reality, but he still wanted to retain Aristotle's view that forms cannot exist apart from matter; individual things, not forms, are the immediate objects of reality.

According to Davidson, the purpose of philosophy is "to unify the world" by uncovering the "unity of the human spirit," thereby revealing God.[15] He argued that Kant demonstrated that Humean skepticism requires us to grant mind a determining role in the construction of the world. Similarly, Zeno's paradox of Achilles and the tortoise shows us that our current understanding of motion is mistaken. It demonstrates that the nature of time and change requires us to postulate an unchanging subject of change that exists outside time. The unchanging subject is a universal mind, and it performs the creative role that Kant had shown to be necessary. Moreover, this universal mind exists in each individual mind. God is an ideality present in all of reality.

Davidson was an idealist and immanentist who denounced materialists, such as Auguste Comte and Herbert Spencer, as obscurationists. Yet, Davidson still retained the Aristotelian belief that spirit cannot exist apart from matter, and forms cannot exist apart from individuals. He criticized the American romantics for considering Being only in its universal aspect, thus losing sight of the individual. He complained that, like Schelling and Hegel, the American romantics "functioned with the forms of thought, disregarding the content, without which the forms have no meaning (as Kant saw); and of course they arrived at a sort of Vedantic or neo-Platonic mysticism."[16] Davidson then replaced Hegel's single, thinking subject with a multitude of sentient individuals. Each individual is a bundle of feelings grouped together and distinguished from others by reference to desires. Feeling, not consciousness or matter, is the fundamental constituent of the world. God is not the formless universal of Hegelianism, since spirit cannot exist apart from monads of feeling.

According to Davidson, individuals have separate identities, but they are also intimately related. Each individual monad seeks to satisfy its desires through actions that have effects that are experienced by other individuals. The world of an individual monad consists of its experiences of the actions of various other desiring monads. As Davidson explained, "I am a feeling or sensibility, modified in innumerable ways by influences which I do not originate," and "these modifications, when grouped, are what I call the world, or *my* world, for I know no other."[17] Equally, the

---

[15] T. Davidson, *The Education of the Wage-Earners: A Contribution toward the Solution of the Educational Problem of Democracy*, ed. C. Bakewell (London: Ginn and Co., 1904), p. 37.

[16] Knight, ed., *Memorials*, p. 149.

[17] T. Davidson, "Education as World Building," *Western Educational Review* 9 (1900): 327.

world of an individual is its consciousness, so when individuals comprehend and classify their sensations, they also construct their world. Thus, Davidson continued, education gives individuals conceptual tools with which to arrange their feelings and so build their worlds. Education can create a new moral order by ensuring that people build harmonious worlds. The propagation of new beliefs can transform society: "We have but to get a new economic faith, laid down in a new economic bible, to transform our cities and our life into something as different from what they are at present as human life is from brute life."[18]

Davidson's proposals for moral reform through education again illustrate his debt to American romanticism. While in America, he taught at summer schools organized by Amos Bronson Alcott. Alcott was a leading exponent of educational and communal reforms. He founded the Temple School in Boston in an attempt to use beautiful surroundings, the imagination, and play to create a new type of schooling that would develop all of a pupil's intellectual, physical, moral, and aesthetic faculties. Alcott's example inspired Davidson to create summer schools initially at Farmington in Connecticut and later at Glenmore in the Adirondacks, upstate New York, where the teachers included Harris. Alcott also inspired Davidson's attempt to bring culture into the lives of the working people of New York by initiating the Breadwinners' College. Like Alcott, Davidson believed that education should promote a broad culture based on physical exercise, morality, and aesthetics. Like Alcott, Davidson wanted education to promote learning through doing in natural, beautiful surroundings.[19]

So, Davidson hoped that a suitable education would inspire a new world that encompassed the values that were taught by the American romantics and lived by the monks at the Rosminian monastery in Domodossola. He wanted to re-create the spiritual life of the monks but to free the religious spirit from the dogmatic institutions of the Catholic Church by infusing it with the tolerant outlook of the American romantics. It was from this perspective that he regularly praised American republicanism as a noble religion that offered more than any other religion had ever offered. He wanted people to adopt a simple communal life guided by a spiritual and ethical ideal free of all dogma. His dream was of "a small devoted band of men and women of fearless character, clear philosophic insight, and mighty spiritual love, who, living a divine life in their relations to each other, shall labour, with all the strength that is in them to lift

---

[18] T. Davidson, *The Moral Aspects of the Economic Question* (London: William Reeves, 1888), p. 25.

[19] T. Davidson, *Aristotle and Ancient Educational Ideals* (London: William Heinemann, 1892), *The Education of the Greek People and Its Influence on Civilization* (London: Edward Arnold, 1895), and *Rousseau and Education According to Nature* (London: William Heinemann, 1898).

their fellows into the same divine life."[20] Yet, Davidson was not a socialist. He criticized socialism for being incompatible with his desire to keep sight of the individual and for being a materialist ideology that ignored the primacy of a moral reformation. He insisted that socialism cannot arise unless the popular mind adopts a new ethic with a new view of the meaning and use of wealth and life, but when people adopt this ethic, the solution will come naturally by itself.[21]

Percival Chubb visited Davidson at Domodossola. Then, when the peripatetic Davidson moved to London in 1882, Chubb led the small group that gathered about him to discuss religion, ethics, and social reform. This small group became the Fellowship of the New Life. The rules of the Fellowship reflected Davidson's utopian views.[22] The members initially were to perfect their individual characters in accord with ethical precepts of simplicity, kindness, and love. Then they were to form a community embodying these principles. And finally they would use the example of this community to regenerate humanity as a whole.

Within the Fellowship, Maurice Adams, Chubb, and Hamilton Pullen were disciples of Davidson, and Havelock Ellis, a young sex therapist, joined Margaret Hinton and her sister Caroline Haddon in preaching James Hinton's evolutionary mysticism.[23] Several other members of the Fellowship, such as H. H. Champion, Edward Pease, and Frank Podmore put social reform before moral regeneration. As we saw in chapter 7, these differences surfaced at the third and fourth meetings of the Fellowship, after which the social reformers departed to found the Fabian Society. Those who remained in the Fellowship then adopted the following spiritual basis:

The Fellowship of the New Life

Object.—The cultivation of a perfect character in each and all.
Principle.—The subordination of material things to spiritual.
Fellowship.—The sole and essential condition of fellowship shall be a single-minded, sincere, and strenuous devotion to the object and principle.[24]

---

[20] Davidson, *Wage-Earners*, p. 48.

[21] Davidson, *Moral Aspects*.

[22] Knight, ed., *Memorials*, pp. 21–25. For a discussion, see K. Manton, "The Fellowship of the New Life: English Ethical Socialism Reconsidered," *History of Political Thought* 24 (2003): 282–304.

[23] Havelock Ellis, *My Life* (London: William Heinemann, 1940). On Hinton and his views, see E. Hopkins, *Life and Letters of James Hinton* (London: Kegan Paul, 1882); J. Hinton, *Life in Nature*, intro. H. Ellis (London: Allen and Unwin, 1932); and J. Hinton, *Philosophy and Religion*, ed. C. Haddon (London: Kegan Paul, 1881).

[24] E. Pease, *The History of the Fabian Society* (London: A. Fifield, 1916), p. 32.

After this spiritual proclamation, there followed statements on simplicity of living, the importance of manual labor, and the desirability of forming a community of fellows. Later, when Davidson returned to America, the members of the Fellowship adopted an explicitly socialist program.

Although Davidson combined American romanticism with the teachings of Rosmini, and although he opposed socialism, his followers in the Fellowship saw him as someone who brought them the teachings of Emerson and Thoreau, teachings that they believed pointed to socialism. Davidson acted as a conduit through which American romanticism reached a number of British ethical socialists. Many of the members of the Fellowship thought of it as an expression of the ideals of American romanticism. Chubb wrote, "England drew upon America for the new ethical inspiration" and, in particular, upon Emerson, whose home in Concord, Massachusetts, was "the citadel of the new truth."[25] Similarly, Pease later described Davidson as a "descendent of the utopians of Brook Farm," a view echoed by Ernest Rhys, who recalled how the Fellowship "aimed, like Hawthorne's Brook Farm, at setting up a colony of workers and craftsmen."[26] A decade after Davidson came to London, *Seed-time*, the official journal of the Fellowship, published an editorial claiming that the Fellowship had been "influenced by Thoreau and Emerson rather than Marx."[27]

Many of the members of the Fellowship adopted an ethical socialism indebted to American romanticism. Chubb defended both an immanentist philosophy expressing a genuine religious conviction and an ethic that identified this religious conviction with the republican ideal. The strength of Chubb's debt to American romanticism is clear from a critical review he wrote of William Morris's utopian novel *News from Nowhere*. Morris's socialist vision drew on British romanticism; it invested nature with imaginative appeal and promoted the skilled craftsmanship of artisans. Chubb's review described the main defect of Morris's book as "the absence in it of anything like a belief in a divine purpose running through nature and history, or in the divine essence of man."[28] Morris was no im-

[25] P. Chubb, *On the Religious Frontier* (New York: Macmillan, 1931), pp. vii–viii, and introduction to *Select Writings of Ralph Waldo Emerson* (London: Walter Scott, 1888), p. xix.

[26] Pease, *History*, p. 26; E. Rhys, *Everyman Remembers* (London: Dent, 1931), p. 2.

[27] *Seed-time*, April 1892.

[28] Ibid., October 1891. Also note Jupp's contrast between the British romantics with their "earthiness" and the American romantics with their belief in "homeliness in relation to things of the body with a view to Heavenliness in relation to things of the mind"; W. Jupp, *Wayfarings: A Record of Adventure and Liberation in the Life of the Spirit* (London: Headley Brothers, 1918), p. 133.

manentist. Morris expressed a paganism that portrayed nature as benefi-
cent but lacked any truly religious impulse. Moreover, Chubb continued,
this defect lay behind problems in Morris's political strategy and socialist
ideal. With regard to political strategy, Chubb argued that Morris failed
to allow for the fact that socialism will arise through the divine purpose
working in history. Morris's optimistic view of nature led him to a faith
in the noble savage or human nature as it is; Morris believed that to
overturn society would be to free the good innate within a humanity
that had been corrupted by society; Morris thus believed that socialism
could arise out of a cataclysmic social revolution destroying bourgeois
society. However, Chubb countered, once we recognize that history is the
working out of a divine purpose, we must acknowledge that socialism
will emerge as the culmination of a process of evolutionary development.
Socialists should seek to remodel society by improving, not abolishing,
contemporary social and political institutions. With regard to the socialist ideal, Chubb argued that Morris neglected the religious dimension of
ethics. Morris's utopian society privileged sensuous delights, neglecting
the religious virtues that are associated with Christianity; Morris did not
appreciate the virtues of love and sympathy as sources of self-denial; he
ignored the importance of the desire to serve others as a motive for action. In contrast, Chubb wanted a socialism infused with a religious ideal,
a social expression of Emerson's concept of the sublime, a community of
people who were consciously aware of being bound together by a common relationship to the divine. This socialist ideal was what he and his
friends meant by "fellowship." The true self is at one with the divine, so
true freedom consists of realizing one's own good through the good of
the community. Elsewhere Chubb described his religion of socialism as
an extension of American republicanism; he wanted "a religious union
parallel with and harmonious with that which unites men under the aegis
of the republican state or party—a religion of Democracy."[29]

The members of the Fellowship equated socialism with a religion of
democracy. Their socialism consisted of a moral ideal of brotherhood.
They defined socialism as a vital moral life, rather than, for example, social and economic institutions. They asked: "Cannot moral life itself glow
with a passion which makes all other passions pale?" They answered:
"We believe it can, and by fellowship and sympathy to raise it to a white
heat, which shall make it a prevailing power in the world, is the ethical
aim of the Fellowship of the New Life."[30] They insisted that the "radical
reform of our social arrangements, which is now being made, will be

[29] Chubb, *Religious Frontier*, p. 29.
[30] M. Adams, *The Ethics of Social Reform* (London: William Reeves, 1887), p. 26.

powerful and salutary just so far as it is based upon a clear and intelligent moral purpose."[31]

As the members of the Fellowship defined socialism as a new religious ideal, so they argued that social change necessarily depended on an ethical transformation. They tried to realize socialism—the religion of democracy—through an ethical transformation within their personal lives. Here they shared the concern of the American romantics with education, communal living, and the simplification of life. Their journal echoed Alcott's belief that schools "ought to be communities, miniature commonwealths or states."[32] The Fellowship founded an alternative school at Abbotsholme, on the edge of the Derbyshire moors. Initially Bob Muirhead and Cecil Reddie shared responsibility for the day-to-day management of the school, but later disagreements led most of the members of the Fellowship to withdraw, leaving Reddie in sole charge.[33]

The members of the Fellowship were also committed to providing an example of communal living. Initially they just tried to live near each other. But later, after much discussion of the relative merits of Latin America and London as possible sites, they rented Fellowship House as a shared residence at 29 Doughty Street in the Bloomsbury district of London. Residents included Havelock Ellis, Edith Lees, Ramsay MacDonald, Sydney Olivier, an anarchist called Agnes Henry, and Mrs. Pagovsky and her daughter from Russia. The residents had separate bed-sitting rooms. They ate their meals together in the basement. Unoccupied rooms were let out to other members of the Fellowship or to friends who needed a temporary base in London. Alas, communal living did not make for harmony. Lees was the dominant figure in the House, and she wrote to Macdonald complaining, "Miss Henry is *awful!*—I hate the place without you."[34] Nonetheless, the Fellowship constantly reiterated the need for individuals to restructure their personal lives according to the precepts of simplicity and comradeship. Even when the Fellowship was dissolved in 1898, the farewell issue of its journal told readers: "It is not to its meetings that the Fellowship must look for the spread of its teaching, but to the lives of those who have received the Fellowship ideal."[35]

[31] New Fellowship, *The New Fellowship: A Statement of Its Constitution and Aims* (Thornton Heath, UK: Sahud, 1890), p. 5.

[32] *Seed-time*, April 1890.

[33] On the founding of the school, see Ibid., July 1889. For later developments, see B. Ward, *Reddie of Abbotsholme*, intro. J. Findlay (London: Allen and Unwin, 1934).

[34] MacDonald Papers, Public Record Office, London. Cited in D. Marquand, *Ramsay MacDonald* (London: Cape, 1977), p. 27. Edith Lees, who later married Havelock Ellis, found inspiration in both Carpenter and Hinton. See E. Havelock Ellis, *Three Modern Seers* (London: Stanley Paul, 1910).

[35] *Seed-time*, February 1898.

Carpenter: Provincial Socialist Societies

> Thoreau [showed] ... it is still possible and profitable
> to live ... in accordance with nature, with absolute
> serenity and self-possession; to follow out one's own
> ideal, in spite of every obstacle, with unfaltering
> devotion; and so to simplify one's life, and clarify one's
> senses, as to master many of the inner secrets.
> — H. Salt, *The Life of Henry David Thoreau*

Edward Carpenter was born in 1844 and educated at the University of Cambridge, where he became a clerical fellow.[36] He held Broad Church beliefs and was ordained despite telling the examining bishop that he rejected the doctrine of the atonement. At Cambridge, Carpenter recognized that he was a homosexual in a moment of revelation that was brought about by his reading of Whitman's poetry. Soon after, in 1873, Carpenter toured Italy with his unorthodox cousin Jane Daubney.[37] To him the ancient statues there seemed to express Whitman's vision of male comradeship. Broad Church Anglicanism now appeared shallow and dogmatic. When he returned to Cambridge, he renounced his Holy Orders, resigned his fellowship, and became a university extension lecturer. In 1876 he wrote to Whitman: "You have made the earth sacred for me."[38] The following year he traveled to the United States, where he spent a night in Concord, Massachusetts, with Emerson before going on to stay in Camden, New Jersey, with Whitman.[39] He returned to the United States in 1884, visiting Walden Pond, where he swam and placed a stone on top of Thoreau's cairn.

When Carpenter first visited the United States, he looked through Emerson's translation of the Upanishads and discussed Oriental literature with Whitman. This shared interest in the religions of India indicates Carpenter's affinity with the American romantics. It is true that British romantics such as Robert Southey found poetic material in the legends of India and in Hindu festivals like the Rath Yaga at Puri. Yet, several

---

[36] E. Carpenter, *My Days and Dreams* (London: Allen and Unwin, 1916). For discussions, see C. Tsuzuki, *Edward Carpenter, 1844–1929* (Cambridge: Cambridge University Press, 1980); and S. Rowbotham, *Edward Carpenter: A Life of Liberty and Love* (London: Verso, 2008).

[37] Carpenter depicted Daubney as Francesca in E. Carpenter, *Sketches from Life in Town and Country* (London: Allen and Unwin, 1908).

[38] H. Traubel, *With Walt Whitman in Camden*, 3 vols. (New York: Mitchell Kennerley, 1906–14), vol. 3: *28 March 1888 to 14 July 1888, and 1 November 1888 to 20 January 1889*, p. 414.

[39] E. Carpenter, *Days with Walt Whitman* (London: G. Allen, 1906), pp. 3–32.

American romantics, such as Emerson, also found religious inspiration in Hindu texts, equating Hinduism with their own immanentist belief in a single God who exists throughout this world.[40] By no means is all Indian philosophy mystical and immanentist. Nonetheless, the American romantics and Carpenter picked out from Indian thought the specific idea that everything contains the divine. Carpenter described how with the Gnani, with whom he studied in Ceylon, "one came into contact with the root-thought of all existence—the intense consciousness (not conviction merely) of the oneness of all life—the general idea which in one form or another has spread from nation to nation, and become the soul and impulse of religion after religion."[41]

Carpenter shared the immanentism of the American romantics. He tried to argue that the logical structure of knowledge implies that there is a fundamental unity to all things. To do so, he divided the very act of knowledge into three constituents: knower, knowledge, and known. He argued that neither object nor subject can be known either independently of the other or outside of an act of knowledge. Objects can be known only by a conscious subject because something "not relative to any ego or subject, but having an independent non-mental existence of its own, cannot be known."[42] And the subject can be conscious of itself only during an act of knowledge because "when there is no act of knowledge there is no consciousness of the Ego."[43] Although Carpenter's argument suggests only that matter cannot be known in the absence of a knower, he assumed that dead matter is impossible. And although his argument suggests only that egos cannot know themselves outside of an act of knowledge, he assumed that egos cannot exist outside of an act of knowledge. So, he continued by arguing that because dead matter is impossible, the objects that people take to be matter must be other egos; and because egos cannot exist outside of an act of knowledge, everything must be united in a fundamental act of knowledge. Carpenter thus concluded that the world consists of a universal subject that is coming to know itself; history is the evolution of an immanent God, the self-revealment of a universal subject. As he explained, "The World, the whole creation, is self-revealment."[44] Carpenter shared the American romantics' vision of God at work in this world, ensuring that history will lead to the fulfillment of a divine pur-

---

[40] R. Emerson, "Brahma," in *Works*, vol. 9: *Poems*, p. 195; and W. Whitman, "Passage to India," in *Walt Whitman: The Complete Poems* (Harmondsworth, UK: Penguin, 1975), pp. 428–37.

[41] Carpenter, *My Days*, p. 143. For his account of his time in India, see E. Carpenter, *From Adam's Peak to Elephanta* (London: Swan Sonnenschein, 1892).

[42] E. Carpenter, *The Art of Creation* (London: G. Allen, 1904), pp. 38–39.

[43] Ibid., p. 42.

[44] Ibid., p. 44.

pose and, more especially, the realization of a society based on the Emersonian sublime, the self-conscious unity of all.

According to Carpenter, the final realization of the unity of all will be socialism. Like Chubb, Carpenter equated socialism not with social institutions and legal arrangements but with a mystical ethic based on the recognition that everything is one. He had converted to socialism as a result of just such a mystical experience.

> I became for the time overwhelmingly conscious of the disclosure within of a region transcending in some sense the ordinary boundaries of personality. ... I almost immediately saw, or rather felt, that this region of Self existing in me existed equally ... in others. In regard to it the mere diversities of temperament which ordinarily distinguish and divide people dropped away and became indifferent, and a field was opened in which all were truly equal.[45]

For Carpenter, socialism is love or comradeship; it is fellowship or democracy. In a socialist society, people will recognize that they are mere outgrowths of a universal self and will be suffused with love and sympathy for their fellows. The triumph of love will establish a universal brotherhood in which there will be no place left for the struggle for personal domination that currently gives rise to political authority and private property. Humanity will live in nongovernmental communities and rely on cooperative systems of production.[46]

Carpenter's socialist vision consciously echoed Whitman's belief that the soul needs religion, the mind needs democracy, the heart needs love, and the body needs nature. Whitman defined his ideal in terms of "the dear love of comrades," arguing that true democracy is of the spirit and consists of "manly love."[47] His poems combined natural simplicity, male comradeship, and democracy in a religious vision of the vitality of human life. Carpenter too suggested that the growth of comradely love will result in a true brotherhood of all, a real democracy based on the recognition of the unity of all things. It is Carpenter's advocacy of an idealized male love that makes him an early voice of homosexual liberation. Carpenter described the meaning and purpose of love as fusion rather than procreation; he tied love to comradeship rather than reproduction. He even suggested that because the love of homosexuals crosses barriers of class, homosexuals might be the harbingers of democracy.

[45] E. Carpenter, *Towards Democracy* (London: Gay Men's Press, 1985), p. 410.

[46] E. Carpenter, "Transitions to Freedom," in *Forecasts of the Coming Century*, ed. E. Carpenter (Manchester, UK: Labour Press, 1897), pp. 174–92.

[47] W. Whitman, "I Hear It Was Charged against Me" and "For You O Democracy," in *Complete Poems*, pp. 161 and 150.

For Carpenter, socialism consisted primarily of a new ethic of comradeship. He tied this ethic to a simple life lived close to nature. In his view, people will embrace the new democratic ethic only when they become aware of the divine within themselves, and they will do that only if they quieten their lower minds and remove the clutter of material existence. They have to eliminate the extraneous wants that drown the true self in the transient waves of the momentary self. To build socialism, people have to simplify and transform their personal lives. They have to connect with their inner selves. Carpenter especially emphasized the importance of returning to nature and undertaking manual labor. Here too he followed the American romantics. He advocated not a return to the greater beauty of hand-made goods but the elimination of as many possessions as possible. And he wanted a commitment to making things oneself even if they turned out to be rough and ready rather than well crafted. Carpenter believed that people should simplify their lives, clear away the debris of convention, and thereby create the space needed for personal expression. He believed that they should return to nature and manual labor, feeling "downwards and downwards through this wretched maze of shams for the solid ground—to come close to the earth itself and those that live in direct contact with it."[48] People should work in the open air, live in simple shelters, and eat a diet of fruit and nuts. They should attempt to practice self-sufficiency. Personal relationships should be a focus of their lives. Carpenter called for the simplification of life, manual labor, and homosexual liberation: "Lovers of all handicrafts and of labour in the open air, confessed passionate lovers of your own sex, Arise!"[49]

According to Carpenter, people's health depended on their developing a proper awareness of the unity of all. Disease is the breakdown of oneness and the consequent disruption of the natural and harmonious balance of the whole. As Carpenter explained, "The establishment of an insubordinate centre—a boil, a tumour, the introduction and spread of a germ with innumerable progeny throughout the system, the enlargement out of all reason of an existing organ—means disease."[50] Disease is rife in modern society because people have lost sight of the fundamental unity of all things. It is because people neglect unity that there are so many doctors, such slow rates of recovery, so many lunatic asylums, and a ubiquitous feeling of unease. Rampant individualism produces mental illness; because people seek their own advantage without considering others, society has set up an arbitrary moral code, and that code stimulates an

[48] Carpenter, *Towards Democracy*, p. 32.

[49] Ibid., p. 33.

[50] Carpenter, *Civilisation: Its Curse and Cure* (London: Swan Sonnenschein, 1902), p. 14.

unnatural sense of sin, and thus mental illness. Similarly, the absence of simple living contributes to physical illness; for example, processed food weakens the teeth, and sedentary lifestyles produce flaccid muscles.

Carpenter thought all kinds of radical groups spread a new religion of democracy. He provided the Marxist Social Democratic Federation with money to begin publishing its newspaper. He joined the Socialist League, albeit briefly. He spoke at meetings of the Fabian Society. He corresponded with the anarcho-communist Peter Kropotkin, sending him notes to help with his research. However, of all the early socialist groups, Carpenter was most at home in the Fellowship, which he joined in 1885. Later he recalled fondly how "those early meetings of the New Fellowship were full of hopeful enthusiasms—life simplified, a humane diet and rational dress, manual labour, democratic ideals, communal institutions."[51]

An overriding concern with comradeship led Carpenter to place special value on small, intimate groups. He put more effort into his local Sheffield Socialist Society than into any national organization. Indeed, his work to establish a socialist movement in Sheffield illustrates the process by which some members of the Fellowship took ethical socialism out of London and into the rest of the country. The Fellowship inspired various groups of local socialists to adopt a new way of life and to build new moral communities among themselves. For example, the Sheffield Socialists concentrated on charitable activities such as teatime outings for slum children, and on enjoyable social gatherings such as those in their Commonwealth Café, where Carpenter played the harmonium while other members sang the songs collected in his *Chants of Labour*.[52] The Sheffield Socialists combined popular culture with a moral belief in the transforming power of a rude simplicity.

Ethical socialism, with its ideal of fellowship, spread throughout the Midlands and northern England in part because of the inspirational example Carpenter provided. Many ethical socialists looked on him and his life as models of the future.[53] They thought that socialism consisted of the

---

[51] Carpenter, *My Days*, p. 223.

[52] E. Carpenter, ed., *Chants of Labour: A Song Book of the People* (London: Swan Sonnenschein, 1888).

[53] Carpenter's influence reached prominent ethical socialists such as Katherine Conway and the Bristol Socialist Society, well-known authors such as D. H. Lawrence and the Nottingham socialists, and less well-known groups such as the small band of Whitman's followers in Bolton. On these groups, see, respectively, S. Bryher, *An Account of the Labour Movement in Bristol* (Bristol, UK: Bristol Socialist Society, 1931); E. Delavenay, *D. H. Lawrence and Edward Carpenter: A Study in Edwardian Transition* (London: Heinemann, 1971); and P. Salveson, *With Walt Whitman in Bolton: Spirituality, Sex and Socialism in a Northern Mill Town* (Huddersfield, UK: Little Northern Books, 2008). For personal reminiscences of his influence, also see G. Beith, ed., *Edward Carpenter: In Appreciation* (London: Allen and Unwin, 1931).

adoption of a new ideal that would transform personal life, and they read his writings for an account of just such an ideal and life. In their view, he was living socialism. Carpenter hoped that his university extension classes would bring him into contact with manual workers, but his audience consisted almost exclusively of artisans and middle-class women. It was not until 1879 that he met Albert Fearnehough, a scythe maker, and his wife and moved in to live with them in the village of Bradway, outside Sheffield. Thereafter Carpenter gave up his extension lecturing, built a roofless hut by the river, and spent his days there writing the first part of *Towards Democracy*, a poem in the style of Whitman. Later he bought some land in rural Derbyshire and built a house in which he lived initially with the Adams family and later with his lover, George Merrill. He tried to become self-sufficient by growing vegetables and selling leftover produce from a stall in the local market.[54] He lived close to nature by taking regular sunbaths and doing his writing in an open-roofed shed built by a stream that ran across the bottom of his garden. This way of life inspired many other socialists. One of these was Harold Cox, who returned to the land at Craig Farm in Tilford, near Farnham, Surrey. When Cox went to India, he sent Carpenter a pair of sandals that provided the model for those Carpenter began to make, in the belief that they liberated the feet.

A belief in the unity of all inspired a general benevolence and sympathy among ethical socialists such as Carpenter. The most prominent organizational expression of this benevolence was founded in 1891 by Henry Salt. The Humanitarian League stood for the principle that "it is iniquitous to inflict suffering on any sentient being."[55] Salt was a member of the Fellowship and a friend of Carpenter's. He was influenced by American romanticism, and he wrote a biography of Thoreau, edited several volumes of Thoreau's writings, and began his plea for vegetarianism by citing Thoreau.[56] Carpenter became increasingly active in the Humanitarian League during the 1890s. Like Salt, Carpenter was a vegetarian who opposed cruelty to humans and animals alike, arguing, for example, that vivisection was immoral because all creatures contained the divine, and besides, even from a utilitarian standpoint, hurting animals did not reduce human suffering but might give rise to new diseases.[57] By

[54] E. Carpenter, *England's Ideal* (London: Swan Sonnenschein, 1902), pp. 95–120.

[55] *Seed-time*, July 1891. Also see H. Salt, *Seventy Years among Savages* (London: Allen and Unwin, 1921).

[56] H. Salt, *The Life of Henry David Thoreau* (London: Bentley, 1890); H. Thoreau, *Poems of Nature*, ed. H. Salt and F. Sanborn (London: Lane, 1895); H. Thoreau, *Selections from Thoreau*, ed. and introd. H. Salt (London: Macmillan, 1895); H. Thoreau, *Anti-Slavery and Reform Papers*, ed. and introd. H. Salt (London: Swan Sonnenschein, 1890); and H. Salt, *A Plea for Vegetarianism and Other Essays* (Manchester, UK: Vegetarian Society, 1885).

[57] E. Carpenter and E. Maitland, *Vivisection* (London: William Reeves, 1893).

the 1890s, Carpenter had also started to champion other humanitarian causes. He initiated a campaign against smoke pollution, pointing to the environmental costs of industry and showing how easily the smoke nuisance could be abated if industrialists would use suitable equipment.[58] In 1890 the Sheffield Socialists made opposition to "the smoke fiend" a condition of their support in the local elections.[59] Soon after, the Sheffield Socialists collapsed following an influx of revolutionary and often violent anarchists, including Fred Charles and John Craghe.

CONCLUSION

Davidson and Carpenter helped bring American romanticism into the British socialist movement. The genuine religious convictions and rough-and-ready ethic of the American romantics inspired many ethical socialists from the Fellowship through various provincial groups, and on, as we shall see, into the personal transformations and socialist churches that provided the background to the rise of the Independent Labour Party. The ethical socialists often modified American romanticism even as they drew on it. In particular, although Davidson remained committed to individualism, ethical socialists were overtly critical of it. They often denied that there was any contradiction between individualism and socialism, appealing to a higher individualism that fused the two. However, it is no coincidence that almost all of their critical comments on American romanticism focused on Thoreau's individualism. Salt argued that Thoreau's "intensely individualistic nature" prevented him from grasping the enormity of the social problem.[60] Chubb complained: "'No concession to society' was the cry of the new Protestants; and so austere were some, that ... they decided to leave society altogether."[61] Yet, although ethical socialists repudiated the individualism of the American romantics, they drew heavily on their immanentist faith, ethic of fellowship, and personal goals of self-reliance, simplicity, and a return to nature.

Themes associated with American romanticism gave a distinctive hue to much ethical socialism. These themes will echo through the next two chapters. One theme was a genuine religious conviction that found the divine in nature. This conviction inspired a range of socialist churches, including the Brotherhood Church and the Labour Church, which we will encounter respectively in chapters 13 and 14. Another theme was a

---

[58] E. Carpenter, "The Smoke Plague and Its Remedy," *Macmillan's Magazine*, July 1890.
[59] For the "smoke fiend" and "anarchists" in Sheffield, see the letters from G. Hukin to E. Carpenter, Edward Carpenter Collection, Sheffield Archives, ECC:362.38 and ECC:362.43.
[60] Salt, *Life of Thoreau*, p. 292.
[61] Chubb, introduction to *Select Writings*, p. xv.

belief in the importance of self-sufficiency and a return to the land. This belief inspired a range of personal and communal experiments, including not only Carpenter's simple life but also the anarchist groups that we will consider in the next chapter.

Before we turn to the new anarchism and the labor churches, we might pause briefly to note the continuing influence of the American romantics on these movements. William Jupp and John Trevor were two immanentists whose thought I examined in the last chapter, and I will pick them up again in ensuing chapters. Jupp was a member of the Fellowship. He wrote the following in its paper:

> When Emerson died a friend said to me, "It was a pity he should have gone. No doubt his work was done; he had no more to say to us. But it was good to think of him there, living on, serene and wise. It had been well if two or three of us could have died instead of him. It was a pity he should die."[62]

Jupp shared the religious sensibility of the American romantics. After his Calvinist youth, he became a Congregationalist minister, but he had serious religious doubts, which began to diminish when he turned to the immanentism of romantics such as Emerson. For Jupp, "*Leaves of Grass* [by Whitman], and *Towards Democracy* took their place with Thoreau's *Walden*, and Emerson's *Essays and Lectures*, and *Conduct of Life* as Scriptures 'given by inspiration of God.'"[63] In 1890 Jupp founded a free religious movement in Croydon, just outside London.[64] A couple of years later, he merged his church into the Brotherhood Church, which I will discuss in the next chapter.

Trevor wrote that Emerson and Whitman "became part of me."[65] He described Whitman as "nearer to God than any man on earth," and he kept a copy of Emerson's book "to read occasionally as a Bible."[66] Trevor too was raised as a Calvinist. But in 1876 he sailed to Australia and renounced the Bible as a religious guide. Soon after, he decided to study in Meadville, Pennsylvania, to become a Unitarian minister. Earlier he had read Emerson. Now he "discovered" him: "What Emerson did for me was, not to give me a formula, but to stimulate my faith—I do not mean faith of any theological sort, but rather that commanding confidence in the soundness of life which is the first step towards true self-confidence,

---

[62] W. Jupp, "Walt Whitman: The Man and His Message," *Seed-time*, July 1892.

[63] Jupp, *Wayfarings*, p. 68. His highly appreciative review of Carpenter's *Towards Democracy* appeared in *Seed-time*, April 1893.

[64] On the formation of the Croydon movement, see *Seed-time*, January 1891.

[65] J. Trevor, *My Quest for God* (London: Labour Prophet, 1897), p. 135.

[66] *Labour Prophet*, July 1896; Trevor, *My Quest*, p. 158.

true courage, and true Religion."[67] Trevor returned to England in 1879, rented a house in the countryside, and experienced the Emersonian sublime through nature. He soon became minister of the Upper Brook Street Free Church in Manchester. Then, in 1891, he went to a Unitarian conference at which Ben Tillett called on the churches to respond to the demands of the workers before the workers left the churches. Soon after, Trevor founded the Labour Church movement, which I will discuss in chapter 14.

[67] Trevor, *My Quest*, p. 135.

CHAPTER THIRTEEN

Ethical Anarchism

MOST VICTORIANS THOUGHT of anarchism as an individualist doctrine lurking in the clandestine organizations of violent revolutionaries. However, by the outbreak of the First World War, a very different type of anarchism had become equally prominent. The new anarchists still opposed the state, but they were communalists, not individualists, and they hoped to realize their ideal peacefully through personal example and moral education, not violently through acts of terror and a general uprising. They took inspiration from Peter Kropotkin and Leo Tolstoy.

The new anarchism overlapped markedly with ethical socialism. From one side, the new anarchists were part of the broad cultural shift away from evangelicalism and classical liberalism, toward immanentist theology and an ethic of fellowship. Almost all of them shared the ethical socialists' concern with personal transformation and communal living. Many of the new anarchists had been inspired by the personal example of ethical socialists such as Edward Carpenter, and several had belonged to ethical socialist groups such as the Fellowship of the New Life. Like the ethical socialists, the new anarchists saw themselves as peaceful and constructive harbingers of a harmonious society based on a higher morality. They had less in common with their anarchist predecessors than with contemporary sex reformers and utopian communalists.

From the other side, the new anarchism drew attention to the bohemianism running through much of ethical socialism. The most prominent ethical socialists and new anarchists were middle-class writers, journalists, and artists. Few artisans or proletarian workers joined them. Moreover, both ethical socialism and the new anarchism were primarily about experiments with unorthodox lifestyles. Their radical politics consisted mainly of a commitment to bohemianism, including free love, voluntary poverty, new religions, and modernist art. Significantly, ethical socialism arose as Victorian culture disintegrated into modernism—a collection of fragmented pieces lacking secure and accepted principles. Some contemporaries saw the disintegration of Victorian culture as a destructive process culminating in decadence. Yet, for those involved, it represented the start of a new cultural renaissance. Contemporaries teetered on a

A version of this chapter appeared as "The Rise of Ethical Anarchism in Britain, 1885–1900," *Historical Research* 69 (1996), 143–165. Published by Blackwell.

parapet, uncertain whether jumping would plunge them into a vile abyss and social catastrophe or propel them up to a higher life and new social order. The fin de siècle was a Janus-faced culture of decadence and optimism. Its optimism shone out of the new anarchism and ethical socialism more generally.

THE RISE OF THE NEW ANARCHISM

Like socialism, anarchism emerged out of nineteenth-century radicalism. Pierre-Joseph Proudhon and Mikhail Bakunin wanted to liberate individuals from the oppression and exploitation that they associated with the state.[1] Anarchists wanted individuals to be free from obtrusive authority and, in particular, free to do as they saw fit with the product of their labor. This individualist anarchism inspired Henry Seymour, a secularist from Tunbridge Wells, Kent, to begin publishing the *Anarchist* in 1885.[2] Like Bakunin, Seymour progressed from a secularist hostility to the church, with its imposition of God on the individual, to an iconoclastic denunciation of a society imposing its values on the individual. Seymour tried to blend Proudhon's mutualism with the extreme individualism of some American anarchists. He envisaged small proprietors cooperating with one another in voluntary schemes. The result would be a free-trade utopia in which "absolutely free competition" made cost "the just limit of price," thereby ensuring that individuals reaped the full benefit of their labor without monopolists or the state exacting a tithe.[3]

Most of Seymour's contributors thought of themselves as libertarian socialists, but not specifically as anarchists. In chapter 8 I discussed the example of George Bernard Shaw. Another example was the ethical socialist Edward Carpenter, whose ideas we explored in the last chapter. As we have seen, the debates among British socialists during the 1880s did much to separate out Marxists, Fabians, and anarchists. For a start, debates within the Marxist Social Democratic Federation led most anarchists to find their way into the Socialist League. Like Seymour, the anarchists of the Socialist League expressed the radical tradition of Proudhon

---

[1] Some historians give anarchy a more ancient lineage. But Proudhon was the first to use the word to describe a political outlook. It became associated with a historical movement only when Marx used it to describe the views of Bakunin and his followers. Even Bakunin described himself as a "collectivist" so as to establish distance from Proudhon. A self-styled anarchist movement first arose in the 1880s. On British anarchism, see H. Oliver, *The International Anarchist Movement in Late Victorian London* (London: Croom Helm, 1983); and J. Quail, *The Slow Burning Fuse* (London: Paladin, 1978).

[2] *Labour Annual* (1899), p. 162.

[3] *Anarchist*, March 1885.

and Bakunin. These anarchists included both refugees, such as Victor Dave, Hermann Jung, and Andreas Scheu, and young Britons influenced by these refugees, such as Frank Kitz and Joseph Lane. In addition, as the Fabians adopted a clear commitment to parliamentary politics and institutional reform, they marginalized the anarchists and ethical socialists among the group. Charlotte Wilson (née Martin) and the other anarchists and ethical socialists among the Fabians rejected Marxism not only as a statist doctrine but also as an immoral one that preached violence and a selfish and sectional ethic of class interest.[4]

Wilson was educated at Cheltenham Ladies' College and Merton Hall (a precursor of Newnham College, Cambridge), after which she married Arthur Wilson, a stockbroker, with whom she set up home on the edge of Hampstead Heath.[5] She became a Pre-Raphaelite bohemian, furnishing her cottage with the objects, fabrics, and prints championed by William Morris and his circle. Like many literary radicals, she joined the Society of Friends of Russian Freedom, which flourished, as the Russian militant and writer Sergei Stepniak proved popular among fashionable Londoners. Wilson wanted to found her own "literary sort of society," to be called the Russian Society, but in the end she settled for a single "drawing-room meeting," since Stepniak told her he saw no role for anything grander or more permanent.[6] By now Wilson had developed a romantic view of the Russian peasantry; she believed that they still retained the "democratic and communistic spirit" of primitive socialism and that "Russia may yet lead the way in social re-organisation."[7]

For several years, Wilson had kept the black flag of anarchism aloft among the Fabians. She wanted the Fabians to remain committed to discussions in which "socialists of every shape of opinion may find a common meeting ground."[8] She argued with them that political action was unnecessary and immoral, and besides, if they really wanted to try political action, they already had a suitable vehicle to hand in the form of the Social Democratic Federation. When the Fabians formed their Parlia-

---

[4] P. Chubb, "The Two Alternatives," *To-day* 8 (1887): 69–77; J. Ramsay MacDonald, "A Rock Ahead," *To-day* 7 (1887): 66–70; and S. Olivier, "Perverse Socialism," *To-day* 6 (1886): 47–55 and 109–14.

[5] Wilson was the model for Gemma in E. Voynich's *The Gadfly* (London: Heinemann, 1897).

[6] Wilson to Pearson, 24 January 1886, Karl Pearson Papers, Bloomsbury Science Library, University College, London, KPP:900.

[7] C. Wilson, "The Condition of the Russian Peasantry," *To-day* 4 (1885): 357.

[8] Wilson to Shaw, 13 September 1886, Shaw Papers, British Library, London, BM:50511. Many anarchists thought that "although the Fabian Society is as yet bourgeois in constitution and sentiment it is the only meeting ground in London for English Socialists of all denominations." See *Anarchist*, July 1885.

mentary League in 1886, she accepted defeat and began to focus almost exclusively on Russia and anarchism.

Wilson conceived of bringing Kropotkin to England to publish an anarchist paper. She began a correspondence with Sophie Kropotkin while the latter's husband was still in Clairvaux Prison. When Kropotkin was released, he came to Britain and joined Seymour to form an editorial collectiveto run the *Anarchist*.[9] However, the collective did not work smoothly together. Seymour still fused Proudhonian mutualism with more extreme forms of individualism. Kropotkin and his followers were anarcho-communists. All kinds of related issues set them against one another. For a start, whereas Seymour believed that anonymity undermined individual responsibility, Kropotkin and his followers regarded anonymous articles as an expression of the communist ethic that they identified with anarchism. Even before the first issue of the *Anarchist* appeared, Seymour was telling Shaw that he preferred signed articles, at the same time as Wilson was telling him that articles should be unsigned.[10] When the paper first appeared, Seymour wrote that "each writer must be alone responsible for his or her views."[11] A year later, he acquiesced in the decision of the editorial collective to publish only anonymous articles.[12] Yet, immediately afterward, he complained publicly that under editorial collectives, "individuality gets extinguished to maintain a 'general tone,' which may for all I know be true Communism, but isn't true Anarchism."[13] More generally, Seymour complained that Kropotkin and his followers demanded an equality that sacrificed the rights of labor to the idle.[14] Because he rejected their social ethic, he could see no way of defending the hardworking against the lazy, so he could not accept their communism. In October 1886, after little more than six months, Kropotkin and Wilson broke with Seymour to start their own newspaper, *Freedom*.

The leading members of the Freedom Group had usually been involved with the Fellowship and the Fabians.[15] Dr. Burns-Gibson was a district police surgeon and a medical officer with the Post Office; he had proposed the resolution that founded the Fellowship, and he had spoken on anarchism to the Hampstead Historic. Mrs. Dryhurst was an Irish

[9] P. Kropotkin, *Memoirs of a Revolutionist*, pref. G. Brandes, 2 vols. (London: Smith Elder, 1899).

[10] Seymour to Shaw, 5 and 6 January 1885, BM:50511; and Wilson to Shaw, 10 December 1884, BM:50510.

[11] *Anarchist*, March 1885.

[12] Ibid., 20 April 1886.

[13] Ibid., 1 June 1886.

[14] Ibid., May 1887.

[15] Wilson's history of the group is in *Freedom*, December 1900. On Dr. Burns-Gibson's talk to the Hampstead Historic, see Wilson to Pearson, 4 March 1886, KPP:900.

Nationalist and an early member of the Fabian Society. Agnes Henry lived in the communal residence of Fellowship members in Bloomsbury, London. Apart from this inner circle, the Freedom Group included various sympathizers and contributors who were generally socialists with acknowledged anarchist leanings. Emma Brooke was an old friend of Mrs. Wilson's from her student and Fabian days. She studied economics with Alfred Marshall but left Cambridge "deeply dissatisfied with orthodox economics."[16] Later she became secretary of the Hampstead Historic. Carpenter was, as we saw in the last chapter, a romantic poet inspired by Whitman, who joined the Fellowship and moved to the north of England in search of a simple life of manual labor and comradely love.

In the early 1890s, the Fellowship inspired a second wave of anarchists who drew their inspiration from Tolstoy.[17] John Bruce Wallace was born in India to a Presbyterian missionary and his wife. He graduated from Dublin University in 1874, studied theology at Bonn University, and returned to Ireland as a Congregationalist minister. In the early 1880s, he heard Henry George speak on land reform, began thinking about social problems, and eventually started a newspaper, *Brotherhood*, to promote the social gospel that he thought could solve these problems. A few years later, Wallace crossed the Irish Sea to found the nondoctrinaire Brotherhood Church in Southgate, London.[18] Other Brotherhood churches soon sprang up nearby in Forest Gate and Walthamstow.

J. C. Kenworthy was born in Liverpool in 1863. In the early 1880s, he read John Ruskin and joined the movement for land reform, becoming honorary secretary of the English Land Colonisation Society. He spent some time working in Mansfield House Settlement, which was part of a movement that aimed to uplift the urban poor by getting middle-class people to live and work in deprived parts of London. By the late 1880s, he was becoming involved with anarchism as a regular contributor to *Freedom*. In 1892 he read Tolstoy's writings while traveling to America and became an instant convert to the latter's social gospel.[19] When Kenworthy returned to England, he and Wallace helped to open yet another Brotherhood church, in Croydon.

The Brotherhood churches sought "to apply the principles of the Sermon on the Mount literally and fully to individual and social conduct, which they interpret into action by efforts to found industries and busi-

---

[16] *Labour Annual* (1895), p. 163.

[17] Not all members of the Fellowship took to Tolstoy. Many were sympathetic and yet critical of his stress on the spiritual and individual at the expense of the physical and social. See H. Rix, "The Later Works of Count Leo Tolstoy," *Seed-time*, January 1893.

[18] *Labour Annual* (1895), p. 191.

[19] J. Kenworthy, *My Psychic Experiences* (London: Office of Light, 1901).

nesses on what may be described as Socialist Co-operative lines."[20] In 1894 Kenworthy and Wallace expanded the movement by forming the Brotherhood Trust. The trust undertook cooperative production and retailing. The profits were put aside to purchase land for anarchist communes. Members of the trust were thereby able to opt out of the capitalist economy. Each member was supposed to recruit a new member every quarter. The hope was that the alternative society of the communes would thereby spread until capitalism and the state were no more. Wallace described the trust as "an organisation of industry and commerce which should substantially and increasingly benefit an ever-widening circle of honest workers, should illustrate the operation of sound moral and economic principles, and should thus serve as an object-lesson and example far more persuasive than many blasts of oratory."[21] The trust opened stores in Croydon, Southgate, and Walthamstow, all of which refused to have any dealings with firms that did not pay a living trade-union wage. Later some of the members of the trust founded Brotherhood House as a communal residence in Croydon.

The followers of Kropotkin and Tolstoy adopted a new anarchism that resembled other bohemian beliefs of the romantic nineties more closely than it did the individualist ideas of Seymour and the Socialist League. Anarchism appealed to them not as a way to assert the rights of the autonomous individual but because they believed that the decay of the old order was giving birth to a new life and because they identified this new life with anarcho-communism.

The Theory of New Anarchism

The new anarchists argued that socialism would bring economic well-being, but something more than material well-being was necessary for human flourishing. They championed a new spirituality and a higher individualism. They wanted to replace the individualism of the Manchester School with a more social individualism. As Wilson explained, the hopes of anarchists rested on the "spread of a higher morality" that reconciled "absolute personal freedom with the growing desire for social unity" by appealing to a "sufficiently enlightened or socialised self-interest."[22] Again, Kenworthy described "the complete Anarchist" as "the perfect idealist"—"the man whose goal is entire freedom of action for all, know-

---

[20] *Labour Annual* (1896), p. 44.
[21] J. Wallace, *Towards Fraternal Organisation: An Explanation of the Brotherhood Trust* (London: Brotherhood Trust, 1894), p. 3.
[22] Wilson to Pearson, 30 October 1884 and 19 December 1884, KPP:900.

ing this to be the only possible condition in which equality and fraternity can exist."[23] The new anarchists hoped to resolve any conflict between the individual and society by allowing people to do as they wished within a framework of mutual cooperation and fraternal comradeship.

A higher individualism dominated the new anarchism. The first issue of *Freedom* defended a concept of liberty as being at "one with social feeling."[24] The new anarchists condemned contemporary social arrangements for suppressing and distorting the social impulses that otherwise would blossom into a higher individualism. Wilson called for the eradication of all forms of domination on the grounds that authority and feelings of superiority corrupt people's fraternal instincts. In her view, western societies had done away with such striking forms of despotism as slavery and serfdom, but they still contained "the spirit of domination in the concrete form of Property, guarded by law, upheld by the organised force of Government, and backed by the yet undestroyed desire to dominate in certain individuals."[25] Like many anarchists, Wilson regarded the state as a double evil. First, the state defended class interests through the rights of property. The law provided a veneer of legitimacy, but when it failed, the police and army dealt with threats to property, thereby revealing the force that actually sustained social inequalities. Second, the state was an evil in its own right, for it allowed others to rule over people. Even democratic states involved "the government of man by man" in a way that reduced the individual to a "slave of the simulacrum that now stands for society."[26] Socialist collectivism could not liberate the human spirit because the continued existence of the state would still perpetuate domination.

Only anarchism could eliminate domination. Wilson rejected all state authority in favor of "the absolute right of every *adult* to do exactly what he *chooses*," provided only that he did not thereby infringe on the equivalent right of others.[27] The existence of a state imposed a pattern of development on the individual. Only in the absence of the state were individuals able to realize a true individuality characterized by social feeling but not subordination to society. The free individual would be able to develop "himself to the utmost," "expanding from within outwards until his soul is one with humanity."[28] The higher individualism had to come from within, so only an anarchic society would do. As *Freedom* explained,

[23] J. Kenworthy, *Tolstoy: His Life and Works* (London: Walter Scott, 1902), pp. 120–21.
[24] *Freedom*, October 1886.
[25] C. Wilson, "Social Democracy and Anarchism," *Practical Socialist* 1 (1886): 11.
[26] C. Wilson, *Anarchism* (Leeds, UK: Anarchist Group, 1900), p. 4.
[27] Wilson to Shaw, 10 December 1884, BM:50510.
[28] Wilson to Pearson, 4 March 1886, KPP:900.

anarchists believed in "self-guidance, voluntary association, general action by the direct and unanimous decision of the persons concerned."[29]

The Tolstoyans placed the higher individualism in a more Christian setting. They condemned the church for having turned its back on Christian morality and taken on the authoritarian garb of the state. They appealed instead to the life of Christ, and especially the Sermon on the Mount. Kenworthy explained how Tolstoy "returned to the principles of conduct taught by Jesus Christ," sweeping aside the dogmas of the churches so as to return to the broad mysticism of John's Gospel.[30] Although all Christian churches teach moral principles, Tolstoy actually put these principles into practice. Besides, Kenworthy continued, Tolstoy alone recognized that Christian morality rests on passive resistance; "the heart of the teaching of Jesus" resides in an insistence on "self-surrender, truth, and perfect love to all," for "self-defence and violent resistance can never establish justice among men."[31]

According to the Tolstoyans, contemporary society denied Christian morality. Capitalism enshrined selfishness and competition, not love and cooperation. It persisted because of the illegitimate power of the state and the failure of the church to preach the true Gospel of Jesus. It was "a false political economy, based upon a perverted philosophy, sanctioned by a venal Church, and enforced by the State's power to kill."[32] The solution was to follow the example of Tolstoy. People should give up their possessions, for even if they tried to use their property for good, they would depend on the force of the police in a way that would implicate them in an immoral society. They should follow Jesus, renouncing property for an ethic of love. They should follow the Sermon on the Mount, replacing the authority of the state with anarchy. Kenworthy equated the Christian principle that we should treat others as we would have them treat us with the complete realization of the revolutionary trinity of liberty, equality, and fraternity. Socialism embodied equality, and communism incorporated fraternity, but only anarchism combined these principles with liberty. Christian morality required anarchy.

The new anarchists believed that the higher individualism would emerge inevitably as the outcome of the evolutionary process. All of history revealed the growth of a spirit of cooperation that would result in an anarchic idyll. The key to future development lay in the extension of this spirit of cooperation into a new sensibility. Thus, changes in institu-

---

[29] *Freedom*, November 1890.

[30] Kenworthy, *Tolstoy*, p. 29. He wrote a commentary on the Sermon on the Mount in *New Order*, December 1897 and January 1898.

[31] Kenworthy, *Tolstoy*, p. 34.

[32] Ibid., p. 130.

tional arrangements were far less important than the growth of a new consciousness. Kenworthy explained that an anarchic society would arise from people's subscribing to a new religious sensibility. He argued that "the Utopia we seek is not a pious hope with which to comfort ourselves, but a practicable reality to be brought about by entering into relationship with the spirit world which is part of the one Nature to which we all belong."[33] He distinguished between wayward "materialists," who wanted to change the system but in the meantime happily profited under it, and right-thinking "mystics," who recognized the system was "the outward manifestation of an indwelling life" and attempted to change the system by living the new life.[34] Similarly, Wilson stressed that "each individual must feel that the responsibility for the realisation of his share in the advance towards his ideal rests with himself alone."[35] Like ethical socialists generally, the new anarchists thus concentrated their energies on transforming their own lives and educating people in the new morality.

Where the new anarchists differed from many ethical socialists was not in their focus on personal transformation but in their refusal to countenance other political action. They argued that to use authority to decree an end to authority was contradictory, immoral, and doomed to failure. Wilson insisted that anarchists "cannot conscientiously take part in any sort of government" because they thereby would strengthen the "idea that the rule of man over man is a right and beneficial thing."[36] The Freedom Group as a whole stood by similar views, arguing, for example, that expropriation would fail if it was undertaken by an organization based on authority.[37] The Tolstoyans were more divided about political action. Kenworthy opposed it on the grounds that "the stage of law, of force, will not cease, cannot cease, while I and others continue to use it."[38] Wallace defended political action in principle even though he thought it probably would prove ineffectual.[39]

New and Old Anarchism

Seymour and the members of the Socialist League approached anarchism from a liberation tradition that wanted to free the individual from the fetters of the state and, at times, capitalism. They believed that individu-

[33] Kenworty, *Psychic*, p. 19.
[34] Kenworty, *Tolstoy*, p. 42.
[35] Wilson to Pearson, 19 December 1884, KPP:900.
[36] C. Wilson, *Anarchism and Outrage* (London: C. M. Wilson, 1893), p. 4.
[37] "Labour Leaflet," *Freedom*, August 1890.
[38] *New Order*, November 1897.
[39] Ibid., December 1897.

als generally should be free to do as they wished without reference to the community. In contrast, the new anarchists wanted to bring the individual into a proper relationship with the community through the spread of a new sensibility. They believed that individuals should recognize that their particular good consists in the good of the community. Kenworthy thought that Tolstoy's great discovery was that "mankind is the creation of a God who is love," and so "love and service to one another are the only relations in which man can exist happily."[40] The different views of the old and new anarchists led to lively debates on the nature of the ideal and on how the ideal can be established.

One debate concerned the nature of the anarchist ideal. Proudhon and Bakunin advocated desert-based concepts of justice according to which individuals consume in proportion to the work they perform, or at least consume only on the condition that they make a productive contribution. Proudhon thought that a just society would keep private property but introduce a mutual credit bank to lend money free of interest and thereby remove the possibility of exploitation.[41] Bakunin believed in a requirement of "work" because "society cannot ... leave itself completely defenceless against vicious and parasitic individuals"; but he hoped to realize his ideal by collectivizing the means of production, and presumably arranging distribution through something akin to a market economy.[42]

Kropotkin offered two reasons for turning instead to a need-based theory of justice.[43] First, he argued pragmatically that desert-based systems could not work. It was not possible to distinguish either the means of production from the means of consumption, or the precise contribution of a particular individual to the process of production. Second, Kropotkin argued morally that a need-based society was preferable to a desert-based one. Private property of any sort encouraged acquisitiveness and self-assertiveness, both of which were detrimental to the ideal of mutual aid. He concluded that consumption should be communal. Everyone should take whatever they needed from a collective store.

Clearly people could become anarcho-communists for either of the two reasons Kropotkin offered. Several of the old anarchists were Proudhonites and Bakuninites who sometimes accepted his pragmatic argument but not his moral one. They were reluctant and pessimistic anarcho-

[40] Kenworthy, *Tolstoy*, p. 28.

[41] P.-J. Proudhon, *What Is Property?* ed. and trans. D. Kelley and B. Smith (Cambridge: Cambridge University Press, 1994).

[42] M. Bakunin, "Revolutionary Catechism," in *Bakunin on Anarchy*, ed. S. Dolgoff, pref. P. Avrich (London: Allen and Unwin, 1973), p. 80.

[43] P. Kropotkin, *Mutual Aid* (London: William Heinemann, 1915) and "The Conquest of Bread," in *The Conquest of Bread and Other Writings*, ed. M. Shatz (Cambridge: Cambridge University Press, 1995).

communists. They became anarcho-communists reluctantly when they realized that their more individualistic ideal could not work. And they were pessimistic about the prospects of anarcho-communism because they retained a fairly individualist view of human nature.[44] In contrast, the new anarchists, whether they followed Kropotkin or Tolstoy, generally accepted both of Kropotkin's arguments.

Seymour never became anything other than a reluctant and pessimistic anarcho-communist. A debate with Kropotkin led him to adopt a "voluntary communism." He accepted that common ownership of the means of production without free consumption required some sort of rule to abolish inheritance and so prevent the private accumulation of wealth leading to a return to inequality; communism was necessary. Yet, he continued to insist that a compulsory system of communism would be antithetical to individualist and anarchist principles; communism must be voluntary. So, although Seymour accepted the validity of Kropotkin's pragmatic argument, his ideal still consisted of autonomous individuals doing as they pleased and reaping the consequences outside of any context of social relations. Indeed, his individualism left him opposing a number of positions that seemed to follow more or less logically from any commitment to anarcho-communism. For instance, he sought a mechanism to prevent idlers from consuming goods that were produced by the hardworking, even though any such mechanism necessarily undermined a need-based system of consumption.[45] Moreover, his radical secularist inheritance prevented him from resolving the tension between anarcho-communism and individualism by appealing to a social instinct that might lead free individuals to strive for the common good. For instance, he remained implacably "opposed to all nonsense known as 'public morality' as set up by a 'public opinion.'" He claimed that "there is no morality but liberty."[46] Even after Seymour became an anarcho-communist, he continued to regard the idea of social solidarity with suspicion and as a threat to the autonomous individual.

In contrast, the new anarchists placed an even greater stress on Kropotkin's moral argument than he did himself. Anarcho-communists needed to explain how their ideal society, in which people's consumption of goods bore no relation to their production of goods, could guarantee that the community could produce a sufficient amount of goods to meet the total demand for consumption. Kropotkin appealed mainly to scientific

[44] Bakuninites criticized Kropotkin's optimism. See E. Malatesta, "Peter Kropotkin—Recollections and Criticisms of an Old Friend," in *Errico Malatesta: His Life and Ideas*, by V. Richards (London: Freedom Press, 1977), pp. 257–68.

[45] *Anarchist*, May 1887.

[46] Ibid., March 1885.

progress, suggesting that technological advances would enable humanity to produce sufficient goods to satisfy any conceivable demand. The new anarchists appealed mainly to a new sensibility: a higher individualism would inspire people to work for the general good and to consume only what they needed. For example, Wilson told Shaw that in an anarchist society the sense of security people currently obtained from owning property would come from "the moral attitude of the public" to the needs and wants of the individual.[47] The new anarchists identified the anarchist ideal not with Seymour's autonomous individual but with a social individual who attained personal freedom through the community: social solidarity was not a threat to the individual but the means of individual self-realization.

Another debate concerned anarchist strategy. Bakunin believed that violence was legitimate only when needed to ensure the triumph of anarchy. His writings on political action concentrated on the nature of the circumstances in which intrinsically immoral violence became morally acceptable as a means to a desirable end. He believed that the masses did not establish anarchy only because a coercive and unjust society kept them ignorant and downtrodden. Anarchists had to break through the stupor of the masses in order to initiate the revolution. Bakunin then argued that human instincts were more powerful and trustworthy than reason. Whereas doctrine killed life, all urges, including the urge to destroy, were creative. Bakunin concluded that violence was legitimate as a means of awakening the revolutionary instincts of the masses. For most of his life, he wanted anarchists to stage a violent uprising designed to initiate a more popular revolution.[48] In 1874 he even led an ill-fated uprising at Castel del Monte. Thereafter, some of Bakunin's followers decided that insurrectionary acts alone might prompt the masses to turn an uprising into a popular revolution. Their faith in insurrectionary acts then gave rise to a doctrine of propaganda by the deed, and so, in the 1890s, to the isolated and pointless acts of terror known as *attentats*.

Kropotkin rejected Bakunin's strategy of using violent putsches to propel the masses into revolution, arguing that it probably would prove unsuccessful, and that even if it was successful, it probably would end in authoritarianism. He accepted that violence might be necessary for the seizure of property during the revolution, and, for a while, he even advocated something akin to propaganda by the deed.[49] None-

[47] Wilson to Shaw, 16 February 1887, BM:50511.

[48] Bakunin, "The Program of the International Brotherhood" and "Letter to Albert Richard," in *Bakunin on Anarchy*, pp. 148–55 and 177–82.

[49] P. Kropotkin, "The Spirit of Revolt," in *Kropotkin's Revolutionary Pamphlets*, ed. R. Baldwin (New York: Dover, 1970), pp. 35–43.

theless, he typically focused on initiating revolution by appealing to people's reason with peaceful persuasion, not appealing to their instincts through violent action.[50]

Many of the anarchists in the Socialist League advocated violent deeds as a form of propaganda. Their emphasis on violence angered those other members of the League who were not anarchists. Morris and his followers finally resigned from the League in 1890 to protest David Nicoll's publication of articles on revolutionary warfare.[51] At times the anarchists in the League seemed to delight in violence, or at least the idea of violence, for its own sake. They wrote joyously of workers throwing stones at the police during a strike in Leeds, complaining only that "no corpses [were] to be seen."[52] They called on the people to start "a fire that would end the whole damn thing."[53] And they argued that an anarchist "should take what he requires of the wealth around him, using violence whenever necessary."[54] This faith in the efficacy of violent deeds led several members of the League to toy with attentats. When in 1893 a bomb exploded at the opera house in Barcelona, killing thirty people, Henry Samuels wrote, "Yes, I am really pleased."[55] Later, on 15 February 1894, Martial Bourdin, a brother-in-law of Samuels, fell over, landed on a bomb that he was carrying, and blew himself up.

The new anarchists eschewed violence even as propaganda. The Tolstoyans rejected all violence as immoral, championing an ideal and a strategy based on passive resistance. The Freedom Group accepted that the revolution probably would be violent, but they opposed violence as a means of preparing people for the revolution, trusting instead to the gradual evolution of a rational morality; they described attentats as understandable but mistaken and unhelpful.[56]

Different attitudes to violent deeds were a source of tension among the anarchists. When *Freedom* and the League organized a meeting in 1891 on behalf of the Chicago Anarchists, a member of the League sniped at the *Freedom* speakers, "We have heard much of the doctrine of brotherhood and love tonight, but the doctrine of hate and vengeance is just as necessary and right."[57] At about the same time, another member of the League complained that although Carpenter wrote poems full of anarchist sentiment, he "disavows all connexion with Anarchists [of the

---

[50] Bakuninites criticized Kropotkin's fatalism. See Malatesta, "Kropotkin."
[51] *Commonweal*, October and November 1890.
[52] Ibid., 12 July 1890.
[53] Ibid., 16 August 1890.
[54] Ibid., 29 November 1890.
[55] Ibid., 25 November 1893.
[56] Wilson, *Outrages*.
[57] *Commonweal*, 21 November 1891.

Socialist League]," and he "has never except in a half-hearted way done anything to support our propaganda."[58]

The issue of violence peaked with the Walsall Anarchist Case. Fred Charles, a member of the League, moved to Walsall in July 1891. He was joined there by Victor Cailes, a French refugee, who had been introduced to the League by Auguste Coulon, a member of the North Kensington branch. Then, in January 1892, six Walsall anarchists were arrested and charged under the Explosives Act with possession of the materials for making a bomb. The six were Cailes, Charles, an Italian refugee called Jean Battola, and three local men, Joe Deakin, William Ditchfield, and John Westley. Battola, Cailes, and Charles were sentenced to ten years' imprisonment, Deakin got five years, and Ditchfield and Westley were found not guilty. Afterward Nicoll wrote an article titled "Are These Men Fit to Live?" attacking Coulon, whom he suspected of being a police agent, and the police officers who had conducted the inquiry.[59] Nicoll was arrested and sentenced to eighteen months' prison for incitement to murder. The League then collapsed, leaving a small circle clustered around *Commonweal,* which steadily lost money until it ceased publication in May 1894. Also in 1894, Wilson resigned from *Freedom* for personal reasons. Without her financial backing, *Freedom* folded in January 1895, only to reappear later that year under the control of some of those who had belonged to the League.

ANARCHISM AND SEX REFORM

When bohemians broke with Victorian mores, they earned the 1890s a plethora of titles such as decadent and naughty. Yet, new anarchists and other bohemians thought of themselves as the prophets of a deeper spirituality and larger morality. They wanted to live their lives in accord with a higher individualism that showed conventional standards to be rigid and arbitrary. As Kenworthy explained, "The part of our 'programme' which differentiates us from others who seek after the ideal society, is the determination that, let the world go in such way as it pleases, we, each one for his own part, for the 'salvation of his soul' must live honestly and fraternally."[60] Personal transformation and communal living were the new anarchists' alternative to violent deeds. The new anarchists believed that an ideal society could arise as a result of the spread of a new ethic based on reason, and that one way of peacefully persuading people

[58] Ibid., 28 November 1891.
[59] Ibid., 9 April 1892.
[60] *Seed-time*, April 1895.

to adopt this new ethic was to put it into practice. They thus became involved in movements from which the old anarchists generally stood aloof. Many members of the Freedom Group became involved in the movement for sex reform. Several Tolstoyans formed utopian communities to embody their new ethic.

The new anarchists and other bohemians rejected what they saw as the fixed rules of the Victorian era for a flexible sensibility that would enable people to relate simply and freely to one another and things. They argued for the right of individuals to control their own development, not follow moral conventions; for personalities, not principles; and for sensibility, not morality. They talked of the virtue of living in accord with one's feelings and developing one's innate character to the highest possible level of perfection. A good life should express one's inner nature. People should expand and beautify their selves and not slavishly follow external codes.

A particularly controversial aspect of fin-de-siècle bohemianism was its challenge to sexual mores. Bohemians believed that people should follow their instincts, including their sexual desires. Pleasure was not suspect. Natural functions were not evil. Sex was there to be enjoyed, perhaps even enjoyed in whatever manner one wished. *Épater la bourgeoisie* became a fashionable sport, with many of the players motivated by a conviction that established conventions imprison the spirit and to break these conventions is to liberate the soul. As Oscar Wilde explained, the higher individualism "converts the abolition of legal restraint into a form of freedom that will help the full development of personality, and make the love of man and woman more wonderful, more beautiful, more ennobling."[61]

The sex reform movement of the 1890s appeared in literature and in various discussion groups. New women authors introduced female characters who were more realistic and vital than the passive and insipid heroines of earlier Victorian literature. Their female characters possessed bohemian glamour, intelligence, sophistication, and sometimes independence. New women authors used fiction to raise feminist issues; they explored the sexual and economic oppression of women through plots that showcased the restricted opportunities available to women.[62] A significant number of the new women writers were active in socialist discussion groups. Most were ethical socialists who emphasized the importance of making socialists both as an end in itself and as a prelude to successful parliamentary action. They thought of socialism and feminism as twin expressions of the new ethic of human emancipation. Some extended this

---

[61] O. Wilde, *The Soul of Man under Socialism* (London: Humphreys, 1912), p. 31.

[62] I. Ford, *Miss Blake of Monkshalton* (London: John Murray, 1890); and O. Schriner, *The Story of an African Farm* (Harmondsworth, UK: Penguin, 1971).

ethic to embrace homosexuals, and a few had an interest in James Hinton's mix of evolutionary mysticism and sexual liberation. But most were happier with the more cautious stance of the Men and Women's Club. This club was founded in 1885 by Professor Karl Pearson, who later became a prominent eugenicist, for the purpose of "free and unreserved discussion of all matters connected with the relations of the sexes."[63] It treated heterosexuality as given and refused to have any dealings with Hinton or others associated with free love.[64] Yet, the formal discussion of sexual matters by women as well as men was a daring enterprise at the time.

New anarchists were prominent in the sex reform movement. Brooke was one of the leading new women novelists. Her heroines rejected the standard Victorian view of their nature and role. *A Superfluous Woman* deals with the gulf between the role that society imposes on women and their natural emotions.[65] The heroine, Jessamine, is an upper-class woman whose upbringing centers on the goal of a materially successful marriage. She flees from the artificial society of London to the Scottish Highlands and to a simple life. Her natural emotions return, and she falls in love with a crofter. He inspires in her a sexual passion that is totally at odds with the conventional ideal of a lady. After a period of emotional turmoil, she returns to London and marries a lord. This capitulation to social norms leads to her nervous breakdown and ultimate death.

Brooke and Wilson were part of the loose circle of socialists and sex reformers inspired by Carpenter. This circle also included Katherine Conway, Isabella Ford, and Enid Stacey, all of whom turned to socialism partly due to the influence of Carpenter. The members of the circle believed that women have to break free of male stereotypes and take control of their own lives. Carpenter argued that women lacked the education and financial independence to be anything other than domestic drudges or prostitutes. Men had reduced women to chattels who could provide sex but not comradeship, and because men could not find comradeship in women, men remained perpetual adolescents. Personal relationships would remain unsatisfactory until women overcame the social forces keeping them passive and dependent. The circle around Carpenter believed that women could take control of their lives only if they were economically independent. They thus became interested in the problems

---

[63] Minute Book of the Men and Women's Club, 1885–89, KPP:10.1.

[64] Wilson believed Hintonianism and anarchism were incompatible. See Wilson to Pearson, 21 February 1886 and 4 March 1886, KPP:900. Brooke described her negative recollection of her personal contact with Hinton in Brooke to Pearson, 4 December 1885, KPP:70.

[65] E. Brooke, *A Superfluous Woman*, 3 vols. (London: William Heinemann, 1894).

of female workers. Ford played a leading role in supporting unionization and strikes among female weavers in Yorkshire.

Carpenter, a homosexual, was something of a prophet of gay liberation. He argued that the Western route to the new ethic would remain the path of love.[66] He treated homosexuality as a model of the comradeship that would define the new ethic. Gay men developed a special comradeship apparent in their unique role through history. In primitive societies, women did domestic chores and men hunted while homosexuals performed the cohesive and caring work of teachers, medicine men, and prophets. The Spartans formalized the teaching role of homosexuals, calling the lover inspirer and the youth hearer. In the modern world, the love of homosexuals crossed class barriers. Homosexuals were the harbingers of democracy.

Brooke and Wilson were also involved in the Men and Women's Club. The club focused on marriage, the possibility of equal relationships between the sexes, prostitution, and the role of the state in such matters. Some of the female members began to articulate a critique of the Victorian concept of womanhood and the relationships it encouraged. For example, Brooke insisted on the reality of female sexuality and argued that problems in sexual relations arose because women had sole responsibility for childbearing.[67] Men had a false image of women as Madonna. Women enjoyed sex just as much as men did, and men wanted children just as much as women did. The only relevant difference was that women suffered the torment of giving birth and men did not. As a result, women desperately tried to avoid perpetual childbearing by means of chastity or preventive checks, whereas men shunned self-control and forced women to have child after child, denying them control over their own bodies. Brooke recommended that both sexes exercise self-control to ensure childbearing occurred only where there was love sanctioned by duty and only when women were able to retain the strength necessary to raise the children they did have.

The new anarchists and their fellow sex reformers altered the suffrage movement. The early suffragists drew on a liberal tradition dominated by John Stuart Mill and Mary Wollstonecraft. They argued for equal legal and political rights mainly by emphasizing the common attributes of men and women.[68] Mill and Wollstonecraft acknowledged that motherhood was an important aspect of many women's lives, but they did not see it

[66] E. Carpenter, *From Adam's Peak to Elephanta* (London: Swan Sonnenschein, 1892).

[67] E. Brooke, "Notes on Karl Pearson's Paper of 9 July 1885 on the Woman's Question," KPP:10.2.

[68] M. Wollstonecraft, "A Vindication of the Rights of Woman," in *A Vindication of the Rights of Men and a Vindication of the Rights of Woman*, ed. S. Tomaselli (Cambridge: Cambridge University Press, 1995); and J. Mill, "The Subjugation of Women," in *The*

as a structural impediment to equality. Similarly, the early suffragists demanded the vote as a right, but they had little to say about the particular social and economic problems facing women. The sex reformers of the 1890s stirred a new suffragism. They encouraged a concern with sexual differences and the way these differences affect relations between men and women. They highlighted issues relating to marriage, prostitution, and venereal disease. Moreover, the emergence of these new issues led some of them to adopt novel arguments for extending the vote to women. They argued that women had particular nurturing characteristics that would benefit the state, especially in an age when welfare legislation was giving it an increasingly caring role.

ANARCHIST COMMUNALISM

New anarchists pinned their hopes on a new ethic that liberated personal and social life. They argued that the new life required an anarchic society composed of a federation of local communes. Each commune should be an autonomous unit of production and distribution. The individual members of each commune should give according to their ability and take according to their need. The new anarchists established several such communes in an attempt to enable people to live in accord with the new ethic. As Hubert Hammond, a Tolstoyan, explained, "We do not desire to press our views upon anyone, but to seek out for ourselves the source of true life and earnestly to strive to live this life."[69]

The first anarchist commune was formed in 1895. The Clousden Hill Communist and Cooperative Colony was a twenty-acre farm. The founders were Frank Kapper and William Key. They had first met at a Cooperative Congress, and they told *Le Temps* that they had been influenced by E. T. Craig, who was a member of the Owenite Commune at Ralahine, County Clare, Ireland.[70] However, their immediate inspiration was Kropotkin; Clousden Hill was to provide a practical confirmation of his theories. Kapper and Key deliberately addressed the prospectus for the commune "To all Friends and Sympathisers of Land Colonisation." Their first six points would have been familiar to the Owenites. The last two reflected their debt to Kropotkin:

Collected Works of John Stuart Mill (Toronto: University of Toronto Press, 1963–91), vol. 21: *Essays on Equality, Law, and Education*, pp. 259–340.

[69] *New Order*, September 1897.

[70] E. Craig, *The Irish Land and Labour Question, Illustrated in the History of Ralahine and Co-operative Farming* (London: Heywood, 1882). For the history of Clousden Hill, see *Le Temps*, 29 September 1897, and the series of occasional reports in both *Newcastle Daily Chronicle* and *Freedom* from 1895 to 1902.

OBJECTS

1. The acquisition of a common and indivisible capital for the establishment of an Agricultural and Industrial Colony.
2. The mutual assurance of its members against the evils of poverty, sickness, infirmity, and old age.
3. The attainment of a greater share of the comforts of life than the working classes now possess.
4. The mental and moral improvement of all its members.
5. The education of the children.
6. To promote or help any organisation to organise similar colonies.
7. To demonstrate the superiority of Free Communist Association as against the Competitive Production of to-day.
8. To demonstrate the productivity of land under intensive culture.[71]

The next anarchist commune to be formed was the Norton Hall Community, just outside Sheffield. This time the inspiration was Carpenter, who, as we saw in the last chapter, had written extensively about his own attempt to live simply as a self-sufficient market gardener. The Norton colonists specialized in horticulture, growing flowers, fruits, and vegetables in five greenhouses and a large garden.

A first Tolstoyan colony appeared in 1896 at Purleigh, Essex.[72] Kenworthy built himself a house on the land. Another prominent resident was Aylmer Maude, the leading translator of Tolstoy, who raised a thousand pounds for the Doukhobors with the help of Vladimir Tcherthoff, a friend of Tolstoy's who arrived at Purleigh in the spring of 1897.[73] The number of colonists rose to over sixty. About a quarter of the residents lived on land owned by the colony. The remainder lived in nearby houses. The members accepted the concept of bread labor that Tolstoy had taken from T. F. Bondareff. Each of them thus had to earn his own livelihood by his own labor, although the community guaranteed him the opportunity so to do. The colonists tried to go back to the land by farming ten acres. They had a kitchen garden, apple trees, and gooseberry bushes, and they kept cows and hens. They did much of the work by hand, although they also had an old horse that had pulled a London bus. In 1899 Kenworthy began to print *New Order*, the main Tolstoyan publication, at Purleigh. For a while, the colony provided vacations to sympathizers who paid for their board and lodging. On Sunday evenings, the

[71] *Torch*, 18 May 1895.
[72] *New Order* carried a regular column of news from Purleigh. Also see P. Redfern, *Journey to Understanding* (London: Allen and Unwin, 1946).
[73] A. Maude, *Life of Tolstoy*, 2 vols. (London: Oxford University Press, 1929–30).

colonists held meetings at which they sang Labour Church hymns and heard readings from works such as Morris's *Dream of John Ball*. Many members also pursued personal fads; "some have decided not to hold legal titles in property, others endeavour not to use money, others not to use stamps, others protest against railways."[74] Yet, as happened so often, the members had difficulty fitting their experiment into the commercial world. When they advertised their products in *New Order*, a correspondent complained that this smacked of competition, arguing that to be true to their principles, they should rely solely on word of mouth and the grace of God.[75]

Other Tolstoyans formed colonies nearby at Ashingdon and Wickford, although many of the latter were "City men" who continued to commute to work in London.[76] In 1898 the Essex colonists divided over the vetting of applicants. The less restrictive ones decamped to Whiteway, Gloucestershire.[77] A few of the Whiteway colonists worked in small industries linked to the nearby village of Sheepscombe. The majority again worked the land. The colony started out with forty acres of farmland, later expanding to include a dairy. The colonists burned the title deed to their land, claiming that land was given "by the Supreme Being for the use of man and therefore should be free to everyone."[78]

A few anarchists formed urban communes. The most important one was in Leeds. In 1897 Albert Gibson helped workers who had suffered in an industrial dispute to establish the Brotherhood Workshop. The workshop made bicycles, repaired electrical goods, and held religious and philosophical discussions.[79] Later the colonists began a publishing venture under the Leeds Free Anarchist Group imprint. They published pamphlets by Kropotkin and Wilson as well as a northern newspaper, the *Free Commune*. In 1899 an offshoot of the Leeds group set up a similar commune in Blackburn, again devoted to the repair of electrical goods.

The anarchist communes embodied a new sensibility that led members to pool their resources and generally, though by no means always, work hard for the common good. Members rejected Victorian conventions in favor of what they thought were free and proper relationships with one another and the natural world around them. Many communes

[74] *New Order*, May 1899.
[75] Ibid., April 1898.
[76] Ibid., March 1898.
[77] Ibid., September 1898. Also see N. Shaw, *Whiteway: A Colony on the Cotswolds* (London: Daniel, 1935).
[78] *New Order*, September 1899.
[79] The latter history of the commune can be traced in the *Free Commune*.

were exclusively vegetarian out of respect for living creatures. Anarchist papers carried advertisements for unusual clothes. Several of the colonists followed Wilde in refusing to wear the tight-fitting fashions of that age. A few even followed Shaw in rejecting the use of vegetable materials in favor of Jaeger's woolens. The colonists generally looked upon marriage as an optional commitment, with many couples preferring to live together rather than, as they saw it, make the woman the chattel of the man. Women typically worked alongside the men, although the men do not seem to have been quite so ready to participate in household chores.

Eventually most of the communes suffered from the difficulties that so often beset such experiments. They attracted idlers. The standard of living went down. Members started bickering. Key figures left. The communes disbanded. Purleigh had endless disputes about who should do what, with each dispute inducing yet more people to leave the colony. The remaining colonists did less and less work. Health inspectors finally closed the colony down after an outbreak of smallpox among the last few cold and undernourished colonists. The organizers of the Leeds colony decided members should work as and when they pleased, but this agreement did not make for financial viability, so they tried to return to regular hours of work, only to meet with hostility from the members and ultimately the collapse of the workshop. Only the Whiteway colony survived far into the twentieth century, and it did so by rejecting communism for a type of mutualism under which individuals owned plots of land.

Conclusion

The 1890s witnessed the growth of a new type of anarchism, significantly different from the radical individualism of Bakunin and Proudhon. The new anarchists were, like the ethical socialists, part of a widespread break with Victorian culture. They championed a spiritual ethic that fused a higher individualism with communalism. They wanted a stateless society based on a communist system of distribution. And they hoped to realize this society by nonviolent means, especially the moral power of their personal example. They thus concentrated on the transformation of personal relationships and the creation of communes.

Ethical socialism was part of a broad cultural shift away from evangelicalism and classical liberalism and toward immanentism and new visions of social reform. Ethical socialism overlapped with a new anarchism and with the bohemianism of the 1890s at least as much as with Marxism and Fabianism. Although there were differences between the ethical socialists, new anarchists, aesthetes, sex reformers, and communalists, there were also significant overlaps of personnel and of ideas. They all sought a new sensibility that would enable individuality to flourish in a context of social harmony without coercion or authority. Often they upheld an immanentist spirituality, an ethic of fellowship, a belief in personal transformation and communal experiments, and a dislike or even rejection of political action. The bohemian world of the 1890s resembled a series of booths at a fair, each with a crier inviting people to join such diverse causes as aestheticism, anarchism, environmentalism, feminism, spiritualism, theosophy, and vegetarianism. A member of Whiteway described early meetings in the colony when "every kind of 'crank' came and aired his views on the open platform"; there were "Atheists, Spiritualists, Individualists, Communists, Anarchists, ordinary politicians, Vegetarians, Anti-Vivisectionists and Anti-Vaccinationists."[80]

---

[80] N. Shaw, *Whiteway*, p. 21.

CHAPTER FOURTEEN

The Labour Church Movement

THE OLD HISTORIOGRAPHY of British socialism tended to discount the persistence of religious belief and to locate the rise of socialism in a process of secularization. Yet, the conference held in Bradford in 1893 to form the Independent Labour Party (ILP) was accompanied by a Labour Church service attended by some five thousand people.[1] The conference took place in a disused chapel then being run as a labour institute by the Bradford labor church as well as the local labor union and the local Fabians. The Labour Church movement was created by John Trevor, who, as we saw in chapters 11 and 12, was a Unitarian minister influenced by the immanentism of the American romantics. Trevor founded the first labor church in Manchester. The church's first service was held on 4 October 1891. A string band opened the event. Then Trevor led those present in prayer. The congregation listened to a reading of James Russell Lowell's poem "On the Capture of Fugitive Slaves." Harold Rylett, a Unitarian minister, read Isaiah 15. The choir rose to sing "England Arise," a popular socialist hymn by Edward Carpenter.

> England arise! the long, long night is over,
> Faint in the east behold the dawn appear;
> Out of your evil dream of toil and sorrow—
>   Arise, O England, for the day is here;
>   From your fields and hills,
>   Hark! the answer swells—
>   Arise, O England, for the day is here.

After the singing stopped, Trevor gave a sermon on the religious aspect of the labor movement. He argued that the failure of existing churches to support labor made it necessary for the workers to form a new movement to embody the religious aspect of their quest for emancipation.[2] The new movement was the Labour Church. It gained adherents rapidly. At its next meeting, Robert Blatchford addressed a crowd that was

A version of this chapter appeared as "The Labour Church Movement, 1891–1902," *Journal of British Studies* 38 (1999), 217–245. Published by The North American Conference on British Studies.

  [1] *Labour Prophet*, February 1893.
  [2] *Workman's Times*, 9 October 1891.

too large to fit into the building. When another Unitarian minister, Philip Wicksteed, led a service in Manchester in early 1892, the congregation numbered over six hundred.[3] Before long, labor churches had sprung up in most large cities in Lancashire and Yorkshire, including, of course, Bradford.

IMMANENTISM—ONCE MORE

Historians have reached something of a consensus about the Labour Church movement and its ethical socialism. Eric Hobsbawm, Henry Pelling, and Stanley Pierson all explain the Labour Church by referring to the impact of secularization and a rise of class politics on nonconformism. They argue that the Labour Church is not a "religious manifestation but rather a symptom of religious decline."[4] In their view, the Labour Church arose as part of a process in which the religious enthusiasm of nonconformists was transferred to the political sphere. This view captures the experience of some members of the Labour Church and even some branches. For example, Trevor was a Calvinist before he discovered Emerson and trained to become a Unitarian minister. He decided to leave the Unitarians and found a labor church when a member of his congregation said he had stopped attending chapel because he felt unable to breathe freely there.[5] Similarly, the Bradford labor church was formed in the run-up to the 1892 general election after wealthy nonconformist ministers sat on the platform at a meeting in support of a Liberal opponent of the socialist candidate, Ben Tillett, and Fred Jowett stood up and warned them, "If you persist in opposing the Labour movement ... we shall establish our own Labour Church."[6]

Yet, as we saw in chapter 11, there are many problems with the claim that ethical socialism was a staging post on the road to secularism and class politics. For a start, most members of the Labour Church retained a strong religious faith. Wicksteed was the most important figure in the

[3] *Labour Prophet*, February 1892.

[4] H. Pelling, *The Origins of the Labour Party, 1880–1900* (Oxford: Clarendon Press, 1966), p. 142. Also see E. Hobsbawm, *Primitive Rebels: Studies in Archaic Forms of Social Movement in the 19th and 20th Centuries* (Manchester, UK: Manchester University Press, 1959), esp. pp. 142–45; and S. Pierson, "John Trevor and the Labour Church Movement in England, 1891–1900," *Church History* 29 (1960): 463–78.

[5] J. Trevor, *My Quest for God* (London: Labour Prophet, 1897), p. 241.

[6] Cited in F. Brockway, *Socialism over Sixty Years: The Life of Jowett of Bradford, 1864–1944* (London: Allen and Unwin, 1946), p. 41. On the formation of the Bradford church, see *Labour Prophet*, August and December 1892. The church soon took over publication of the *Bradford Labour Echo*.

movement after Trevor, and he remained a practicing Unitarian minister long after joining it. The Bolton labor church was formed when B. J. Harker led his congregation in affiliating with the movement "so far as their constitution as a congregational church would allow."[7] In addition, the Labour Church attracted people who did not have backgrounds in nonconformism. The second general secretary of the Labour Church Union, Fred Brocklehurst, was a Broad Church Anglican who considered taking holy orders before he turned to socialism.[8] The London church was formed by Paul Campbell, an Anglican who edited the *Christian Socialist* and played an active role in the settlement movement.[9] J. A. Fallows, a former minister in the Church of England, was secretary of the Birmingham church.[10] Walter Morse became secretary of the Union in 1896, and he was an Anglican until he joined the Leeds church.[11] The editor of the movement's newspaper, the *Labour Prophet*, was R. A. Beckett, the son of an Anglican clergyman.[12] Some people joined the Labour Church from less Christian backgrounds. The Keighley church was formed by Swedenborgians.[13] Finally, most members of the Labour Church were not on the road to secularism. Their religious beliefs were powerful, and, as we will see, they held them, or ones like them, until their death. A firm and lasting religious commitment characterized the Labour Church just as it did ethical socialism more generally.

The Labour Church was less part of a process of secularization than an expression of the type of ethical socialism we have explored in the last three chapters. Its members responded to the crisis of faith with an immanentist theology, an ethic of fellowship, and an emphasis on making socialists. Many drew inspiration from American romantics, and several were involved with the new anarchists and their efforts at personal transformation and communal living.

Labour Church members often experienced the crisis of faith in their own lives. D. B. Foster grew up as a Wesleyan and became a local preacher at the tender age of seventeen before experiencing severe doubts about the compatibility of his faith with modern science and, above all, about the morality of the atonement. He responded to these doubts by following "the revelation of life" offered him by Jesus until he learned to "trust to the great creative forces."[14] He briefly committed himself to the Wes-

---

[7] *Labour Prophet*, May 1892.

[8] *Labour Annual* (1895), p. 163.

[9] *Labour Prophet*, April 1892.

[10] *Labour Church Record*, October 1899.

[11] *Labour Prophet*, August 1896.

[12] *Labour Annual* (1898), p. 193.

[13] *Clarion*, 11 January 1893.

[14] D. Foster, *Socialism and the Christ* (Leeds, UK: Foster, 1921), pp. 27 and 28.

leyan missions, but before long he left them for the labor church in Leeds. Percy Redfern, a secularist until he turned to the Labour Church movement, the cooperative movement, and Tolstoyism, spoke for many when he complained that secularism offered only a "negative" liberation, when people needed a "truth *now*, a whole truth, a truth they can live by."[15] For the members of the Labour Church, this truth was that God existed as a presence in the spontaneous life of the world.

The Labour Church embodied an immanentist faith. The divine was present in everything, and it was evolving to take us, in Trevor's words, to "the great source of all things."[16] What distinguished the Labour Church from other forms of immanentism was the conviction that the labor movement was the means of realizing socialism and so the Kingdom of God. The divine life was present in the labor movement and its battle to realize the truth of universal brotherhood. Indeed, "the Labour Church was founded for the distinct purpose of declaring that God is at work, here and now, in the heart of the Labour Movement."[17] In this view, the labor movement did not represent the workers alone. It stood for a labor consciousness that pointed to a growing sense of brotherhood among the downtrodden of the world. Trevor explained that the labor movement pointed to a "human consciousness, world consciousness, God consciousness."[18] Similarly, Foster argued that the trade-union movement made "specific trade interests subservient to the general interest of all the workers," thereby promoting the "co-operation of the whole people in owning and controlling the means of life."[19] No doubt critics would argue that the labor movement did not always seem to embody a "democratic spirit." Yet, Wicksteed responded:

It would no doubt be easy to show that a great deal of what announces itself as belonging to the Labour Movement ... is in fact opposed to this [democratic] principle. ... But, nonetheless, whenever the Labour Movement looks into its own principles, and formulates its goal, it is the abolition, not the maintenance, of privilege which inspires it; and we may fearlessly assert that, so far as the Labour Movement means anything, it means the organisation of society in the interest of the unprivileged producers.[20]

[15] P. Redfern, *Journey to Understanding* (London: Allen and Unwin, 1946), p. 70.
[16] Trevor, *My Quest*, p. 152.
[17] *Labour Prophet*, September 1894.
[18] Trevor, *My Quest*, pp. 235–36.
[19] D. Foster, *The Logic of the Alliance* (Leeds, UK: Foster, n.d.), pp. 5 and 6.
[20] P. Wicksteed, "What Does the Labour Church Stand For?" *Labour Prophet Tracts*, 2nd ser., no. 1 (1896): 6.

Members of the Labour Church disagreed about the relationship of a commitment to the labor movement to belief in Christ. Some contrasted the two. Beckett complained that Christ had made no "contribution to sociology," merely advocating indiscriminate charity; and Trevor wanted to temper a "Christian tenderness of suffering" with a "Pagan joy in life."[21] Others conjoined them. Foster argued that "the realisation of the Christ ideal is the greatest force for Socialism in the world," and John Kenworthy insisted that the brotherhood of man was the central message of Christ, as well as of the Labour Church.[22]

Immanentism led Labour Church members to an ideal of universal brotherhood and fellowship. Redfern contrasted "fraternity with the universe, under one maker, to conquest over it through the mind used as a weapon."[23] Socialism appealed as a higher individualism that recognized the importance of each individual, but it did so in the context of an understanding of the unity of all. Foster believed that "sociality, the spirit which demands the socialisation of the necessaries of human life, is but individuality fuller grown."[24] The members of the Labour Church defined the socialist ideal in terms of fellowship, rather than economic reforms. Moreover, the economic reforms for which they did call typically derived from an ethic of fellowship, not an economic analysis of capitalism. Foster described how after he became a socialist, he saw "the way to that Kingdom of God on earth for which I have prayed and worked so long"; he saw "why Love was the fulfilling of the Law," and this altered his view of "my relation to my fellows" so that "the men whom I employed became my comrades in life, whose needs constituted their right to wages rather than their ability to make profit for me."[25] This emphasis on a new life of the spirit explains why the labor churches often provided platforms for speakers advocating other humanitarian causes, including antivivisection, ethical culture, theosophy, Tolstoyism, and vegetarianism.

Finally, the Labour Church adopted a political strategy based on the making of socialists. Once people felt the divine in themselves, they would accept the relationship of brotherhood that linked them to others, and so they would create a new fellowship. Missionaries would spread the religion of socialism, converting others to the cause, thereby leading them to transform their personal lives and eventually to create God's kingdom on earth. Rachel McMillan simply proclaimed that people "are 'bound to do

---

[21] *Labour Prophet*, September 1896; J. Trevor, *Labour Prophet Tracts* (London: Labour Prophet, 1896), tract 1, p. 13.

[22] Foster, *Socialism*, p. 1; *Labour Prophet*, September 1896.

[23] Redfern, *Journey to Understanding*, p. 70.

[24] Foster, *Socialism*, p. 1.

[25] Ibid., p. 27.

it' if they think at all."[26] Here too the Labour Church gave a special role to the labor movement as the agent of change. Labour Church activists often argued that labor needed an independent party and an independent church to distance itself, respectively, from Conservatives and Liberals and from the Church of England and nonconformity. Because the labor movement expressed the divine life, it must avoid the corrupting effects of the traditions embodied in the elder parties and churches.

PRINCIPLES AND ACTIVITIES

The principles and activities of the Labour Church reflect an immanentist faith rather than a process of secularization. Its "Statement of Principles" certainly expresses a belief in an immanent God and an ethic of fellowship apparent in the labor movement.

The Labour Church is based upon the following principles:

1. That the Labour Movement is a religious movement.
2. That the Religion of the Labour Movement is not a Class Religion, but unites members of all classes in working for the Abolition of Commercial Slavery.
3. That the Religion of the Labour Movement is not Sectarian or Dogmatic, but Free Religion, leaving each man free to develop his own relations with the Power that brought him into being.
4. That the emancipation of Labour can be realised so far as men learn both the Economic and Moral Laws of God, and heartily endeavour to obey them.
5. That the development of Personal Character and the improvement of Social Conditions are both essential to man's emancipation from moral and social bondage.[27]

Yet, although the Labour Church was based on a particular set of religious and ethical doctrines, the importance of these doctrines can be obscured by the fact that they inspired an antitheological perspective. Within the Church of England, the *Lux Mundi* theologians and others approached their immanentism through theological discussions about the relationship of faith to reason and about the character of the Incarnation and the Bible.[28] In contrast, Labour Church writers characteristically derided theology as an attempt to suppress life with doctrine. Belief in an immanent God led some members of the Labour Church to dismiss theol-

[26] M. McMillan, *The Life of Rachel McMillan* (London: Dent, 1927), p. 39.
[27] *Labour Prophet*, January 1892.
[28] C. Gore, ed., *Lux Mundi* (London: J. Murray, 1890).

ogy as insignificant and even damaging. They showed no interest in theological disputes about whether God was a person or a principle, whether Christ was the son of God, or whether Christ founded a visible church based on apostolic succession. They argued that all these disputes mattered little compared with the great truth that God's presence on earth binds people together in universal brotherhood. Sam Hobson argued that Christ "was essentially a practical teacher" who constantly expressed his "detestation of mere theology."[29] Trevor argued more generally that when "Life appears on the scene, Tradition is compelled to weakly follow."[30] The labor movement incorporated the divine spirit because it embodied life, whereas the old churches expressed a sterile theological tradition.

A rejection of dogma and a belief that the whole labor movement embodied the divine could leave members of the Labour Church confused by its apparent lack of clear commitments. For example, Mr. Gutteridge of the Nottingham Church complained that he was "puzzled by the multiplicity of the ideas of their speakers," for "one Sunday, they would have an orthodox speaker, and ... the next an aggressive secularist."[31] Yet, most members recognized, as did Gutteridge, that the Labour Church had its own orthodox set of commitments: an immanentist faith sustaining an ideal of universal brotherhood that was thought to be embodied in the labor movement. Despite its opposition to theology, the Labour Church adhered to a clear set of beliefs, including most notably what Tom Mann called "the DEITY or NATURE."[32] It treated God as an "intense reality in which all life was united into one whole-souled harmony."[33]

The antitheological doctrines of the Labour Church proved very appealing. More than a thousand Labour Church hymnals sold in just one day during the movement's second annual meeting in Birmingham in 1894.[34] The total number of labor churches exceeded one hundred, although many were short-lived, so the number of active branches peaked at just over fifty around 1895. The most important church was in Manchester; in 1893 and 1894 it held three services each Sunday, and they usually had full houses.[35] Most churches had congregations of 300 to 500. Bradford had 300 members, attracted more to its services, and often sold five thousand copies of its newspaper.[36] Dundee had an average

[29] S. Hobson, *Possibilities of the Labour Church* (Cardiff: Chappie and Kemp, 1893), pp. 4 and 5.
[30] Trevor, *Tracts*, tract 1, p. 8.
[31] *Labour Church Record*, July 1899.
[32] *Labour Prophet*, January 1892.
[33] Trevor, *Tracts*, tract 2, p. 17.
[34] *Labour Prophet*, November 1894.
[35] Ibid., December 1893.
[36] *Labour Annual* (1897), p. 166.

congregation of 400, although it had to turn people away when Keir Hardie spoke at its inaugural meeting.[37] Halifax generally attracted 500 participants. Oldham's average attendance was 300, of whom 100 were regulars. Plymouth regularly filled a hall with a capacity of about 250. When 120 people attended a service of the Birmingham church in 1893, its members were disappointed, saying that the turnout was not "very good."[38] There were also many smaller labor churches. Wolverhampton generally had an attendance of about 100 at its monthly meetings, and Barnsley rarely attracted more than 40.[39] Famous speakers boosted attendance, but many churches reported "a difficulty in getting speakers, especially on the moral and religious side of the work."[40]

Membership of the Labour Church included people of both sexes and a variety of ages and social classes. Yet, young lower-middle-class and upper-working-class males predominated. The most notable characteristic of the members was probably their shared religious experience. Several wrote spiritual autobiographies, and these have a similar structure. Many Labour Church members were raised in traditional structures of faith but then experienced profound doubts before coming to believe again through an encounter with romantics such as Emerson, a personal sense of oneness with their fellows, or a new religious movement such as theosophy or spiritualism, all of which led to immanentism.

Labor churches attracted some people who were raised as Anglicans, Catholics, or even secularists, but the majority had nonconformist backgrounds. The predominance of nonconformists reflects the religious experiences and ideas informing the movement. So, secularists would not have experienced evolutionary theory, historical criticism, and the like as dilemmas requiring them to change their religious beliefs. Similarly, although Anglicans often experienced a crisis of faith and responded to it with immanentism, the Church of England provided more outlets than did nonconformity for those who rejected the evangelicalism that had dominated the early Victorian era. The Church of England included organizations, such as the Guild of Saint Matthew and the Christian Social Union, that were based on a mix of immanentism and social concern. Besides, of course, nonconformists came from a tradition in which independent churches already had a well-established place.

The predominance of nonconformists in the Labour Church does much to explain its geographic distribution. The Labour Church thrived in the industrial centers of nonconformity. Of the fifty or so branches that lasted for more than a year, more than half were in Lancashire or

---

[37] *Labour Prophet*, January 1893.
[38] Ibid., February 1894.
[39] Ibid., March–April 1894; *Labour Church Record*, April 1899.
[40] *Labour Prophet*, September 1894.

the West Riding of Yorkshire. In the first four months of 1894, four new churches sprang up in South Lancashire alone.[41] In addition, there were several branches in South Wales and Scotland, a small group around Birmingham, a slightly larger group in the Potteries, and others dotted all around the country.

Religious services in the labor churches expressed the immanentism on which the movement was founded. The ideal service was supposed to consist of "(1) Hymn (2) Reading (3) Prayer (4) Solo or Music by the Choir (5) Notices and Collection (6) Hymn (7) Address (8) Hymn (9) Benediction."[42] In practice, however, few labor churches bothered with anything other than hymns, readings, addresses, and short prayers. The *Labour Church Hymn Book* contained few traditional hymns, being composed mainly of socialist songs by writers such as Carpenter and William Morris and poems by romantics such as Emerson and Charles Kingsley.[43] These writers were also the source of most of the readings in the Labour Church. Trevor complained that "the Bible is so frightfully and falsely conventionalised ... it is difficult to make a Bible reading a real and helpful thing to a Labour Church audience."[44] The labor churches often relied on local activists to give the addresses. The most popular speakers were those who proved most successful for the ILP. Sam Hobson, a Quaker born in Ireland who joined the Cardiff church and sat on the council of the Labour Church Union, later recalled that Philip Snowden was the most popular speaker, Hardie attracted larger crowds but spoke less frequently, and Katherine Conway and Enid Stacey had more select audiences.[45] Clearly, the hymns, readings, and addresses of the Labour Church relied heavily on ethical socialists and the romantics who inspired them. They celebrated both the divine presence in this world and the joyful fellowship it implied. The same was true of the prayers and benedictions used in labor churches. Benedictions were brief and simple, composed of a phrase such as "May the strength and joy of God's presence be with all who love their brethren in sincerity, Amen."[46]

The members of the Labour Church believed they could bring socialism about by making socialists. If they convinced others of the unity of all and the reality of universal brotherhood, these others would transform

[41] Ibid., May 1894.

[42] Ibid., June 1895.

[43] J. Trevor, ed., *The Labour Church Hymn Book* (London: Labour Prophet, 1895). Several labor churches printed their own hymn sheets. The Birmingham church reportedly printed a hymnbook.

[44] *Labour Prophet*, June 1895.

[45] S. Hobson, *Pilgrim to the Left: Memoirs of a Modern Revolutionist* (London: E. Arnold, 1938), p. 41.

[46] *Labour Prophet*, June 1895.

their lives in accord with the fellowship ideal and thereby create socialism. Apart from religious services, the leading activities of the Labour
Church were, therefore, educational and philanthropic ones. With respect
to education, the churches tried both to improve their own understanding
of the theoretical principles underlying socialism and to bring others, particularly the workers, to an inner conversion to socialism. The churches
often founded their own Sunday school or took over one established by
a *Clarion* group. Many also organized adult education classes in religion, economics, and ethics. The London church was especially active in
outreach education, under the guidance of Campbell and McMillan.[47]
When McMillan moved to Yorkshire, she lectured at the Leeds church
in 1896 on the French Revolution and in 1897 on modern economists.[48]
The churches also used the resources provided by the Fabian Society to
educate themselves. Trevor explained that "there is the greatest need for
education in our movement, and the Fabian Society is taking the work
in hand."[49] The movement's newspapers regularly urged members to join
Fabian correspondence classes. The Birmingham church joined with the
local Fabians to establish the Socialist Lecture Committee.[50]

The philanthropic activities of the churches varied considerably. The
Bradford church collected ten pounds and ten shillings for the local cotton operatives.[51] The Hanley church led a campaign against local lead
poisoning.[52] Foster worked tirelessly to publicize and improve the condition of the slums in Leeds, a task he continued after being elected a local
councillor.[53] The Manchester church organized a shelter for the homeless
and the Cinderella Club for underprivileged children in the Deansgate
area of the city.[54] Many of the movement's Sunday schools were tied to
Cinderella Clubs, which raised money to provide treats for children.[55]
The Manchester Cinderella Club organized an annual picnic in the city
park, a Christmas feast in the schoolroom, and outings to the country-

[47] Ibid., April 1892; and McMillan, *Rachel McMillan*, pp. 38–41.

[48] *Clarion*, 28 March 1896; 4 and 11 April 1896; 6, 20, and 27 March 1897; and 24
April 1897.

[49] *Labour Prophet*, September 1893.

[50] Minute Books of the Birmingham Labour Church, 1894—1910, Birmingham Central
Library, mss. 538059-62:ZZ72A, 1896.

[51] *Labour Prophet*, April 1893.

[52] *Labour Church Record*, July 1899.

[53] D. Foster, *Leeds Slumdom* (Leeds, UK: Foster, 1897).

[54] *Labour Prophet*, February 1893.

[55] The idea of the Cinderella Club originated in the Clarion movement, but clubs were
also established or taken over by labor churches. The first Cinderella supplement designed
for children appeared in *Labour Prophet*, May 1893.

side.[56] The Birmingham club outlived the Birmingham church, and it ran a holiday cottage for disabled children.[57]

Although the educational and philanthropic activities of the churches were intended to provide a cultural basis for socialism, the churches themselves eschewed political action on the grounds that if they made socialists, politics would look after itself. The annual meeting of 1899 passed a resolution "deprecating the taking of political action by Labour Churches as such, although heartily approving of such action by individual members."[58] John Sneyd of the Hanley church proposed the resolution, arguing that "where there was no political party they [the Labour Church] ought to make their position known, but where a political party existed they could leave it to them."[59]

The Labour Church had particularly close ties with the ILP. As the Labour Church played a role in the formation of the ILP, so it later drew strength from the ILP. The two organizations attracted similar memberships, relied on the same speakers, and embodied similar beliefs. In 1894 the council of the ILP even recommended that all its branches form labor churches to promote the religious side of the movement. Moreover, the available evidence suggests that most labor churches had close ties with the local ILP. There was considerable overlap of personnel. Brocklehurst was on the National Administrative Council of the ILP as well as general secretary of the Labour Church Union. Harker led the Bolton church, and he was elected president of the local ILP. Hobson was a leading member of the Cardiff church, and he was elected chairman of the ILP in Wales.[60] Many labor churches, including the one in Oldham, met in the clubroom of the local ILP. The *Labour Prophet* relied heavily on articles written by leading figures in the ILP, with Conway, Hardie, McMillan, Mann, and Tillett all contributing pieces in its first year of publication. Even the services in labor churches closely resembled branch meetings of the ILP. Both gatherings usually consisted of a hymn or song, a reading from a religious or political book, and an address by a prominent speaker. The main difference was that church services usually included a short prayer. It even seems probable that some labor churches were formed largely to get around a law that forbade political meetings on Sundays. The Dundee labor church was established explicitly to keep "the religious element in the cause robust" and to allow "lecturers to obtain a hearing

[56] Redfern, *Journey to Understanding*, p. 111.

[57] For the activities of the Birmingham Cinderella Club, see Annual Reports of the Birmingham Cinderella Club, 1896–1928, Birmingham Central Library, mss. 154722:L41.23.

[58] *Labour Church Record*, July 1900.

[59] Ibid.

[60] *Labour Prophet*, May 1892 and November 1894.

on Sundays."[61] If a labor church ran into difficulties with the local ILP, the result was normally a disaster for the church. For example, the Dundee church reported opposition from the local ILP in April 1895, and it seems to have fallen apart by January 1896.[62]

The ILP was not the only political organization with which labor churches associated themselves. Indeed, although Trevor welcomed the ILP "unhesitatingly," in the movement's newspaper he published an article in favor of the ILP by Mann and another one by Rylett arguing against independent political action and for cooperation with the Liberal Party.[63] Often the allegiances of labor churches reflected those of the areas in which they were located. Lancashire and London provided the main source of support for the Marxist Social Democratic Federation (SDF), and the Bolton church had close ties with the local SDF. However, after the ILP, the organization with which labor churches most often aligned themselves was the Fabian Society. In Liverpool, Fabians organized church meetings. In Cardiff, the church was formed by a group of young men who earlier had formed a local Fabian Society. In Leek, the church was opened by an address by Fred Whelan, who described what the Fabian Society could do to aid labor churches.[64] Perhaps we should not distinguish too sharply between the ILP and other socialist organizations, for at least at the local level their membership often overlapped. Local Fabian groups, in particular, provided congenial homes for many of the ethical socialists who joined the ILP. As Redfern later recalled, "In the northern regions then dominant in Labour politics, the British socialism at this time [before 1906] was the Fabianism of the idealists of the Independent Labour Party."[65]

The close links between the Labour Church and other socialist organizations meant that its fortunes fluctuated alongside theirs. From 1893 to 1895, an enthusiastic optimism encouraged people to believe that the good news of socialism would spread rapidly through the working class and bring a new life into being. But a more realistic determination characterized the period from 1895 to 1900, with attacks on trade unions, changes in the scale and organization of industry, and the growth of commercialized leisure pursuits all making socialists aware of a gulf between their aspirations and the daily concerns and activities of most workers.

---

[61] D. Lowe, *Souvenirs of Scottish Labour* (Glasgow: W. and R. Holmes, 1919), p. 97. Redfern later wrote: "'A jolly good idea, this Labour Church,' said one of its destroyers. 'With a prayer and a couple of hymns thrown in you get a socialist lecture to thousands whom otherwise you'd never see.'" Redfern, *Journey to Understanding*, p. 71.

[62] *Labour Prophet*, April 1895.

[63] Ibid., March 1892.

[64] Ibid., May 1893; *Leek Times*, 12 December 1896.

[65] Redfern, *Journey to Understanding*, p. 100.

So, the number of labor churches rose each year from 1891 to 1895, but then fell from about 50 in 1895 to 40 in 1897, 30 in 1898, and 20 in 1902. Moreover, the 1895 election suggested that socialists had to meet the exacting demands of more sustained political activity. Many ethical socialists shifted their focus from making socialists to the structure and finance of a new political party and the opportunities and costs of collaborating with existing parties. The failure of the Labour Church to embody this shift of focus meant that other socialists began taking a more jaded view of its role. In Halifax, Yorkshire, for example, the ILP started to compete with the church; it argued that the church was not practical enough and organized political meetings to coincide with services, leading to the dissolution of the church in 1901.

Despite occasional conflicts between churches and other local socialist groups, the main political role of the labor churches always remained to provide a cultural basis for activity undertaken elsewhere. As Edwin Halford, of the Bradford church, explained, "The Churches were formed for education, and for the stimulation of action on the part of Socialists," so "political action" lay "outside their sphere of work."[66] The cultural activities of the churches often focused on socialism as a way of life as much as any overtly religious theme. Few labor churches bothered with the rites of passage traditionally performed by the other churches. The Leeds church was unusual in that it performed christenings, devised a ceremony "equivalent to the orthodox baptism," and acquired a marriage license.[67] Most labor churches were worried that the people who performed rites of passage might acquire a priestly status of which they disapproved. Their immanentist belief that God was present in all inspired a strongly democratic and anticlerical outlook.

A democratic ethos informed the organizational structure of the Labour Church. The branches relied on fellowship rather than priesthood. As labor churches held that everyone had a place in the divine order, so they believed that everyone had a part to play in organizing, managing, and leading the movement. The typical church had no priest, pulpit, or Bible. It was just a congregation of believers held together by a chairman with no special status. Hanley and a few others had a constitution, but many did not.[68] There were no rituals or organized forms of worship. Each church adopted the activities best suited to its own nature and needs. Many churches, including Dundee, allowed speakers to choose whatever form of service they wished.[69]

---

[66] *Labour Church Record*, July 1899.
[67] *Labour Prophet*, May 1895 and December 1897.
[68] *Labour Church Record*, July 1899.
[69] *Labour Prophet*, January 1893.

Central organization of the movement was kept to a minimum in an attempt to ensure that it represented a spontaneous eruption of life, not the dead weight of theology. Local churches did not even have to subscribe to the five principles on which the national movement was based. The Birmingham church replaced them with a demand making faith in the divine optional. Its members had to accept only "the moral and economic laws that may be adduced from the Fatherhood of God or the Brotherhood of Man."[70] After the *Labour Prophet* first appeared in January 1892, it provided the main centralizing force in the movement. A full-time general secretary was appointed briefly, but the post did not last long because the local churches could not afford to pay a suitable salary. In 1893 about twenty branches came together to form the Labour Church Union, which held annual meetings, but the union had little power and never attracted many more than the initial twenty affiliates.

DISPUTES AND DECLINE

Historians typically argue that the Labour Church collapsed because the process of secularization led its members to drift away from even the quasi-religion it embodied. More particularly, they suggest that this process of secularization led to the rise of cycling clubs and other "sport and entertainment at the expense of religion and serious political discussion."[71] Yet, this suggestion ignores the fact that labor churches often sponsored new leisure pursuits. The Clarion Cycling Club arose from a meeting held in the Birmingham labor church in 1894, and many other labor churches formed cycling clubs. The Birmingham labor church discussed the reasons for falling attendances in some detail, but at no point did it seem to relate the problem to the rise of the local cycling club.[72]

It is also difficult to find evidence for the general argument that the decline of the Labour Church reflects a process of secularization. Immanentism often provided a stable response to the crisis of faith rather than a halfway house on the way to secular beliefs. So, most members of the Labour Church remained immanentists long after the movement collapsed. Trevor upheld an immanentist faith in the South Place Ethical Society until his death.[73] Wicksteed struggled to find a theological explanation of the Boer War and the First World War, but he still contributed

---

[70] *Labour Church Record*, July 1900.

[71] Pelling, *Origins of the Labour Party*, p. 138.

[72] Minute Books of the Birmingham Labour Church, esp. 1904–10.

[73] See the few surviving letters written by Trevor held in the Modern Records Centre, University of Warwick, UK, mss. 143.

to the Unitarian newspaper the *Inquirer* as late as 1923.[74] Redfern was a Tolstoyan mystic, rejecting all institutional affiliations and affirming the divine presence in everything.[75] Hobson joined the New Europe Group, which combined occultism with psychology and social reformism to express his faith in "a profound humanity that moves to its appointed end [the reign of love] uninfluenced by the schools."[76] Foster still thought that "the ever-growing public life around me was a far truer interpretation of the spirit of Jesus than the narrow self-serving ideas common in the churches."[77] Hugh Gore of the Bristol church worked in a boys' club trying to infuse into the young a sense of the divine spirit and human brotherhood.[78] Finally, the histories of the surviving branches of the Labour Church also suggest that immanentism persisted as a basis for social action. Several branches joined the Ethical Culture Movement. The Aberdeen church was absorbed by the local Unitarians. The Keighley church returned to its Swedenborgian origins. The Croydon church remained part of the Brotherhood Church movement. And the Hyde church continued as a labor church until the Second World War.

An adequate account of the decline of the Labour Church should suggest why some members withdrew from politics in the name of their faith and why others came to regard the Labour Church as of little political use. It seems likely that the collapse of the Labour Church reflects the limits of immanentism when used as a political doctrine. In very general terms, the problem is that immanentists usually have to appeal to a wider audience if they are to acquire the support necessary for effective political action, but to make such an appeal, they have to play down their religious faith. If they remain true to their faith, there remains little effective political activity they can undertake, but if they try to formulate a clear political stance, they risk undermining their religious identity. So, any organization akin to the Labour Church is likely to face a conflict between religious purity and political effectiveness, and this conflict often leads to sterility and the decline of the organization.

Competing claims of religious purity and political effectiveness pulled apart the Labour Church. Once the growth of socialism slowed and ethical socialists paid more attention to political strategy, an immanentist faith sometimes conflicted with the political needs of the socialist movement. The theology of the Labour Church implied that the divine was working through the labor movement, and any attempt to theorize that

---

[74] *Inquirer*, November 1923.
[75] Redfern, *Journey to Understanding*, esp. pp. 54–55 and 103–4.
[76] Hobson, *Pilgrim*, p. 290.
[77] Foster, *Socialism*, p. 56.
[78] *Labour Prophet*, May 1895.

process was likely to create a tradition that would inhibit the natural expression of life. Yet, if God was present in the labor movement, the Labour Church could not question the activities of the movement. If the labor movement expressed divine life in a way that theological reflection could only hinder, the Labour Church had no business theorizing the labor movement. The Labour Church thus aimed only "to set free the tremendous power of religious enthusiasm and joy which is now pent-up in the great labour movement."[79] Its only role was to proclaim the labor movement a religious one embodying the divine life in its immediate intensity and veracity. Trevor often explained that the Labour Church existed not to bring a religious dimension to the labor movement but only to witness the religious nature of that movement. Yet, if the Labour Church existed only to glorify the labor movement, there was little point in its having a separate identity, and if it nonetheless had a separate identity, this identity might bring it into conflict with the labor movement.

The Labour Church thus became torn between an absorption in the political movement, which would undermine its religious identity, and a repudiation of the political movement, which would contradict its theology. Trevor and his allies, including Foster and Redfern, wanted the Labour Church to retain a religious identity. Brocklehurst and others wanted to reduce its mission to the "Labour programme," which they defined as the "socialisation of wealth through the election of independent Labour candidates to all representative bodies."[80] They argued that "neither religious faith nor want of religious faith should debar any man from joining our ranks."[81] These theoretical differences led to disputes over the form of services. In 1895 Trevor introduced a formal benediction, including a reference to God, at the end of services in Manchester, and he recommended that other churches do likewise. But few labor churches followed his lead, and some members opposed the use of the word "God." A similar dispute arose over whether to have prayers in services. Trevor argued that prayer "should not be lightly abandoned," since its absence was "a weakness in a religious service."[82] But several labor churches did without prayer, and some members opposed the adoption of any such religious practice.[83]

One particularly divisive issue was whether to use the word "God" in the Labour Church's pronouncements. Trevor defended the word "God" on the grounds that it was the best way of conveying the idea of a "Su-

---

[79] *Workman's Times*, 23 October 1891.

[80] *Labour Prophet*, December 1893.

[81] Ibid., January 1894.

[82] Ibid., June 1895.

[83] The issue of prayer eventually was left to the discretion of individual chairmen. See *Labour Prophet*, June 1895.

preme Power we all must recognise."[84] In contrast, people such as Brock-lehurst argued that the word "God" was irrelevant. The first struggle here concerned the motto of the *Labour Prophet*. Initially the front page carried the phrase "God is our King," but after four issues this was replaced by a phrase taken from Giuseppe Mazzini, "Let Labour be the basis of civil society.[85] Later, in 1894, Brocklehurst and his allies extended the fight to the movement's statement of principles. Their proposed statement made no reference to God: "The Labour Church movement is a union of all those who, by organised or individual effort, are emphasising or developing the moral and ethical aspect of the Labour movement." The Labour Church Union voted to retain the word "God," but only by eleven votes to nine.[86] Moreover, despite Trevor's apparent victory, an official journal of the movement still reported that "Labour Church folk do not bother much about God," and Foster still complained that he saw little sign of "God consciousness" in the movement.[87] The more the Labour Church turned its back on religious forms, the more it denied itself a distinct identity.

Just as the demands of political action challenged the religious identity of the Labour Church, so its religious identity weakened its political effectiveness. Some of the members who wanted to bolster its religious identity even thought that socialists had to avoid all political action if they were to retain spiritual integrity. As Redfern recalled, "I began to think that it was in the nature of a struggle for political power to produce just that 'bankruptcy' of the socialist ideal."[88] Immanentism generally led the members of the Labour Church to neglect questions of political strategy. Immanentism suggested that social transformation had to come from within, but once people learned to listen to the divine within, socialism would follow automatically. Conway told the Leek church that socialism was "the form of society which must inevitably come into being when men believe, that is to say live by, the truth of the unity of life."[89] Likewise, Trevor argued that the way to create socialism was simply "to make life from within, to keep on making it."[90]

Many members of the Labour Church believed that an inner transformation would suffice to bring about the ideal. They could be dismissive of organizations that engaged in the more mundane activities necessary

---

[84] Ibid., August 1893.

[85] G. Mazzini, "From the Council to God," in *The Duties of Man and Other Essays,* ed. E. Rhys (London: J. M. Dent, 1907), p. 320.

[86] Ibid., December 1894.

[87] *Labour Church Record,* April 1899; Foster, *Socialism,* p. 33.

[88] Redfern, *Journey to Understanding,* p. 101.

[89] *Leek Times,* 19 December 1896.

[90] Trevor, *Tracts,* tract 4, p. 5.

to obtain political power. And they could be severely critical when the pursuit of political power seemed to lead these organizations to deviate from their high moral ideals. Trevor denounced the ILP as follows:

> To a man who has any sense of the vast range of life, and of the intricate interaction between the laws of human progress, the I.L.P. must of necessity appear to be attempting the salvation of the world in appallingly cheap fashion. Making converts at the low price of a penny a head, winning elections by listening to tickling speeches, ... jealous and suspicious of any extension of their own principles where they touch man's deeper needs and higher aspirations—all this I have been watching with perplexity and sorrow during the past twelve months.[91]

The Labour Church often favored religious purity over political effectiveness. It was unable to take political action, since to have done so would have been to depart from its religious principles. Members of the Labour Church placed more emphasis on the labor movement, joining it, and being a good socialist than on obtaining power and using it to make a better world. Often the only role available to the labor churches was preaching. Yet, several members soon recognized the limitations of this role. As Gore explained, "What exercises the minds of some of us ... is a kind of consciousness that we have not considered the road at all"; "we have pictured the ultimate condition of Society, we have urged the wisdom, even the necessity, of its accomplishment, but we have failed so far to explain the rule of the road thither."[92]

Actually, the Labour Church did little to fill in its picture of the ultimate condition of society. Immanentism could encourage a neglect of questions of policy as well as of political agency. Labour Church members regularly implied that institutions and policies were likely to become fossilized traditions and, as such, to hinder the work of the divine. Hobson argued for "a complete absence of dogma" so that life might flourish; he trusted in "a new concept of life wide enough to encompass existing creeds."[93] The theology of the Labour Church gave it the difficult task of sustaining fellowship while trying to avoid a commitment to particular traditions or practices. Of course, the Labour Church arose out of a particular tradition, but organizations generally will sustain the commitment and unity of their members only if they are rather more self-conscious about the substantive beliefs and practices for which they stand. Labor churches became little more than public spaces in which socialists could gather to hear inspirational speakers.

---

[91] *Labour Prophet*, May 1895.
[92] Ibid.
[93] Hobson, *Pilgrim*, p. 264.

A member of the Labour Church complained, "I find Labour Churches generally weak, unbusiness-like, and quarrelsome."[94] The conflict between religious purity and political effectiveness led to a sense of purposelessness. A *Clarion* investigation into the causes of the decline of the movement highlighted the fact that many people found "practically no difference between a Labour Church meeting and an I.L.P. meeting."[95] The *Labour Prophet* continued publication until 1898, when it was replaced by the smaller quarterly *Labour Church Record*, which survived until 1902. Yet, these publications signaled not the vitality of the movement but Trevor's activity and Wicksteed's financial support. When Trevor's wife and younger son died in 1894, his energies began to flag. When his proposals for a system of discipleship were defeated in 1900, he withdrew from the movement to farm chickens, study the sex question, and then to try to establish a free-love community called Oasis.[96] Allan Clarke of the Bolton church took over Trevor's editorial duties. Clarke immediately began a campaign to highlight the "spiritual" side of the movement, even proposing changing its name to Goodwill Church on the grounds that "'labour' shuts out so many people."[97] Foster became president of the Labour Church Union, and he too hoped to revive the religious identity of the movement. He visited numerous local churches, only to conclude sadly that "the purely material interpretation of life so far dominated the Labour Churches as to unfit them for any great spiritual leadership."[98] Some local churches still thrived, and a few new ones were formed after the relative success of the Labour Party in the 1906 general election, but the movement had ceased to be an effective force as early as 1902.[99]

Conclusion

The Labour Church was neither a stopover on the way to a mature secular socialism nor an organization fulfilling the emotional role of religious faith without being tied to any doctrinal content. Rather, it was an expression of an immanentist faith. Indeed, the immanentist theology of the Labour Church was what prevented its taking on an effective political role. More generally, ethical socialism was neither a transient stopover on the way to a mature secular socialism nor a religious aspiration that

[94] *Labour Church Record*, April 1901.
[95] Cited in Pierson, "John Trevor and the Labour Church," 475.
[96] See J. Trevor, *The One Life* (Horsted Keynes, UK: Trevor, 1909).
[97] *Labour Church Record*, January 1901.
[98] Foster, *Socialism*, p. 49.
[99] *Clarion*, 9 February 1906.

became the prisoner of a cautious party machine. Rather, it was a historical tradition that emerged in the 1890s as an immanentist response to the crisis of faith, inspired many of those who worked to form the Labour Party, got remade and appropriated in new contexts, and continued to play a role alongside other traditions in the British socialist movement.

Ethical socialism initially relied heavily on an immanentism according to which God is in the world, revealing himself through the evolutionary process. Immanentism supported ethical socialism in several ways. For a start, immanentism undermined the evangelical distinction between secular and sacred. It suggested that the divine is present in this world, so the nature of social life is a religious matter. Foster noticed how the members of the Labour Church rejected "the 'other worldliness'" of evangelicals.[100] In addition, immanentism implied that everyone contained a divine spark that united them in a universal brotherhood. Ethical socialists believed that the evolutionary unfolding of the divine led to the realization of an ethic of fellowship. Finally, immanentism often brought a renewed interest in the Incarnation and Christ the man. Ethical socialists evoked Jesus as the son of a simple carpenter who sided with the downtrodden and lived in fellowship with his disciples. Fred Henderson described the workers as "Gaunt Christs, whose thorns are not yet hid with bays."[101]

[100] Foster, *Socialism*, p. 33.
[101] *Workers' Cry*, 2 May 1891.

Socialism, Labor, and the State

HISTORIANS HAVE OFTEN DISCUSSED socialism as a product of the rise of a secular society and class-based politics. Socialism and the social democratic welfare state appeared as the inevitable results of a process of socioeconomic modernization. Today, however, the old historiography might seem simplistic and even implausible in the presence of a growing suspicion of any vestige of teleology and determinism. New historiographies might turn instead to the contingent processes by which people made socialism. Socialism was not a byproduct of the growth of a secular or class-based society. On the contrary, people actively made socialism as they struggled to make sense of their world and their aspirations.

British socialism arose as a result of the contingent ways in which people modified their inherited intellectual traditions in response to dilemmas. Historians can understand how and why people made socialism by examining the relevant traditions and dilemmas. British socialism then appears as a contingent and varied product of the radical milieu of the 1880s and 1890s. In the late nineteenth century, socialists and others broke with the evangelicalism and classical liberalism that had dominated earlier in the century. Evolutionary theory and a general crisis of faith precipitated a shift from evangelicalism to an ethical positivism and immanentist theologies that encouraged humanitarianism and an ethic of fellowship. The collapse of classical economics precipitated a greater focus on new policy instruments and utopian visions including state action and nationalization.

Socialism arose contingently, and also variously. People were not bound to respond to the crisis of faith and the collapse of classical economics in any one way; nor did they do so. Socialism had no correct or developed form that was bound to come to the fore and triumph over more primitive rebellions. On the contrary, people made socialism differently, depending on the traditions on which they drew, but also on their own situated agency. The making of socialism thus involved debates and exchanges between and among Marxists, Fabians, and ethical socialists. Even the leading Fabians never settled on a single agreed set of ideas; rather, they debated economics and strategy with one another and changed their individual views in response to those debates and to their experiences.

British socialism was not bound to result in a new class-based party and a social democratic welfare state. Indeed, historians should avoid tying socialism to any core idea, historical essence, or teleological path. They might treat socialism as a constantly shifting product of particular contexts. This concluding chapter provides an overview of the making and the remaking of socialism. It draws out some of the patterns of socialist debate and thought on labor and the state that emerged in the 1880s and 1890s. It points to the persistence and transformation of these patterns during the twentieth century. And it suggests how the legacy of these patterns may still be relevant to us today.

SOCIALISM AND THE STATE

Victorian Britain contained diverse traditions of thought. Yet, the dominant ones were an evangelicalism that treated classical political economy as an elucidation of divine laws and a liberalism that was wedded to classical political economy. The Enlightenment and romanticism resulted in the reinvention, not marginalization, of these traditions. The Enlightenment undoubtedly included deistic and agnostic themes. However, evangelicals typically reinvented their theology to accommodate the social and economic theories of the Scottish Enlightenment. They described natural social laws as the creations of God. God had created social mechanisms that rewarded the virtuous and punished the immoral. Later a romantic organicism eroded the legacy of the Enlightenment, with David Ricardo shifting classical political economy from mechanistic approaches and metaphors toward developmental ones, and with John Stuart Mill modifying utilitarianism to accommodate notions of individual and social development derived from romanticism and positivism. However, Victorian organicism proved compatible with the social and economic ideals of the Enlightenment. Whig histories in particular restated Enlightenment ideals as the telos of an organic process; history developed progressively toward an enlightened liberty that was based on personal freedom in a civil society, market economy, and constitutional democracy.

Evangelicalism and classical political economy dominated through much of the nineteenth century. Even popular radicals accepted the ideal of a harmonious and self-regulating market economy. The radicals' critique of British society drew here on a republican tradition that traced social ills back to a corrupt political system, not the inner workings of the economy. The popular radicals argued that a ruling oligarchy used the political power of the state to perpetuate an unnatural and unjust system of land ownership that kept a virtuous people in poverty. It was only in the late nineteenth century that the collapse of classical political economy and evangelicalism created the space in which socialism then appeared. In a first phase, a few popular and Tory radicals moved toward Marxism. In a second phase, a few liberal radicals moved toward humanitarianism, engaged Marxist and anarchist ideas, and forged a distinctive Fabian socialism. In a final phase, a general cultural shift toward immanentism led to the rapid spread of an ethical socialism based on an ideal of fellowship and attempts at personal and communal transformation.

British socialists held widely disparate views of the state. The Marxists generally came from traditions of secularism and Tory and popular radicalism. They had long been skeptical of evangelicalism and the more liberal strands of classical political economy. In the 1880s, their discovery of Karl Marx encouraged them to identify social ills less with political corruption and the monopoly of land than with capitalism itself. They adopted Marx's catastrophist vision of capitalist development. Capitalism did not lead to wealth, happiness, and peace. It resulted in crises of overproduction, the immiseration of workers, and imperial rivalries and wars over foreign markets. Capitalism was self-destructive, not self-regulating. Many British Marxists argued that the failings of capitalism made state intervention in civil society essential; the state had to intervene in civil society to secure a just and stable society. Many British Marxists also wanted to reform the state to create an appropriate instrument for such intervention; socialism and freedom depended on a properly democratic political system. So, the Social Democratic Federation (SDF) demanded not only a parliament based on universal suffrage but also popular control of this parliament to be reinforced through measures such as annual elections, referenda, a principle of delegation, the abolition of the House of Lords, and an elected civil service.

Although many Marxists accepted the need for a more interventionist state, their economic theories did not necessarily require state intervention. Marxists believed that the evils of capitalism arose from private ownership of the means of production. Some Marxists suggested that if private ownership were eradicated, civil society might indeed come to resemble the older liberal ideal of a harmonious and self-regulating system. So, the Marxists debated the nature of common ownership of the means of production. Henry Mayers Hyndman and the Tory and popular radicals in the SDF believed that a democratic state could act as a suitable vehicle for common ownership. The few Marxist converts from liberal radicalism generally remained more hostile to the state. Anarcho-communists such as William Morris suggested that the absence of private property would remove almost all cause of disagreement; thus civil society could become a self-regulating sphere from which political authority would be almost absent. Syndicalists such as Tom Mann gave a role to democratic authority, but they located it in industrial units composed of producers, not geographic units composed of citizens.

Marxism attracted more popular and Tory radicals than it did liberal radicals. When liberal radicals turned to socialism, they generally joined the Fabian Society, and they did so following the collapse of classical economics. The Fabians drew on new marginalist, neoclassical, and positivist economics to devise theories of rent as exploitation. George Bernard Shaw and Sidney Webb, in particular, argued that any economy necessarily would produce land rent and possibly other related social surpluses. Rent is unearned; it comes from the permanent or temporary monopolies that arise from natural and social variations of fertility and industrial situation. The Fabians also argued that rent was not needed to ensure the supply of land or capital and thus an efficient economy. They even suggested that rent enabled inefficient companies to flourish. More generally, many Fabians came to argue that capitalism was an uncoordinated industrial system composed of numerous fragmented centers of management that knew little about each other's activities, and that this lack of coordination led to duplication, temporary blockages, and other unnecessary forms of waste.

Fabian economic theories, unlike those of the Marxists, almost required their adherents to call for an interventionist state. Insofar as Marxists believed that surplus value arose from the buying and selling of labor, they could conclude that the collective ownership of the means of production would eliminate exploitation irrespective of the particular role the state played. In contrast, the Fabians believed that rents could not be eliminated, since they arose from the variable productivity of different pieces of land and capital. The only solution seemed to be for the state to collect rent and use it for the collective good. Of course, if the state were to play a greater role in society, its integrity and efficiency would have to be vital. The Fabians thus wanted "through Democracy to gather the whole people into the State, so that the State may be trusted with the rent of the country."[1] Here the Fabians' debt to liberal radicalism, rather than the republicanism of the popular radicals, meant that they defined democracy almost wholly in terms of representative government to the exclusion of other forms of popular control over the executive.

The third strand to make up British socialism was an ethical one based on a moral critique of capitalism. Ethical socialists denounced the free market and competition in favor of a moral economy and cooperation. Proponents of the moral economy denied that a market economy would promote prosperity, happiness, and peace. They associated capitalism

[1] G. Shaw, "The Transition to Social Democracy," in *Fabian Essays*, ed. G. Shaw, introd. A. Briggs (London: Allen and Unwin, 1962), p. 182.

with poverty, urban squalor, immorality, and social dislocation. Even if capitalism did bring material benefits, these were outweighed by its social costs. Besides, many of the commodities produced by a capitalist economy satisfied artificial wants because the market responded primarily to the changing whims of the wealthy, not to people's genuine needs. Worst of all, capitalism encouraged individualism and competition. It brought to the fore people's mean and selfish instincts. It elevated material greed above human fellowship.

Ethical socialists rarely appealed to economic analyses of capitalism. Edward Carpenter even dismissed the debate over the nature of value as being akin to disputes among medieval scholastics.[2] For ethical socialists, the important task was not to provide some formal theory of abstract economic processes but to examine the results of these processes and then to assess their moral acceptability. Capitalism stood condemned for its failure to ground economics on an ethic of cooperative fellowship. Ethical socialists wanted people to accept that, in Wilfrid Richmond's words, "economies are within the sphere of conscience."[3] An ethic of fellowship required people to concern themselves with others in all their daily activities. Capitalists, consumers, and workers all had to put the well-being of their fellows before their selfish interests in profits, prices, and wages. Yet, the idea of a moral economy had perilously little to say about the role of the state under socialism. Ethical socialists typically defined socialism simply as the enactment of a spirit of democracy and fellowship in which relationships were based on equality and love. The role of the state was of little importance compared with personal transformation. On the one hand, if economic interactions were governed by suitable moral values, there would be little need for the state to intervene. Some ethical socialists even propagated a nongovernmental utopia, focusing on a new way of living personally and in community. On the other hand, debates about the economic role to be played by the state should not be allowed to detract from the vital need for a moral revolution. Some ethical socialists even associated the new ethic with state intervention of the kind advocated by the SDF and the Fabians.

Socialism and Independent Labor

As Marxists, Fabians, and ethical socialists debated the role of the state, they tried to decide on an appropriate relationship to the labor movement. Many thought socialism involved eliminating the exploitation of

[2] E. Carpenter, "The Value of the Value Theory," *To-day* 11 (1889): 22–30.

[3] W. Richmond, *Christian Economics* (London: Rivingtons, 1888), p. 25.

workers, or at least saving the workers from a grinding poverty. Yet, to want to save the workers was not necessarily to believe that the workers were the best instrument of their own salvation. Some socialists were skeptical of the trade-union movement, believing, for example, that it remained mired in liberalism, that it represented the interests only of the skilled elite among the workers, or even that it was a factional group standing in the way of collective goods. Almost all socialists wanted the workers to become socialists. Most hoped to establish socialism by convincing the workers of the need for political action for socialist ends. But they did not necessarily want to combine with a new labor party if doing so would dilute the socialist message.

To some extent socialist debates over an independent labor party reflected those over state intervention. The more socialists believed in state action, the more likely they were to stress the importance of a political party to take control of the state and so to look to the labor movement for support for a new party. Only a few purists, anarchists, and nongovernmental utopians opposed the very idea of an independent labor party. Most socialists accepted the ideal of an independent labor party while worrying about the practical extent to which such a party would be able to secure funding and be properly socialist. The main debate among the Marxists of the SDF concerned the extent to which they should merge with an independent labor party instead of remaining separate as a clear socialist vanguard. The main debates among Fabians were about the ability of a new party to raise funds from the trade unions, and the extent to which they themselves might be able to promote socialism through an alternative progressive alliance. The main debates among ethical socialists concerned the extent to which an organized political party would dilute the moral example and power of socialism as a personal way of life.

Some trade unions debated similar issues. Historically, the trade unions had allied themselves with the Liberal Party. Yet, during the late 1880s some unionists, inspired in part by socialists such as H. H. Champion, began to promote more independent action. A leading example is Keir Hardie.[4] Hardie had gone down the pit in 1866 at the age of ten. In 1878 he became the Hamilton district agent of the Lanarkshire miners' union. An unsuccessful strike in 1880 forced him to leave the pits, move to Ayrshire, and eke out a living as a radical journalist. At that time, Hardie was a liberal radical who spoke regularly at the Cumnock Junior Liberal Association. In 1886 he became secretary of the newly formed Ayrshire Miners' Union and a leader in another strike. The employers

[4] B. Holman, *Keir Hardie: Labour's Greatest Hero?* (Oxford: Lion Hudson, 2010); and Kenneth Morgan, *Keir Hardie: Radical and Socialist* (London: Weidenfeld and Nicolson, 1975).

reacted brutally, and the Liberal government backed the employers by sending in the Hussars to preserve order. Hardie was dismayed. At the 1887 Trades Union Congress (TUC), he proposed a motion calling for a labor party in order to promote the parliamentary representation of the workers. Yet, Hardie remained a liberal radical; he supported most Liberal policies but wanted the Liberal Party to adopt more working-class candidates, and his proposed party was really a pressure group to advance that end. In 1888 Hardie tried to become the Liberal candidate for Mid-Lanark, but the Liberal caucus rejected him, so he decided to stand as an independent candidate backed by the Labour Electoral Association. After Hardie lost the election, he founded the Scottish Labour Party and, finally, four months later, in September 1888, announced that he had become a socialist.[5]

By the early 1890s, several provincial Fabians and ethical socialists were also thinking about a new party to represent the interests of the workers. The Labour Church was especially important here. John Trevor's claim that God was working through the labor movement bypassed some of the awkward questions about the extent to which socialists should dilute their message in order to cooperate with trade unions. In May 1892 Trevor and Robert Blatchford established the Manchester Independent Labour Party. Soon after, Joseph Burgess led a campaign to unite such local organizations into a national body.[6] On 13 January 1893, a conference at the Bradford Labour Institute founded the national Independent Labour Party (ILP). Trevor was present as a delegate from Manchester and, as we saw in the last chapter, led the associated Labour Church gathering. Hardie, who had just been elected to Parliament for West Ham South, chaired the conference.

The ILP may have attracted trade unionists such as Hardie, as well as ethical socialists such as Trevor, but it was a clearly socialist organization, with little appeal to trade unionists who were not socialists.[7] To simplify, we might say that the socialism of the ILP fused ethical socialism with Fabian economics and sociology. All the leading members of the ILP were directly influenced by ethical socialists from the Fellowship of the New Life, the Sheffield Socialists, and the Labour Church movement. Ramsay MacDonald belonged to the Fellowship and for a while lived in its communal residence in London. Katharine Conway later recalled, "I came under Carpenter's influence as a morbid High Churchwoman with

[5] *Miner*, September 1888.

[6] *Workman's Times*, 30 April 1892.

[7] D. Howell, *British Workers and the Independent Labour Party, 1888–1906* (Manchester, UK: Manchester University Press, 1983); and D. James, T. Jowitt, and K. Laybourn, eds., *The Centennial History of the Independent Labour Party* (Keele, UK: Keele University Press, 1992).

vague humanitarian impulses and the lead he gave me was literally from darkness and bondage out into life and liberty."[8] Moreover, the Sheffield Socialists inspired numerous other local groups, including those in Bristol and Nottingham, and these groups often later became branches of the ILP.[9] In the previous chapter I discussed the close ties between the ILP and the Labour Church movement. A list of the main preachers at Labour Church meetings reads like a who's who of the early ILP; Blatchford, Conway, Hardie, and Margaret MacMillan were regular favorites.

An immanentist faith and an ethic of fellowship dominated the ILP. Socialists such as Hardie, MacDonald, and Philip Snowden now condemned capitalism in much the same terms as ethical socialists had done earlier. Snowden complained that capitalism brought out people's "animal instincts," not their moral ones; capitalism "makes men hard, cruel, selfish, acquisitive economic machines."[10] MacDonald defended the idea of "buying in the best market," provided that the concept of "best" included the welfare of producers, not just cheapness.[11] Hardie suggested that socialism is, "if not a religion in itself, at least a handmaiden to religion, and as such entitled to the support of all who pray for the coming of Christ's kingdom upon earth."[12]

The ILP differed from earlier ethical socialist organizations mainly in its far stronger reliance on explicitly Christian ideas and symbols. Appeals to the Sermon on the Mount and the coming of the Kingdom of God were commonplace. Carpenter and Trevor had drawn from romantics such as Ralph Waldo Emerson to forge an immanentist faith based on a spiritual view of nature. The members of the ILP shared their immanentism, arguing, in Hardie's words, that "there must be some principle of beauty and perfection in the Universe towards which all creation is reaching out."[13] But the leading members of the ILP further bolstered the religious content of their socialism through appeals to Christ and his incarnation on earth. Some of them, including Hardie, were practicing Christians who believed that Christ was the son of God. Others, including John Bruce Glasier, had rejected Christianity but still appealed to the

---

[8] G. Beith, ed., *Edward Carpenter: In Appreciation* (London: Allen and Unwin, 1931), p. 183.

[9] S. Bryher, *An Account of the Labour and Socialist Movement in Bristol* (Bristol, UK: Bristol Socialist Society, 1931); E. Delavenay, *D. H. Lawrence and Edward Carpenter: A Study in Edwardian Transition* (London: Heinemann, 1971).

[10] P. Snowden, *Socialism and Syndicalism* (London: Collins, 1913), p. 84.

[11] J. Ramsay MacDonald, *The Zollverein and British Industry* (London: Grant Richards, 1903), p. 163.

[12] J. Hardie, "From Serfdom to Socialism," in *From Serfdom to Socialism*, ed. J. Hardie (London: G. Allen, 1907), p. 44.

[13] Ibid., p. 87.

moral example of the human Jesus. Glasier likened capitalists who "cry communist" to those who crucified Christ.[14]

Most of the leading members of the ILP had belonged to the Fabians as well as to ethical socialist groups. They increasingly fused ethical socialism with Fabian economic theories. Snowden adopted Webb's theory of interest as analogous to land rent, arguing that "just as the landlord gets an unearned income from the increase in the value of land, so the capitalist gets an unearned increment from improvements in productive methods and in other ways not the result of his own efforts or abilities."[15] Similarly, MacDonald followed Webb's denunciation of the uncoordinated nature of the market, arguing that capitalism relied on a chaotic and haphazard clash of interests, whereas socialism would eliminate waste by organizing economic life on a scientific basis.[16]

As the ILP increasingly relied on Fabian economics, it came explicitly to reject any association of socialism with an unregulated civil society. Socialism required state intervention, quite possibly beginning with legislation to enforce the eight-hour day. The existence of an unearned increment present in all economies made it necessary for the state to collect this surplus and use it for the benefit of the community. Over time, Hardie, MacDonald, and Snowden advocated a range of measures to deal with the social surplus in the economy. They wanted to collect the surplus through taxation, but also through legislative restrictions on property rights and eventually public ownership of the means of production. And they wanted to use the surplus for communal benefit through an extension of social-welfare legislation.

The leading figures in the ILP turned to the state to correct the failings they believed were inherent in the economy. They rejected traditional fears about a powerful state by stressing the ethical nature of a truly democratic state. Liberals had been right to oppose state intervention at a time when the state was a corrupt aristocratic one, but the establishment of democracy had now made the state trustworthy. MacDonald explained that "the democratic State is an organisation of the people, democratic government is self-government, democratic law is an expression of the will of the people who have to obey the law."[17] The leading figures within the Labour Party defined democracy in terms taken, again,

[14] J. Glasier, *On the Road to Liberty: Poems and Ballads*, ed. J. Wallace (London: National Labour Press, 1920), p. 33.

[15] Snowden, *Socialism*, p. 117.

[16] J. Ramsay MacDonald, "Socialism," in *Ramsay MacDonald's Political Writings,* ed. B. Barker (London: Allen Lane, 1972).

[17] J. Ramsay MacDonald, *Socialism and Society* (London: Independent Labour Party, 1905), p. 70.

from the ethical socialists and the Fabians. They equated democracy with a spirit of fellowship and representative institutions, rarely showing enthusiasm for other forms of popular control.

Precisely because the ILP was a socialist group, it still faced some awkward questions about the extent to which socialists might cooperate with other political parties, and the extent to which socialists might dilute their message in order to appeal to labor. Its founding conference made it possible for members to vote for, and even to join, other parties, most obviously the Liberals. And the conference also rejected the title Socialist Labour Party so as to appeal to the trade unions. Ben Tillett said that he "would sooner have all the solid, progressive, matter of fact, fighting Trades' Unionism of England than all the hare-brained chatterers and magpies of Continental revolutionists."[18] However, the ILP included some members who were less sympathetic to liberalism and labor. Some Tory socialists, mainly from the Manchester branch, wanted to pass a motion requiring members to abstain in elections in which there was no ILP candidate. Similarly, the more secular socialists, who did not equate the labor movement with the divine spirit, complained that the labor alliance involved a betrayal of socialism for mere electoral advantage. The Clarion group called for a united socialist party to take precedence over links with trade unions.

By the end of the nineteenth century, the challenges to the ILP leadership had largely faded. In 1898 Hardie, Glasier, MacDonald, and Snowden were elected to the National Administrative Council, where they remained, taking turns as chairman, until 1909. Earlier, in 1895, the ILP had entered twenty-eight candidates in the general election, and when they all lost, the leadership had become even more convinced of the need for a labor alliance. Hardie and the others called for a clear and almost exclusive focus on the labor issue of working-class representation in Parliament while also trying to present socialism as a mere extension of liberalism.[19] But despite the overtures of the ILP, the unions remained coy.

Finally the TUC of 1899 passed a resolution calling for a congress to discuss how to return more labor members to Parliament. The Labour Representation Committee (LRC) was created. The ILP blocked the attempts of the SDF to get a commitment to socialism as well as labor representation. A secret pact with the Liberals ensured that the LRC had a free run against the Conservative Party in about thirty constituencies in

---

[18] Independent Labour Party, *Annual Conference Report*, 1893, p. 3.

[19] *Labour Leader*, 12 November 1898; J. Hardie and J. Ramsay MacDonald, "The Independent Labour Party's Programme," *Nineteenth Century* 53 (1899): 142–49.

return for a prior commitment to support the Liberals in other seats and in government. This pact helped secure the return of twenty-nine LRC candidates. At their first meeting, in February 1906, these new members of Parliament and one other took the title of the Labour Party.[20]

SOCIALISM AND MODERNISM

The LRC and the Labour Party brought socialists together with the trade unions. The inaugural meeting of the LRC included three socialist groups: the SDF, Fabians, and ILP. The SDF withdrew in 1901, believing that the real need was for a united and fully socialist party, rather than a labor alliance. The ILP and the Fabians remained involved, although the leading Fabians initially remained somewhat distant. The Labour Party continued to grow, winning forty-two parliamentary seats in 1910 and playing a small role in government during the First World War. At the end of the war, the Labour Party adopted a constitution, drafted by Webb, which included the famous Clause IV, committing it to the socialist goal of "common ownership of the means of production, distribution, and exchange."

By the time Webb drafted Clause IV, the Fabians had become a leading source of Labour Party policy. To some extent the role of the Fabians merely continued that which they had played for the ILP. The leading socialists in the Labour Party came from the ILP, including Hardie, MacDonald, and Snowden. Most merged ethical socialism with Fabianism. Several were members of the Fabian Society. As the Labour Party thought about policy, it occasionally got inspiration from Marxists, who had long championed an eight-hour day, or ethical socialists, several of whom wanted to make vivisection illegal, but it typically fell back on the Fabian ideas of greater taxation, the collective provision of social goods, and the rational organization of industry. The Labour Party's mock budget of 1907 spoke in Fabian terms of introducing "taxation" to collect "unearned ... increments of wealth" and then use them "for communal benefit."[21] Again, the Labour Party came to adopt common ownership of the means of production as a solution to the anarchic nature of capitalist production.

[20] R. McKibbin, *The Evolution of the Labour Party, 1910–24* (Oxford: Clarendon Press, 1974); H. Pelling, *The Origins of the Labour Party, 1880–1900* (Oxford: Clarendon Press, 1965); and D. Tanner, *Political Change and the Labour Party, 1900–1918* (Cambridge: Cambridge University Press, 1990).

[21] P. Snowden, "The Socialist Budget 1907," in *From Socialism to Serfdom*, ed. Hardie, p. 7.

The role of the Fabians in Labour Party policymaking also reflected their concern with questions of governance. Most Marxists focused primarily on an economic analysis of capitalism's downfall and on political action to prepare for the consequent revolution. Most ethical socialists focused primarily on moral ideals, personal transformation, and communal experiments. In contrast, several Fabians tied socialism to an evolutionary sociology, thereby focusing on public administration. When the Labour Party leaders thought about how to implement policies, they found that the Fabians were the main socialists who consistently and creatively addressed questions of public administration. It is one thing to believe in socialism as an economic inevitability or a moral ideal and quite another to have an account of institutions and policies that can advance socialism. The Fabians alone had compelling answers to questions about governance. They wanted the state and other collective organizations to take control, organize, and regulate social life. And they thought representative democratic institutions could do so through a hierarchical bureaucracy differentiated along functional lines.

Yet, although the Fabians addressed issues of public governance, even they had perilously little to say about economic governance. The Fabians often expressed their faith in the collectivist future, and they spent considerable energy devising collectivist policies that might attain immediate political backing, but between these two activities lay the unresolved issues of how to cope with economic and social difficulties prior to the adoption of collectivist solutions. The spread of collectivism would eliminate shortages, temporary blockages, and the other problems associated with anarchic competition, but a faith that cooperation and coordination would solve problems did nothing to alleviate them prior to collectivism. In particular, the Fabians' long-term goal of collectivism was of little help in dealing with the interwar depression. Webb's belief in collectivism had long led him, for example, to dismiss any long-term role for relief work.[22] The field lay open for alternative proposals for economic governance, and perhaps even for social reform. Just as the Fabians' evolutionary positivism had broken with utilitarianism, so it in turn gave way to an atomistic and analytical modernism.

Modernism had precursors prior to 1914, but it flourished when the First World War undermined earlier organicist and evolutionary theories.[23] Although the demise of beliefs in development and progress was a

---

[22] S. Webb, *The Government Organisation of Unemployed Labour* (London: Fabian Society, 1886).

[23] R. Adcock, M. Bevir, and S. Stimson, eds., *Modern Political Science: Anglo-American Exchanges since 1880* (Princeton, NJ: Princeton University Press, 2007); W. Everdell, *The First Moderns: Profiles in the Origins of Twentieth Century Thought* (Chicago: University of Chicago Press, 1997); T. Porter, *Trust in Numbers: The Pursuit of Objectivity in Science*

gradual, drawn-out process that stretched far into the twentieth century, the First World War did much to undermine the link between technological development and moral improvement that had sustained earlier ideas of the rational and progressive nature of history. It thereby lent a fillip to modernist modes of knowing that based correlations, classifications, and models on atomistic facts and other such units. The earlier focus on wholes and their evolution increasingly gave way to atomistic and analytical approaches to discrete and discontinuous elements and their assemblage. At the edges of modernism, moreover, there arose ideas of self-reference, incompleteness, and radical subjectivity. Out went the organicism and moralism that had thrived during much of the nineteenth century with its belief in a historical rationality. In came a new technical expertise based on more ahistorical economic and sociological concepts of rationality. Modernism enshrined the expertise of liberal socialists, Keynesians, and planners.[24] The creation of the social democratic state after the Second World War depended less on ethical positivism or evolutionary sociology than on these modernist forms of expertise.[25]

The Labour Party, like the ILP, drew primarily on those socialist traditions that supported a labor alliance and state intervention. It initially fused ethical socialism with Fabianism before turning increasingly toward new modernist forms of expertise. Yet, the Labour Party, again like the ILP, also contained various critical, oppositional voices that drew on traditions of socialism that were more hostile to state intervention, formal expertise, and a liberal concept of democracy as representative government. To simplify, we might say that although the dominant outlook in the Labour Party long combined ethical socialism with Fabian and modernist forms of expertise to emphasize the role of the state, this dominant outlook was criticized by other socialists influenced by either syndicalist forms of Marxism or nongovernmental forms of ethical socialism. The Labour Party followed the Fabians and many Marxists in suggesting that the state had to play a more active role for the common good and that a democratic state could be trusted to do so. Syndicalists and nongovernmental socialists called instead for the democratization of associations within civil society.

---

and Public Life (Princeton, NJ: Princeton University Press, 1995); and M. Schabas, *A World Ruled by Number: William Stanley Jevons and the Rise of Mathematical Economics* (Princeton, NJ: Princeton University Press, 1990).

[24] E. Durbin, *New Jerusalems: The Labour Party and the Economics of Democratic Socialism* (London: Routledge, 1985); and D. Ritschel, *The Politics of Planning: The Debate on Economic Planning in Britain in the 1930s* (Oxford: Clarendon Press, 1997).

[25] J. Tomlinson, *Democratic Socialism and Economic Policy: The Attlee Years* (Cambridge: Cambridge University Press, 1997), and R. Toye, *The Labour Party and the Planned Economy, 1931–1951* (Woodbridge, UK: Royal Historical Society, 2003).

The leading British syndicalists, including Tom Mann and James Connolly, were Marxists who had belonged to the SDF.[26] They argued, first, that the cure for capitalism lay in a transformation of industry and society without any state involvement. Marxist economics did not require a greater role for the state. The syndicalists could thus envisage a harmonious civil society in which the capitalist system of private property had been replaced by one based on worker-owned industrial units. They rejected the idea of realizing socialism through a parliamentary party in favor of industrial action by trade unions. The syndicalists argued, second, that any leadership tended to become a self-serving bureaucracy unless it was subject to strong democratic controls. Even worker-owned industrial units should institutionalize popular control in, for example, a principle of delegation. The syndicalists opposed the Labour Party's restricted view of democracy as requiring little other than representative government. They wanted to extend popular control by introducing the initiative and referenda into the institutions with which they were concerned.

Some ethical socialists associated their ideal of fellowship with a world of craftsmen conjoined in guilds. A. J. Penty explicitly drew on Carpenter and John Ruskin to describe just such a romantic medievalism in *The Restoration of the Gild System*. Penty then inspired other guild theorists, notably S. G. Hobson and A. R. Orage.[27] The early guild theorists drew on themes from the ethical socialist tradition. They argued, first, that the ideal of fellowship consisted of a social spirit of democracy. Individuals should have full control over their daily activities in a cooperative and decentralized society. Penty explained that "it is necessary to transfer the control of industry from the hands of the financier into those of the craftsman."[28] The guild theorists argued, second, that the cure for capitalism lay in an ethic of fellowship. The state was irrelevant and perhaps even detrimental to this ethic, because a moral economy did not require state intervention, and state-owned industries might develop a commercial ethic akin to that of private companies. Guild theorists thus wanted to focus not on parliamentary politics but on the creation of the ideal of fellowship. They too rejected the Labour Party's view of democracy as representative government. Democracy depended on local control of institutions in civil society that were autonomous from the state.

Socialists remained divided, therefore, between those who looked to correct the failings of the market primarily through the action of a

---

[26] R. Holton, *British Syndicalism, 1900–14: Myths and Realities* (London: Pluto Press, 1976).

[27] A. Penty, *The Restoration of the Gild System* (London: Swan Sonnenschein, 1906).

[28] Ibid., p. 57.

democratic state and those who looked more to the democratization of civil society itself.[29] The Labour Party believed that Fabian and modernist experts could guide state action so as to eliminate, or at least limit, the inequities and inefficiencies of capitalism. Other socialists defended socialist visions based more on voluntary associations than on the state. They criticized the Labour Party for the statist nature of its ideal and its limited concept of democracy. Between the wars, for example, pluralists such as G.D.H. Cole and Harold Laski fused guild socialism with syndicalism—and also some Fabian themes—in an attempt to revitalize the democratic impulses in the Labour Party.[30]

SOCIALISM TODAY

In the late nineteenth century, British socialists made a new ideology. They rejected the evangelicalism and classical political economy that had infused so much of nineteenth-century liberalism. Many turned to immanentist and humanitarian ideas that supported a new ethic focused on fellowship, cooperation, and social welfare. Some also developed economic and sociological theories of the ills of capitalism and the collective action needed to cure these ills. Later, many socialists joined with the trade unions to make a new instrument of change. The Labour Party was meant to realize the ideals of the socialists, as well as to promote the interests of the workers. Later still, the Labour Party played a prominent role in making a new state formation. The social democratic welfare state replaced the liberal state of the nineteenth century. Modernist expertise guided the state as it took on new functions and became increasingly centralized. The state concentrated decision making in itself, added to its jurisdictions, increased taxation, extended its powers of surveillance, developed new strategies of economic management, oversaw massive growth in the public sector, and accepted responsibility for the welfare of its citizens. Socialism appeared to be moving inexorably forward along with a class-based politics and state intervention.

By the late twentieth century, the forward march of socialism, labor, and the state had come to an abrupt halt. Neoliberalism was ascendant. No doubt the Labour Party could have tried slowly to move from the

[29] L. Barrow and I. Bullock, *Democratic Ideas and the British Labour Movement, 1880–1914* (Cambridge: Cambridge University Press, 1996).

[30] C. Labourde, *Pluralist Thought and the State in Britain and France, 1900–25* (Basingstoke, UK: Macmillan, 2000); and M. Stears, *Progressives, Pluralists, and the Problems of the State: Ideologies of Reform in the United States and Britain* (Oxford: Oxford University Press, 2002).

modernist expertise of the Keynesians to the modernist expertise of the monetarists; after all, the Labour government under James Callaghan made the initial move toward monetarism. However, monetarism was widely associated with the far broader free-market agenda of the neo-liberals, and, after 1979, the Conservative governments of Margaret Thatcher pursued that agenda. They challenged the legal privileges of the trade unions, and they attempted to roll back the state and to pro-mote markets.

The future of socialism looked bleak. When the Labour Party eventu-ally returned to power in 1997, it had rejected Webb's Clause IV, and its leaders were wary of the very word "socialist."[31] However, the future of socialism looked bleak only because socialism had become so closely tied to the labor movement and, more importantly, to bureaucratic state intervention. Even if the industrial working class and the bureaucratic state were in decline, socialism need not have been. British socialism had never been reducible to a commitment to acting in conjunction with the labor movement to secure state action to promote welfare and equality. The Marxists, Fabians, and ethical socialists had made socialism as a set of ideas while debating and disputing its relationship to the organized labor movement and the state. The old historiography mistakenly tied socialism to a narrative of the rise of class-based politics and the welfare state; it neglected or dismissed as primitive those bits of the history of socialism that did not fit. A new historiography should recover the diver-sity, contingency, and contestability of socialist ideas and the movements they inspired.

Pessimism about the effectiveness of the bureaucratic state and the decline of the industrial working class needs to be tempered with opti-mism about the possibilities for rediscovering other parts of the socialist heritage. A new historiography can help to shift attention from social-ism's involvement with industrial labor and state action toward its in-volvement with liberal progressivism, radical democracy, and personal and communal utopianism.

British socialism emerged in a close, overlapping relationship with a new social or progressive liberalism.[32] Many Fabian and ethical social-ists came from a tradition of liberal radicalism that continued to influ-ence their socialist ideas. Similarly, many liberal radicals responded to the crisis of faith and the collapse of classical economics in ways that paralleled the socialists. T. H. Green reacted to the crisis of faith with

---

[31] M. Bevir, New Labour: A Critique (London: Routledge, 2005).

[32] P. Clarke, Liberals and Social Democrats (Cambridge: Cambridge University Press, 1978); and M. Freeden, The New Liberalism (Oxford: Clarendon Press, 1978).

an idealist and immanentist philosophy that supported an ethic of social welfare and the common good. J. M. Keynes reacted to the collapse of classical economics by challenging the concept of a natural market equilibrium and by promoting state action in response to macroeconomic imbalances. During the early twentieth century, many progressive liberals moved easily into the Labour Party.[33] Socialists and liberal radicals alike believed in representative democracy and modernist expertise. They formed a progressive movement that promoted social justice through economic planning, Keynesian demand management, progressive taxation, and state provision of welfare. Socialism arose, in other words, less as a new class-based politics than as part of a shift in liberal and radical thought toward a greater concern with social justice and a greater acceptance of state intervention. Neoliberals sometimes try to bind liberalism to individual choice, free markets, and a minimal state. Yet, historically liberalism has been more consistently linked with representative government, the rule of law, and toleration. Most socialists remained committed to these liberal values. It was just that socialists and progressive liberals increasingly combined these values with a stronger commitment to social justice. Socialists may have defended a more robust economic egalitarianism than even social liberals, but they were, and are, part of a broader progressivism.[34]

Many Fabian and ethical socialists owed a debt to liberal radicalism, which was apparent in their identifying democracy with representative democracy. Other socialists drew on the republican inheritance of popular radicalism. They championed more radical forms of democracy that received little support from progressive liberals. Too many progressives tried to promote social justice through a modernist expertise located within a bureaucratic state. Neoliberals sometimes try to equate socialism with just such state intervention and bureaucratic red tape. Yet, historically, socialism included not only a strand that hoped to use liberal government to promote social justice, but also a strand that promoted a radical democratic critique of state action and modernist expertise alike. Today this later strand of socialism may inspire progressive alternatives to both the historic social democratic state and the neoliberal alternative. Here, although neoliberals oppose the bureaucratic state, they still remain wedded to modernist expertise. They suggest that formal

---

[33] D. Blaazer, *The Popular Front and the Progressive Tradition: Socialists, Liberals and the Quest for Unity, 1884–1939* (Cambridge: Cambridge University Press, 1992); and Tanner, *Political Change and the Labour Party.*

[34] B. Jackson, *Equality and the British Left: A Study in Progressive Political Thought, 1900–64* (Manchester, UK: Manchester University Press, 2007).

economic models of rational individual action provide a scientific basis for a public policy based on markets. In contrast, some socialists have long challenged expertise and state action as inimical to the democratic ideal of self-rule. These socialists have advocated a radical extension of democratic principles throughout civil society. Some have advocated more pluralist arrangements. Others have championed nongovernmental forms of governance. There is here a stubborn resistance to the state's or experts' telling people how they should govern their activities. There is a vision of people collectively making, implementing, and adjudicating the rules that define their social activities. Many socialists have hoped to empower people so as to enable them to participate effectively in self-governing practices.

Socialists promote justice and democracy. Many also want a transformation of personal life. It is true, of course, that some socialists have followed the liberal tradition not only in equating democracy with representative government but also in focusing on the public sphere. Yet, other socialists broke with classical liberalism precisely in that they looked for a transformation of private life. Ethical socialists in particular typically emphasized ideals such as the simplification of life and a return to nature. Their message resonates even louder today as we realize the extent to which humans are devastating the environment. We do not have to believe in an immanent God to see that individuals are ineluctably connected both to others in a community and to the natural world of which they are just a part. And we do not have to believe in a natural harmony to believe in the importance and benefits of a simpler life more in tune with the environment. Neoliberals sometimes promote the free market as a mechanism that effectively allocates resources in accord with the choices people make following their desires. Yet, politics is not just a matter of how we can most effectively get whatever we happen to want. Politics is, at least as importantly, a matter of debating and deciding what we should want. Socialist utopias seek to educate aspirations. They prompt people to think beyond materialism and consumerism. They offer accounts of alternative pleasures found in alternative lives and communities. Perhaps socialist utopias still may inspire us too to transform ourselves—to live more richly on less.

Socialists are part of a broader progressivism. Some bring to progressivism a distinctive concern with class-based politics and state intervention. Others contribute a rather different emphasis on radical democracy and utopian transformation. In the late twentieth century, neoliberals tried to identify socialism with the rise of a bureaucratic state and even totalitarianism. Neoliberal governments aggressively promoted markets. Inequalities then became increasingly stark as the gap widened between the richest and the poorest members of society. Democracy suffered as marketization and contracting out blurred lines of accountability, and as some collective decisions were handed over to nonmajoritarian institutions. Environmental devastation continued to worsen as deregulation enabled private-sector firms to exploit and pollute the earth. Some socialists have reacted to neoliberalism by defending the continuing relevance of class-based politics, modernist expertise, and state action. A new historiography may encourage others to insist equally firmly on social justice, collaborative governance, and a simpler life.

Bibliography

ARCHIVES

Annual Reports of the Birmingham Cinderella Club. Birmingham Central Library, UK.
Edward Carpenter Collection. Sheffield Archives, UK.
Fabian Papers. British Library of Political and Economic Science, London, UK.
Hyndman Collection. Harry Ransom Center, Austin, Texas, U.S.
Karl Pearson Papers. Bloomsbury Science Library, University College, London, UK.
MacDonald Papers. Public Record Office, London, UK.
Minute Books of the Birmingham Labour Church. Birmingham Central Library, UK.
Passfield Papers. British Library of Political and Economic Science, London, UK.
Scheu Papers. International Institute of Social History, Amsterdam, Netherlands.
Shaw Collection. Harry Ransom Centre, Austin, Texas, U.S.
Shaw Papers. British Library, London, UK.
Tawney Papers. British Library of Political and Economic Science, London, UK.
Wallas Papers. British Library of Political and Economic Science, London, UK.
William Morris Papers. British Library, London, UK.

NEWSPAPERS AND MAGAZINES

Anarchist
Bradford Labour Echo
Christian Socialist
Church Reformer
Clarion
Commonweal
Co-operative News
Daily Herald
Daily News
Echo
Free Commune
Freedom
Inquirer
International Herald
Justice
Labour Annual
Labour Church Record
Labour Leader

Labour Prophet
Labour Prophet Tracts
Labour Standard
Leek Times
Link
Macmillan's Magazine
Miner
National Reformer
Newcastle Daily Chronicle
New Order
New Statesman
Observer
Our Corner
Pall Mall Gazette
Poor Man's Guardian
Practical Socialist
Radical
Republican
Reynolds's
Seed-time
Star
St James's Gazette
Le Temps
Times
To-day
Torch
Workers' Cry
Workman's Times

BOOKS AND ARTICLES

Adams, M. *The Ethics of Social Reform*. London: William Reeves, 1887.

Adcock, R., M. Bevir, and S. Stimson, eds. *Modern Political Science: Anglo-American Exchanges since 1880*. Princeton, NJ: Princeton University Press, 2007.

Alexander, J. *Shaw's Controversial Socialism*. Gainesville: University of Florida Press, 2009.

Annan, N. *Leslie Stephen*. London: MacGibbon and Kee, 1951.

Arnot, R. *William Morris: The Man and the Myth, Including the Letters of William Morris to J. L. Mahon and Dr. John Glasse*. London: Lawrence and Wishart, 1964.

Auerbach, J. *The Great Exhibition of 1851: A Nation on Display*. New Haven, CT: Yale University Press, 1999.

Aveling, E. "An Atheist on Tennyson's 'Despair.'" *Modern Thought* 4 (1882): 7–11.

———. "'Nora' and 'Breaking a Butterfly.'" *To-day* 1 (1884): 473–80.

Bagehot, W. *The Collected Works of Walter Bagehot.* Edited by N. John-Stevas. 15 vols. London: Economist, 1965–86.

Bailey, P. *Popular Culture and Performance in the Victorian City.* Cambridge: Cambridge University Press, 1998.

Bakunin, M. "Revolutionary Catechism." In *Bakunin on Anarchy*, edited by S. Dolgoff, preface by P. Avrich. London: Allen and Unwin, 1973.

Bancroft, G. *A History of the United States from the Discovery of the American Continent to the Present Time.* 6 vols. New York: Appleton, 1885.

Barker, E. *Political Thought in England, 1848–1914.* Oxford: Oxford University Press, 1928.

Barnes, J. "Gentleman Crusader: Henry Hyde Champion in the Early Socialist Movement." *History Workshop* 60 (2005): 116–38.

Barrow, L., and I. Bullock. *Democratic Ideas and the British Labour Movement, 1880–1914.* Cambridge: Cambridge University Press, 1996.

Bax, E. "The 'Collective Will' and Law." *Social-Democrat* 1 (1897): 368–71.

———. *Essays in Socialism: New and Old.* London: Grant Richards, 1906.

———. *The Ethics of Socialism.* London: Swan Sonnenschein, 1889.

———. *The Fraud of Feminism.* London: Grant Richards, 1913.

———. *A Handbook of the History of Philosophy.* London: George Bell, 1886.

———. "Hartmann's 'Religious Consciousness of Humanity.'" *Modern Thought* 4 (1882): 177–81.

———. "How I Became a Socialist." In *How I Became a Socialist: A Series of Biographical Sketches*, edited by H. Hyndman et al. London: Twentieth Century Press, n.d.

———. Introduction to *Kant's Prolegomena and Metaphysical Foundations of Natural Science.* London: George Bell, 1883.

———. Introduction to *Selected Essays of Arthur Schopenhauer.* London: George Bell, 1891.

———. *Jean Paul Marat: The People's Friend.* London: Charing Cross, 1882.

———. "Leaders of Modern Thought—XX: Richard Wagner." *Modern Thought* 3 (1881): 243–49.

———. "Leaders of Modern Thought—XXIII: Karl Marx." *Modern Thought* 3 (1881): 349–54.

———. *The Legal Subjection of Men.* London: New Age, 1908.

———. "Modern Socialism." *Modern Thought* 1 (1879): 150–53.

———. *Outlooks from the New Standpoint.* London: Swan Sonnenschein, 1891.

———. *Outspoken Essays on Social Subjects.* London: W. Reeves, 1897.

———. *The Problem of Reality.* London: Swan Sonnenschein, 1892.

———. *Problems of Men, Mind, and Morals.* London: Grant Richards, 1912.

———. *The Real, the Rational and the Alogical, Being Suggestions for a Philosophical Reconstruction.* London: Grant Richards, 1920.

———. *The Religion of Socialism.* London: Swan Sonnenschein, 1887.

———. *Reminiscences and Reflexions of a Mid and Late Victorian.* London: Allen and Unwin, 1918.

———. "Reply to Criticism of Modern Socialism." *Modern Thought* 1 (1879): 196–98.

———. *The Roots of Reality.* London: Grant Richards, 1907.

Bax, E. *A Short History of the Paris Commune*. London: Twentieth Century, 1895.

———. *The Social Side of the Reformation in Germany*. 3 vols. London: Swan Sonnenschein, 1894–1903.

———. "The Word 'Religion.'" *Modern Thought* 1 (1879): 67–69.

Bax, E., and C. Bradlaugh. *Will Socialism Benefit the English People?* London: Freethought Publishing, 1887.

Bax, E., and H. Hyndman. "Socialism, Materialism and the War." *English Review* 19 (1914): 52–69.

Bax, E., and J. Levy. *Socialism and Individualism*. London: Personal Rights Association, 1904.

Bebbington, D. *The Mind of Gladstone: Religion, Homer and Politics*. Oxford: Oxford University Press, 2004.

———. *The Nonconformist Conscience: Chapel and Politics, 1870–1914*. London: Allen and Unwin, 1982.

Beer, M. *Fifty Years of International Socialism*. London: Allen and Unwin, 1935.

———. *A History of British Socialism*. London: George Bell, 1929.

Beith, G., ed. *Edward Carpenter: In Appreciation*. London: Allen and Unwin, 1931.

Bentham, J. *The Works of Jeremy Bentham*. Edited by J. Bowring. 11 vols. Edinburgh: Tait, 1833–43.

Berlin, I. *Political Ideas in the Romantic Age: Their Rise and Influence on Modern Thought*. Edited by H. Hardy. Introduction by J. Cherniss. Princeton, NJ: Princeton University Press, 2006.

Bernstein, E. "Kant against Cant." In *Evolutionary Socialism*, translated by E. Harvey. London: Independent Labour Party, 1909.

Besant, A. "The Fabian Conference." *To-day* 6 (1886): 8–14.

———. *Radicalism and Socialism*. London: Freethought, 1887.

———. *The True Basis of Morality*. London: Freethought, n.d.

Besant, A., and G. Foote. *Is Socialism Sound?* London: Freethought, 1887.

Bevir, M. *The Logic of the History of Ideas*. Cambridge: Cambridge University Press, 1999.

———. *New Labour: A Critique*. London: Routledge, 2005.

Bevir, M., and F. Trentmann, eds. *Critiques of Capital in Modern Britain and America: Transatlantic Exchanges, 1800 to the Present Day*. Basingstoke, UK: Palgrave Macmillan, 2002.

———, eds. *Markets in Historical Contexts: Ideas and Politics in the Modern World*. Cambridge: Cambridge University Press, 2004.

Biagini, E., ed. *Citizenship and Community: Liberals, Radicals and Collective Identities in the British Isles, 1865–1931*. Cambridge: Cambridge University Press, 1996.

———. *Liberty, Retrenchment, and Reform: Popular Liberalism in the Age of Gladstone, 1860–1880*. Cambridge: Cambridge University Press, 1992.

Biagini, E., and A. Reid, eds. *Currents of Radicalism: Popular Radicalism, Organised Labour, and Party Politics in Britain*. Cambridge: Cambridge University Press, 1991.

Blaazer, D. *The Popular Front and the Progressive Tradition: Socialists, Liberals and the Quest for Unity, 1884–1939.* Cambridge: Cambridge University Press, 1992.

Bland, H. *Essays by Hubert Bland.* Edited by E. Nesbit. London: Goschen, 1914.

———. "The Need of a New Departure." *To-day* 8 (1887): 131–41.

———. "The Socialist Party in Relation to Politics." *Practical Socialist* 1 (1886): 94–95.

Blau, J. "Rosmini, Domodossola and Thomas Davidson." *Journal of the History of Ideas* 18 (1957): 522–28.

Boos, F., and W. Boos. "The Utopian Communism of William Morris." *History of Political Thought* 7 (1986): 489–510.

Booth, C. *Life and Labour of the People of London.* 2 vols. London: Macmillan, 1902–3.

Bradlaugh, C., and H. Hyndman. *Will Socialism Benefit the English People?* London: Freethought, 1884.

Brailsford Bright, J. "English Possibilists." *Practical Socialist* 2 (1887): 8–11.

Briggs, A. *The Age of Improvement, 1783–1867.* London: Longman, 1959.

Britain, I. *Fabianism and Culture: A Study in British Socialism and the Arts, c. 1884–1918.* Cambridge: Cambridge University Press, 1982.

Brockway, F. *Socialism over Sixty Years: The Life of Jowett of Bradford, 1864–1944.* London: Allen and Unwin, 1946.

Brooke, E. *A Superfluous Woman.* 3 vols. London: William Heinemann, 1894.

Brown, G., ed. "Documents: Correspondence from H. M. Hyndman to Mrs. Cobden Sanderson, 1900–1921." *Labour History Bulletin* 22 (1971): 11–16.

Brown, J. "Attercliffe 1894—How One Local Liberal Party Failed to Meet the Challenge of Labour." *Journal of British Studies* 14 (1975): 48–77.

Bryher, S. *An Account of the Labour and Socialist Movement in Bristol.* Bristol, UK: Bristol Socialist Society, 1931.

Burke, E. *Reflections on the Revolution in France.* Harmondsworth, UK: Penguin, 1970.

Burrow, J. *Evolution and Society: A Study in Victorian Social Theory.* Cambridge: Cambridge University Press, 1966.

———. *Whigs and Liberals: Continuity and Change in English Political Thought.* Oxford: Clarendon Press, 1988.

Burton, A. *Burdens of History: British Feminists, Indian Women, and Imperial Culture, 1865–1915.* Chapel Hill: University of North Carolina Press, 1994.

Cain, P., and A. Hopkins. *British Imperialism: Innovation and Expansion, 1688–1914.* London: Longman, 1993.

Campbell, R. *The New Theology.* London: Chapman and Hall, 1907.

Capaldi, N. *John Stuart Mill: A Biography.* Cambridge: Cambridge University Press, 2004.

Carlyle, T. *The Works of Thomas Carlyle.* 30 vols. London: Chapman and Hall, 1896–99.

Carpenter, E. *The Art of Creation.* London: G. Allen, 1904.

———, ed. *Chants of Labour: A Song Book of the People.* London: Swan Sonnenschein, 1888.

Carpenter, E. *Civilisation: Its Curse and Cure*. London: Swan Sonnenschein, 1902.

———. *Days with Walt Whitman*. London: G. Allen, 1906.

———. *England's Ideal*. London: Swan Sonnenschein, 1902.

———, ed. *Forecasts of the Coming Century*. Manchester, UK: Labour, 1897.

———. *From Adam's Peak to Elephanta*. London: Swan Sonnenschein, 1892.

———. *My Days and Dreams*. London: Allen and Unwin, 1916.

———. *Sketches from Life in Town and Country*. London: Allen and Unwin, 1908.

———. *Towards Democracy*. London: Gay Men's Press, 1985.

———. "The Value of the Value Theory." *To-day* 11 (1889): 22–30.

Carpenter, E., and E. Maitland. *Vivisection*. London: William Reeves, 1893.

Carter, M. *T. H. Green and the Development of Ethical Socialism*. Exeter: Imprint Academic, 2003.

Chadwick, O. *The Victorian Church*. 2 vols. London: A. and C. Black, 1971.

Channing, W. *An Address delivered before The Mercantile Library Company of Philadelphia*. Philadelphia: Crissy, 1841.

Chubb, P. Introduction to *Select Writings of Ralph Waldo Emerson*. London: Walter Scott, 1888.

———. *On the Religious Frontier: From an Outpost of Ethical Religion*. New York: Macmillan, 1931.

———. "The Significance of Thomas Hill Green's Philosophical and Religious Teaching." *Journal of Speculative Philosophy* 22 (1888): 1–21.

———. "The Two Alternatives." *To-day* 8 (1887): 69–77.

Claeys, G. *Citizens and Saints: Politics and Anti-politics in Early British Socialism*. Cambridge: Cambridge University Press, 1989.

———. *Machinery, Money, and the Millennium: From Moral Economy to Socialism, 1815–60*. Princeton, NJ: Princeton University Press, 1987.

———. *Thomas Paine: Social and Political Thought*. London: Unwin Hyman, 1989.

Clark, A. *The Struggle for the Breeches: Gender and the Making of the British Working Class*. Berkeley: University of California Press, 1995.

Clarke, P. *Liberals and Social Democrats*. Cambridge: Cambridge University Press, 1978.

Cobbett, W. *History of the Protestant Reformation in England and Ireland*. London: James Duffy, 1868.

Cole, G. *British Working Class Politics, 1832–1914*. London: Routledge, 1941.

Cole, M. *The Story of Fabian Socialism*. London: Heinemann, 1961.

———, ed. *The Webbs and Their Work*. London: F. Muller, 1949.

Coleridge, S. *On the Constitution of the Church and State*. London: Hurst, 1830.

Collini, S. *Public Moralists: Political Thought and Intellectual Life in Britain, 1850–1930*. Oxford: Oxford University Press, 1991.

Collins, H. "The Marxism of the Social Democratic Federation." In *Essays in Labour History, 1886–1923*, edited by A. Briggs and J. Saville. London: Macmillan, 1971.

Collins, H., and C. Abramsky. *Karl Marx and the British Labour Movement*. London: Macmillan, 1965.

Crompton, L. Introduction to *The Road to Equality: Ten Unpublished Lectures, 1884–1918*, by G. Shaw. Boston: Beacon Press, 1971.

Comte, A. *The Catechism of Positive Religion.* Translated by R. Congreve. London: Chapman, 1858.

———. *The Positive Philosophy.* Translated by H. Martineau. 2 vols. London: George Bell, 1853.

———. *System of Positive Polity.* Translated by J. Bridges. 4 vols. London: Longmans, 1875–77.

Cowley, J. *The Victorian Encounter with Marx.* London: British Academic Press, 1992.

Crafts, N. *British Economic Growth during the Industrial Revolution.* Oxford: Clarendon Press, 1985.

Craig, E. *The Irish Land and Labour Question, Illustrated in the History of Ralahine and Co-operative Farming.* London: Heywood, 1882.

Crick, M. *The History of the Social Democratic Federation.* Keele, UK: Keele University Press, 1994.

Crowley, B. *The Self, the Individual, and the Community: Liberalism in the Political Thought of F. A. Hayek and Sidney and Beatrice Webb.* Oxford: Clarendon Press, 1987.

Darwin, J. "Imperialism and the Victorians: The Dynamics of Territorial Expansion." *English Historical Review* 112 (1997): 614–42.

Daunton, M. *Progress and Poverty: An Economic and Social History of Britain, 1700–1850.* Oxford: Oxford University Press, 1995.

Davidson, T. *Aristotle and Ancient Educational Ideals.* London: William Heinemann, 1892.

———. "Autobiographical Sketch." Edited by A. Lataner. *Journal of the History of Ideas* 18 (1957): 531–56.

———. "Education as World Building." *Western Educational Review* 9 (1900): 325–45.

———. *The Education of the Greek People and Its Influence on Civilization.* London: Edward Arnold, 1895.

———. *The Education of the Wage-Earners: A Contribution toward the Solution of the Educational Problem of Democracy.* Edited by C. Bakewell. London: Ginn and Co., 1904.

———. *The Moral Aspects of the Economic Question.* London: William Reeves, 1888.

———. *Rousseau and Education According to Nature.* London: William Heinemann, 1898.

Delavenay, E. *D. H. Lawrence and Edward Carpenter: A Study in Edwardian Transition.* London: Heinemann, 1971.

The Democratic Federation. *Socialism Made Plain: Being the Social and Political Manifesto of the Democratic Federation.* London: W. Reeves, 1883.

Dickens, C. *Dombey and Son.* London: Bradbury and Evans, 1848.

Disraeli, B. *Sybil.* Harmondsworth, UK: Penguin, 1954.

———. *A Vindication of the English Constitution.* London: Saunders and Otley, 1835.

Dixon, J. *Divine Feminine: Theosophy and Feminism in England.* Baltimore: Johns Hopkins University Press, 2001.

Driver, C. *Tory Radical: The Life of Richard Oastler.* Oxford: Oxford University Press, 1946.

Durbin, E. "Fabian Socialism and Economic Science." In *Fabian Essays in Socialist Thought,* edited by B. Pimlott. London: Heinemann, 1984.

———. *New Jerusalems: The Labour Party and the Economics of Democratic Socialism.* London: Routledge, 1985.

Edelstein, M. *Overseas Investment in the Age of High Imperialism: The United Kingdom, 1850–1914.* London: Methuen, 1982.

Eliot, G. *The Mill on the Floss.* New York: Penguin, 1979.

Ellis, Havelock. *My Life.* London: William Heinemann, 1940.

Ellis, E. Havelock. *Three Modern Seers.* London: Stanley Paul, 1910.

Emerson, R. *The Complete Works of Ralph Waldo Emerson.* Edited by E. Emerson. 12 vols. London: George Routledge, 1903–4.

Engels, F. *Anti-Dühring.* Moscow: Progress Publishers, 1947.

———. *The Condition of the Working Class in England.* Harmondsworth, UK: Penguin, 1987.

———. *Dialectics of Nature.* Moscow: Progress Publishers, 1972.

Everdell, W. *The First Moderns: Profiles in the Origins of Twentieth Century Thought.* Chicago: University of Chicago Press, 1997.

Faber, R. *Young England.* London: Faber and Faber, 1987.

Feinstein, C. "What Really Happened to Real Wages? Trends in Wages, Prices, and Productivity in the United Kingdom, 1880–1913." *Economic History Review* 43 (1990): 329–55.

Fichman, M. *Evolutionary Theory and Victorian Culture.* New York: Humanity Books, 2002.

Finn, M. *After Chartism: Class and Nation in English Radical Politics, 1848–1874.* Cambridge: Cambridge University Press, 1993.

Flatau, P. "Jevons's One Great Disciple: Wicksteed and the Jevonian Revolution in the Second Generation." *History of Economics Review* 40 (2004): 69–107.

Foote, G. *The Labour Party's Political Thought.* London: Croom Helm, 1986.

Forbes, D. *The Liberal Anglican Idea of History.* Cambridge: Cambridge University Press, 1952.

———. "Sceptical Whiggism, Commerce, and Liberty." In *Essays on Adam Smith,* edited by A. Skinner and T. Wilson. Oxford: Clarendon Press, 1976.

Ford, I. *Miss Blake of Monkshalton.* London: John Murray, 1890.

Foster, D. *Leeds Slumdom.* Leeds, UK: Foster, 1897.

———. *The Logic of the Alliance.* Leeds, UK: Foster, n.d.

———. *Socialism and the Christ.* Leeds, UK: Foster, 1921.

Freeden, M. *The New Liberalism.* Oxford: Clarendon Press, 1978.

Freemantle, A. *This Little Brand of Prophets.* London: G. Allen, 1960.

Gilbert, A. *Religion and Society in Industrial England: Church, Chapel and Social Change, 1740–1914.* London: Longman, 1976.

Glasier, J. *On the Road to Liberty: Poems and Ballads.* Edited by J. Wallace. London: National Labour Press, 1920.

————. *William Morris and the Early Days of the Socialist Movement*. London: Longmans, 1921.

Goodway, D. *Anarchist Seeds Sown beneath the Snow: Left-Libertarian Thought and British Writers from William Morris to Colin Ward*. Liverpool: Liverpool University Press, 2006.

Gore, C. *Buying up the Opportunity*. London: Society for Promoting Christian Knowledge, 1895.

————. *The Incarnation of the Son of God*. London: J. Murray, 1891.

————, ed. *Lux Mundi*. London: J. Murray, 1890.

————, ed. *Property: Its Duties and Rights*. London: Macmillan, 1913.

————. *The Reconstruction of Belief*. 3 vols. London: J. Murray, 1921–24.

————. *The Sermon on the Mount: A Practical Exposition*. London: J. Murray, 1896.

————. *Strikes and Lock-Outs: The Way Out*. London: P. King, 1926.

Gould, F. *Hyndman: Prophet of Socialism*. London: Allen and Unwin, 1928.

Green, T. *Prolegomena to Ethics*. Edited by A. Bradley. Oxford: Clarendon Press, 1884.

————. *The Works of Thomas Hill Green*. Edited by R. Nettleship. 3 vols. London: Longmans, 1885–88.

Haakonssen, K. *The Science of a Legislator: The Natural Jurisprudence of David Hume and Adam Smith*. Cambridge: Cambridge University Press, 1981.

Hall, C. "The Early Formation of Victorian Domestic Ideology." In *Fit Work for Women*, edited by S. Burman. London: Croom Helm, 1979.

————. *White, Male, and Middle Class: Explorations in Feminism and History*. Cambridge: Polity Press, 1992.

Hall, S. "The Great Moving Right Show." In *The Politics of Thatcherism*, edited by S. Hall and M. Jacques. London: Lawrence and Wishart, 1980.

Hamer, D. *Liberal Politics in the Age of Gladstone and Roseberry*. Oxford: Oxford University Press, 1972.

The Hammersmith Socialist Society. *Statement of Principles*. London: Hammersmith Socialist Society, 1893.

Hardie, J., ed. *From Serfdom to Socialism*. London: G. Allen, 1907.

Hardie, J., and J. Ramsay MacDonald. "The Independent Labour Party's Programme." *Nineteenth Century* 53 (1899): 142–49.

Harris, J. *Private Lives, Public Spirit: A Social History of Britain, 1870–1914*. Oxford: Oxford University Press, 1993.

————. *Unemployment and Politics: A Study in English Social Policy, 1886–1914*. Oxford: Clarendon Press, 1972.

Harrison, R. *Before the Socialists*. London: Routledge and Kegan Paul, 1965.

————, ed. *The English Defence of the Commune, 1871*. London: Merlin Press, 1971.

————. *The Life and Times of Sidney and Beatrice Webb, 1858–1905: The Formative Years*. Basingstoke, UK: Palgrave, 2001.

Henderson, A. *George Bernard Shaw: His Life and Work*. London: Hurst and Blackett, 1911.

Hill, C. *Understanding the Fabian Essays in Socialism*. Lewiston, UK: Edwin Mellen, 1996.

Hilton, B. *The Age of Atonement: The Influence of Evangelicalism on Social and Economic Thought, 1785–1865*. Oxford: Clarendon Press, 1991.

———. "The Politics of Anatomy and an Anatomy of Politics." In *History, Religion, and Culture: British Intellectual History, 1750–1950*, edited by S. Collini, R. Whatmore, and B. Young. Cambridge: Cambridge University Press, 2000.

Hinton, J. *Life in Nature*. Introduction by H. Ellis. London: Allen and Unwin, 1932.

———. *Philosophy and Religion*. Edited by C. Haddon. London: Kegan Paul, 1881.

Hobsbawm, E. *Labouring Men: Studies in the History of Labour*. London: Weidenfeld and Nicolson, 1964.

———. *Primitive Rebels: Studies in Archaic Forms of Social Movement in the 19th and 20th Centuries*. Manchester, UK: Manchester University Press, 1959.

Hobsbawm, E., et al. *The Forward March of Labour Halted*. London: New Left Books, 1981.

Hobson, S. *Pilgrim to the Left: Memoirs of a Modern Revolutionist*. London: E. Arnold, 1938.

———. *Possibilities of the Labour Church*. Cardiff: Chappie and Kemp, 1893.

Holman, B. *Keir Hardie: Labour's Greatest Hero?* Oxford: Lion Hudson, 2010.

Holmes, C., ed. "Documents: H. M. Hyndman and R. D. Blumfield Correspondence, 1913." *Labour History Bulletin* 24 (1972): 25–32.

Holroyd, M. *Bernard Shaw*. 3 vols. London: Chatto and Windrus, 1988–92.

Holton, R. *British Syndicalism, 1900–14: Myths and Realities*. London: Pluto Press, 1976.

Hont, I., and M. Ignatief, eds. *Wealth and Virtue: The Shaping of Political Economy in the Scottish Enlightenment*. Cambridge: Cambridge University Press, 1983.

Hopkins, E. *Life and Letters of James Hinton*. London: Kegan Paul, 1882.

Howe, A. *Free Trade and Liberal England, 1846–1946*. Oxford: Clarendon Press, 1997.

Howell, D. *British Workers and the Independent Labour Party, 1888–1906*. Manchester, UK: Manchester University Press, 1983.

Hulse, J. *Revolutionists in London: A Study of Five Unorthodox Socialists*. Oxford: Clarendon Press, 1970.

Hummert, P. *Bernard Shaw's Marxian Romance*. Lincoln: University of Nebraska Press, 1973.

Hunt, K. *Equivocal Feminists: The Social Democratic Federation and the Women Question, 1884–1911*. Cambridge: Cambridge University Press, 1996.

Hutchison, T. *A Review of Economic Doctrines, 1870–1929*. Oxford: Oxford University Press, 1953.

Hyndman, H. "The Bankruptcy of India." *Nineteenth Century* 9 (1881): 443–62.

———. *The Coming Revolution in England*. London: W. Reeves, 1884.

———. "The Dawn of a Revolutionary Epoch." *Nineteenth Century* 9 (1881): 1–18.

———. *The Economics of Socialism*. London: Twentieth Century, 1896.

———. "The English Workers as They Are." *Contemporary Review* 52 (1887): 122–36.

———. *The Evolution of Revolution*. London: Grant Richards, 1920.

———. *Further Reminiscences*. London: Macmillan, 1912.

———. *The Future of Democracy*. London: Allen and Unwin, 1915.

———. *The Historical Basis of Socialism in England*. London: Kegan Paul, 1883.

———. *The Indian Famine*. London: E. Stanford, 1877.

———. *The Record of an Adventurous Life*. London: Macmillan, 1911.

———. *Social Democracy: The Basis of Its Principles and the Cause of Its Success*. London: Twentieth Century Press, 1904.

———. "Social Democrat or Socialist?" *Social-Democrat* 1 (1897): 227–31.

———. *Socialism and Slavery*. London: Modern Press, 1884.

———. *Socialism vs Smithism*. London: Modern Press, 1883.

———. *The Text Book of Democracy: England for All*. London: E. Allen, 1881.

Hyndman, H., and W. Morris. *A Summary of the Principles of Socialism*. London: Modern, 1884.

Hyndman, R. *Last Years of H. M. Hyndman*. London: Grant Richards, 1923.

Illingworth, J. *Divine Immanence*. London: Macmillan, 1898.

Independent Labour Party. *Annual Conference Report*. 1893.

Inglis, K. *Churches and the Working Classes in Victorian England*. London: Routledge, 1963.

Jackson, B. *Equality and the British Left: A Study in Progressive Political Thought, 1900–64*. Manchester, UK: Manchester University Press, 2007.

Jaffe, J. *Striking a Bargain: Work and Industrial Relations in England, 1815–1865*. Manchester, UK: Manchester University Press, 2000.

James, D., T. Jowitt, and K. Laybourn, eds. *The Centennial History of the Independent Labour Party*. Keele, UK: Keele University Press, 1992.

Jevons, W. *The Theory of Political Economy*. Edited by R. Collison Black. Harmondsworth, UK: Penguin, 1970.

Johnson, G. *Social Democratic Politics in Britain, 1881–1911*. Lampeter, UK: Edwin Mellen, 2002.

Jones, P. "Henry George and British Socialism." *American Journal of Economics and Sociology* 47 (1988): 473–91.

Joyce, P. *Visions of the People: Industrial England and the Question of Class*. Cambridge: Cambridge University Press, 1991.

Jupp, W. *The Forgiveness of Sins and the Laws of Reconciliation*. London: P. Green, 1903.

———. *The Religion of Nature and of Human Experience*. London: P. Green, 1906.

———. *Wayfarings*. London: Headley Brothers, 1918.

Kautsky, K. *The Economic Doctrines of Karl Marx*. London: Black, 1925.

———. *Selected Political Writings*. Edited by P. Goode. London: Macmillan, 1983.

Keane, J. "Despotism and Democracy: The Origins and Development of the Distinction between Civil Society and the State, 1750–1850." In *Civil Society and the State*, edited by J. Keane. London: Verso, 1988.

Kenworthy, J. *My Psychic Experiences*. London: Office of Light, 1901.

———. *Tolstoy: His Life and Works*. London: Walter Scott, 1902.

Keynes, J. "Alfred Marshall." *Economic Journal* 34 (1924): 311–72.

Kinna, R. "The Jacobinism and Patriotism of Ernest Belfort Bax." *History of European Ideas* 30 (2004): 463–84.

———. "William Morris and Anti-Parliamentarianism." *History of Political Thought* 15 (1994): 593–613.

Kitson Clark, G. *The Making of Victorian England.* Cambridge, MA: Harvard University Press, 1962.

Knight, W., ed. *Memorials of Thomas Davidson, the Wandering Scholar.* London: Fisher Unwin, 1907.

Kropotkin, P. *The Conquest of Bread and Other Writings.* Edited by M. Shatz. Cambridge: Cambridge University Press, 1995.

———. *Memoirs of a Revolutionist.* Preface by G. Brandes. 2 vols. London: Smith Elder, 1899.

———. *Mutual Aid.* London: William Heinemann, 1915.

———. "The Spirit of Revolt." In *Kropotkin's Revolutionary Pamphlets*, edited by R. Baldwin. New York: Dover, 1970.

Labourde, C. *Pluralist Thought and the State in Britain and France, 1900–25.* Basingstoke, UK: Macmillan, 2000.

Lane, J. *Anti-Statist Communist Manifesto.* London: International Revolutionary, 1887.

Lawrence, J. "Popular Radicalism and the Socialist Revival in Britain." *Journal of British Studies* 31 (1992): 163–86.

Lee, H., and E. Archbold. *Social-Democracy in Britain.* London: Social Democratic Federation, 1935.

Leno, J. *Drury Lane Lyrics.* London: J. Leno, 1868.

Letwin, S. *The Pursuit of Certainty.* Cambridge: Cambridge University Press, 1965.

Levy, C., ed. *Socialism and the Intelligentsia, 1880–1914.* London: Routledge, 1987.

Lieberman, D. "Economy and Polity in Bentham's Science of Legislation." In *Economy, Polity, and Society: British Intellectual History, 1750–1950*, edited by S. Collini, R. Whatmore, and B. Young. Cambridge: Cambridge University Press, 2000.

Lowe, D. *Souvenirs of Scottish Labour.* Glasgow: W. and R. Holmes, 1919.

MacCarthy, F. *William Morris: A Life for Our Time.* London: Faber and Faber, 1994.

MacDonald, J. Ramsay. *Ramsay MacDonald's Political Writings.* Edited by B. Barker. London: Allen Lane, 1972.

———. "A Rock Ahead." *To-day* 7 (1887): 66–70.

———. *Socialism and Society.* London: Independent Labour Party, 1905.

———. *The Zollverein and British Industry.* London: Grant Richards, 1903.

Macintyre, S. *A Proletarian Science: Marxism in Britain, 1917–33.* London: Lawrence and Wishart, 1986.

Mack, M. "The Fabians and Utilitarianism." *Journal of the History of Ideas* 16 (1955): 76–88.

MacKenzie, N., and J. MacKenzie. *The First Fabians.* London: Weidenfeld and Nicolson, 1979.

Maitland, E. *The New Gospel of Interpretation.* London: Lamley, 1892.

Malatesta, E. "Peter Kropotkin: Recollections and Criticisms of an Old Friend." In *Errico Malatesta: His Life and Ideas*, edited by V. Richards. London: Freedom Press, 1977.

Mandler, P. "Tories and Paupers: Christian Political Economy and the Making of the New Poor Law." *Historical Journal* 33 (1990): 81–103.

Mann, T. *Memoirs*. London: Labour Publishing, 1923.

Manton, K. "The Fellowship of the New Life: English Ethical Socialism Reconsidered." *History of Political Thought* 24 (2003): 282–304.

Marquand, D. *Ramsay MacDonald*. London: Cape, 1977.

Marshall, A. *Industry and Trade: A Study of Industrial Technique and Business Organisation*. London: Macmillan, 1919.

———. *Principles of Economics*. Edited by C. Guillebaud. London: Macmillan, 1961.

Marshall, M. *What I Remember*. Cambridge: Cambridge University Press, 1947.

Marx, K., and F. Engels. *Letters to Americans, 1848–1895*. Translated by L. Mins. New York: International Publishers, 1953.

Maude, A. *Life of Tolstoy*. 2 vols. London: Oxford University Press, 1929–30.

Mayhew, H. *Report Concerning the Trade and Hours of Closing Usual among the Unlicensed Victualling Establishments at Certain So-Called "Working Men's Clubs."* London: Judd and Co., n.d.

Mazzini, J. "From the Council to God." In *The Duties of Man and Other Essays*, edited by E. Rhys. London: J. M. Dent, 1907.

McBriar, A. *Fabian Socialism and English Politics, 1884–1918*. Cambridge: Cambridge University Press, 1962.

McKibbin, R. *The Evolution of the Labour Party, 1910–24*. Oxford: Clarendon Press, 1974.

McMillan, M. *The Life of Rachel McMillan*. London: Dent, 1927.

Meacham, S. *Toynbee Hall and Social Reform, 1880–1914: The Search for Community*. New Haven, CT: Yale University Press, 1987.

Meier, P. *William Morris: The Marxist Dreamer*. 2. vols. Sussex, UK: Harvester, 1978.

Mendilow, J. *The Romantic Tradition in British Politics*. London: Croom Helm, 1986.

Milburn, J. "The Fabian Society and the British Labour Party." *Western Political Quarterly* (1958): 319–40.

Milgate, M., and S. Stimson. *After Adam Smith: A Century of Transformation in Politics and Political Economy*. Princeton, NJ: Princeton University Press, 2009.

Mill, J. *The Collected Works of John Stuart Mill*. Edited by J. Robson. 33 vols. Toronto: University of Toronto Press, 1963–91.

Moneypenny, W., and G. Buckle. *The Life of Benjamin Disraeli, Earl of Beaconsfield*. London: John Murray, 1929.

Moore, J. *The Post-Darwinian Controversies: A Study of the Protestant Struggle to Come to Terms with Darwin in Great Britain and America, 1870–1900*. Cambridge: Cambridge University Press, 1979.

Morgan, Kenneth. *Keir Hardie, Radical and Socialist*. London: Weidenfeld and Nicolson, 1975.

Morgan, Kevin. *The Webbs and Soviet Communism*. London: Lawrence and Wishart, 2002.

Morris, W. *The Collected Works of William Morris*. Edited by M. Morris. 24 vols. London: Longmans, 1910–15.

———. *The Collected Letters of William Morris*. Edited by N. Kelvin. 4 vols. Princeton, NJ: Princeton University, 1984–87.

———. *The Letters of William Morris to His Family and Friends*. Edited by P. Henderson. London: Longmans, 1950.

———. *Socialist Diary*. Edited by F. Boos. London: Journeyman, 1982.

———. *William Morris: Artist, Writer, Socialist*. Edited by M. Morris. 2 vols. Oxford: Blackwell, 1936.

Morris, W., and E. Bax. *Socialism: Its Growth and Outcome*. London: Swan Sonnenschein, 1893.

Morrow, J. *Coleridge's Political Thought: Property, Morality and the Limits of Traditional Discourse*. London: Macmillan, 1990.

———. "Liberalism and British Idealist Political Philosophy." *History of Political Thought* 5 (1984): 91–108.

Murray, C. *A Letter to Mr. George Jacob Holyoake*. London: Pavey, 1854.

Nairn, T. "The Fateful Meridian." *New Left Review* 60 (1970): 3–35.

National Reform League Tract No. 5. November 1855.

The New Fellowship. *The New Fellowship: A Statement of Its Constitution and Aims*. Thornton Heath, UK: Sahud, 1890.

Nicholson, P. "T. H. Green and State Action: Liquor Legislation." *History of Political Thought* 6 (1985): 517–50.

Norman, E. *The Victorian Christian Socialists*. Cambridge: Cambridge University Press, 2002.

Oakey, T. *A Basketful of Memories*. London: J. Dent, 1930.

O'Brien, J. *The Rise, Progress, and Phases of Human Slavery*. London: W. Reeves, 1885.

———. "Bronterre's Second Letter to the People of England." *Political Letters and Pamphlets*, 12 February 1831.

Oliver, H. *The International Anarchist Movement in Late Victorian London*. London: Croom Helm, 1983.

Olivier, S. "Capital and Land." *Fabian Tract* 7 (1888).

———. "John Stuart Mill and Socialism." *Today* 2 (1884): 490–504.

———. "Perverse Socialism." *To-day* 6 (1886): 47–55 and 109–14.

———. *Sydney Olivier: Letters and Selected Writings*. Edited by M. Olivier. London: Allen and Unwin, 1948.

Oppenheim, J. *The Other World: Spiritualism and Psychological Research in England, 1850–1914*. Cambridge: Cambridge University Press, 1985.

Owen, J. "Dissident Missionaries? Re-narrating the Political Strategy of the Social Democratic Federation, 1884–1887." *Labour History Review* 73 (2008): 187–207.

Parry, J. *The Rise and Fall of Liberal Government in Victorian Britain*. New Haven, CT: Yale University Press, 1994.

Pearson, H. *George Bernard Shaw: A Full Length Portrait*. New York: Harper, 1942.

Pease, E. "Ethics and Socialism." *Practical Socialist* 1 (1886): 16–19.

———. *The History of the Fabian Society*. London: A. Fifield, 1916.

Pelling, H. "H. H. Champion: Pioneer of Labour Representation." *Cambridge Journal* 6 (1953): 222–38.

———. *The Origins of the Labour Party, 1880–1900*. Oxford: Clarendon Press, 1965.

Penty, A. *The Restoration of the Gild System*. London: Swan Sonnenschein, 1906.

Perkin, H. *Origins of Modern English Society, 1780–1880*. London: Routledge, 1969.

Perren, R. *Agriculture in Depression, 1870–1940*. Cambridge: Cambridge University Press, 1995.

Pierson, S. *British Socialists: The Journey from Fantasy to Politics*. Cambridge, MA: Harvard University Press, 1979.

———. "Ernest Belfort Bax, 1854–1926: The Encounter of Marxism and Late Victorian Culture." *Journal of British Studies* 12 (1972): 39–60.

———. "John Trevor and the Labour Church Movement in England, 1891–1900." *Church History* 29 (1960): 463–78.

———. *Marxism and the Origins of British Socialism*. Ithaca, NY: Cornell University Press, 1973.

Plummer, A. *Bronterre: A Political Biography of Bronterre O'Brien, 1804–1864*. London: Allen and Unwin, 1971.

Pocock, J. *Virtue, Commerce, and History: Essays on Political Thought and History, Chiefly in the Eighteenth Century*. Cambridge: Cambridge University Press, 1985.

Porter, T. *Trust in Numbers: The Pursuit of Objectivity in Science and Public Life*. Princeton, NJ: Princeton University Press, 1995.

Prestige, G. *The Life of Charles Gore*. London: Heinemann, 1935.

Proudhon, P.-J. *What Is Property?* Edited and translated by D. Kelley and B. Smith. Cambridge: Cambridge University Press, 1994.

Pugh, M. "The Rise of Labour and the Political Culture of Conservatism, 1890–1945." *History* 87 (2002): 514–37.

Pugh, P. *Educate, Agitate, Organise*. London: Methuen, 1984.

Quail, J. *The Slow Burning Fuse*. London: Paladin, 1978.

Rappaport, E. *Shopping for Pleasure: Women in the Making of London's West End*. Princeton, NJ: Princeton University Press, 2000.

Readman, P. *Land and Nation in England: Patriotism, National Identity and the Politics of Land, 1880–1914*. Woodbridge, UK: Boydell and Brewer, 2008.

Redfern, P. *Journey to Understanding*. London: Allen and Unwin, 1946.

Reid, A. *The Tide of Democracy: Shipyard Workers and Social Relations in Britain, 1870–1950*. Manchester, UK: Manchester University Press, 2010.

Report of the First General Conference of the I.L.P. Held at Bradford on 13 and 14 January 1893. Glasgow: Labour Literature Society, 1893.

Rhys, E. *Everyman Remembers*. London: Dent, 1931.

Ricardo, D. *Works and Correspondence*. Edited by P. Sraffa. Cambridge: Cambridge University Press, 1951.

Ricci, D. "Fabian Socialism: A Theory of Rent as Exploitation." *Journal of British Studies* 9 (1969): 105–21.

Richmond, W. *Christian Economics*. London: Rivingtons, 1888.

Richter, M. *The Politics of Conscience: T. H. Green and His Age*. London: Weidenfeld and Nicolson, 1964.

Ritschel, D. *The Politics of Planning: The Debate on Economic Planning in Britain in the 1930s*. Oxford: Clarendon Press, 1997.

Robbins, L. *The Evolution of Modern Economic Theory and Other Papers on the History of Economic Thought*. London: Macmillan, 1970.

Robertson, J. "Scottish Political Economy beyond the Civic Tradition: Government and Economic Development in *The Wealth of Nations*." *History of Political Thought* 2 (1983): 451–82.

Robinson, R., and J. Gallagher. *After the Victorians*. London: Macmillan, 1961.

Rothstein, A. *A House on Clerkenwell Green*. London: Marx Memorial Library, 1983.

Rowbotham, S. *Edward Carpenter: A Life of Liberty and Love*. London: Verso, 2008.

Rowell, G. *Hell and the Victorians*. Oxford: Clarendon Press, 1974.

Royle, E. *Radicals, Secularists, and Republicans*. Manchester, UK: Manchester University Press, 1980.

Ruskin, J. *The Works of John Ruskin*. Edited by E. Cook and A. Wedderburn. 39 vols. London: G. Allen, 1903–12.

Salt, H. *The Life of Henry David Thoreau*. London: Bentley, 1890.

———. *A Plea for Vegetarianism and Other Essays*. Manchester, UK: Vegetarian Society, 1885.

———. *Seventy Years among Savages*. London: Allen and Unwin, 1921.

Salveson, P. *With Walt Whitman in Bolton: Spirituality, Sex and Socialism in a Northern Mill Town*. Huddersfield, UK: Little Northern Books, 2008.

Samuel, R. "The Workshop of the World: Steam-Power and Hand-Technology in Mid-Victorian Britain." *History Workshop* 3 (1977): 6–72.

Saul, S. *The Myth of the Great Depression, 1873–1896*. London: Macmillan, 1969.

Schabas, M. *A World Ruled by Number: William Stanley Jevons and the Rise of Mathematical Economics*. Princeton, NJ: Princeton University Press, 1990.

Schriner, O. *The Story of an African Farm*. Harmondsworth, UK: Penguin, 1971.

Scotland, N. *Squires in the Slums: Settlements and Missions in Late Victorian London*. London: I. B. Taurus, 2007.

Scott, J. *Gender and the Politics of History*. New York: Columbia University Press, 1988.

Searle, G. *Morality and the Market in Victorian Britain*. Oxford: Clarendon Press, 1998.

Semmel, B. *The Rise of Free Trade Imperialism*. Cambridge: Cambridge University Press, 1970.

Shaw, G. "Bluffing the Value Theory." *To-day* 11 (1889): 128–35.

———. *Collected Letters, 1874–1897*. Edited by D. Laurence. London: Reinhardt, 1965.

———. "Concerning Interest." *Our Corner* 10 (1887): 162–75 and 193–207.

———. *The Doctor's Dilemma*. Harmondsworth, UK: Penguin, 1946.

————. "The Fabian Election Manifesto." *Fabian Tract* 40 (1892).

————, ed. *Fabian Essays*. Introduction by A. Briggs. London: Allen and Unwin, 1962.

————. "A Fabian Manifesto." *Fabian Tract* 2 (1884).

————. "The Fabian Society: What It Has Done and How It Has Done it." *Fabian Tract* 41 (1892).

————. "George Bernard Shaw." In *Forecasts of the Coming Century*, edited by E. Carpenter. Manchester, UK: Labour Press, 1897.

————. "The Hyndman-George Debate." *International Review* 2 (1889): 50–57.

————. *John Bull's Other Island; How He Lied to Her Husband; and Major Barbara*. London: Constable, 1931.

————. *The Perfect Wagnerite*. London: Richards, 1898.

————. *The Quintessence of Ibsenism*. London: Walter Scott, 1891.

————. "Report on Fabian Policy." *Fabian Tract* 70 (1896).

————. *The Sanity of Art*. London: New Age Press, 1908.

————. *Sixteen Self Sketches*. London: Constable, 1949.

————. "The True Radical Programme." *Fabian Tract* 6 (1887).

————. *An Unsocial Socialist*. London: Constable, 1930.

Shaw, G., and S. Webb. "To Your Tents, O Israel." *Fortnightly Review* 60 (1893): 569–89.

Shaw, N. *Whiteway: A Colony on the Cotswolds*. London: Daniel, 1935.

Shipley, S. "Club Life and Socialism in Mid-Victorian England." *History Workshop Pamphlet* 5 (1971).

Simon, W. "Auguste Comte's English Disciples." *Victorian Studies* 8 (1964): 161–72.

Smith, A. *The Wealth of Nations*. Edited by E. Cannan. London: Methuen, 1961.

Snowden, P. *Socialism and Syndicalism*. London: Collins, 1913.

The Socialist League. *The Manifesto of the Socialist League*. London: Socialist League, 1885.

Southey, R. *Letters of Robert Southey*. Edited by M. Fitzgerald. London: World's Classics, 1901.

Stansky, P. *Redesigning the World: William Morris, the 1880s, and the Arts and Crafts Movement*. Princeton, NJ: Princeton University Press, 1985.

Stead, W. "The Labour Party and the Books That Helped to Make It." *Review of Reviews* 33 (1906): 568–92.

Stears, M. *Progressives, Pluralists, and the Problems of the State: Ideologies of Reform in the United States and Britain*. Oxford: Oxford University Press, 2002.

Stedman Jones, G. "The Determinist Fix: Some Obstacles to the Further Development of the Linguistic Approach to History in the 1990s." *History Workshop* (1996): 19–35.

————. *Outcast London: A Study in the Relationship between Classes in Victorian Society*. Oxford: Oxford University Press, 1971.

————. "Rethinking Chartism." In *Languages of Class: Studies in English Working-Class History, 1832–1982*. Cambridge: Cambridge University Press, 1983.

Tanner, D. "The Development of British Socialism, 1900–1918." *Parliamentary History* 16 (1997): 48–66.

Tanner, D. *Political Change and the Labour Party, 1900–1918.* Cambridge: Cambridge University Press, 1990.

Taylor, M. "The Beginnings of Modern British Social History." *History Workshop* 43 (1997): 155–76.

Thomas, W. *The Philosophic Radicals: Nine Studies in Theory and Practice, 1817–1841.* Oxford: Clarendon Press, 1979.

Thompson, E. *The Making of the English Working Class.* Harmondsworth, UK: Penguin, 1981.

———. *The Poverty of Theory and Other Essays.* London: Merlin Press, 1978.

———. *William Morris: Romantic to Revolutionary.* London: Lawrence and Wishart, 1955.

———. *William Morris: Romantic to Revolutionary.* London: Merlin, 1977.

Thompson, P. *Socialists, Liberals and Labour.* London: Routledge and Kegan Paul, 1967.

Thompson, W. *Postmodernism and History.* Basingstoke, UK: Palgrave Macmillan, 2004.

Thoreau, H. *Anti-Slavery and Reform Papers.* Edited and with an introduction by H. Salt. London: Swan Sonnenschein, 1890.

———. *Poems of Nature.* Edited and with an introduction by H. Salt and F. Sanborn. London: Lane, 1895.

———. "Resistance to Civil Government." In *Political Writings*, edited by N. Rosenblum. Cambridge: Cambridge University Press, 1996.

———. *Selections from Thoreau.* Edited and with an introduction by H. Salt. London: Macmillan, 1895.

———. *Walden.* Edinburgh: David Douglas, 1884.

Tomlinson, J. *Democratic Socialism and Economic Policy: The Attlee Years.* Cambridge: Cambridge University Press, 1997.

Toye, R. *The Labour Party and the Planned Economy, 1931–1951.* Woodbridge, UK: Royal Historical Society, 2003.

Traubel, H. *With Walt Whitman in Camden.* 3 vols. New York: Mitchell Kennerley, 1906–14.

Trentmann, F. *Free Trade Nation.* Oxford: Oxford University Press, 2008.

Trevor, J., ed. *The Labour Church Hymn Book.* London: Labour Prophet, 1895.

———. *Labour Prophet Tracts.* London: Labour Prophet, 1896.

———. *My Quest for God.* London: Labour Prophet, 1897.

———. *The One Life.* Horsted Keynes, UK: Trevor, 1909.

Tsuzuki, C. *H. M. Hyndman and British Socialism.* Oxford: Oxford University Press, 1961.

———. *Edward Carpenter, 1844–1929.* Cambridge: Cambridge University Press, 1980.

Turner, F. *Between Science and Religion: The Reaction to Scientific Naturalism in Late Victorian Britain.* New Haven, CT: Yale University Press, 1974.

Ulam, A. *Philosophical Foundations of English Socialism.* Cambridge, MA: Harvard University Press, 1951.

Vernon, J. *Politics and the People: A Study in English Political Culture.* Cambridge: Cambridge University Press, 1993.

Vincent, A., and R. Plant. *Philosophy, Politics and Citizenship*. Oxford: Blackwell, 1984.

Voynich, E. *The Gadfly*. London: Heinemann, 1897.

Walker, F. "The Source of Business Profit." *Quarterly Journal of Economics* 1 (1887): 265–88.

Walkowitz, J. *City of Dreadful Delight*. Chicago: University of Chicago Press, 1992.

Wallace, J. *Towards Fraternal Organisation: An Explanation of the Brotherhood Trust*. London: Brotherhood Trust, 1894.

Wallas, G. "Aristotle on Wealth and Property." *Today* 10 (1888): 16–20 and 49–53.

———. "The Chartist Movement." *Our Corner* 12 (1888): 111–18 and 129–40.

———. "An Economic Eirenicon." *To-day* 11 (1889): 80–86.

———. "L. T. Hobhouse." In *Men and Ideas*. London: Allen and Unwin, 1940.

———. "Personal Duty under the Present System." *Practical Socialist* (1886): 118–20 and 124–25.

Ward, B. *Reddie of Abbotsholme*. Introduction by J. Findlay. London: Allen and Unwin, 1934.

Ward, P. *Red Flag and Union Jack: Englishness, Patriotism and the British Left, 1881–1924*. Woodbridge, UK: Royal Historical Society, 1998.

Waters, C. *British Socialists and the Politics of Popular Culture, 1884–1914*. Manchester, UK: Manchester University Press, 1990.

Watmough, P. "The Membership of the Social Democratic Federation, 1885–1902." *Labour History Bulletin* 34 (1977): 35–40.

Weaver, S. *John Fielden and the Politics of Popular Radicalism*. Oxford: Oxford University Press, 1987.

Webb, B. *The Co-operative Movement in Great Britain*. London: Swan Sonnenschein, 1891.

———. *The Diary of Beatrice Webb*. Edited by N. and J. Mackenzie. 4 vols. London: Virago, 1982–85.

———. *My Apprenticeship*. Harmondsworth, UK: Penguin, 1938.

———. *Our Partnership*. Cambridge: Cambridge University Press, 1975.

Webb, S. "The Difficulties of Individualism." *Fabian Tract* 69 (1896).

———. "The Economics of a Positivist Community." *Practical Socialist* 1 (1886): 37–39.

———. "An Eight Hours Bill." *Fabian Tract* 9 (1889).

———. *English Progress towards Social Democracy*. London: Modern, 1888.

———. "Facts for Socialists." *Fabian Tract* 5 (1887).

———. *The Government Organisation of Unemployed Labour*. London: Fabian Society, 1886.

———. *The London Programme*. London: Swan Sonnenschein, 1891.

———. "The Rate of Interest." *Quarterly Journal of Economics* 2 (1888): 469–72.

———. "Rate of Interest and Laws of Distribution." *Quarterly Journal of Economics* 2 (1888): 188–208.

———. "Rome: A Sermon in Sociology." *Our Corner* 12 (1888): 53–60 and 79–89.

Webb, S . *Socialism in England*. Baltimore: American Economic Association, 1889.

———. "The Truth about Leasehold Enfranchisement." *Fabian Tract* 22 (1890).

———. "Twentieth Century Politics: A Policy of National Efficiency." *Fabian Tract* 108 (1901).

———. *Wanted a Programme: An Appeal to the Liberal Party*. London: Labour, 1888.

———. "What Socialism Means: A Call to the Unconverted." *Practical Socialist* 1 (1886): 89–93.

Webb, S., and B. Webb. *A Constitution for the Socialist Commonwealth of Great Britain*. Edited by S. Beer. Cambridge: Cambridge University Press, 1975.

———. *English Local Government from the Revolution to the Municipal Corporations Act*. 8 vols. London: Longmans, 1906–29.

———. *The History of Trade Unionism*. London: Longmans, 1894.

———. *Industrial Democracy*. London: Longmans, 1920.

———. *The Letters of Sidney and Beatrice Webb*. Edited by N. MacKenzie. 3 vols. Cambridge: Cambridge University Press, 1978.

Wells, H. *The New Machiavelli*. London: Bodley Head, 1911.

Whitman, W. *Walt Whitman: The Complete Poems*. Harmondsworth, UK: Penguin, 1975.

Wicksteed, P. *The Common Sense of Political Economy, and Selected Papers and Reviews on Economic Theory*. Edited by L. Robbins. London: Routledge, 1935.

Wilde, O. *The Soul of Man under Socialism*. London: Humphreys, 1912.

Willey, B. *Nineteenth Century Studies*. Harmondsworth, UK: Penguin, 1964.

Wilson, C. *Anarchism*. Leeds, UK: Anarchist Group, 1900.

———. *Anarchism and Outrage*. London: C. M. Wilson, 1893.

———. "The Condition of the Russian Peasantry." *To-day* 4 (1885): 353–57.

———. "Social Democracy and Anarchism." *Practical Socialist* 1 (1886): 7–12.

Wilson, C., et al. "What Socialism Is." *Fabian Tract* 4 (1886).

Winch, D. *Adam Smith's Politics*. Cambridge: Cambridge University Press, 1978.

———. *Wealth and Life: Essays on the Intellectual History of Political Economy in Britain, 1848–1914*. Cambridge: Cambridge University Press, 2009.

Wolfe, W. *From Radicalism to Socialism*. New Haven, CT: Yale University Press, 1975.

Wollstonecraft, M. *A Vindication of the Rights of Men and a Vindication of the Rights of Woman*. Edited by S. Tomaselli. Cambridge: Cambridge University Press, 1995.

Wooton, D. *Republicanism, Liberty and Commercial Society, 1649–1776*. Stanford, CA: Stanford University Press, 1994.

Wright, T. *The Religion of Humanity*. Cambridge: Cambridge University Press, 1986.

Yeo, S. "A New Life: The Religion of Socialism in Britain, 1883–1896." *History Workshop* 4 (1977): 5–56.

Young, G. *Victorian England: Portrait of an Age*. London: Oxford University Press, 1936.

Index